WHO DO YOU SAY
THAT I AM?

In Honor of Jack Dean Kingsbury

WHO DO YOU SAY THAT I AM?

ESSAYS ON CHRISTOLOGY

MARK ALLAN POWELL AND DAVID R. BAUER,
EDITORS

WESTMINSTER JOHN KNOX PRESS
LOUISVILLE, KENTUCKY

© 1999 Westminster John Knox Press

Scripture quotations, unless otherwise indicated, are from
the New Revised Standard Version of the Bible,
copyright © 1989 by the Division of Christian Education
of the National Council of the Churches of Christ in the
U.S.A., and are used by permission.

Book design by Sharon Adams
Cover design by Koechel Peterson & Associates

First edition
Published by Westminster John Knox Press
Louisville, Kentucky

This book is printed on acid-free paper that meets the American
National Standards Institute Z39.48 standard. ∞

PRINTED IN THE UNITED STATES OF AMERICA

Library of Congress Cataloging-in-Publication Data

99 00 01 02 03 04 05 06 07 08 — 10 9 8 7 6 5 4 3 2 1

Library of Congress Cataloging-in-Publication Data

Who do you say that I am? : essays on Christology / Mark Allan Powell
and David R. Bauer, editors. — 1st ed.
    p.   cm.
Includes bibliographical references and indexes.
ISBN 0-664-25752-6 (alk. paper)
1. Jesus Christ — Person and offices — Biblical teaching.
I. Powell, Mark Allan, 1953–   . II. Bauer, David R.
BT205.W46   1999
232—dc21   99-14863

This volume is affectionately dedicated to

Jack Dean Kingsbury

Aubrey Lee Brooks Professor of Biblical Theology

Union Theological Seminary, Richmond, Virginia

presented to him by his students on the occasion

of his sixty-fifth birthday, November 19, 1999

———•·•———

Luke 6:40a is true, we know
We pray 6:40b may be also

———•·•———

David R. Bauer

John Blumenstein

Joseph R. Dongell

John Jay Dozier

Frances Taylor Gench

Jeffrey A. Gibbs

Blake Grangaard

Sheila Klassen-Wiebe

William H. Malas

Mark Allan Powell

Keith H. Reeves

Daniel W. Ulrich

Michael E. Vines

Dorothy Jean Weaver

Ronald D. Witherup

Gary Yamaski

CONTENTS

FOREWORD

Frederick W. Danker

When biblical scholars in the third millennium commemorate achievements in the second, the name of Jack Dean Kingsbury will be listed among the seminal contributors to the interpretation of the first three Gospels.

As a seminarian, Jack exhibited a determined interest in discerning the spirits of hermeneutical inquiry. After tracking the main artery of Rudolf Bultmann's hermeneutical theory, he examined numerous aspects of the Marburg professor's approach to the explication of biblical texts. He did not become a disciple of this school—whose days were certain to be numbered—but he did collect proceeds from the enterprise. Among these was a liberation from confinement to a diachronic approach that viewed biblical books as a collection of minuscule syntactical parts without the adequate thematic ligaments to function as an articulated entity.

Renewed for further research, Jack traveled with his wife, Barbara, to Basel, Switzerland, where he took seriously the preposition *kata* ("according to") in the title of what we demystifiers call the first Gospel. With theory from the start grounded in primary grammatical grasp, and with close attention paid to the hermeneutical implications of Matthew 1:1, Kingsbury began his probe of what he considered the most challenging matter in Matthew's story not simply of Jesus but of "Jesus Christ, son of David, son of Abraham." Interests rooted in this explicit and marvelously succinct summary would lead eventually to Kingsbury's treatment of Christology, kingdom, and the problem of a divided course in the fortunes of Israel. But prior to such comprehensive inquiry, other work had to be done.

Following the lead of *Redaktionsgeschichte,* which had been stimulated by nineteenth-century debate concerning the probability that Mark's sequence of events suggested development of plot, Kingsbury wished to clear away much of the flotsam and jetsam washed up by high waves of ecclesiastical thought. "Matthew's Gospel itself," he wrote in the first chapter of *The Parables of Matthew in Matthew 13: A Study in Redaction-Criticism* (St. Louis: Concordia Publishing House, 1969), "becomes the norm for interpreting the parables in chapter 13 . . . not some preconceived theory regarding the nature and function of parables and not the whole of the scriptures or the later dogmatics of the Church."

Never leaving Matthew's first verse out of sight, Kingsbury proceeded further to explore Matthew's thematic interests and their literary articulation.

The results appeared in *Matthew: Structure, Christology, and Kingdom* (Philadelphia: Fortress Press, 1975). Kingsbury had treated the canonist's titular *kata* with a respect rarely enjoyed by such an unassuming semantic marker. In doing so, he directed attention with unerring focus onto Matthew's protagonist as thematic initiator of numerous dramatic moments that make Matthew's work a classic literary production. Through analysis of the principal players' interaction on Matthew's literary stage, Kingsbury offers an alternative exposition of what Bultmann proclaimed as the focal challenge to claims of faith. In *Matthew as Story* (2d ed.; Philadelphia: Fortress Press, 1988), all is gathered in a climactic exhibition of awareness that any great story must have a beginning and a middle that provide the basis for a convincing end. To state such an obvious fact would appear ludicrous, were it not that American biblical interpreters had—with few exceptions—become experts in dissection of the Gospels at the expense of their ostensible claims as literary units.

After picking up the lines of Matthew's plot, it was a short step to concentration on the motif of conflict itself. What better streamlined literary container for such material than the Gospel *kata* Mark (*Conflict in Mark: Jesus, Authorities, Disciples* [Minneapolis: Fortress Press, 1990])? The nineteenth-century seed of the plot here found a sturdy plant. Then it was on to the Gospel *kata* Luke (*Conflict in Luke: Jesus, Authorities, Disciples* [Minneapolis: Fortress Press, 1991]), where conflict seems to exude from every syntagmatic pore.

Finally we come full circle. Kingsbury had begun his decades of work on the Gospels with a survey and critique of nineteenth-century and early twentieth-century hermeneutical inquiry. Appropriately, he climaxed his critical inquiry and exposition with *Gospel Interpretation: Narrative-Critical and Social-Scientific Approaches* (Valley Forge, Pa.: Trinity Press International, 1997). Bultmann would have liked that thrust. Even more, he would have congratulated Professor Kingsbury, as I am privileged to do, for his unceasingly restless study of the evangelists' focus on Jesus Christ, not as one to be probed by exegetical maneuvering but as the proclaimed agent of God, whose very person spells hermeneutical adequacy for all who are on the quest for discovery of ultimate meaning in a world conflicting with God.

Let it last be stated, and last so that there be no forgetting: The congruence that Kingsbury highlighted in the evangelists' writings received further exposition in his own commitment to solid scholarship within the confessional framework of the various academic institutions he has served. He has not used placement in academe as a point of privilege for private intellectual enterprise that makes Jesus Christ a hermeneutical option. And for this reason we can look with hope for more products from his searching mind and spirit. Paul Shorey, master of Platonic lore, at times complained of books that urged the world's heeding but in which he found "no food for thought." The same cannot be said of our honoree's productions.

Near the beginning of the nineteenth century, a prominent biblical scholar, Benjamin Bacon, asked, "Is theology scientific?" The same question appears to have been on the mind of Claude Lévi-Strauss. At a meeting of educators in 1946,[1] he proposed an answer:

> I heard somebody telling somebody that the purpose of education was to improve the lot of mankind, and I was reminded of another definition which was given several centuries ago by the most materialistic and down-to-earth philosopher, Francis Bacon. He said that education was to glorify God *and* to improve the lot of mankind. If, while improving the lot of mankind, we forget to glorify God, then we are lost and our children are lost.

Jack Dean Kingsbury's life and work are accurate commentary on those words.

---

1. Claude Lévi-Strauss, "France's View," *Humanistic Values for a Free Society,* Proceedings of the Third Regional Conference on the Humanities, Estes Park, Colorado, June 1946 (Denver: University of Denver, 1947), 166–67.

LIST OF CONTRIBUTORS

Elizabeth Achtemeier
Adjunct professor of Bible and homiletics, retired
Union Theological Seminary in Virginia

Paul J. Achtemeier
Jackson Professor of biblical interpretation, emeritus
Union Theological Seminary in Virginia

C. K. Barrett
Emeritus professor of divinity
Durham University

David L. Bartlett
Lantz Professor of preaching and academic dean
Yale Divinity School

David R. Bauer
Ralph W. Beeson Professor of inductive biblical studies
Asbury Theological Seminary

Carl E. Braaten
Executive director
Center for Catholic and Evangelical Theology

Lisa Sowle Cahill
J. Donald Monan, S.J. Professor of theology
Boston College

R. Alan Culpepper
Dean
Mercer School of Theology

Frederick W. Danker
Christ Seminary-Seminex Professor of New Testament, emeritus
Lutheran School of Theology at Chicago

Birger Gerhardsson
Professor emeritus
Lund University

CONTRIBUTORS *(continued)*

Terence E. Fretheim
Elva Lovell Professor of Old Testament
Luther Seminary

Luke Timothy Johnson
Woodruff Professor of New Testament and Christian origins
Emory University

Leander E. Keck
Winkley Professor of biblical theology, emeritus
Yale Divinity School

Elizabeth Struthers Malbon
Professor and director of religious studies
Center for Interdisciplinary Studies
Virginia Polytechnic Institute and State University

Pheme Perkins
Professor of theology
Boston College

Mark Allan Powell
Robert and Phyllis Leatherman Professor of New Testament
Trinity Lutheran Seminary

John Reumann
Ministerium of Pennsylvania Professor of New Testament, emeritus
Lutheran Theological Seminary at Philadelphia

Marion L. Soards
Professor of New Testament studies
Louisville Presbyterian Theological Seminary

Charles H. Talbert
Distinguished Professor of religion
Baylor University

Ben Witherington III
Professor of New Testament
Asbury Theological Seminary

INTRODUCTION

Mark Allan Powell and David R. Bauer

The editors of this volume, both of whom wrote their doctoral dissertations under the direction of Jack Dean Kingsbury at Union Theological Seminary in Virginia, considered it unthinkable that Professor Kingsbury's sixty-fifth birthday should pass without a commemorative volume published in celebration of this milestone. Over the past twenty-five years Professor Kingsbury has been recognized as a New Testament scholar of global significance who has been especially influential in the interpretation of the Synoptic Gospels, in hermeneutics, and in New Testament Christology. Throughout his career, Professor Kingsbury has pursued these academic interests from the perspective of a strong theological commitment and with a view toward serving the church. It is most appropriate, therefore, that this commemorative volume should deal with Christology according to the various witnesses of the New Testament, give attention to the relationship between New Testament Christology and the Old Testament, and include essays that explore the significance of New Testament theology for systematic theology, ethics, pastoral ministry, and preaching.

The contributors to this volume are among the most prominent biblical and theological scholars active in the world today. They set out the main contours of Christology in the various areas assigned to them, but in the process they also suggest new and exciting ways of understanding Christology, thus making this volume both useful for introducing persons to New Testament Christology and valuable for scholars who wish to explore innovations in the field. Unlike many *Festschriften,* this book is designed to be used as a classroom text, in appropriate recognition of Professor

Kingsbury's commitment to theological education and his unusual gifts in that area.

We dedicate this volume to Professor Kingsbury with the profoundest professional regard and personal affection, and with every wish that the work he continues to pursue will outstrip even his already impressive contributions to New Testament Christology.

This volume begins where Christology itself began, with Jesus' own understanding of his person and mission. Ben Witherington III notes that in the ancient world persons' social relationships determined their identity, and he uses this insight to probe how Jesus thought about himself and how others would have understood his teachings and activities. Witherington concludes that Jesus' social relationships surrounding his geographical location and family connections would suggest to no one anything like messianic greatness, and thus the fact that the issue of his messiahship emerged indicates something extraordinary, and even remarkable, about his life and ministry. Moreover, Witherington avers that Jesus refused ultimately to understand himself in terms of these mundane social relationships, opting instead for a self-identity reflected in the christological titles "Son of man" (emphasizing humanness in interpersonal relationship, rather than beastliness), "Son of God" (emphasizing his being named by God and his relationship with God), "Christ" (emphasizing his anointing by God for eschatological work), and "Lord" (emphasizing his relation to his subjects).

Birger Gerhardsson insists that Matthew presents a coherent portrait of Jesus from the diverse material he inherited. Matthew employs christological titles, in a significant yet limited way, to elucidate this portrait of Jesus. The central affirmation comes from Peter, speaking on behalf of the disciples: "You are the Christ/Messiah, the Son of the living God," an affirmation to which Matthew gives specific content in terms of Jesus' servanthood. In addition, through the story he tells, Matthew presents his Christology as having a didactic character, a therapeutic aspect, an ethical dimension, and support of the scriptures. In the process, Matthew describes the various components of the relationship between Jesus and the disciples/church.

Employing the method of literary criticism, or more specifically, narrative criticism, Elizabeth Struthers Malbon argues against the generally held position that the point of view of the narrator of Mark's Gospel and that of the Markan Jesus are identical. Malbon insists, on the contrary, that while the narrator of the Gospel, as well as the various characters presented throughout the Gospel, focus on the person of Jesus and make liberal use of christological titles to describe Jesus, the Markan Jesus is reticent about himself and, with the exception of "Son of man," does not make use of christological titles. Rather, the Markan Jesus prefers to speak of God and to focus attention on God's kingdom. Malbon concludes that scholars must come to understand that Markan Christology includes (in creative tension) both the perspective of the narrator and various characters and that of Jesus.

In his contribution dealing with Luke-Acts, Luke Timothy Johnson also utilizes the method of narrative criticism. Johnson insists that Luke-Acts is a consistent literary composition in the form of a coherent two-volume work, and that the second volume, the book of Acts, is especially expressive of Luke's Christology, since Luke was relatively unencumbered by reliance on traditional materials in its production and was thus freer to weave his own Christology into the narrative than was the case with the Gospel. Johnson posits, then, that one should begin the pursuit of Lukan Christology with the book of Acts and use the presentation of Jesus in Acts to interpret that found in the Gospel. Using this procedure and carefully analyzing several lines of evidence, Johnson concludes that Luke presents Jesus primarily as a prophet who is sent a first time to the people of Israel for their salvation. After he is killed, raised from the dead, and exalted at the right hand of God, he sends his Spirit on his disciples, who continue his prophetic work among the people, offering them another chance for salvation. This salvation involves being included in the restored people that God is forming around his prophet Jesus. Luke sets forth the story of Jesus in this way to show that God was faithful to the promises he made to Abraham, and that God is thus worthy of the trust that Gentiles place in him.

R. Alan Culpepper reminds us that scholars have generally explored Johannine Christology by pursuing one of two dominant approaches, namely, the tracing of stages in the development of Johannine Christology that correspond to the history of the Johannine community and the investigation of the several christological titles in the Gospel (and the epistles). But Culpepper objects that the focus on developmental theories is inadequate to explain how the various stages or strands of thought are related in the final form of these texts, and that the investigation of christological titles has often involved treating these titles in isolation from one another and with little attention to their narrative contexts. Culpepper argues that when one studies seriously the relationship of the titles to each other within the composition of the Johannine material, one will find that the Logos Christology, which scholars generally regard as representing a late stage in the development of Johannine theology, actually forms the foundation of John's understanding of Jesus, beginning already with the prologue. "Son of God," which is the preeminent christological title for John, is linked in profound ways to this central Logos concept.

Marion L. Soards addresses Pauline Christology by an investigation into the narrative substructure of the story of Jesus that one might construct from the varied and, for the most part, isolated remarks that Paul sprinkles throughout his epistles. Soards identifies these narrative materials, lists these elements in the order of their canonical occurrence, reconstructs the story from the various isolated elements, examines the meaning of the major components of the story of Jesus that Paul presents, and draws inferences from all these data regarding Paul's knowledge and beliefs about Jesus Christ. In short, Soards concludes that Paul tells the story of Jesus in such a way that the origins and destiny of all creation are bound up in the most profound way with the historical revelation of God in God's Son, Jesus Christ. Finally, Soards reflects on the significance of Paul's story of Jesus Christ for the church today.

For his part, C. K. Barrett posits that the epistle to the Hebrews might well have emerged from the same community of Christian diaspora Jews that claimed Stephen and the other seven (Acts 6—7) as its most visible and notable leaders, a community responsible not only for the Stephen Speech of Acts 7 but also for the Areopagus Speech of Acts 17 (inaccurately attributed by Luke to Paul) and for the Decree of Acts 15 (inaccurately attributed by Luke to James). Barrett follows the suggestion of William Manson that this community, with Stephen at its head, initiated a Gentile mission responsible for the spread of Christianity as far as Alexandria and Rome, and that Hebrews was written to the Roman church at a time when it was still a part of the synagogue and was overemphasizing the Jewish element in Christianity, with the purpose of making this church aware of the deeper implications of the newness of the Christian faith. An examination of the speeches of Acts 7 and 17 reveals that this community of Christian diaspora Jews thus responsible for the church at Rome was originally somewhat theologically deficient in two key areas: the temple and Christology. The epistle to the Hebrews was written to supply what was lacking in these areas, and in the process the writer was concerned to understand the one in relation to the other. Barrett carefully traces the christological argument of the epistle from the perspective of his hypothesis, demonstrating both the plausibility of the hypothesis and its significance for a more penetrating interpretation of the Christology of Hebrews.

When assignments for this book were made, John Reumann drew the wild card and agreed to comment on the Christology of James. Popular opinion often holds that this epistle is void of Christology and, for that matter, rather weak on theology as well. Nevertheless, Reumann applies his considerable exegetical skills to the limited data that are present, reflecting on passages that might refer to Christ when they employ such terminology as "the Lord" (James 5:7–11, 14–15), "the word" (1:18, 21), and "the righteous one" (5:6). Reumann ultimately concludes that the letter of James remains the sole literary monument to a first-century Christology that does not fit typical categories. While displaying no interest in salvation history or justification, James does present a Christology in a wisdom mode that views the Lord as shaping faith and ethical activity in his people. It serves as a reminder of how varied images for understanding Jesus Christ have been, even from the beginning.

In his study of the Christology of 1 Peter, Paul J. Achtemeier notes that the presentation of Jesus in this letter reflects early Christian traditions generally and is thus essentially that which we find in the New Testament as a whole: Although Christ was innocent of any wrongdoing he suffered and died on the cross, was subsequently raised from the dead by God, ascended into heaven at God's right hand with all powers subjected to him, and all of this according to God's eternal plan. But 1 Peter develops certain aspects of this rather general portrait by drawing on the cultic language of Israel, which leads the epistle to speak of Christ as a sacrificial "lamb without defect or blemish" (1:19) and as a "living stone" (2:4), and on the image of "chief shepherd" (5:4), used in the Old Testament to speak of God but now applied to Jesus. Yet 1 Peter does more than simply develop aspects of general early Christian reflection on the person of Jesus. The epistle also presents a Christology that stems from its own purpose of establishing a theological justification for the appropriation of the language of Israel for the Christian community by insisting that the Spirit of Christ was present with the prophets of Israel, who therefore bore witness to Christ for the sake of those who were to be his people, that is, the church. In line with that theological purpose, this epistle, alone among the writings of the New Testament, presents Jesus and his significance for the Christian community in terms of a sustained application of the prophetic portrait of the Suffering Servant of Isaiah 52 and 53.

As for 2 Peter and Jude, Pheme Perkins insists that Christology plays only a subordinate role in the theology of these epistles. Both epistles adopt traditional language to speak of Jesus as the Lord and Savior who is the agent of the salvation enjoyed by believers who express their loyalty to God (and to Christ) in a life of godliness and moral reform. Jude assimilates Christ to God as the judge who will, at the end, grant faithful Christians mercy and eternal life, whereas 2 Peter abandons Jude's appeal to judgment as the motivation for faithful Christian behavior and prefers to speak instead of Christ as the agent by whom Christians share in the divine nature now and thereby will participate in the eternal kingdom yet to come. Both epistles emphasize that Jesus is the powerful but distant master known to Christians only through his agents, the apostles, and thus submission to the apostolic tradition is the one thing most necessary.

The book of Revelation presents more data for christological reflection than does the letter of James, but like that epistle, it does not offer a complete or ordered account to facilitate an easy understanding of the data. Charles H. Talbert organizes what is present under five headings. First, he describes the *names* given to Christ, the *titles* used for him, and the *functions* ascribed to him in the final book of the New Testament canon. Next, he discusses the two *faces* of Christ (human and heavenly) that are assumed throughout Revelation, even though the book's writer makes no apparent effort to relate these to each other. Finally, Talbert describes two *contexts* in which all the preceding data must be interpreted: (1) the implied narrative of Christ's past, present, and future activity and (2) the presupposed beliefs of the ancient Mediterranean world that comprised the book's intended audience. Attention to the latter context leads Talbert to conclude that the idea of a human being becoming identified with a divine being, sharing the throne of God, and executing a final judgment would have been typical. The innovative element in Revelation's Christology for the Mediterranean world would have been the soteriological significance assigned to Christ's death, though this was traditional for Christianity. Thus, the Christology of the Apocalypse can be understood as a Christian adjustment of a typical pattern that, in turn, established a trajectory that found fuller expression in the "angelomorphic Christologies" of later Christianity.

Once all major witnesses of the New Testament canon have been analyzed, we call in Leander E. Keck to question the legitimacy of such investigations—or at least, to help us consider where all this is supposed to lead. Keck describes the difference between the task of describing the various Christologies of individual New Testament writers and that of defining *a* New Testament Christology that may serve the academy or the church when articulating theology or mission. Keck offers a historical overview of the problem, with emphasis on the role of William Wrede, who favored discernment of "connections and effects" over description of the thoughts of individual writers. Keck himself thinks that Christology must be reconceived as "a theological discipline with historical horizons." Thus, all the views described in the first eleven chapters of this book must be considered from the perspective of a developed rationale that the New Testament authors themselves may not have understood. This rationale derives from the grammar of christological discourse that they created but also includes reflection on the centuries of debate that their discourse spawned. The implications of such an approach are numerous. As one example, Keck demonstrates how one may eschew an artificial quest for unity in the New Testament witness to focus instead on persistent features or common traits that mark the variety of witnesses. Keck lists five of these, which he thinks may serve as "channel markers" to safeguard the integrity of continuing christological thought.

Terence E. Fretheim would expand the diversity of biblical witnesses to Christology even further. In the opening sentence of his essay, he lays to rest the common notion that Christology is a subset of New Testament theology: "Without the Old Testament, there would be no adequate Christology." In elucidating this argument, furthermore, he goes well beyond reminding us of the fairly obvious (though oft-neglected) recognition that the New Testament writers developed their christological views with reference to Old Testament texts. Fretheim claims that the Old Testament must also serve as a guide for continuing christological reflection. Contemporary theologians will find the Old Testament indispensable in ways that go beyond what was explicitly taken up by New Testament authors. In developing this thesis, Fretheim notes several points of contact between the story of Jesus and the Old Testament story of God. Israel's God is consistently presented as being in relationship with creation, as being active and present in the world and even *within* the world. Indeed, Old Testament theophanies provide an especially fruitful basis for understanding incarnation and testimonies to a suffering God speak decisively on atonement. Put simply, biblical Christology must recognize that God did not become human or suffer for the sins of the world for the first time in Jesus. The New Testament story of Jesus is not unique or surprising but wholly consistent with the Old Testament story of God.

The book could end here, but that would not be appropriate for its honoree. Jack Dean Kingsbury has always been a scholar interested in moving out of the academic ivory tower and engaging the persistent question "So what?" If any asks that question after our first thirteen chapters, here are four responses. We have asked four specialists in other fields of religious studies (systematic theology, ethics, pastoral ministry, homiletics) to reflect on the significance of New Testament Christology for their respective disciplines.

Carl E. Braaten begins his essay by noting a "prevailing alienation" today between exegesis and systematic theology. The rift he perceives is similar to that described in Keck's chapter, for exegetes stereotypically describe the various Christologies of individual writers while systematicians seek to define a transcendent, unified Christology that may be regarded as founda-tional in broader theological tasks. The two chapters make for an interest-ing comparison, especially since the one is written by a biblical scholar (Keck) and the other by a systematician (Braaten). For his part, Braaten views the development of Christology as necessitating involvement of three equally important trajectories: Gospel narratives, New Testament kerygma, and church dogma. Furthermore, the development of critical method has produced a primacy of historical interest that requires preliminary attention to the historical Jesus. Nevertheless, Braaten insists that starting Christol-ogy "from below" (with the historical Jesus) does not necessitate conclud-ing with a low Christology. He attempts to show, in brief compass, how it is possible to start with recognition of a Jewish eschatological prophet and conclude with confession of a triune God. The "high Christology" of Paul's letters and John's Gospel are important steps along the way. For Braaten, the ability to make such a transition is far from academic; what is perhaps most significant is whether one has interest or motivation for making it. Ul-timately, the question is sharpened to an inquiry of what this world needs: a Redeemer or a role model.

Lisa Sowle Cahill presents a study highly compatible with that of Braaten but with specific interest in ethics. She notes immediately that the focus of modern ethics has shifted from personal virtue to social change and indicates that for the latter, the lifestyle and message of Jesus has been deemed especially important. In particular, social-historical research such as that of Marcus Borg has helped define a distinctive orientation for Chris-tian ethics. The question arises, however, if it makes any difference for ethics whether this Jesus is in fact considered to be "the Christ," as the New Testament pluralistically but unanimously maintains. Cahill develops the thesis that such christological claims are what place Jesus' moral message "against the horizon of a new reality that warrants and empowers the moral life." To illustrate, she contrasts the ethical position of Richard Hays, whose christological understanding leads him to accent suffering as a key-stone of the moral life, and that of Mary Solberg, whose understanding leads her to prioritize love. Then, Cahill concludes with an appeal based on yet another example of how Christology affects ethical vision. Many ur-gent issues confronting humanity today transcend specifically Christian concerns and are not well served by traditional understandings of the lim-ited character of God's election in Christ. Rather, the ethical tasks before us require christological formulations that emphasize the universal char-acter of divine love mediated through Christ's resurrection.

David L. Bartlett also chooses a paradigmatic approach to his topic, the significance of New Testament Christology for pastoral ministry. He selects three particular New Testament writings that present diverse Son of God Christologies and demonstrates how the christological claims of each shape pastoral understanding and practice. The Gospel of Mark emphasizes that sonship requires suffering; pastoral ministry that takes this Christology seriously knows the costs of discipleship and avoids the easy pitfalls of theologies of glory. The Gospel of John emphasizes the strong sense of unity between Son and Father and subsequent unity between believers and God through Christ. Pastoral ministry built on this Christology will recognize its implicit affirmation of unstructured egalitarian community, according to which all believers may relate directly to the Father through the Son (though even in John, this model is held in tension with another; compare John 10 to John 21). Paul's letter to the Galatians emphasizes the Son's identity as heir and thus as the one through whom believers have access to the family of God. Pastoral ministry informed by this Christology articulates and embodies the inclusivity of equal access without acquiescing to a secular universalism that fails to define such inclusion as being always and only through Christ.

Elizabeth Achtemeier, finally, considers the significance of New Testament Christology for preaching. She distinguishes quickly between the biblical task of "releasing the active, effective Word of God" and the widespread practice of "therapeutic preaching," which may simply reassure or interest the audience with sagacious insight. Christological preaching presents Jesus Christ, who is found in biblical narrative and interpretation of history. In a manner that would probably be pleasing to Fretheim, Achtemeier elucidates key ways in which Jesus Christ must be understood from the standpoint of Old Testament scripture: He is the new Moses, the Suffering Servant who died in accordance with scripture, the incarnation of the entire word of the Old Testament. He is, further, the true Israel who fulfills God's will such that "in him every one of God's promises is a 'Yes'" (2 Cor. 1:20). To illustrate her thesis pragmatically, Achtemeier goes on to present a few selected "pericope studies," demonstrating in each case how proclamation on a New Testament text may be informed by a christological understanding grounded in the canon as a whole.

THE CHRISTOLOGY
OF JESUS

Ben Witherington III

Almost a decade ago, I published a book with the same title as this chapter,[1] which, accordingly, might more properly be called "The 'Christology of Jesus' Revisited." When that book was written, the reaction of scholars was predictably mixed.[2] There was some awkward silence; there was some enthusiastic acceptance; and there was some rather vehement rejection. I remember well the wry smile of one member of the Society of New Testament Studies Historical Jesus section when I suggested "the Christology of Jesus" as a topic for discussion. It was assumed that Rudolf Bultmann had long ago pronounced the benediction on this topic, when he said that we could know next to nothing with any certainty about the historical Jesus other than that he was crucified under Pontius Pilate. As things have turned out, quite a lot of New Testament scholars, including a wide variety of contributors to the third quest for the historical Jesus, have chosen to disagree with Bultmann not only in general about the historical Jesus but on the specific question of Jesus' self-understanding. To choose but one example, John Meier has argued, as I did, that much remains to be learned about Jesus' self-understanding by examining his relationships with various other significant figures, such as John the Baptist, the Pharisees, and the first disciples.[3]

One of the questions I have pondered a good deal of late is whether we really have framed the questions about Jesus' relationships properly. Have we not simply assumed that ancient persons related to one another much as we do today? Have we not presumed that ancient persons and personalities were not essentially different from ourselves and our personas, and thus that we can evaluate Jesus as if he were a candidate for modern or post-modern Western psychological evaluation?[4] The problem of this anachronism has all too often been ignored, even though we know that nurture as well as nature, culture as well as genetics, affect the sort of person one turns out to be. It is in this area of the social and cultural conditioning of human personality that I think the exploration of Jesus' self-understanding has been lacking. I propose, then, to do two things in this study: (1) focus the discussion of Jesus more closely on his social context and relationships, and (2) make some introductory suggestions about how this sort of social data and approach might illuminate the discussion of the so-called christological titles found in the Synoptic Gospels.

TO KNOW AS ONE IS KNOWN

One of the areas in which distinct progress has been made in Gospel studies since I wrote *The Christology of Jesus* is in genre studies. The crucial work of R. A. Burridge has provided a strong case that at least three of the four Gospels fall into the category of ancient Greco-Roman biography.[5] One of the most striking features of these sorts of ancient biographical works, whether one thinks of Plutarch's *Lives* or Josephus's *Against Apion* or Tacitus's *Agricola* or Mark's Gospel, is that instead of presenting womb-to-tomb analyses of the development of a particular human personality, the authors regularly assumed that a person's character does not develop over time at all. To the contrary, time was thought simply to reveal the character a person had always had. Human personality was viewed as static, and therefore, most ancient biographers would have viewed a change in one's personality, a conversion, or chameleon-like behavior with extreme skepticism. Knowing what we now know on this front, it becomes very difficult to psychoanalyze Jesus on the basis of texts that by and large do not believe in developmental theories of personality and do not present us with anything like adequate data about such things as Jesus' early childhood influences.[6] What we can say about the historical Jesus must stand or fall on the data revealed in the Gospels about the adult Jesus during the last three or so years of his life. It is not the stuff of modern biographical portraits, for it provides us few opportunities to speculate about how he grew or changed over time.

The study of ancient Mediterranean persons and personalities reveals that it was assumed that "normal" persons were not what we would call unique individuals at all, but rather mirrors of the virtues and vices, the strengths and flaws, of some particular ancient group. What we might call stereotypes ancients would see as character types, or traits that explain both individuals and the groups of which they are a part. The remarks we find at Titus 1:12 ("Cretans are always liars, vicious brutes, lazy gluttons")—a quote from a famous Cretan, no less—and at John 1:46 are frankly typical of this sort of ancient literature. Human identity was established by the group and was confirmed to the individual by members of the group. Life was not, by and large, about establishing one's unique place in the world, discovering one's distinctive character, or making personal claims for oneself.

In antiquity it was widely assumed that gender, generation, and geography for the most part determined one's identity,[7] and with good reason. Corporate, or group, identity rather than individual identity was primary. A person who sought to stand out from his ethnic or familial or geographical or gender group was seen as a deviant, not as a person simply "being himself." In this sort of environment, even a remarkable and somewhat distinctive person like Jesus would seek to identify himself by indicating the relationships that were formative for him and would seek to have his identity confirmed to him by his most intimate dialogue partners, since it was normal that someone other than oneself had a crucial say in who one was and could be (see Mark 1:11; 8:27–30).

As it turns out, there is nothing very surprising about a first-century person choosing to speak only indirectly or elliptically about himself, if at all. This is what one would expect in a culture where corporate identity was not merely prominent but dominant. If Mark's messianic secret and silencing motif does to some degree go back to the historical Jesus' situation, it does not suggest that Jesus had doubts about his identity or was seeking to veil it or was being coy. It merely indicates that Jesus was an ancient person who played out his life in a setting where "whose child one was" was far more important than "who one was" (one's inner self or uniqueness).

Something must be said at this juncture about Jesus as a change agent in a patriarchal world and about Jesus' relationships with his family. It has become a commonplace of discussion of Jesus' environment that he lived in a male-dominated and androcentric world. Slim evidence to the contrary, coming from Jewish colonies outside Israel, does not change the basic picture that has been usually painted of Galilee and Judea.[8] I know of no evidence of women in the Holy Land as synagogue leaders or elders or teachers of Torah with disciples prior to or during the time of Jesus. Still-extant traditional Near Eastern or Far Eastern cultures in our world are better analogies for what we find in Jesus' environment than anything in the West today. In this sort of environment it is no surprise that Jesus had twelve male disciples as his inner circle. What is very surprising is that he also apparently had various women disciples, something that would have scandalized many in his setting.

Clearly, Jesus was not a person who simply followed the flow of his culture, but equally clearly, he was able to relate to others in this male-dominated environment. This must tell us something about how Jesus viewed himself and his place in his Jewish world. His social approach to relationships was such that he could relate well to both men and women and could attract both men and women to his circle of disciples. This is, in part, why I suggested in my earlier work on women in Jesus' ministry that he must be seen as some sort of reformer within Judaism,[9] creating a community with differing values within that society, not as a revolutionary building base camps in Galilean villages in preparation for a revolt against the dominant Roman or client-king power structures.[10] He is eschatological and theocratic in orientation in a somewhat similar fashion to the Qumran community, and unlike the Zealots.[11]

One must admit that in Jesus' culture, his gender is probably part of why he was able to attract a following of both men and women in his social setting, why he was able to be a public person and build his social network as he did, why he was able to conjure up conjectures by various people about whether he was some sort of a messianic figure. Note, however, that his own teaching and way of relating suggest that he believed the in-breaking dominion of God was in the process of changing some of the social stereotypes and constrictions that especially plagued women and other subordinate members of society in this culture. This Jesus still does not fit neatly into modern pigeonholes of chauvinist or feminist.

If his gender was an asset as he strove to be some sort of leader figure in Israel, Jesus' geographical location and family connections would seem to have been liabilities. Jesus lived in a culture where people had no last names to distinguish one from another. Rather, a patronymic or a geographical tag was used to distinguish one person from another who had the same personal name. From start to finish in the Gospels, Jesus is regularly identified as Jesus of Nazareth (John 1:45–46; Mark 16:6). This cannot be accidental. Such an identifying label would seem to have ruled out any likelihood of Jesus being some kind of messianic figure (John 1:46). Yet in spite of this geographical tag, Jesus managed to raise eyebrows and messianic questions anyway. This indicates, albeit in an indirect fashion, that Jesus' words, deeds, and relationships must have been extraordinarily suggestive to overcome this sort of geographical identity marker. Surely no one was looking for God's eschatological Anointed One to come from a backwater town in Galilee such as Nazareth, and yet Jesus' followers enshrined this part of his identity repeatedly in the Gospels. One must ask how Jesus overcame this geographical determinism to stir up hopes and fears, curses and blessings, during his ministry. That Jesus was not simply dismissed by all and sundry suggests he did overcome this initial obstacle, at least in the minds of some.

Perhaps most important is the whole question of Jesus' family. What do we make of the fact that Jesus is rarely identified by a patronymic label—indeed, is sometimes identified by a matronymic label—in a culture where the question "Who is your father?" was always critical to figuring out identity? We do have texts such as John 1:45 or the variant reading of Mark 6:3, but in both cases it would appear that we are meant to think those speaking are not in the best position to know the full truth about Jesus' relationship with Mary's husband, Joseph. Indeed, both texts are laden with irony, for in Mark 6 the hometown crowd goes on to reject Jesus on the basis of what they think they know about his true identity, and in John 1 we have just begun a long trek through various attempts to name Jesus properly, a trek that does not come to a fully satisfactory conclusion until the confession of Thomas in John 20 matches up with that of the prologue in John 1.[12]

Furthermore, the most likely reading in Mark 6:3 is "the carpenter, the son of Mary," and there is some reason to suspect that this is meant as a disparaging identity statement.[13] If Jesus' parentage was open to question, it is very hard to see how he could have appeared to anyone in this culture to be a potential messianic figure *unless* something was dramatically impressive about his words, deeds, and relationships. The overcoming of traditional identity markers and boundaries is a telltale sign that Jesus did not present himself as just one of the crowd.

If we probe a bit further in regard to Jesus' relationship with his family, we note that it is plainly admitted in both the Synoptic and Johannine traditions that there was a certain distance between Jesus and his family during his ministry (Mark 3:21, 31–35; John 7:5); indeed, his family could not really be said to be followers of Jesus at this time. This is frankly a shocking admission in an environment where family, including extended family, was perhaps the chief building block of Jewish society, and where after the death of a father, the eldest son, in this case presumably Jesus, would be expected to take over as head of the kinship group. This was a critical matter in the times in which Jesus lived, precisely because, as Richard Horsley has suggested, enormous pressures were brought to bear on artisan-class family units in Galilee due to the stresses on the economy by tax farmers, client rulers, and others trying to raise funds.

To make matters worse, the Gospels suggest that Jesus actually befriended some of the tax and toll collectors in the region, even making them his disciples. This would surely have been seen as a betrayal by many Jews, perhaps even by members of Jesus' own family.[14] What one must ask is: How did Jesus during his itinerant ministry overcome the negative stigma of being considered a bad Jew, one who was a social deviant, one who associated with the wrong sorts of people, one who did not properly honor his parents and family by living among them and serving them? How, in spite of the fact that the text freely admits that Jesus apparently refused to be taken home by his family when he was causing too much controversy (Mark 3:31–35), did Jesus implant positive impressions in the minds and hearts of early Jews that suggested to some of them that he was a messianic figure?[15] Again, the more we know about the social matrix out of which Jesus came, the more it seems likely that Jesus must indeed have made some sort of messianic claims, indirectly or directly, to overcome so much and so many ordinary ancient beliefs about what established identity. I argue that only a strongly implanted suggestion during Jesus' lifetime to the effect that he was some sort of prophet or sage or messianic figure could have overcome all these obstacles and led those who knew Jesus before his death to proclaim him after the Easter events as the Jewish Messiah.[16]

It needs to be understood that it was expected to some degree for prophets and kingly figures and sages to deviate somewhat from the norm. For example, many in Israel would have seen John the Baptist as a true prophet despite his abnormal lifestyle. In Jesus' case, we must ask what sort of person, in this androcentric culture built on extended families, leaves home and family; itinerates with women and men; calls his own followers his family; fraternizes with women, slaves, minors, and tax collectors; and yet overcomes geographical and familial drawbacks to announce the arrival of the dominion of God. With this set of credentials it is not surprising so many saw Jesus as someone out of the ordinary either in a good way or a bad way.[17] What *is* surprising is that the positive viewpoint prevailed even after Jesus' execution.

The so-called big bang theory of Easter, which suggests that the appearances of Jesus are what created much of the later christological speculation, does not account for the social matters we have just discussed. It does not adequately deal with Jesus in his own social setting, and it is especially inadequate at dealing with the fact that the first post-Easter witnesses for Jesus had been pre-Easter followers whose hopes had been shattered, as the Gospels freely admit, on Good Friday (Luke 24:21). Note, too, that the social networks of Jesus continued to operate for him after his death. Indeed, to judge from Acts 1:14, the previously unpersuaded family members became persuaded. An adequate explanation must be given for all these remarkable facts. Bearing these things in mind, we turn to the so-called titles of Christ.

ENTITLED TO A NAME

Naming in antiquity was not very much like the modern practice in which a husband and wife gather together a list of names that they like and then choose a moniker for their child. It was often and widely assumed in antiquity that a name, and perhaps especially a nickname or self-chosen form of identification, revealed something about someone's nature. Names were not mere distinguishing labels in antiquity; they were badges of honor or dishonor. And the exercise of naming established a social relationship of power flowing in a particular direction from one person to another (Matt. 16:16–17; Mark 1:11). This process is different from title or honor recognition or from name-calling in the pejorative sense (John 8:48). It needs to be seen, then, that the titles Son of man, Son of God, Lord, and Christ are not names for Jesus or names that Jesus uses. In each case they represent claims to honor, and they are relational in character.

The first of these titles deserves the closest scrutiny. Whatever else one may wish to say about the endlessly debated phrase *bar enasha* ("son of man"), it is clearly not a proper name or a nickname in either Daniel 7 or the Gospels. In Daniel 7 it is intended as a description, functioning as part of an analogy. Furthermore, it says something about the relationship of the person in question to human beings. As with other Semitic phrases that use the expression "son of . . ." and then a qualifier, the qualifier is meant to inform us about something crucial or definitive that characterizes or shapes the person in question. For example, *Boanerges,* or "sons of thunder," was meant to tell us something about the Zebedees that shaped or characterized them in their actions or attitudes or words, just as the phrases "sons of light" and "sons of darkness" in the Qumran literature indicate persons whose lives are characterized by one or the other of these qualities. The idea is that an outside force or group is shaping or defining a person's identity.

In Daniel 7 the phrase *bar enasha* must be interpreted in the larger context of what is suggested about the evil empires discussed in the previous chapters—namely, that they are beastly in character when compared to this figure. The one "like a son of man" has a human face and can truly represent human beings, particularly God's people, in the presence of God. He is *representative* of these human beings (hence he is said to be like them), and he represents them. He, in turn, is given tasks and dominion somewhat reminiscent of those given Adam (compare Dan. 7:14 to Gen. 1:28).

Perhaps, then, the first question to be asked about Jesus' use of the phrase *bar enasha* of himself, especially when coupled with his regular pronouncements about God's dominion, is: Why did he most often choose this term to identify himself instead of, for instance, "son of David"?[18] The latter would have more clearly had a messianic ring to it, at least in some quarters. Perhaps the answer lies in the fact that Jesus believed he represented humankind with a different vision of kingdom than that of the beastly kingdoms. God's dominion, which Jesus would proclaim and seek to inaugurate, would be a place where things dehumanizing would have no place, and where even the least, last, and lost would be able to be all they were meant to be. In other words, "Son of man" is a relational phrase, but it indicates that Jesus saw himself as defined or characterized not by humanness as opposed to divineness but rather, to judge from Daniel 7, by humanness as opposed to subhumanness or beastliness, especially in the form of the structured evil found in empires and their tyrannical rulers. To put it another way, the coming of God's dominion was about humanity gone right in the Son of man as opposed to humanity gone beastly and wrong in Adam and his kin—or perhaps in Jesus' day, in Caesar and his kin or in Herod and his. This is what God had promised in Daniel 7.

The second phrase, "Son of God," will be more controversial, but it needs to be said that the Synoptic Gospels all suggest this phrase was first applied to Jesus by an outside source—namely, by a voice from heaven at his baptism (Mark 1:11 and parallels).[19] This phrase is known to have messianic overtones,[20] but here we are talking about the act of being named by a divine power. Identity is being confirmed or established through this experience, and it is suggested that who Jesus is will perhaps best be revealed by the sort of relationship he has with God. It is in this light that the shorter phrase "the Son" and the use of the term *Abba* take on fresh meaning.

We are being told that if one wants to know who Jesus is, one should contemplate how he relates to and names God and how, as a basis of that, he sees himself as being named by God. One is not Son of God in isolation but rather in constant relationship to the Divine. It is this idea, rather than his being son of Joseph or son of David, that characterized Jesus and how he viewed himself. Like other ancients, he is named by others, and like other ancients, he identifies himself by the group he sees himself representing. Yet for Jesus it is not finally gender, geography, or ethnic generation that is the determinant but even more basic determinants, both human and divine.

In many ways the scene we find in Mark 8:27–30 is a typical ancient naming story. Rather than Jesus telling his disciples who he is, he asks them what the word is on the street, so to speak. Having heard that answer, he then asks the disciples directly what they think. Their response, represented by Peter, is said to be that they thought Jesus was God's Anointed One, that is, the person especially imbued by God with power and mission to bring in God's reign among God's people. Once again, this is not a case of Jesus making a claim and then responding to challenges. Jesus operates like other ancients and is told how he is viewed, and then he can concur or disagree or conclude the discussion. In the earliest form of this story in Mark, Jesus appears not to disagree with the disciple's suggestion, though it is treated as a dangerous suggestion and apparently because of this is silenced. Notably, this title is the one closest to what seems to have appeared on the *titulus* at Jesus' death.

What would it have meant for Jesus to accept the acclamation that he was God's Anointed One, as he apparently did on this or some other occasion? It would mean that he recognized that his commission, his mission, his power, his authority came from God, and that he had certain eschatological tasks to perform for God and on behalf of God's people as a royal figure. It is telling that this term *mashiach,* which would more narrowly limit Jesus' scope to his relationship to Israel, is not his own preferred self-designation.[21] Yet he appears not to have simply rejected the suggestion that claiming this relationship for him was in some way appropriate.

Last, there is the term *Lord.* Apart from the fact that Jesus may have been called *mare* as a teacher or Jewish leader, indicating he was a respected figure, the Synoptics do not suggest that others named Jesus this during his ministry with a meaning other than the mundane sense of the term. It does appear, however, that Jesus may well have prompted such an exalted form of naming after he engaged in debate with other Jewish leaders about the significance of Psalm 110:1. Perhaps Jesus in this debate was suggesting that Davidic connections are not necessarily the most crucial issue when one is talking about one who is David's Lord (Mark 12:35–37 and parallels). If this is so, it comports with Jesus' efforts elsewhere to make clear that generation and geography should not be the final determinants of identity for someone such as this person that the scriptures describe. In short, it would make clear that Jesus was acting as an ancient person and dealing with relational language in a way that his social world would find understandable. A great deal more could be said along these lines, but it is appropriate to draw some conclusions at this point.

CONCLUSIONS—AND SO?

It is no accident that all the major titles used of Jesus in the Synoptics (Son of man, Son of God, Christ, Lord) refer to relationships that Jesus was believed to have had. One can only be a son in relationship to another or others; one can only be an anointed one in relationship to an anointer; and finally, one can only be a lord in relationship to some subjects. These titles attempt to tell us who Jesus was, not in isolation but in his social and religious relationships. The christological issue is framed in this fashion because of the social contours of the world out of which both Jesus and the Gospels came.

Whether we call it dyadic personality, as modern sociologists would, or group-formed identity, the christological discussions in the Gospels clearly manifest a world in which a person's identity was largely determined by whose child one was, what group one was an indigenous part of, and what locale one lived in. Into this world where gender, generation, and geography were major determinants of identity came Jesus, who at least in regard to the matter of generation and geography seems to have chosen to swim against the current. Then, too, he rejects various of the basic assumptions about what roles are appropriate in Jewish society for men and women. This is not because he could even remotely be thought of as being like a late-twentieth-century Western individual. It is because Jesus chose a different sort of social network in which to flesh out his identity, one where he would primarily and properly be named by God and by his own disciples, and by himself rather than by his parents, his hometown people, or even his fellow male leaders in early Judaism. It is the way in which Jesus modifies the social assumptions and networks of his day that reveals, more than any ordinary close scrutiny of titles could, that Jesus stood out from the crowd, chose to create his own community or family, and thereby made at least implicit and indirect claims about himself that were rightly interpreted by the earliest Christians as messianic or christological in character.

Jesus did not come on the scene of first-century Judaism to conform to anyone's preconceived expectations about prophets, sages, or messiahs, much less to our expectations at the end of the twentieth century. He came to make known something about God and something about humankind and something about their interrelationship in the crucible of a volatile environment, in which proclamations about the intervening saving reign of God were dangerous and could get one crucified because of what such messages implied about one's own relationships of power to both God and God's people. The names Jesus chose for himself, as well as the ones he accepted from others, both divine and human, are meant to help us locate Jesus on the social map of Jewish messianic pretenders and contenders. They distinguish Jesus from many other contemporary claimants, but they also identify him with basic elements embedded in the Hebrew scriptures as part of the hopes of God's people. The more we learn about Jesus' social matrix, the more clearly the christological questions seem to come into focus.

What this greater clarity does not do is settle whether we will name Jesus as the evangelists did. It is always possible that one may become convinced that though Jesus made a christological claim in the way in which he related to others (receiving and offering names), this claim was not justified. The truth about the historical issues does not settle whether we will conclude that the theological claims are also true.

Finally, whatever else we may say, it is clear enough from the recent sound and fury of the third quest for the historical Jesus that the Western world is still a Jesus-haunted place, with many wishing to claim Jesus for their own causes and caucuses.[22] In our own social context a bit more light on the historical Jesus is always welcome, especially when the hysterical Jesus is the one who seems to appear most frequently in the Western media.

Perhaps *fides quaerens intellectum* is, after all, not such a bad mode of pursuing and perusing this issue of Jesus' names and claims, since we know very well there is no such thing as pure objectivity in such matters. This Anselmian model appears to be the sane and sober one our honoree has offered us in his own work and in his works on the Christologies of the New Testament. It is my wish that his tribe may increase and his legacy to us all be appreciated and appropriated.

NOTES

1. See Ben Witherington III, *The Christology of Jesus* (Minneapolis: Fortress Press, 1990).

2. In the past twenty years, the writing of books and articles on the Christologies of and in the New Testament has proved to be a growth industry. Far before it was fashionable, however, some scholars were working very hard to discern the perspectives of the different New Testament writers on Jesus. Among those who concentrated on the perspectives of the Synoptic writers, none has contributed more to our understanding than Jack Dean Kingsbury. It is therefore a privilege to offer a chapter on Christology to this fine scholar, as part of a volume honoring his contribution to New Testament studies. I hope he will find this essay on Jesus' self-understanding an exercise in fertility rather than futility.

3. See John Meier, *A Marginal Jew: Rethinking the Historical Jesus,* vol. 2 (New York: Doubleday, 1994).

4. This seems, surprisingly enough, to be the assumption behind the recent effort by John W. Miller, *Jesus at Thirty: A Psychological and Historical Portrait* (Minneapolis: Fortress Press, 1997). There are some helpful insights in the work, in spite of Miller's attempt to explain Jesus on the basis of a midlife crisis.

5. See R. A. Burridge, *What Are the Gospels? A Comparison with Greco-Roman Biography* (Cambridge: Cambridge University Press, 1992). The case for Luke as biography is not convincing, not least because of the preface and opening chapter to that Gospel, which are crucial in defining its literary kind. See the introduction to my *The Acts of the Apostles: A Socio-Rhetorical Commentary* (Grand Rapids: Wm. B. Eerdmans Publishing Co., 1997).

6. On this latter front we would be able to deduce next to nothing from Mark or John, and even Matthew's and Luke's birth narratives leave us very little to work with. Luke 2:41–52 is a very slender foundation on which to build, and it sends a mixed signal. On the one hand, Jesus sees it as his duty to be doing what he was doing in the temple, even after his parents have left; on the other hand, he obeys his parents and goes home with them. Again, on the one hand, his growth in wisdom and stature is linked to obedience to his parents; on the other, he responds to the "your father and I" remark with a distinguishing reference to "my Father." In short, this is not a typical picture of a dutiful son enmeshed in the social and patriarchal webs of his culture.

7. See the discussion of this matter in B. J. Malina and J. H. Neyrey in *Portraits of Paul: An Archaeology of Ancient Personality* (Louisville, Ky.: Westminster John Knox Press, 1996). I owe the summary triad of gender, generation, and geography to them.

8. On which, see my *Women and the Genesis of Christianity* (Cambridge: Cambridge University Press, 1990).

9. The same sort of give and take with the dominant Jewish culture can be seen in Jesus' approach to the law. Sometimes he affirms it; sometimes he intensifies it; sometimes he offers new teaching; sometimes he suggests, by deeds or words, that portions of the law have been fulfilled or have had their day and no longer apply now that the dominion of God is breaking in. It is precisely because Jesus believes that God is bringing about divine rule by eschatological intervention that he feels no compulsion to lead a revolt.

10. Compare what I have suggested on this matter in *Women in the Ministry of Jesus* (Cambridge: Cambridge University Press, 1984) to what is said by E. P. Sanders in *The Historical Figure of Jesus* (London: Penguin Books, 1993).

11. Note that if it is the case that Jesus envisioned himself and his twelve disciples playing a role in the future judging of the twelve tribes of Israel and in the judgment that would come on sin in Israel, this would not distinguish him from the Qumranites, who, like Jesus, were not taking such action in

the present but were prepared to be a part of it as the "sons of light" later, when the final intervention came.

12. See my discussion on these texts in *John's Wisdom: A Commentary on the Fourth Gospel* (Louisville, Ky.: Westminster John Knox Press, 1995).

13. See my *Women in the Ministry of Jesus,* 85–92.

14. See Richard Horsley, *Galilee: History, Politics, People* (Valley Forge, Pa.: Trinity Press International, 1995), and idem, *Archaeology, History, and Society in Galilee* (Valley Forge, Pa.: Trinity Press International, 1996).

15. Nothing in the Gospels suggests that we should think Jesus' parents were not good and loving parents. A text such as Luke 2:41–52 should not be read with modern eyes. This is not about child neglect by Mary and Joseph. It is about the fact that Jesus was part of an extended family, not just a nuclear family, and in that situation it was perfectly understandable for the parents to assume Jesus was with other relatives and townspeople making the pilgrimage home from Jerusalem. The story also, as a side note, suggests strongly how devoted to Torah Galilean Jews were, that they came and went from feasts in Jerusalem in great numbers.

16. Indeed, they were so bold as to proclaim him Messiah in Jerusalem—where there were numerous witnesses to his execution, which presumably should have scotched the rumor that he was more than an ordinary mortal.

17. Note the suggestion in Mark 3:22 that Jesus is in league with the devil, that his social networks provide him power from a nefarious source; and in John 6:41–51 that Jesus is at best merely the son of Joseph, that he was not from God (compare 9:16).

18. I am assuming, with most scholars, that Jesus did use the phrase "Son of man" of himself in various contexts, and that in view of his proclamation of dominion it is likely that Daniel 7 lies somewhere in the background of the use of this phrase by Jesus. On this, see my *Christology of Jesus,* 238.

19. The earlier Markan form of the text is crucial here and makes clear that it is likely this was originally part of some sort of apocalyptic vision Jesus had at his baptism, not unlike the visions recorded in the book of Revelation. See my *Christology of Jesus,* 148–55.

20. This is evident from the discoveries in cave 4 at Qumran. See J. A. Fitzmyer, *The Gospel of Luke 10—24* (New York: Doubleday, 1981), 347.

21. Note how in Mark 14:61–62 he does not reject the suggestion of the high priest but immediately shifts the discussion to his preferred form of self-identification, "Son of man."

22. See my analysis in *The Jesus Quest: The Third Search for the Jew from Nazareth,* 2d ed. (Downers Grove, Ill.: Inter-Varsity Press, 1997).

THE CHRISTOLOGY
OF MATTHEW

Birger Gerhardsson

In a well-known pericope in the Synoptic Gospels, Jesus asks his disciples who people say he is. They mention some current guesses: in the Matthean version, John the Baptist, Elijah, Jeremiah, or one of the prophets. When Jesus then asks them their own opinion, their spokesman Peter answers: You are the Christ/Messiah, the Son of the living God—an answer that Jesus confirms (16:13–16). According to Mark, Peter answers that Jesus is the Christ/Messiah (8:27–30); according to Luke, the Christ/Messiah of God (9:18–21). The text reflects that Jesus was an enigmatic man, evoking the question of who he could be, and also that early Christianity could answer in somewhat diverse ways.

In this chapter, which I dedicate to Jack Kingsbury in gratitude for old friendship as well as for many fine studies from his hand both about the Gospel of Matthew and about Christology, I shall discuss Matthean Christology.

INTRODUCTION

Christology is, in traditional theological language, the doctrine of the person of Jesus as Christ, God's only Son, the Lord. The doctrine of his salvific work is usually taken by itself and called soteriology. This distinction is less helpful if we want to study historically the Christology of the New Testament books. The church fathers' penetrating questions about the secret of Jesus' person (how he could be both true God and true man, or how the relation between the Father, the Son, and the Spirit should be understood) were not even asked in the church in New Testament times. The questions about Jesus' identify were, at the beginning, of a more general nature and concerned mostly his life and achievement. It may in fact be said that the Christology of Matthew's Gospel represents the main content of the book. The Gospel of Matthew is from beginning to end a christological book.

Matthew is—like the other Gospels—a unity. A definite protagonist is in focus on each and every page of this writing. It is composed of motley materials; most of the constituents—narratives, aphorisms, parables, and so forth—were originally short, independent texts. In the edited, completed Gospel, however, these items belong together and are calculated to give a combined portrait of Jesus Christ, his work and message. We must respect the fact that the evangelist gives his witness about Jesus Christ this variegated form and this composite yet coherent content. If we choose to isolate one specific type of text and describe its Christology, we make an artificial analysis. What disappears is the fact that in Matthew (as in all other early Christian sources we know of), the material is diverse and obviously calculated to give a composite, many-sided picture of Jesus Christ. The source dissections and methodological distinctions we introduce are hypothetical. When the fictive sources we construct (Q, M, L, or whatever) are treated as fixed entities, which often happens, we are working on quagmire.

My main theme is thus the Christology of the first Gospel, read as it appeared in its final form between 80 and 100 C.E. It is important to remember that at that time Jesus Christ had, for forty or fifty years, been the object of profound pondering among the Christians, of constant conversation and penetrating reflection in the light of the ancient Holy Scriptures. Matthew wants to present an overall view of a Lord of whom his first readers have already rich ideas and living knowledge. It should not be taken as an elementary book.

It is hard to know whether the Gospel of Matthew was written to interact with already-existing collections of Jesus tradition or to stand entirely on its own. Much suggests, for instance, that the Gospel of Mark had been read and interpreted in the Matthean community for a decade, perhaps more, before the Gospel of Matthew received its final form. Did the evangelist presuppose that the Gospel of Mark would continue to be used and therefore needed only to be complemented, much as Kings continued to be read alongside Chronicles? Or did Matthew write a comprehensive book calculated to replace its predecessors and become the only Gospel in those congregations for which he was writing? We would very much like to have answers to such questions. When one wants to say everything, one does not write in the same way as when one wants only to make a supplementary contribution. One definite conclusion, anyhow, is that we cannot assume that Matthew repudiates those Christian views that he does not mention in his Gospel.

Matthew has no interest in telling his readers how Jesus *became* Jesus Christ, the Lord. From the beginning of his narrative, he regards Jesus as the Christ, the crucified and exalted Lord. It is foreign to Matthew to suggest some development in Jesus' person. From the first line of his book, Matthew presents the "complete," authentic Christ, the Son of the living God (16:16), to whom the Father has handed over all things (11:27) and to whom he has given all *exousia* (authority, power) in heaven and on earth (28:18). Luke, by comparison, narrates without hesitation that the child Jesus grew and increased in wisdom (2:40, 52), but Matthew does not touch even on a childhood development of that innocent and self-evident kind. He does not start with a *Vorgeschichte* (prehistory), with a narrative about Jesus' birth and childhood; in his first prologue (1:1–2:23), Matthew simply elucidates certain messianic and christological details that legitimize Jesus with the aid of the Holy Scriptures.[1] I will return to this point. After these passages, the evangelist, in a second prologue, proceeds with the forerunner John the Baptist and the baptism and testing that Jesus has to undergo before his public ministry in Israel (3:1–4:11). Both John and Jesus are by this point grown men. Of course, Matthew cannot give a complete picture of Jesus at once. Insights into his secrets must be introduced successively in the course of the narrative. But the motivation here is pedagogical. Jesus himself is the same throughout the Gospel.[2]

THE NAME OF JESUS

Before discussing various christological appellations in Matthew, I must briefly touch on Jesus' personal name, *Iēsous,* Hebrew *Jeshûa'*. This was a rather common Jewish male name in New Testament times. When the Synoptics narrate about the protagonist of their Gospels, they call him Jesus. Luke calls him the Lord at two or three places (7:13; 16:8 [?]; 22:61), but these are exceptions without parallel in Matthew (or Mark). Matthew always calls the leading character of his Gospel Jesus (and only twice Jesus Christ).[3] For the writer of the first Gospel, no christological title has received a status that allows it to function alone as the name of Matthew's protagonist, not even the titles "Christ" or "the Lord." The development, however, is on its way in this direction.

It was inevitable that, in the course of time, the name Jesus should receive christological connotations. We can see in Matthew that this process has started. When the name is mentioned the first time (1:21), its meaning is interpreted: "You are to name him Jesus, for he will save his people from their sins." This is not a simple rendering of the meaning of the name; it is an interpretation. The idea of salvation (*jāsha'*)   lay in the very name, but not that salvation freed people from their sins. In Matthew, the name Jesus has started to receive christological dimensions.[4]

It is interesting that Matthew brings in the savior name Emmanuel in this context. This name is not mentioned elsewhere in the New Testament. The fact that Joseph, at a heavenly command, gives the child the name Jesus is taken as a fulfillment of the ancient prophecy that the son of the virgin would receive the name Emmanuel (1:23). Both Jesus and Emmanuel have deep meaning for Matthew: Jesus comes to save his people from their sins (1:21), to serve and to give his life as a ransom for many (20:28), and his arrival means Emmanuel, that in him *God is with us* (1:23)—always, to the end of the age (28:20).

The name Emmanuel is thus adduced in this context even though Jesus did not actually receive that name. This is one example among innumerable others of the creative role that the Holy Scriptures play in early Christian thinking about Jesus. At the same time, both the name Jesus and the use of the name Emmanuel show that neither Jesus' person nor his fate is simply *created* by the words of the scriptures. The scriptures are quoted, but the fulfillment in Jesus was allowed to retain its own historically given profile. It is perfectly clear that statements and formulations from the scriptures not only elucidate and support but also color and fill out the presentation, but neither the person nor the story of Jesus is simply *taken* from the scriptures. A partly set picture of Jesus and his ministry existed even before it was all brought together with the statements of the prophetical books. The Christ of early Christianity was always Jesus of Nazareth, never anybody else. Important characteristics of his person and work made his picture resistant to interpretations of him that were too "fictional."

CHRISTOLOGY—INCLUSIVE THINKING

It is a great mistake to imagine that there ever existed a Christian congregation that gave Jesus only one title, that somewhere in early Christianity existed an exclusive, clear-cut son of David Christology, Messiah Christology, Kyrios Christology, Son of God Christology, or the like. We have no evidence of that. Here the analyses of modern New Testament scholars have created hypothetical entities that now live their own life in the learned debate, without ever having existed in antiquity. Everything shows that the enigmatic Jesus was identified with the aid of numerous titles and appellations even at the first Christian Easter. One needed a large cluster of such titles. These were allowed to function together; they did not normally compete against each other but simply complemented each other. Nor did they prevent new titles from being added, making the picture even richer. Christology was based on inclusive thinking.

In time, the different titles became essentially synonymous in the church. They referred—all of them, as the creeds of the church refer even today—to the same Jesus, the "whole" Jesus, from his preexistence to all eternity. But we can see that these titles were originally taken from different contexts, and we may presume that they had somewhat different content to begin with. When we ask to what extent these appellations affected one another and came to receive more or less the same meaning, however, we face a very complicated issue. Here scholars sin abundantly; many exegetes presume both that christological appellations which were taken into use for describing Jesus retained the value they had before being applied to him and that they continued to retain the same value after they became designations of Jesus. This, I think, is a gross misunderstanding. To early Christian teachers, the ancient appellations and motifs were only interesting insofar as they could say something about Jesus, and their individual, distinctive meanings became pliant and overlapping once they came to characterize him and nobody else.

The christological appellations appear in many different contexts. They are in the foreground in certain passages, but the focus is normally not on the titles themselves. This observation shows that they did not, in their early Christian context, retain much of an original, specified meaning that the Christian teachers were concerned to preserve.

In what follows, I try to elucidate the Christology of Matthew from these points of departure: *It is all about one single character, interpreted from different angles; one single Christology with many aspects.*

THE CONFESSIONAL TITLES

Matthew mentions quite a number of appellations of Jesus; they are all important, though not all equally important. For example, Jesus is called son of David more often in Matthew than in the other Gospels, especially in the narratives about his therapeutic activity, yet this title still has a limited significance.[5] Two of the titles are in a class of their own: the "Messiah/Christ" and the "Son of God."[6]

The designation *christos* (Messiah/Christ) became basic indeed for the Christians; in its Greek form, it soon became frozen as a second name of Jesus. The main reason was presumably that Jesus was crucified as a false messiah (Matt. 27:37; cf. Mark 15:26; Luke 23:38; John 19:19). Therefore, those who challenged the sentence had to insist that Jesus was indeed the Messiah, profess his messiahship, spread it, illustrate it, and present arguments for it.[7] The second significant reason was certainly that, with this title, the Christians could monopolize the Old Testament prophecies about a future final and decisive savior. Jesus was the one who was to come; nobody else should be waited for.[8] The title "Messiah/Christ" served the exclusivity of early Christian belief. Both these inducements are easily discernible in Matthew.

The designation "Messiah" is a title calculated to identify. Its centrality and importance can be seen in questions such as "Are you (is he? is this man?) the Messiah/Christ?" as well as in professing and confirming statements such as "You are (this one is) the Messiah/Christ." This title received a fixed place in the creeds of the church. Nonetheless, it was insufficient; it had to be specified and complemented.

The importance of the title *ho huios tou theou* (the Son of God) is clear from the fact that it, too, is found in confessional statements ("You are the Son of God") and in searching questions ("Are you the Son of God?"). But this title was not equally self-evident. "Son of God" was not a set title of an expected savior; it was an interpretive title with various applications. It gave, however, a basic answer to the question of who Jesus was, and it provided a better base than the title "Messiah/Christ" for a closer identification of Jesus. Therefore, it was soon combined with Christ, and this pairing became central for the church.[9]

In Paul, by comparison, the pattern is different. We can see in his letters that the predication "Lord" (*kyrios*) was an essential confessional title of Jesus. The credal statements "You are the Messiah/Christ" and "You are the Son of God" are both missing in Paul. Instead we find the creedlike acclamation "Jesus is Lord" (Rom. 10:9; 1 Cor. 12:3; Phil. 2:11). This is somewhat puzzling. The title "Lord" was vague and flexible; it could function as a very high predication but also as a colloquial title. Yet it could be used as a distinctive appellation of Jesus (notably, 1 Cor. 8:6). In Matthew (as well as in Mark) the flexible term *kyrios* is applied to Jesus only as a form of address, only in vocative form. That ought to mean that this word had not yet received any proper christological connotation for Mark and Matthew and in their congregations. It meant "sir" (certainly very respectfully).

The confession that Jesus is the Christ/Messiah, the Son of the living

God, is in Matthew first expressed by Jesus' leading disciple, Peter.[10] Jesus confirms Peter's identification and declares that it stems from heaven; it has been revealed to the disciple by Jesus' heavenly Father (16:13–20). Only Matthew makes this emphatic point in this pericope. In the baptism narrative, all three Synoptics narrate that heaven reveals the divine sonship of Jesus, but only the Baptist and Jesus are present on this occasion (Matt. 3:13–17; Mark 1:9–11; Luke 3:21–22). The same heavenly identification of Jesus is recorded in the transfiguration narrative; there, the witnesses are Peter, James, and John (Matt. 17:1–8; Mark 9:2–8; Luke 9:28–36). These texts, too, show what an essential role the identification of Jesus as the Son of God plays in the Christology of Matthew.

We are certainly to read Peter's confession at Caesarea Philippi as the core creed of Matthew and his church: "You are the Christ/Messiah, the Son of the living God."

THE SELF-TESTIMONY OF JESUS

The expression *ho huios tou anthrōpou* (the Son of man) is not like any other designation of Jesus in the Gospels. It is not a title; nobody calls him this, not even the narrator. The "Son of man" appears only as Jesus' self-appellation, as his circumlocutional way of saying "I."[11] We may discuss whether this designation with its double determinateness ("the Son of the man") also was calculated to suggest something more than the content "I," and whether in that case it suggested associations with an expected figure. But the two important points I recall now are just that the appellation is used by Jesus himself, but nobody else; and that it is an "I" designation. I do not think we have reasons for taking the expression "the Son of man" in the Gospels as a messianic title.

If we are asking for the Christology of Matthew, Jesus' self-testimony must be examined. First, then: What does Jesus say about himself in the Son of man sayings? None of Matthew's twenty-nine Son of man sayings is concerned with who Jesus *is*. Seven of them are pronouncements about his position and situation, powers and tasks, at the present time (for instance, that the Son of man has nowhere to lay his head, has *exousia* [authority/power] to forgive sins, is Lord of the Sabbath).[12] In seven other of these sayings, Jesus predicts his imminent passion, death, and resurrection.[13] And finally, fifteen of them concern Jesus' coming on the clouds in splendor and glory at the time of judgment.[14]

To summarize: *In the Gospel of Matthew, the status of Jesus—both in his humiliation and in his exaltation—and his entire work are covered by Son of man sayings.*[15] Self-testimonies of this type from Jesus' lips elucidate in Matthew the whole, composite picture of Christ. Yet none of these sayings addresses directly the question of who he *is*.

The Son of man sayings may be combined with other pronouncements in which Jesus speaks about himself: the so-called "I" sayings.[16] They address aspects of Jesus' work or details from it. Close to these are the sayings about the aim of Jesus' coming, statements introduced by *ēlthon* ("I have come").[17] These pronouncements, too, have something to say of interest for Matthean Christology.

Of special importance is the solemn declaration that the resurrected Jesus makes at the end of the Gospel: "All *exousia* [authority/power] in heaven and on earth has been given to me [by my Father]" (28:18; see also 11:27a).

In substance, even Jesus' pronouncement "You have one teacher [*didaskalos, kathēgētēs*]" in 23:8, 10 is a self-testimony, and a significant one. Samuel Byrskog has shown that the idea conveyed by these words has profoundly influenced the Gospel of Matthew—its revising of the transmitted material and its design as a whole. *The Matthean Christology has a strongly didactic character,* stronger than that of the other Gospels.[18]

Perhaps I should mention that the *parables* seem to have nothing to say of substantial christological interest.[19]

THE SON OF GOD
AND SERVANT OF GOD

The christological aspect that is beyond all comparison the most important to Matthew when he formulates his book about Jesus and his ministry is— as Jack Kingsbury wants to underline—the Son of God aspect.[20] I have myself always worked along the same line.[21]

The Gospel of Matthew starts with a double prologue, or two prologues. Prologue 1 (1:1–2:23) contains an account of the genealogy of Jesus Christ (vv. 1–17), followed by a pericope that clarifies the last member of the genealogy, the birth of Jesus (vv. 18–25). The question Matthew takes up here is how Jesus can be both God's son, conceived by Holy Spirit, and David's son. This question is asked by Jesus himself later on in the Gospel, in the controversy with the Pharisees in 22:41–46: If David calls him Lord, how can he be his son? Matthew's readers get to know the answer from the start.

Prologue 2 concerns Jesus' forerunner, the Baptist (3:1–12), followed by the double pericope about the baptism and testing of Jesus (3:13–4:11). At the end of the baptism narrative (3:13–17), Matthew narrates that Jesus, when he comes up from the water, sees the heavens open to him and the Spirit of God descending like a dove and alighting on him. Furthermore, a voice from heaven enunciates his great secret: "This is my Son, the Beloved, with whom I am well pleased." In Matthew, these heavenly words are not addressed to Jesus; they are said *about* him (to the readers of the Gospel). Matthew has even from the beginning indicated that Jesus is the Son of God, but now this is said expressly, and said from heaven. The heavenly Father confesses with his own voice his Son. The baptism is an act of consecration. Jesus sees the Spirit coming to him from above. But the Spirit has been with him even from his mother's womb. *Matthean Christology is not one of adoption.*

Nothing is said in the baptism narrative of how Jesus reacts to this proclamation from heaven. That which is missing in the baptism story comes, however, in the following pericope, in which Jesus is tested by the devil (4:1–11). It is done in simple, clear words. "The tempter," or "the tester" (*ho peirazōn*), addresses three provocative proposals to Jesus, following the model: If you are the Son of God, do this. . . . [22] Jesus' answers show that he does not want to exploit his Sonship to seek his own good. He wants to serve his heavenly Father in obedience and love. The three testing acts reveal that he obeys and loves his Father with his whole heart (first test), his whole soul (second test), and all his might (outer resources) (third test). In short, the double pericope about the baptism and testing of Jesus shows that Jesus is the Son of God and in everything intends to be the servant of God. The narrative illustrates with what mind-set he has come to serve and give his life a ransom for many (20:28).[23]

With the prologue about Jesus' baptism and testing, the evangelist has given his readers an introductory identification of Jesus. He has handed over the master key to Matthean Christology. Thus the readers know with what eyes the following presentation of Jesus' life and work should be read. It is made clear from the start that *Jesus Christ is the Son of God* and that *he goes about in Israel to work as the servant of God.*[24]

I have also tried to show along what tracks Matthew thinks when he depicts Jesus' history on earth. Jesus' ministry is divided into two very different periods. In the first period, the longest one (4:12–25:46), Jesus is successful and fortunate. Nothing can fail for him; nobody can withstand him. Matthew could not interpret this situation as chance, luck, or good fortune; it was the result of grace from God. It was said in traditional Jewish language about a human being in a situation of this kind that God was with him or her, that he or she was working in strength, or that he or she stood under the blessing or under the measure of God's kindness. Jesus works under these conditions during the first period of his ministry. But during the second period of his life on earth (26:1–27:56), his lot changes. When the hour comes, his enemies can attack him and do to him whatever they want. Matthew could not take this situation as a coincidence or blind fate either. Jesus' defeat had to be interpreted as permitted by God. The apple of God's eye could be crushed only because he was "delivered up" by God (16:21; 17:22–23; 20:17–19; 26:2, 24, 45), abandoned by God (27:46), and given into the hands of his enemies.[25] He was now in a situation of weakness, under the curse, experiencing God's severity, the measure of God's punishment. The theological interpretation of Jesus' situation on Golgotha is presented in the only statement that Jesus expresses in the crucifixion narrative: God has abandoned his Son (27:46).[26]

I have also tried to show that the crucifixion narrative in Matthew (27:32–56) should be read in the light of the prologue pericope about the testing of Jesus after his baptism (4:1–11). Matthew has, with the aid of small adjustments of the transmitted text, indicated that the hours of crucifixion are also hours of testing. Jesus is tested with regard to heart, soul, and might (outer resources) (27:33–34, 35–37, 38–54). And he stands the test: He accepts his lot from God without rebellion, in irreproachable obedience and love for God (4:1–11). The great event on Golgotha is that Jesus Christ gives his life a ransom for many (20:28; 26:28), but the testing reveals that his sacrifice is made in obedience and love and therefore without blemish or spot, blameless, perfect; it is therefore acceptable as a ransom.

Jesus shows, both in his time of strength and in his time of weakness, both when preserved and when delivered up by God, both under the divine blessing and under the divine curse—in rabbinic terms, both under God's measure of kindness and under God's measure of punishment—that he is the Son of God and in everything the servant of God.[27]

This also means that the second part of the saying that Jesus came to serve and give his life a ransom for many is illustrated more penetratingly in Matthew than is usually noticed. *Matthew portrays Jesus as the servant of God not only in his period of strength but also in the period when he becomes crucified in weakness,* if I may use Paul's expression (2 Cor. 13:4). In this way Matthew makes it clear that the salvific death is the climactic point in the earthly ministry of Jesus.

CHRIST'S SERVING IN STRENGTH

The classical creeds of the church—both the Nicene and the Apostles Creed—have a large lacuna. They have nothing to say about Jesus' *active* ministry on earth. They go directly from his birth to his passion. This is strange, considering the portrait of Christ's life and work in the Gospels, not least in the Gospel of Matthew.

Jesus' task on earth was, according to his self-testimony in Matthew 20:28, "to serve [*diakonēsai*], and to give his life a ransom for many." Matthew is, as I said, anxious to illustrate what his serving meant—he records numerous narratives and sayings—but he also summarizes in brief, pregnant words what Jesus' active ministry in Israel included under his period of strength, before he was delivered up to his enemies. Let us take a quick look back at that.

Two of Matthew's summarizing notices about Jesus' work in Israel have an inclusive, programmatic character. The evangelist states to what Jesus dedicated himself. He narrates that Jesus went throughout Galilee, "teaching [*didaskein*] in their synagogues and proclaiming [*kēryssein*] the good news of the kingdom and curing [*therapeuein*] every disease and every sickness among the people" (4:23; 9:35). In Matthew the verb *therapeuein* means "to heal" or "to cure," but it certainly retains also its general sense "to serve." When Jesus heals the sick, he fulfills the prophecy about the Suffering Servant in Isaiah 53 (Matt. 8:16–17).

Matthew has also words about Jesus' success during this part of his ministry. He says at the end of the Sermon on the Mount that Jesus taught the people as one having *exousia* (authority/power) and not as their scribes did (7:29), and he records in one of the narratives the opinion of the people that Jesus' therapeutic miracles outshone everything that had been seen earlier in Israel (9:33).

Similar to Mark and Luke, Matthew also indicates in a short formula what the message of Jesus was all about: "From that time Jesus began to proclaim, 'Repent, for the kingdom of heaven has come near'" (4:17). This summary is astonishingly general and vague. Matthew summarizes the message of the Baptist with the same words (3:2). The reason Matthew finds himself free to use this general summary in both cases (see also 10:7) is presumably that he accounts for Jesus' preaching and teaching with so much concrete material in what follows. I have already touched upon parts of it.

The second main task in Jesus' ministry was to cure sick people. When presenting Jesus' therapeutic acts, Matthew makes use of two types of text: nine summarizing notices telling that Jesus heals many sick at a place, and fourteen pericopes narrating how Jesus cures in individual cases.

In these summaries, Matthew provides large, generalizing information: Jesus heals all kinds of sickness and all who are sick, and he does so with ease. If we put together what is said in these notices, we receive the impression that Jesus eradicated all illness from Galilee. Here, theology has prevailed over historical correctness. The evangelist resorted to great words.[28]

These comprehensive passages depict Jesus Christ as "Israel's healer."

Matthew does not use this ancient divine predication (Ex. 15:26), but it would describe well Jesus' role in the Matthean summaries. *Matthean Christology has a conspicuous therapeutic aspect,* which should not be overlooked.

The fourteen concrete narratives about Jesus' therapeutic acts relate how Jesus heals in individual cases; each concerns one or two people who are sick or possessed (or dead). Matthew focuses especially on two things: Jesus' sovereign *exousia* (authority/power) from heaven and what happens when help-seeking people turn to him in faith. Their prayer is immediately heard. Yet in none of the depicted cases are they adherents, but always outsiders.[29]

Matthew tells that Jesus' care for the harassed and helpless crowds is dictated by compassion, that is, love (9:35–38, cf. 14:14; 15:32). His therapeutic acts are answers to prayers for pity.

THE ETHOS OF JESUS CHRIST: JESUS AS THE MODEL

None of the evangelists is so keen to account for the ethos of Jesus—his righteousness in life and action—as is Matthew. In his teaching, the Matthean Jesus criticizes above all that pious ethos which is but surface and appearance, and he calls for a piety that dominates the heart and thus the person in all that he or she is and does.

The ideal attitude in life is that required in the two great commandments in God's law, the commandments of love for God and for one's neighbor (Deut. 6:5; Lev. 19:18). Jesus' demand for authenticity and genuineness from within and all the way out is basic; the child of God must be whole and perfect (*teleios*). Certainly this ideal stems from the Shema: "with all your heart, and with all your soul, and with all your might" (Deut. 6:5). In much of the teaching material in Matthew, Jesus inculcates loving-kindness in different forms: taking pity, sacrificing, helping, forgiving, and so forth. The parable of the sower in Matthew 13 ends with a picture of the ideal listener to the words of the kingdom: Such a one hears and understands and therefore also performs what the heavenly words say.

This is not only teaching. Throughout the Gospel, Matthew is anxious to show that Jesus himself measures up to the demands. He depicts Jesus as a righteous man, as one who loves God with his whole heart, his whole soul, and all his resources. Jesus' mission of teaching and healing is dictated by compassion (love); his mighty acts are answers to prayers for pity. The Matthean Jesus lives as he teaches. He is therefore also a model—*the* model—for his believers. The typical invitation is: "Follow me!"[30]

The innermost secret of Jesus' ethos is presented in the pericope on how Jesus is tested by the devil after his baptism (4:1–11). There the three main aspects of his love for God are tested. And when the crucifixion narrative is read in the light of this prologue text, it becomes clear that Jesus shows perfect love for God, blameless obedience and righteousness, until death.

Matthean Christology has thus a conspicuous ethical dimension. It was important (especially as long as the church retained contact with her Jewish mother milieu) to show that Jesus, who had been condemned and executed as a criminal, was pure and innocent and righteous (*dikaios*). He fulfilled in life and work the law's decisive demand of *agapē*.

THE VINDICATION OF JESUS CHRIST

When Jesus Christ has taken the way of the servant to the end, his humiliation is over. His dead body is treated with piety; he receives a worthy funeral (27:57–61). Moreover, his Father vindicates him in accordance with his teaching: Everyone who has left precious things for Christ's name's sake will receive a hundredfold (19:29); whoever humbles self will be exalted (23:12); and whoever loses life for Christ's sake will find it (10:39). Jesus proves right. God recognizes him and acknowledges him, showing that he was not a transgressor but a righteous man. But now the case lies on the highest level. Jesus becomes "exalted and lifted up and very high," as is said of the Suffering Servant in Isaiah 52—53.

Matthew's narrative about the vindication of Jesus is based on the Easter material in the early Christian tradition, with some adjustments and additions. Most important is the grandiose final pericope about the farewell of the resurrected One to his disciples on the holy mountain in Galilee, a passage found only in Matthew (28:16–20).

This final pericope shows that Jesus Christ stands in the foreground to the very end of the Gospel of Matthew. Here the resurrected one elucidates his position in the world and gives his directives for the work that now must go on in his name: the work of the rule of God, exercised as the rule of Christ. The Son has received from his Father all *exousia* (authority/power) in heaven and on earth. His work will now be extended to all peoples; the borderline between Israel and the Gentiles is abolished.[31] The apostles are sent out to make disciples from all nations. In this work, the representatives of Jesus are not thrown on their own resources. Jesus will be with them— always, to the end of the age.

Here the evangelist obviously joins up with his introductory chapter, where the secret of Jesus is elucidated by the ancient Emmanuel prophecy.

That Jesus Christ is born on earth means that God has come near and is near to God's people. When Jesus has finished the earthly part of God's salvific work, the Emmanuel promise is made more precise: God, the Father, is near in the Son—and in the Spirit (28:19).

The grand finale is prepared from the beginning of the Gospel in other ways as well. In the first line of the book Jesus is called the Christ/Messiah, the son of David, the son of Abraham. Abraham is mentioned not only because he is the ancestor of Israel but also because the great promise he received from God included prospects for all the families of the earth (Gen. 12:3; 18:18). The openness toward other peoples appears over and over in the course of Matthew's narrative, starting with the wise men's adoration of the child in contrast with the hostile attitude of Israel's king and the leading men in Jerusalem (2:1–23). We are used to speaking of a "Gentile bias" in Matthew.

THE *EXOUSIA* OF JESUS CHRIST
AND HIS DISCIPLES

The relation between Jesus and his disciples, Jesus and the church, is a very important aspect of Matthew's presentation. Jesus starts his public ministry by calling disciples—the first four cases are recorded (4:18–22)—and finishes his work after his resurrection by giving the Eleven renewed confidence and sending them out to all peoples (28:16–20). Between these poles, the disciples are with Jesus, hearing and seeing, learning and practicing. At a central place in the Gospel, Jesus says to Peter that he will build his church upon him (16:13–20).

In Matthew's view, the disciples must grow and mature in Jesus' company. During his earthly ministry he empowers them to assist him in his work by proclaiming (*kēryssein*) the gospel of the kingdom and curing (*therapeuein*) the sick (10:1–15); but they cannot receive the crowning task of teaching (*didaskein*) prior to the farewell ceremony on the mountain in Galilee. Their education is not completed. Nor can the full commission be given to them until then. Jesus is and remains, according to Matthew, the Only Teacher (23:8, 10). The mission of the disciples is to teach the nations to obey that which the Only Teacher has commanded them, that is, everything that Matthew has accounted for in his book.

One group of pericopes about the mighty acts of Jesus in Matthew fulfills the function of elucidating Jesus' unlimited *exousia* (authority/power) and the part the disciples have in it. These are the six or seven pericopes about Jesus' nontherapeutic miracles.[32] These miraculous acts are all, in contrast to the therapeutic miracles, performed for Jesus' disciples or for one of them (Peter). Jesus reveals by these events how unlimited his divine *exousia* is—this authority and power that they have access to themselves—and reproaches them for their weak faith (*oligopistia*) and lack of insight. These pericopes, too, concern *exousia* and faith, but the faith at stake in these cases is that faith which the disciples need in order to execute Jesus' commission—that faith which can move mountains.

These mighty acts are not included in any of the nine notices in which Matthew summarizes Jesus' miraculous work in Israel. Thus they do not belong to that which defines Jesus' ministry. Yet they are important passages about the mission of the disciples and the church. *Their contribution to Christology in the first Gospel is that they illuminate the fullness of Jesus' divine* exousia.[33]

ACCORDING TO THE SCRIPTURES

Nowhere in the Old Testament do we find a comprehensive messiah picture that accords with the early Christian picture of Jesus Christ. Yet practically every page of the New Testament witnesses to the early Christians' eagerness to show that the ministry of Jesus took place "according to the scriptures." They were bent on finding that his appearance, work, and fate accorded even in its details with the Law and the Prophets: The scriptures were fulfilled in him and he fulfilled the scriptures. The efforts are most strikingly evident in the Gospel of Matthew, especially in the eleven so-called formula quotations ("All this took place to fulfill what had been spoken by the Lord through the prophet").[34]

Exegesis during our century has shown great interest in analyzing how the New Testament writers interpreted the fulfillment of the ancient prophecies—not only explicit prophetical words but also other Old Testament words that they could read prophetically. The question of to what extent and how Jesus fulfilled the Law—the Torah—has not evoked the same attention. Yet this question must have been of utmost importance for Jesus' first adherents. He had been executed, and a sentence to death must have been based on the law. In Matthew, his leading Jewish enemies call him an impostor, a deceiver (*planos,* 27:63; cf. 9:34; 12:24).

According to the adherents of Jesus, all the accusations against him were false. Jesus refutes in the Gospel of Matthew the allegation that his intention is to abolish the Law and the Prophets; he has come to fulfill them (5:17–48). Nowhere in the Gospel of Matthew does Jesus speak against the law or act against it. The accusations that his forgiveness of sins is blasphemy, that he transgresses the Sabbath commandment, and that he casts out demons by Beelzebul are repudiated (9:1–8; 12:9–14; 12:22–31). The accusation at the trial that he had spoken outrageous words against the temple did not prevail, according to Matthew. Jesus did not transgress the law.[35]

Nor was he condemned by the great council because his intentions were misunderstood; the basis of the verdict was his own explicit confession that he was the Messiah/Christ, the Son of God, who would soon come on the clouds of heaven. *This* was taken as blasphemy (26:57–68).

Matthew keeps always in mind that Jesus fulfills the Law and the Prophets. I have already mentioned the programmatic section of the Sermon on the Mount (5:17–48). Let me also recall the Synoptic pericope about the foremost commandment. Matthew has revised this text so that it presents a hermeneutic program for a right exposition of the Law and the Prophets (22:34–40). The basic principle is that all other commandments are to be considered as "hanging" on the demands of the two love commandments, that is, as being derived from them. This shows what the words "not to abolish but to fulfill" mean. The antitheses of the Sermon on the Mount give us six examples of how this hermeneutic program functions in practice. The ancient individual commandments are made total and absolute at the same time as their character is changed: They are now *agapē*-demands.[36] *That is the way in which the scriptures are to be interpreted according to Matthew;* so Jesus Christ taught and so he conducted his own life.

SUMMARY

Christology was, from the very beginning, based on inclusive thinking. There never existed an exclusive, clear-cut Messiah Christology, son of David Christology, Son of God Christology, or the like. Nor did any Christian group ever exist that could content itself with a Christology of one specific kind. All groups needed a cluster of appellations to identify Jesus. The different high designations were taken from different contexts and may originally have had somewhat different points, but when applied to Jesus they became pliant and shaded into one another to suit their new function. In the long run they became essentially synonymous; all of them signify the "whole" Jesus.

Matthew paints a composite and yet coherent picture of Jesus with the aid of diversified material. His Gospel is from beginning to end a christological book. I have in this chapter tried to give a sketchy account of the evangelist's Christology, in which the christological *appellations* fulfill but a limited function. We meet its core form in the first confession of the leading disciple, Peter: "You are the Christ/Messiah, the Son of the living God." Jesus' ministry is well summarized in the saying that he "has come to serve and give his life a ransom for many." Matthew narrates about his serving both during the first, "strong" period of his life and then in his period of "weakness." The narratives of the testing after his baptism and on the cross are calculated to reveal that he is the true Son of God, who works in everything as the servant of God. His mission during his period of strength consists of preaching, teaching, and curing the sick. Jesus' period of weakness and humiliation is followed by vindication from heaven, exaltation.

Among the typical characteristics of Matthean Christology, we may mention that it is inclusive, that it has a strongly didactic character, that it has a conspicuous therapeutic aspect, and that it has an important ethical dimension. It can also in all its details be supported by the Holy Scriptures. Furthermore, Matthew elucidates the relations between Jesus Christ and his disciples/the church, not least how his *exousia* is to function with the disciples, as well as the way in which the message of the rule/kingdom of God is to find its way to all peoples. The work of Jesus Christ must now be carried on in the name of the Father and the Son and the Holy Spirit.[37]

NOTES

1. K. Stendahl has drawn our attention to the fact that the first chapter in Matthew comments on some *names* and the second on some *places* connected with Jesus. His birth and childhood are not presented. See K. Stendahl, "Quis? et Unde? An Analysis of Matthew 1–2," in *Judentum, Urchristentum, Kirche*, ed. W. Eltester (Berlin: Töpelmann, 1960), 94–105.
2. S. Byrskog, "Slutet Gott, allting Gott. Matteus 28:16–20 I narrativt Perspektiv," in *Matteus och hans läsare—Förr och nu*, ed. B. Olsson, S. Byrskog, and W. Übelacker (Lund: Teologiska Institutionen, 1997), 85–98.
3. Matthew 1:1, 18. Note that only 1:18 is properly narrative. Compare Mark 1:1.
4. Note also how Jesus' name is used in 7:22 and 18:20.
5. Jesus is not called son of David by his disciples, nor by his prominent opponents, but only by ignorant outsiders: a heathen woman, four blind men, the crowds, and some children in the temple. See J. Kingsbury, "The Title 'Son of David' in Matthew's Gospel," *Journal of Biblical Literature* 95 (1976): 591–602; and my own book *The Mighty Acts of Jesus according to Matthew* (Lund: Gleerup, 1979), 86–88.
6. See, for example, H. F. von Campenhausen, "Das Bekenntnis im Urchristentum," *Zeitschrift für die neutestamentliche Wissenschaft* 63 (1972): 217–19.

7. See W. Kramer, *Christ, Lord, Son of God,* Studies in Biblical Theology 50 (London: SCM Press, 1966), 19–44. He makes the observation that in the Pauline material (and even earlier) the title "Christ" is firmly associated with Jesus' death.

8. Note the expression "the one who is to come" in 11:3.

9. B. Gerhardsson, "Den äldsta kristna bekännelsen och dess rötter," in B. Gerhardsson and P. E. Persson, *Kyrkans bekännelsefråga* (Malmö: Liber Förlag, 1985), 9–106, 201–9, 212–23.

10. Note, however, the spontaneous exclamation of the disciples in the boat, after having seen Jesus and Peter walking on the sea: "Truly you are the Son of God" (14:33).

11. The exception in John 12:34 is only apparent; the people react with a question to Jesus: What do you mean with your talk of the Son of man?

12. Matthew 8:20; 9:6; 11:19; 12:8, 32; 13:37; 20:28.

13. Matthew 17:12, 22; 20:18; 26:2, 24 (twice), 45.

14. Matthew 10:23; 12:40; 13:41; 16:27, 28; 17:9; 19:28; 24:27, 30 (twice), 37, 39, 44; 25:31; 26:64.

15. Jack Kingsbury emphasizes that Jesus employs this "technical term" in public, especially in the full view of his opponents. See J. D. Kingsbury, *Matthew as Story,* 2d ed. (Philadelphia: Fortress Press, 1986), 95–102.

16. Matthew 5:17; 10:34–39, 40; 11:18–19; 15:24. Note also 8:10; 10:16; 10:37, 38; 11:27–30; 12:27, 28; 16:8–11; 18:20; 19:28; 28:18–20. Compare R. Bultmann's classical discussion of these sayings in *The History of the Synoptic Tradition* (Oxford: Basil Blackwell Publisher, 1963), 150–66.

17. Matthew 5:17 (twice); 9:13; 10:34 (twice), 35; cf. 11:19; 18:11; 20:28.

18. See S. Byrskog, *Jesus the Only Teacher: Didactic Authority and Transmission in Ancient Israel, Ancient Judaism and the Matthean Community,* Coniectanea biblica, New Testament 24 (Stockholm: Almqvist & Wiksell International, 1994).

19. See my analyses of the message of the parables in "Illuminating the Kingdom: Narrative Meshalim in the Synoptic Gospels," in *Jesus and the Oral Gospel Tradition,* ed. H. Wansbrough, Journal for the Study of the New Testament Supplement Series 64 (Sheffield: JSOT Press, 1991), 283–91.

20. See especially Kingsbury, *Matthew as Story.*

21. See especially my book *The Testing of God's Son (Matt. 4:1–11 and Par),* Coniectanea biblica, New Testament 2 (Lund: Gleerup, 1966); and those articles that have been republished in my book *The Shema in the New Testament: Deut. 6:4–5 in Significant Passages* (Lund: Novapress, 1996).

22. Even the third proposal is meant as a testing of Jesus' Sonship. It was, however, necessary to vary the wording in this case. The devil could not reasonably say, "If you are the Son of God, fall down and worship me!"

23. See Gerhardsson, *Testing of God's Son.* There I tried to show that Jesus is not tempted in this pericope but tested, that he is not tested as the Messiah

but as the Son of God, and that the greatest commandment in the law (Deut. 6:4–5) was used as the criterion for the testing. Today, I think many colleagues agree with me on the first two points; very few, however, seem to ask the question concerning the criterion of the testing.

24. See my article "Gottes Sohn als Diener Gottes," in *Shema in the New Testament*, 139–72.

25. Compare the Johannine reflection in John 7:30; 8:20b.

26. Jesus' cry does not express what he *feels*. He only classifies his situation and asks God: Why? See my articles "Jesus, ausgeliefert und verlassen—nach dem Passionsbericht des Matthäusevangeliums" in *Shema in the New Testament*, 109–38 (esp. 124–32); and "Gottes Sohn als Diener Gottes," in *Shema in the New Testament*, 139–72 (esp. 162–69).

27. Gerhardsson, "Jesus, ausgeliefert," 124–34; and idem, "Gottes Sohn," 162–69.

28. See Gerhardsson, *Mighty Acts of Jesus*, 20–37.

29. Ibid., 38–51.

30. See my book *The Ethos of the Bible* (Philadelphia: Fortress Press, 1980; London: Darton, Longman & Todd, 1981), 33–62 (esp. 54–60); and my article "'An ihren Früchten sollt ihr sie erkennen' in die Legitimitätsfrage in der matthäischen Christologie," in *Shema in the New Testament*, 173–86.

31. I do not think that the address to all peoples here excludes Israel. The meaning is presumably that Israel has lost its position as the favorite child, without, however, being rejected.

32. Matthew 14:13–21; 15:29–39; 8:23–27; 14:22–27, 32; 14:28–31; 17:24–27; 21:18–22.

33. See Gerhardsson, *Mighty Acts of Jesus*, 52–67.

34. Matthew 1:22–23; 2:5–6, 15, 17–18, 23; 4:14–16; 8:17; 12:17–20; 13:14–15, 35; 21:4–5; 27:9–10; compare 26:56.

35. See above, note 30.

36. See my article (from 1976) "The Hermeneutic Program in Matthew 22:37–40," in *Shema in the New Testament*, 202–23.

37. Stephen Westerholm polished my English; I thank him.

THE CHRISTOLOGY OF MARK'S GOSPEL: NARRATIVE CHRISTOLOGY AND THE MARKAN JESUS

Elizabeth Struthers Malbon

A PERSONAL PREFACE

I am pleased and honored to be invited to join with others to honor Jack Dean Kingsbury on the occasion of his sixty-fifth birthday. Neither a student of nor a student or local colleague with Kingsbury, I have been one of his many national colleagues who have been engaged in lively interpretive debates through the meetings of the Society of Biblical Literature. I am also challenged in a way the others who honor him here are not—by writing a chapter on a topic on which Professor Kingsbury wrote the book *The Christology of Mark's Gospel*. When he published this significant scholarly monograph in 1983, Kingsbury explained that he had "undertaken a balancing act":

> While keeping the reader in touch with the plot of Mark by tracing the development of the motif of the secret of Jesus' identity, I have also attended to what I perceive to be the more stubborn problem of ascertaining the meaning and function of major titles of majesty.[1]

My own, more limited goal here will also be a balancing act, but I will be balancing my own perspectives with Kingsbury's. Not wishing to repeat all that we hold in common, and not being able to cover in my brief chapter all that he has covered in his full book, I wish to highlight some different ways of approaching the problem of "Christology" in Mark's Gospel.

While we hold in common a literary-critical—or more specifically, a narrative-critical—approach, I will not be balancing this approach with a more traditional focus on "major titles of majesty." After my recent and third reading of *The Christology of Mark's Gospel*—and there are relatively few scholarly monographs I have found it profitable to read three times—and my second reading of the closely related book "for pastors and students," *Conflict in Mark: Jesus, Authorities, Disciples* (1989), I appreciate more fully how Kingsbury has identified with the point of view of the narrator of the Markan Gospel. My essay, in balancing that perspective, will draw greater attention to the point of view of the protagonist of the Markan Gospel, the character Jesus.

I have been asked why (unlike Kingsbury) I have never written specifically about Jesus or Christology. I have been observing Markan characters for quite some time and have written on the disciples and the crowd,[2] the women characters and the broader category of fallible followers,[3] the Jewish leaders,[4] and the so-called minor characters[5]—nearly all the characters around Jesus. I have also written about the significance of the spatial settings throughout which those characters and Jesus move in Mark's story.[6] It is from this perspective that I now turn my attention to the Gospel's central character, Jesus, whom the narrator presents (as Kingsbury explicates so well) as "Jesus Christ, the Son of God" (1:1).

ENACTED CHRISTOLOGY

I am less comfortable than Kingsbury in thinking of Christology as something the Gospel of Mark explicitly *has*. Kingsbury's use of the term *identity,* for example, seems too reified when applied to Mark's story of Jesus. "Who Jesus is" comes across, in Kingsbury's explication, as some unchanging essence, not unrelated to but in distinction from Jesus' particular actions. Thus, Kingsbury can distinguish Jesus' "identity" (made known chiefly through what Kingsbury identifies as the title "Son of God," applied by the Markan narrator and characters other than Jesus) and Jesus' "destiny" (referred to by what Kingsbury designates as the technical term "Son of man," employed by Jesus alone). I find more helpful the title phrase of Robert Tannehill's classic essay on this topic, "The Gospel of Mark as Narrative Christology,"[7] because in that phrase recognition is explicitly given to the implicit nature of any Markan Christology. Because Mark's Gospel is a narrative, whatever Christology it offers is presented narratively, that is, through the plotted actions of the characters as narrated. Whereas Kingsbury pursues questions of Jesus' identity, Tannehill discusses Jesus' "commission" from God.

Both Kingsbury and Tannehill consider the actions of the Markan Jesus a crucial aspect of Markan (narrative) Christology. Because Jesus' actions are so intertwined with the actions of other characters, Kingsbury does a fuller job of discussing them in *Conflict in Mark,* where his three stories (the story of Jesus, the story of the authorities, and the story of the disciples) parallel Tannehill's three commissions (the commission Jesus receives from God, the commission the disciples receive from Jesus, and the commission of Jesus' "opponents"). With considerable overlap with Kingsbury's two books, and even more with Tannehill's article, I observe that the Christology of Mark's Gospel is "enacted Christology."

Throughout the first half of the Gospel, the Markan Jesus' primary activities are teaching, preaching, healing, and exorcising demons. All these actions serve as evidence for the reality of Jesus' archetypal preaching statement: "The time is fulfilled, and the kingdom of God has come near" (1:15a). Kingsbury has little to say about the kingdom (or rule) of God in his discussion of Markan Christology. The in-breaking rule of God is implicit in Tannehill's judgment that "Jesus' commission [from God] is central in Mark" and Jesus' "basic role" is that of "eschatological salvation bringer."[8] It is Jesus' teaching and preaching and his healing and exorcising, along with his calling of disciples, that appear to be summed up in the dialogue between Jesus and Peter that leads to Peter's words "You are the Christ" (8:29; NRSV, "Messiah"; Greek, *christos*). Clearly this statement, which echoes the first half of the narrator's opening statement about "Jesus Christ, the Son of God" (1:1) and occurs about halfway through the narrative, is a significant marker of narrative Christology. Both Kingsbury and Tannehill offer simple outlines of the Markan Gospel as part of their discussions of Christology, and both outlines indicate the beginning of a major subunit of the narrative with the story of "Peter's confession" (8:27–30).

Both outlines also illustrate the interrelations of one's outline and one's overall interpretation. Each scholar suggests three divisions:

Kingsbury		*Tannehill*
1:1–13	beginning	1:1–8:26
1:14–8:26	middle	8:27–10:52
8:27–16:8	end	11:1–16:8

Kingsbury's "beginning" section is very short, which creates the awkward situation of having the "middle" section begin at the fourteenth verse of the narrative, but the division thereby draws attention to the baptism scene: "the centerpiece of the first main part of Mark's story. Here God, participating as 'actor' in the story, formally identifies for the reader 'who Jesus is.' "[9] Since the narrator has already identified Jesus as "the Son of God" in 1:1, God's calling Jesus "Son" at 1:11 shows the narrator's point of view to be aligned with God's point of view. (I do not disagree with this interpretation, but there is much more to the story.) Kingsbury's "middle" and "end" sections are basically the two halves of the Gospel: the first shows Jesus' powerful actions as teacher and healer, the second shows Jesus' willingness to suffer. Tannehill's outline also manifests this twofold division of Jesus' actions: 1:1–8:26, teaching and healing, and 11:1–16:8, suffering, with a middle section, 8:27–10:52, in which Jesus attempts to prepare his disciples for the significant shift. Both outlines emphasis *the* "christological" surprise of Mark's Gospel: The powerful one who teaches and heals with God's authority accepts his suffering and death at human hands as the will of God.

My Markan outline, which can only be sketched here, naturally also correlates with my overall interpretation of Mark, but it may suggest some aspects of Markan narrative Christology that the other two do not, especially if the focus is on "enacted Christology."

1:1–45	Jesus and the rule of God
2:1–3:6	Jesus and the established community
3:7–35	Jesus and the new community
4:1–34	Jesus' powerful words: the rule of God (seed-time)
4:35–8:26	Jesus' powerful deeds: for Jews and Gentiles
8:27–10:52	Jesus and disciples (leaders of the new community) "on the way"
11—12	Jesus and the established community
13	Jesus' powerful words: the rule of God (harvest) (the passion of the new community)
14—16	Jesus' passion

I have argued elsewhere that the spatial settings of 4:35–8:26, for example, call attention to the symbolic extension of Jesus' ministry to both Jews and Gentiles.[10] If Mark's question were "Who is Jesus?" and if a dominant answer of the first half of the narrative were "He is the Christ," an additional answer, narrated in 4:35–8:26, would be "He is the Christ for all those he teaches, heals, and feeds—both Jews and Gentiles." This is a christological statement, not merely a geopolitical one. However, I think Mark's question is more appropriately put "What does it mean for Jesus to be the Christ, the Son of God?"—stressing not identity but implication. It means that Jesus' proclamation of the nearness of God is good news for both Jews and Gentiles; go tell.

In his attempt to balance a literary-critical, or perhaps narrative-critical, approach with a study of christological titles in Mark, Kingsbury privileges the two titles, and especially the second one, privileged by the Markan narrator in the title of the narrative: "The beginning of the gospel [NRSV, 'good news'] of Jesus Christ, the Son of God" (1:1). If one is going to privilege christological titles (or titles of majesty) in a discussion of Christology and yet also wishes to take the narrative itself into consideration, this interpretive move makes sense.[11] I am more concerned to examine all the ways the narrative employs to disclose its central character, Jesus: not only what Jesus does—the actions he initiates ("enacted Christology") and what the narrator and other characters say about him (Kingsbury's focus)—but also what Jesus says, and does, in response to what these others say about him ("deflected Christology"); what Jesus says about himself and God ("refracted Christology"); and how what other characters do is related to what Jesus says and does ("reflected Christology"). I have introduced the concept of enacted Christology above. Below I present my understanding of deflected Christology. Discussion of refracted and reflected Christology must await another occasion.

DEFLECTED CHRISTOLOGY

At least since William Wrede's challenging work on the "messianic secret" (first published in 1901), commentators have been unable to overlook the puzzling commands for secrecy made by the Markan Jesus.[12] Scholars have not agreed on exactly which data are to be included as part of the messianic secret in Mark, nor on how these data are to be interpreted, but Kingsbury judged the issue of such importance to Markan Christology that he made discussion of it primary (chapter 1) and foundational for his study. Kingsbury sees the secret of Jesus' "identity" in Mark as linked more with the title "Son of God" than with the title "Messiah" (Christ); and although he recognizes that the secret is not really a secret to the readers, since the narrator makes it plain in 1:1, he takes care to show how various statements in the narrative that might seem to "break" the secret (Jesus' "Son of man" statements and Bartimaeus's cry of "son of David") in fact do not. Kingsbury discusses the secrecy motif in terms of Jesus' identity, and he admits, although it is not of central importance to his argument, that "it is more accurate to say that it is from the standpoint of the reader that Mark depicts the progressive disclosure of Jesus' identity."[13] A thoroughgoing narrative analysis suggests another way to look at the evidence of the messianic secret in Mark but confirms the importance of this material for a Markan narrative Christology.

Characters are revealed to their audience (a term I use in preference to "readers" because of its inclusivity of hearers as well) by what they say and do and by what others say and do—to and about them and in relationship with them. Mark's narrative manifests a significant gap between what the character Jesus says about himself and what other characters and the narrator say about him. Here we consider Jesus' responses that *deflect* away from himself the recognition, honor (sincere or sarcastic), or attention a character, group of characters, or the narrator intends to give. The words of the Markan Jesus do not echo the words (titles? labels? descriptions?) of the Markan unclean spirits, crowds, John the Baptizer, Herod, Peter, Bartimaeus, high priest, Pilate, chief priests and scribes, centurion, or narrator. We begin with a look at what the unclean spirits and demons have to say, along with the crowds, because these two character groups are most involved with the so-called messianic secret.

From the beginning the unclean spirits (and demons) know who "Jesus of Nazareth" is—"the Holy One of God" who has "come to destroy" them (1:24). How they come into this knowledge is not stated explicitly, but it is implicitly connected to the coming near of the kingdom (rule) of God that Jesus proclaims (1:15) and the breaking up of the kingdom of Satan to which Jesus alludes (3:23–27). Three times this knowledge is narrated in direct speech: the unclean spirit possessing the man in the synagogue in Capernaum, quoted above (1:24); the unclean spirits described in a summary passage (3:11, "You are the Son of God!"); and the legion of unclean spirits inhabiting the Gerasene (5:7, "Jesus, Son of the Most High God"). Once the narrator simply states that "the demons . . . knew him [Jesus]" (1:34). In each of the four cases, the response of the Markan Jesus is to silence them: "But Jesus rebuked him, saying, 'Be silent, and come out of him!'" (1:25); ". . . and he would not permit the demons to speak, because they knew him" (1:34); "But he sternly ordered them not to make him known" (3:12); and in the case of the Gerasene demoniac, the noisy silencing comes by their negotiated sending into the swine, who rush down the steep bank and are drowned in the sea. All four responses are reported by the narrator, who seems thereby well aware of Jesus' reticence in being made known (at the very least by *these* characters, and perhaps more broadly) as the Son or Holy One of God.

Throughout at least the first half of Mark's narrative, people in general, or the crowds, respond to Jesus in amazement, awe, or wonder—especially in response to his healings. Over and over the narrator reports Jesus' commands to the healed (and their families) to "say nothing to anyone" (1:44; compare 5:43; 7:36; 8:26). Twice Jesus even isolates the person before the healing (7:33 and 8:23), apparently to deflect attention. However, no one seems surprised when these impossible commands are not obeyed; it would be pretty difficult, for example, for Jairus and his wife not to tell the mourners (5:38) that their daughter's funeral is off! But the point here is that the Markan narrator repeatedly gives evidence of Jesus' reticence to be known as a healer and of his desire to deflect such attention.

Repeatedly the narrator notes that Jesus tried to escape the attentions of the crowds. Alone he "went out to a deserted place" to pray (1:35); he invited his disciples, "Come away to a deserted place all by yourselves and rest a while" (6:31). He even requested the disciples "to have a boat ready for him because of the crowd, so that they would not crush him" (3:9; compare 4:35 and 8:13). Later "he made his disciples get into the boat and go on ahead to the other side" of the Sea of Galilee "while he dismissed the crowd" and "went up on the mountain to pray" (6:45–46). To state the obvious: The Markan Jesus' prayer was to God; his retreats from the crowd, and sometimes even from the disciples, were made to attend to God. In the "region of Tyre," Jesus "entered a house and did not want anyone to know he was there." "Yet," the narrator admits, "he could not escape notice" (7:24).

The narrator imparts to Jesus' apparent "shyness" a theological motive: The Markan Jesus wishes to *deflect* the attention given to him, especially as healer, to the true source of the healing, God. Two occasions make this explicit. The narration of an early healing of a (Jewish) leper concludes with Jesus' command for secrecy and his command that thanksgiving be offered to God, following Jewish sacrificial tradition: "See that you say nothing to anyone; but go, show yourself to the priest, and offer for your cleansing what Moses commanded, as a testimony to them" (1:44; compare the response of the people in the synagogue in Capernaum to Jesus' healing of the paralytic: they "glorified God," 2:12). The narration of a later healing of a (Gentile) demoniac concludes with Jesus' command for containing the news of the exorcism (You may not go with me; "Go home to your friends") but attributing it to the Lord God: "Tell them how much the Lord has done for you, and what mercy he [God] has shown you" (5:19).

Although reporting Jesus' attempts to direct attention to God—hence, deflected Christology—the narrator seems more aligned with the point of view of the Gerasene demoniac, who "went away and began to proclaim in the Decapolis [the "Ten Cities" were hardly his "home"] how much Jesus [the Lord?] had done for him" (5:20).[14]

Jesus' reticence and the Markan deflected Christology are not restricted to the healing ministry. When, at Jesus' own query, Peter stated, "You are the Christ" (8:29; NRSV, "Messiah"), Jesus "sternly ordered them not to tell anyone about him" (8:30). After the transfiguration in the presence of Peter, James, and John, Jesus "ordered them to tell no one about what they had seen, until after the Son of Man had risen from the dead" (9:9). Jesus' negative commands for "christological" secrecy (Don't tell about me) are balanced by his positive statements of theology (Tell about God): "Why do you call me good? No one is good but God alone" (10:18); "For mortals it is impossible, but not for God; for God all things are possible" (10:27); "Have faith in God" (11:22); "Give to the emperor the things that are the emperor's, and to God the things that are God's" (12:17); "But about that day or hour no one knows, neither the angels in heaven, nor the Son, but only the Father" (13:32).

Such a deflected Christology is not shared by the Markan characters who present statements about or questions to Jesus. John the Baptizer says, "The one who is more powerful than I is coming after me" and "he will baptize you with the Holy Spirit" (1:7–8).[15] Ironically, the Markan narrator never directly reports Jesus' baptizing others by the Holy Spirit (but see 13:11), but Jesus himself seems almost baptized with the (Holy) Spirit (1:10). Linked to the views of John are those of Herod, because Herod assumes Jesus is John resurrected after his beheading. What Herod says about Jesus is contrasted with what other people say: Jesus is Elijah or a prophet (6:14–16). What people say (that Jesus is John the Baptist or Elijah or one of the prophets, 8:28) is later contrasted with what Peter, speaking for the disciples, says: "You are the Christ" (8:29). Jesus says, Don't tell (8:30).

Outside Jericho, blind Bartimaeus calls out to Jesus: "Jesus, Son of David, have mercy on me!" (10:47); and even though many try to silence him, he calls out again, "Son of David, have mercy on me!" (10:48). Neither the Markan Jesus nor the Markan narrator comments directly on this "title" at this point (but see 12:35–37),[16] but when Jesus stops and speaks to him, Bartimaeus calls Jesus "My teacher" (Aramaic *Rabbouni*, 10:51); and when Jesus restores his sight, Bartimaeus follows Jesus "on the way" (10:52).

The Markan Jesus is not in a position to ignore what the high priest and Pilate say to and about him. Thus Jesus does accede somewhat cryptically to the "christological" depiction of the high priest and begrudgingly to that of Pilate, both in settings that lead to his death, when to respond otherwise might well "save" his life (see 8:35). The high priest asks, "Are you the Christ [NRSV, 'Messiah'], the Son of the Blessed One?" (14:61), being too religiously observant to pronounce the name of God. Jesus answers, "I am" (Greek, *Egō eimi;* 14:62). Unlike Kingsbury, I cannot imagine how this *Egō eimi* can be free of the connotations of the divine recognition formula (Ex. 3:14, LXX) so clearly called on in its one other Markan usage, when Jesus, walking on the sea, tells the disciples *egō eimi* (6:50; NRSV, "it is I"). On the one hand, the Markan Jesus is reticent to speak of himself or defend himself (see 14:61a); but on the other hand, when he does speak he echoes the words of God—which could also be considered religiously observant. Pilate, of course, asks a Gentile question: "Are you the King of the Jews?" (15:2). The Markan Jesus responds, "You say so" (15:2), a response positive enough to seal his death but noncommittal enough to disvalue the discourse. Whereas others speak sarcastically of Jesus as "*King* of the Jews"—Pilate (15:2, 9, 12; compare 15:26), the soldiers (15:18), and even the chief priests and scribes (15:32, "the Christ [NRSV, 'Messiah'], the King of Israel")—Jesus speaks seriously of the *king*dom of God. The Markan Jesus consistently deflects honor away from himself and toward God.

Not sarcasm but irony—profound irony—surrounds what the centurion says about Jesus. Clearly the centurion's point of view is aligned with those of the narrator and God (discussed below). It is in seeing how Jesus died that the Roman centurion comes to know that Jesus was "Son of God" (15:39; NRSV, "God's Son"). Jesus says nothing in response, having "breathed his last," and his last words serve to underline the reality of his death: "My God, my God, why have you forsaken me?" (15:34). The Markan Gospel has been building to this point from the beginning. In the first half of the narrative, the Markan Jesus tries to avoid acclamation and deflect honor to God; in the passion narrative, Jesus accedes to those acclamations that lead to his death, accepted as the will of God (see 14:36; compare 10:45).

God is the one the Markan Jesus wishes to speak about, but twice God enters the Markan narrative as a character—or rather as a voice[17]—and speaks to or about Jesus: at the baptism and at the transfiguration. The scenes are clearly and strongly interrelated. At the baptism scene the heavens split, the Spirit descends, and a voice comes from heaven saying, "You are my Son, the Beloved; with you I am well pleased" (1:10–11). Jesus says nothing; "and the Spirit immediately drove him out into the wilderness" (1:12). At the transfiguration scene, on "a high mountain" (9:2) a cloud overshadows Jesus (whose clothes are dazzling white) and Peter, James, and John; and a voice comes from the cloud saying,"This is my Son, the Beloved; listen to him!" (9:3–8). Jesus says nothing; but "as they were coming down the mountain, he ordered them to tell no one about what they had seen, until after the Son of Man had risen from the dead" (9:9). The two scenes are impressively high in drama but amazingly low in content concerning what it *means* for Jesus to be called God's Son. The actions of Jesus ("enacted Christology") and the words of Jesus about God ("deflected Christology") confirm that the widespread Jewish understanding of the person obedient to God as a "son of God" is shared by the Markan Jesus. The Markan Jesus, of course, never says "I am the Son of God." Kingsbury makes much of Jesus' use of the term *son* in the parable of the wicked tenants (12:1–11),[18] but it is good to remember that this is a parable. The Markan Jesus speaks of "the Son" in the third person in the eschatological discourse—precisely in order to deflect honor from "the Son" to "the Father": "But about that day or hour no one knows, neither the angels in heaven, nor the Son, but only the Father" (13:32). And Jesus calls God "Abba, Father" in his prayer in Gethsemane (14:36), seeking release but accepting suffering and death in deference to God's will. Whoever responds similarly—that is, "whoever does the will of God" (3:35)—is family to Jesus. Not "I am God's Son" but "Here are" (3:34) "my brother and sister and mother" (3:35) is the heart of the deflected Christology of Mark's Jesus.

The Markan narrator knows all this. The narrator is aware of Jesus' reticence to receive attention and his desire to deflect honor to God, but the Markan narrator does not entirely share that reticence. The narrator opens the narrative boldly: "The beginning of the gospel [NRSV, 'good news'] of Jesus Christ, the Son of God" (1:1). This opening verse serves as a title for the entire narrative. All that is told here—from baptism through resurrection—is but the *beginning* of the gospel; the good news continues beyond the narrative world into the world of the audience, which is also the world of the narrator. The narrator asserts from the beginning that Jesus is the Christ, the Messiah. Peter comes to this affirmation at midpoint (8:29), prompted and then silenced by Jesus. Jesus reticently accepts the assignation from the high priest in order *not* to "save" his own life. The chief priests and scribes apply the term sarcastically to the only Jesus it really fits: the crucified Jesus. The narrator also asserts from the beginning that Jesus is the Son of God.[19] God, so it is narrated, confirms this point of view (1:11; 9:7), and the unclean spirits share it (1:24, 34; 3:11; 5:7). Jesus deflects attention from "the Son" to "the Father" (13:32), whose will is accepted and for whom "all things are possible" (10:27). The centurion comes to this affirmation at the narrative's climax, at the only point from which it is really true: the crucifixion.

I am not saying that the narrator's point of view is dramatically at odds with the point of view of the Markan Jesus, but they are clearly distinguishable. The narrator boldly asserts that Jesus is the Christ, the Son of God. Jesus is reticent. Perhaps this is why it is so important that God confirm the narrator's point of view; the Markan Jesus hardly does so! Yet the Markan Jesus makes assertions about the Son of man, about which the narrator is silent, and boldly proclaims the kingdom of God, about which the narrator speaks directly just once, and that after Jesus' death (15:43). There is thus a tension between the Markan narrator who wants to talk about Jesus and the Markan Jesus who wants to talk about God.

In his classic, and now also twenty-year-old, essay on "'Point of View' in Mark's Narrative," Norman Petersen asserts that the Markan narrator's "ideological standpoint is identical with that of his central character, Jesus, with whom he shares the power of knowing what is in the minds of others."[20] In fact, he argues that "through this commonality of psychologically internal points of view, and with the support of the plotting of the story by which one actor is rendered central, the narrator is aligned—if not identified—with the central actor."[21] At least three significant differences between Petersen's assumptions and mine lead him to this conclusion. First, the central argument of Petersen's 1978 essay is that the "intrusive omniscience of the narrator in Mark's Gospel [and his unified point of view] is the principal guarantee that it is a literary narrative, and that its author is a bona fide narrator."[22] It no longer seems necessary—thanks in part to the work of Petersen, Kingsbury, Tannehill, and others—to argue that Mark's Gospel is a narrative (except perhaps with undergraduates and laity). And I argue that expressing more than one point of view would seem to add to a narrative's complexity, rather than challenging its narrativity. Second, Petersen assumes that "Mark [as narrator] never explicitly claims any title [for Jesus] as his own, except for the name 'Jesus' ('son of God' in 1:1 is textually suspect)."[23] While there is textual variation with regard to the presence of *huiou theou* in 1:1, it is included (in brackets) in the current United Bible Societies text.[24] And what of "Christ" in 1:1? That is not "textually suspect." Third, and more problematic, Petersen asserts the Markan narrator's "ideological, temporal and spatial, and psychological identification of his point of view with Jesus', aligns him with the one appellation used only by Jesus, 'Son of Man.'"[25] I find just the opposite. It is the narrator's failure to pick up this significant term (as well as *kingdom of God*, except for 15:43) that draws attention to the distinction between the

Markan narrator and the Markan Jesus, a distinction also noted in the reticence or refusal of the Markan Jesus to pick up the narrator's terms *Christ, the Son of God*.

Contrary to what has generally been observed about Mark's Gospel,[26] the narrator is not identical with the implied author. Both the Markan narrator and the Markan Jesus are under the control of the implied author. A narrative Christology of Mark's Gospel should reflect not just the point of view of the narrator (as Kingsbury tends to do) but the creative tension between the point of view of the narrator and that of the Markan Jesus. It is the implied author who juxtaposes the "Christology" of the Markan Jesus and the "Christology" of the Markan narrator, and it is the Markan implied audience that has to hold the two together. The tension is essential to the enacted and deflected Christology of Mark's Gospel. A Jesus who talked like the narrator could hardly be a Jesus who "came not to be served but to serve" (10:45).

CONCLUSION

In developing the narrative Christology of Mark's Gospel, one has to consider not only what the narrator and other characters say about Jesus (Kingsbury's focus, perhaps "titular Christology") but also what the character Jesus does—the actions he initiates (also addressed by Kingsbury, my "enacted Christology"); what Jesus says—and does—in response to what these others say about him ("deflected Christology"); what Jesus says about himself and God ("refracted Christology"); and how what other characters do is related to what Jesus says and does ("reflected Christology"). Here I have touched on enacted and deflected Christology; I can only suggest what I mean by refracted and reflected Christology, which must be taken up at some other point. Not only does the Markan Jesus attempt to deflect attention and honor away from himself and toward God, but the Markan Jesus also *refracts*—or bends—the "Christologies" of other characters and the narrator. The image comes from the way a prism refracts "white" light and thus shows its spectral colors. When a thing is bent and looked at from another angle, something different appears. The most obvious way in which the Markan Jesus bends the "Christologies" of others is by his statements about the Son of man, especially in juxtaposition with christological titles offered by other characters. However, the Markan Jesus' statements about the kingdom of God may also be seen as refracting the Christologies of other characters and the narrator. No other character or the narrator speaks of the Son of man; no other character speaks of the kingdom of God, and the narrator does so but once, just after Jesus' death (15:43). *Son of man* and *king-*

dom of God depict the Markan Jesus' distinctive point of view. Reflected Christology, for its part, might be investigated in two complementary ways: (1) by sketching out a general schema of the entire Markan cast of characters, highlighting who is in conflict with whom and who models whom; and (2) by focusing on minor characters who serve as exemplars of Jesus' words and deeds for the rest of his followers. In both the overview of all the interrelated characters and the close-up view of minor characters, one would see mirrored the "Christology" implied in Jesus' words and deeds.

I have tried to present something of a narrative Christology of Mark's Gospel by focusing on the character Jesus. In the background has been Kingsbury's *Christology of Mark's Gospel,* in which concern for the "titles of majesty" applied to Jesus by the other characters, and especially by the narrator, dominates. Kingsbury takes "the narrator's point of view" to be the only "correct" point of view on Christology in the Gospel of Mark. All differing points of view expressed by characters (Jesus is not considered in the same way) are wrong; all similar points of view, including God's, are congruent and thus "correct." I have come to appreciate a more complicated narrative arrangement, whereby the protagonist Jesus presents a unique point of view about himself in relation to God (surely central for Christology). It is a point of view *enacted* in his words and deeds, as separate from what others say about him (for example, titles). It is a point of view from which honor and attention are *deflected* from himself to God and from which traditional understandings (and titles) applied to him are *refracted* or bent into new meanings. And it is a point of view that can be *reflected* in the actions of other characters who share, even if in one exemplary moment, the deflected and refracted Christology enacted by the Markan Jesus.

One could say that the narrator controls all the characters and thus that Jesus' point of view is absorbed into the narrator's point of view. But to do so would be to lose a distinction that does make a difference. Much of what Kingsbury sees in Mark's Christology is there in the Markan *narrator's* Christology. I hope others will judge that much of what I see in the narrative Christology of Mark's Gospel—in relation to the character Jesus—is there as well. Thus, I propose that we employ a distinction we have had all along but have not generally found helpful or necessary—that between the implied author and the narrator—to make sense of this new distinction in Markan narrative Christology. The implied author controls the narrator and all the characters. The implied author is the one who allows a character, even the main character, to have a point of view distinct from the narrator—and for a good purpose.

In the Gospel of Mark the tension between the narrator's point of view and Jesus' point of view enables the implied author to present a Jesus whose focus is always on God, even though the narrator keeps focusing on Jesus. One could hardly present the story of Jesus without focusing on Jesus; the narrator is thus not to be blamed. But neither is the implied author to be ignored in creating the gap, the tension, between the narrator's point of view and that of the main character, Jesus. It is not the Markan Jesus' point of view nor the Markan narrator's point of view that is the point of view of Mark's Gospel. It is the implied author's point of view. Thus the tension between the narrator and Jesus is not a problem to be resolved or a gap to be filled in but a narrative christological confession, to be heard in all its silence.

Let anyone with ears to hear listen!

NOTES

1. Jack Dean Kingsbury, *The Christology of Mark's Gospel* (Philadelphia: Fortress Press, 1983), ix.
2. Elizabeth Struthers Malbon, "Disciples/Crowds/Whoever: Markan Characters and Readers," *Novum Testamentum* 28 (1986): 104–30; idem, "Texts and Contexts: Interpreting the Disciples in Mark," *Semeia* 62 (1993): 81–102.
3. Elizabeth Struthers Malbon, "Fallible Followers: Women and Men in the Gospel of Mark," *Semeia* 28 (1983): 29–48; idem, "The Poor Widow in Mark and Her Poor Rich Readers," *Catholic Biblical Quarterly* 53 (1991): 589–604.
4. Elizabeth Struthers Malbon, "The Jewish Leaders in the Gospel of Mark: A Literary Study of Marcan Characterization," *Journal of Biblical Literature* 108 (1989): 259–81.
5. Elizabeth Struthers Malbon, "The Major Importance of the Minor Characters in Mark," in *The New Literary Criticism and the New Testament,* ed. Elizabeth Struthers Malbon and Edgar V. McKnight (Sheffield: Sheffield Academic Press, 1994; paperback with editors' names reversed, Valley Forge, Pa.: Trinity Press International, 1994), 58–86.
6. See especially Elizabeth Struthers Malbon, *Narrative Space and Mythic Meaning in Mark* (San Francisco: Harper & Row, 1986; reprint, Sheffield: Sheffield Academic Press, 1991).
7. Robert C. Tannehill, "The Gospel of Mark as Narrative Christology," *Semeia* 16 (1979): 57–95.
8. Ibid., 62, 63.
9. Kingsbury, *Christology,* 60.
10. Elizabeth Struthers Malbon, "Echoes and Foreshadowings in Mark 4–8:

Reading and Rereading," *Journal of Biblical Literature* 112 (1993): 213–32; idem, "Narrative Criticism: How Does the Story Mean?" in *Mark and Method: New Approaches in Biblical Studies,* ed. Janice Capel Anderson and Stephen D. Moore (Minneapolis: Fortress Press, 1992), 23–49.

11. "My principal (though not exclusive) method, then, is that of literary criticism, and by this I mean no more than that I shall endeavor to read Mark by looking to the story it tells for the primary clues of meaning" (Kingsbury, *Christology,* 45).

12. William Wrede, *The Messianic Secret,* trans. J. C. C. Grieg (Cambridge and London: James Clarke & Co., 1971).

13. Kingsbury, *Christology,* 90, commenting on Mark 8:27–16:8.

14. At 1:3b the narrator (or implied author) changes the LXX reading of "his," meaning God's, to "of the Lord," leaving open reference to Jesus. At 5:19 the narrator reports Jesus using the term *Lord* as a probable reference to God, but at 5:20 the narrator reports the Gerasene acting as if "Lord" means Jesus. At 7:28 the narrator reports the Syrophoenician woman addressing Jesus as "Lord" (NRSV, "Sir"). And by 11:3 the narrator reports what may be intended as a self-reference of Jesus as "Lord"; Jesus tells the disciples to tell the one whose colt they are to take, "The Lord needs it and will send it back here immediately." Thus the narrator (or implied author) becomes increasingly bold in the suggestion that Jesus is Lord.

15. Perhaps in relation to the John of Matthew, the Markan John deflects honor to God. People come to John and are baptized, "confessing their sins" (1:5); Jesus comes to John and is baptized (1:9)—is confessing his sins implied? This possibility worries the Matthean John but not the Markan John. Matthew's story of Jesus' baptism thereby stretches the distance between Jesus and other human beings and closes the distance between Jesus and God that Mark's baptismal story assumes.

16. Contra Kingsbury (*Christology,* 102–14), I argue that the Markan Jesus first ignores (10:47–48), then deflects (12:35–37) the title "son of David." The scribe in the pericope preceding 12:35–37 is clearly portrayed as exceptional. The scribes in the succeeding pericope (12:38–40) are portrayed as (stereo-)typical, and the view that the Christ is the son of David is attributed to them (12:35) and thus rejected (cf. 11:10).

17. As Kingsbury rightly observes, "One thing Mark does not do: he does not deal with God in the same manner in which he deals with the other characters of his story. With respect to the latter, Mark assumes the posture of the 'omniscient narrator.' . . . With respect to God, however, Mark does not permit the reader to imagine that he has 'unmediated access' either to heaven— God's abode (11:25)—or to his 'mind'" (*Christology,* 48). I might add that the Markan narrator seems to follow the lead of the Markan Jesus on this point; not even Jesus claims to know what God knows (13:32; compare 10:40).

18. Kingsbury, *Christology,* 114–18.

19. On evaluating the textual variants of 1:1, that is, the presence or absence of *huiou theou,* "Son of God," see Bruce M. Metzger, *A Textual Commentary on the Greek New Testament* (London: United Bible Societies, 1971), 73.

20. Norman R. Petersen, " 'Point of View' in Mark's Narrative," *Semeia* 12 (1978): 97–121; quotation from 107.

21. Ibid., 102.

22. Ibid., 97.

23. Ibid., 111.

24. See note 19 above.

25. Petersen, " 'Point of View' in Mark's Narrative," 111.

26. Even by me: "The distinctions between the implied author and the narrator and between the narratee and the implied reader were developed in secular literary criticism for the close analysis of nineteenth- and twentieth-century novels. . . . Most narrative critics of the first-century Gospels have not found these distinctions as useful. Most narrative critics have observed little or no difference between the implied author and narrator or between the narratee and implied reader of Matthew, Mark, Luke, and John. The implied author of *Moby Dick* knows more than Ishmael, but a similar separation is not obvious in Mark" (Malbon, "Narrative Criticism," 28). "Not obvious" indeed—but subtle and important!

THE CHRISTOLOGY OF LUKE-ACTS

Luke Timothy Johnson

Jack Dean Kingsbury's name is rightly associated with the effort to connect Christology to literary analysis of the Gospels.[1] This modest chapter
seeks to sort through some of the important questions that need to be asked
if one seeks the Christology of Luke-Acts. In other places I have advanced
some of my ideas on the subject, arguing in particular for the importance
in Luke's presentation of Jesus as prophet.[2] But I have not before this had
the opportunity to consider other dimensions of Christology in Luke-Acts.
The way to that broader consideration can be prepared by answering some
basic questions.

WHAT IS THE TOPIC?

The obvious first question is by no means the easiest: What is it we seek when
we inquire into a composition's "Christology"? Do we mean to discover the
manner in which the writing demonstrates that Jesus is the Jewish Messiah?
This has its own complications, including the diverse messianic expectations
within Judaism of the first century against which our writing needs to be measured. But the task itself is relatively straightforward. We can treat the composition as a species of apologetics over against Judaism: Here are the
messianic job qualifications, here is how Jesus meets them. Deciding the
topic in this fashion also determines the choice of materials and methods.
The use of messianic titles, for example, would appear of obvious importance, as would statements describing Jesus' functions. These are compared
to diverse messianic images in Judaism.[3] In the case of Luke-Acts, we would

give our attention to titles such as "Son of man" and "Christ" and "prophet" and "son of David." Since all are used in considerable profusion, we might find ourselves trying to determine which was most important—to our author as well as to Jews of the first century—and might even conclude that our author was correcting messianic misperceptions by the use of such titles. Thus, in Luke 24:19–26, we might think Luke had such a strategy in mind when the disciples call Jesus a prophet and Jesus responds by referring to himself as Messiah.[4]

We might also come at the question of Christology from quite a different angle, asking now not how Luke's Jesus fits the categories of Jewish expectation but how Luke's presentation of Jesus fits within the belief structure of earliest Christianity. Thus, "Christian Christology"—to employ an awkward phrase—is the topic within which Luke is studied. From this perspective, it might be asked whether Luke's presentation of Jesus is more "human" or more "divine," using the categories of a developed Christian theology. On one side, perhaps his presentation of the resurrection in the speeches of Acts suggests an "adoptionistic" Christology;[5] on another side, perhaps his infancy account moves in the direction of a high, "incarnational" Christology.[6]

Each of the foregoing approaches works within a framework outside the text of Luke-Acts and suffers from three fairly obvious limitations. First, asking questions from one perspective excludes those from another; they are two distinct frames of reference. Second, we do not know enough about either of the two frames to make the pursuit finally satisfying. Third, reading Luke-Acts only with reference to the world outside the composition leads to the neglect of the world constructed by the composition.

A more adequate way of defining the topic, therefore, is in terms of the presentation of Jesus in the literary composition we call Luke-Acts. This approach cannot entirely avoid questions pertinent to the other two definitions of the topic, for the simple reason that Luke's words are contextualized by the symbolic world of Torah (and all the literature generated by Torah in first-century Judaism) as well as by the literature of nascent Christianity. But the focus here stays on what Luke's composition itself gives us. We seek to discover what this composition has constructed as *christos* (messiah) or as *prophētēs* (prophet), rather than make appeal to what those terms necessarily must have meant to Jews or Christians in that world. By asking about the presentation of Jesus within the composition, furthermore, our investigation can include a range of evidence that neither of the other approaches allows, such as that provided by the characterization of Jesus and those with whom he interacts within the narrative.

WHAT IS THE LITERARY COMPOSITION?

If our analysis of Luke's Christology is bounded by his literary composition rather than by the symbols and convictions of Judaism and the early church respectively, then we must be clear on exactly what our sense of that composition is. Decisions at this stage can be decisive. If, for example, we follow Hans Conzelmann in reading Luke apart from Acts and apart from the Lukan infancy accounts, we come up with a very different portrait than if those elements are included.[7] Likewise if we focus, as C. F. D. Moule did, only on the Christology of Acts, with no real reference to the Gospel except for points of contrast, our results are again affected by this preliminary literary decision.[8]

The decision to read Luke-Acts as a literary and thematic unity is one that has, until recently, won wide general approbation but less systematic application.[9] Remarkably few narrative studies of both volumes read as a single literary project have been undertaken by one scholar.[10] Yet this is the sort of reading that promises the greatest yield. The recent question put to the unity of Luke-Acts on the basis of generic difference is, in my view, mistaken.[11] The evidence that Luke has constructed a single composition in two volumes is overwhelming at every level, and if this position is seriously to be refuted, then the hypothesis of literary unity needs to be challenged in detail at each of these levels.

The decision to read Luke-Acts as a literary unity is not based on a theoretical conviction concerning "canonical criticism," for the logic of a canonical criticism actually moves in the other direction: The early separation of the Gospel and Acts in the process of canonization would argue for their separate treatment.[12] Luke-Acts is simply a case in which the premise of narrative criticism that a narrative in its finished form ought to be treated as a coherent and intelligible whole unless the evidence forces an opposite conclusion is magnificently rewarded by the results.

Another way of asking the question "What is the composition?" is by inquiring specifically into literary genre. Although one part of Luke's story or another might be read as a novel[13] or as a biography,[14] it seems correct to conclude as a whole that he sets out to write some sort of historical composition, and that the sort of history he does is best compared to Greco-Roman and Jewish histories of the apologetic sort.[15] Like most such histories, Luke's concern was less to persuade outsiders than to reassure insiders. Although elements in his narrative can support the suggestion that he is writing a defense of the Christian movement over against Rome—or even for Rome over against apocalyptically minded Christians—and although other elements can support his writing in defense of Paul with an eye either toward Roman authorities or toward a theologically influential Jewish segment within the Christian movement, the narrative makes the most sense when read as an apologia for God's ways in history.[16]

IS CHRISTOLOGY THE MAIN TOPIC?

It may seem odd to ask whether the presentation of Jesus is really the most important thing going on in a Gospel, but the answer is not as obvious as we might at first think. Each Gospel's way of presenting Jesus ought to be evaluated within the context of that composition's discernible aims and concerns.

That Jesus is a central character in Luke-Acts is clear enough, although the way he continues to function as a character in the book of Acts requires some study. But is Jesus the point of Luke-Acts in the way he is the point of the fourth Gospel, let us say, or the Gospel of Mark? In the fourth Gospel, everything focuses on Jesus as the revealer of the Father. Mark likewise directs the reader's attention above all to the drama of Jesus and his disciples. Luke-Acts — in this respect resembling Matthew — opens the narrative to wider concerns. The way in which the good news reaches the Gentile world and the consequences of this extension for historical Israel form the central narrative theme of Luke-Acts.[17] And within that theme, the issue of God's fidelity to Israel and to the promises God made to Israel is critical. Luke is writing an apologia for God.[18]

What Luke has to say about Jesus, in other words, must be placed within his overarching literary and religious purposes. We can legitimately expect that Luke's presentation of Jesus will serve those larger purposes, and we can test to see if in fact it does.

HOW DOES NARRATIVE MEAN?

Literary theory has exposed how complex reading is. I will not enter that hall of mirrors but will only make a couple of observations of rudimentary and fairly obvious significance in reading a narrative with the question "What is the presentation of Jesus in this narrative?" The first and most obvious assumption behind this question is that the ancient author had control of the materials deployed in the story. Even if, as in the case of Luke-Acts, some earlier sources are used, the working premise must be that the author approved those materials included without change and made alterations to other materials deliberately. This is a powerful assumption, and a necessary one for the task to be undertaken at all. If we do not understand the shaping, we conclude that the author made sense but we cannot find it. Once we assume that an author did not have control over the materials and was simply handing over traditions in a haphazard or "clumsy construction,"[19] then it is senseless to ask about the consistency of a composition on any point at all.

In the case of Luke-Acts, it is reasonable to suppose, furthermore, that Luke had proportionately greater freedom in the composition of the story in Acts than in that in his Gospel. We may suspect that he used sources for Acts, but we have not been able to determine them;[20] it is most probable that he was, in any case, the first to tell the story as we find it in Acts. Even if he was using earlier traditions, in other words, the shaping was his. For the Gospel, in contrast, we know that he used Mark as well as the source material designated as Q. In the Gospel portion of the story, we are able to observe the range of Luke's creativity both in his use of Mark and by comparison with Matthew's redaction of their shared materials. The implication of Luke's being the first to continue the story into another complete volume and of having a correspondingly greater compositional freedom is that we should consider Acts as Luke's own interpretation of the first part of his story. What he has to say about Jesus in the Gospel looks forward to Acts, and what he has to say about Jesus in Acts looks back to the Gospel.[21]

The next assumption is that narrative expresses meaning through the form of the story itself; a narrative is not simply a package containing propositions or a setting for the presentation of examples but, as Aristotle already recognized (*Poetics* 6.19–22), through the interplay of *ethos* (character) and *mythos* (plot) expresses *dianoia* (theme, or meaning).[22] If this is so, then every element of a narrative is significant for understanding every other element: Just as the theme is expressed through characters and plot, so does characterization have plot implications and so does plotting serve the shaping of characters.

In narratives written for purposes other than sheer entertainment, furthermore—as its prologue shows Luke-Acts manifestly was—narrative can legitimately be read as a form of rhetoric: The way the story is told expresses an argument.[23] In the case of Luke, the argument concerns God's fidelity to God's promises and is intended to secure *asphaleia* (truth) in the readers (Luke 1:1–4). The prologue further indicates that the narrative argument involves the order in which the story is told. It is because the events are recounted *kathexēs* (in order) that Theophilus can be expected to have *asphaleia* (see Acts 11:4). The reader can therefore expect more than a normal importance to the sequence in Luke-Acts. Where something occurs in the story is as important as what occurs. The literary shaping of the story, in short, serves the religious purposes of the composition.[24]

HOW IS CHARACTER DETERMINED?

Speaking about the presentation of Jesus in Luke-Acts implies that the focus of reading is the determination of the character within the story who is named Jesus, a character constructed in the act of reading by means of the textual clues provided by the narrative and the ways in which these are processed by the reader.[25] Among textual clues are those modes of "telling" that directly characterize: what a character says about himself, what other characters say about him, and what the narrator says about him. The various titles and functions claimed by Jesus or ascribed to Jesus by others are obviously of considerable importance. Equally important are the modes of "showing" that are forms of indirect identification, such as the use of language echoing biblical stories in the construction of scenes involving Jesus, as well as how language is used to suggest lines of resemblance or continuity between other characters and Jesus.

The more rounded and complex a character within a narrative, the more difficult it is to reduce its presentation to a simple formula. The best advice is to "learn the character by reading through the narrative." Analysis can, however, identify salient features that help distinguish or determine the shape of a specific character. The more an analysis depends on the convergence of multiple lines of evidence, the more adequate it will be. A statement about Jesus in Luke-Acts that relied solely on the use of titles or that ignored what was said about Jesus in the speeches of Acts, for example, must on that very basis be considered deficient. The more different kinds of evidence from different kinds of discourse and from different angles of vision converge, the more likely it is that a characterization is worth considering.

THE PRESENTATION OF
JESUS AS A PROPHET

Analysis of the presentation of Jesus as a prophet[26] in Luke's character-construction best begins with the narrative of Acts as the freer and fuller development of themes anticipated in the Gospel. It begins with attention to how Luke portrays Jesus' followers as prophets. The Holy Spirit actively intervenes throughout Acts (8:29, 39; 10:19; 11:15; 13:2; 15:28; 16:6; 20:23), and Luke shows five separate outpourings of the Spirit (2:1–4; 4:28–31; 8:15–17; 10:44; 19:6) on believers. But Luke's most important characters—those who fundamentally advance the plot (Peter, John, Philip, Stephen, Barnabas, and Paul)—are "people of the Spirit" in a special way. They are not designated as *prophets,* for that term is reserved for relatively minor players within the way (11:27; 13:1; 15:32; 21:10). Instead, Luke describes these protagonists with language that clearly identifies them as prophets. Each is "filled with the Holy Spirit" (4:8; 5:32; 6:3; 7:55; 11:24; 13:9). Each is "bold" in proclamation (4:13; 13:46; 28:31) of "the good news" (5:42; 8:4, 12, 25, 40; 11:20; 13:32; 14:7; 15:35) or the "word of God" (4:29; 8:14; 13:5). Each is a "witness" (2:32; 10:41; 13:31; 22:20) who works "signs and wonders" (4:30; 6:8; 14:3; 15:12) among the "people" (*laos*), that is, the Jewish population considered as the people of God (3:12; 4:1; 6:8; 13:15). In the symbolic world of Torah, this composite of characteristics belongs unmistakably to the prophet.

Luke's characterization of the apostles in Acts connects them explicitly to Moses and to Jesus. By having Peter amend the Joel citation with which he begins his Pentecost sermon, Luke shows his readers that the outpouring of the Spirit is eschatological ("in the last days"), is explicitly prophetic (he adds "they shall prophesy" in 2:18), and works "signs" and "portents" (wonders) (2:19). This last touch establishes a clear allusion to the prophet Moses, with whom the tag "signs and wonders" is associated in the LXX (Ps. 77:11–12, 32, 43) and above all in Deuteronomy 34:10–12: "Never since has there arisen a prophet in Israel like Moses . . . for all the signs and wonders that the Lord sent him to do." When Peter then identifies Jesus as "a man attested to you by God with deeds of power, wonders, and signs that God did through him among you" (2:22–24), the reader naturally makes the connection between Jesus, Moses, and the apostles, especially since Luke consistently emphasizes that the power active in the words and works of his followers is precisely the Spirit of Jesus (2:33; 3:13; 4:10; 13:30–33). The link is forged most explicitly when Luke has Stephen—himself portrayed as a prophet—speak of Moses' working "wonders and signs" in the wilderness after his empowerment by God (7:36). The apostles are therefore portrayed as prophets like Jesus, and Jesus is portrayed as a prophet like Moses. But this is not a simple linear succession. Moses was "raised up" by God as a prophet only in the sense that God chose him. Jesus, by contrast, is the prophet whom God "raised up" in resurrection as the source of the eschatological outpouring of the Spirit, and the apostles are dependent on that Spirit of Jesus for their prophetic activity. The superiority of Jesus to Moses is intimated in 3:22 and above all in Stephen's speech, which declares:

> It was this Moses, whom they rejected when they said, "Who made you a ruler and a judge?" and whom God now sent as both ruler and liberator through the angel who appeared to him in the bush. He led them out, having performed wonders and signs in Egypt, at the Red

Sea, and in the wilderness for forty years. This is the Moses who said to the Israelites, "God will raise up a prophet for you from your own people as he raised me up." (7:35–37)

In that part of the Stephen Speech devoted to Moses, moreover, Luke provides a narrative key to his two-volume work. The story of Moses, as Luke has Stephen tell it, has two main stages with an interlude. He is sent a first time to the people Israel but is rejected because they do not understand that he was "visiting" them for their salvation (7:17–22). Moses must go into exile, but he encounters God and is empowered to return to his people a second time (7:30–34). Moses leads the people out of Egypt with "wonders and signs" (7:35–37), but the people reject him a second time by worshiping the golden calf. This time, the rejection of the prophet leads to their own rejection by God, expressed by their being sent into exile (7:39–43). Thus Luke frames two visitations of the people, the first time in weakness, the second in power, and two offers of salvation to the people, the first, rejected in ignorance, leading to a second chance to hear the prophet.

The pattern of the Moses story provides the basic framework for Luke's two-volume composition. The Gospel tells the story of God's first sending of the prophet Jesus to "visit" the people for their "salvation" (see Luke 1:68; 7:16; 19:44), of their rejection of this salvation out of their ignorance (see Acts 3:17), and of Jesus being "raised up" out of death. Acts recounts Jesus' establishment in power, manifested by the outpouring of the Holy Spirit (Acts 2:33–36), the sending out of the witnesses empowered by that Spirit (Luke 24:48–49; Acts 1:7–8), and the second offer of salvation to Israel in his name (4:12; 5:41). This time, however, the cost of rejecting the "prophet whom God has raised up" is being cut off from the people God is forming around the prophet himself (Acts 3:22–23).

By taking seriously the interpretive key offered by the speeches of Acts, we can appreciate more fully Luke's portrayal of Jesus as prophet in the Gospel narrative. We see, for example, that although Luke does not use the title "prophet" with overwhelming frequency, he does employ it more vigorously than the other Gospels and in narratively strategic places.[27] It is a title, furthermore, that Jesus applies to himself (Luke 4:24; 13:33) and that is used with reference to him by his enemies (7:39; see also 22:64) and as a designation by both the receptive *laos* (7:16; 9:8, 19) and his disciples (24:19; Acts 3:22). Even more important are the ways in which readers recognize Jesus as a prophet from how Luke shapes episodes within the narrative. Thus, the prophetic connotations are readily grasped in the prediction by Simeon that Jesus would be a "sign that will be opposed" and destined to cause "the falling and the rising of many in Israel" (Luke 2:34), and by the repeated insistence that, in Nazareth, Jesus was "full of the Holy Spirit" (see 4:1, 14) as he opened the scroll of Isaiah to read "The Spirit of the Lord is upon me because he has anointed me" (4:18) and then declare that this reading was fulfilled in him (4:21). But only in light of the development in Acts can the reader fully appreciate that in Luke's version of Jesus' transfiguration, Moses and Elijah not only appear with Jesus but also discuss the exodus that he will accomplish in Jerusalem (Luke 9:31), and recognize in God's command "Listen to him" (9:35) the anticipation of the citation from Deuteronomy 18:15 found in Acts 3:22 and 7:37.

The mention of Elijah at the transfiguration reminds us how complex Luke's prophetic imagery is, not least because of how the biblical figures of Elijah and Elisha in Kings were themselves modeled on the prophetic succession of Moses and Joshua. The way in which Joshua received Moses' prophetic spirit (Deut. 34:9) and Elisha received a double portion of Elijah's spirit (2 Kings 2:9–15) obviously provided Luke with a precedent in Torah for how the Spirit at work in Jesus during his ministry was even more powerfully active in his apostles after his resurrection and ascension. Not only Moses, therefore, but also Elijah and Elisha help shape Luke's portrayal of Jesus. Indeed, the first prophet in Luke's narrative is Jesus' cousin John the Baptist, whom the angel Gabriel declares will be filled with the Holy Spirit from the womb, will turn many of the children of Israel back to their God, and "with the spirit and power of Elijah . . . will go before him [Jesus]" to "make ready a people prepared for the Lord" (1:15–17). John's preaching and prophetic action of baptizing for repentance follow "the word of God" coming upon "John son of Zechariah in the wilderness" (3:2), and Jesus himself acknowledges John as a "prophet . . . and more than a prophet" (7:26).[28]

It is clear that for Luke, John is not Elijah *redivivus* any more than Jesus is Moses *redivivus*. Luke simply uses all the prophetic imagery available for the depiction of his main characters. Note how the wonders of Elijah and Elisha in Luke 4:25–27 (the raising of the widow of Zarephath's son and the healing of the Gentile soldier Naaman) are echoed by Jesus' own miracles of healing the servant of a Gentile soldier and raising the widow of Nain's son (7:1–16), a connection recognized by the crowd that cries, "A great prophet has risen among us!" and "God has looked favorably on his people!" (7:16).[29] Elijah reappears at the transfiguration in the company of Moses (9:30). The tiny incidents in the journey narrative involving the threat of fire from heaven (9:54) and Jesus' saying about putting one's hand to the plow (9:62) appear to echo stories from the Elijah-Elisha cycle (see 2 Kings 1:10–12 and 1 Kings 19:20). And the most likely explanation for the presence of the "two men in dazzling clothes" at the empty tomb (Luke 24:4) and the "two men in white robes" at the ascension (Acts 1:10) is that they represent once more, at the time of Jesus' *exodos,* the prophetic figures of Moses and Elijah.[30] Certainly the literary signals planted by Luke himself support such a conjecture, particularly when the very construction of the ascension scene recalls the ascension of Elijah and the subsequent bestowal of the Spirit on Elisha.[31]

The characteristic actions of Jesus in the Gospel narrative also lead to perceiving him as a prophetic figure. His gestures of healing are twice connected to his prophetic mission. His inclusive table fellowship challenges the accepted piety of his opponents, climactically so in the case of Zacchaeus. His provocative acts at table serve to raise the question of his prophetic character. His entry into the city and his cleansing of the temple are intentionally symbolic acts.

No less does Jesus' speech characterize him as prophet. His parabolic discourse is designated as "the word of God." He issues warnings of judgment and calls for conversion. And most decisively, he makes predictions. Luke carefully redacts the eschatological discourse he inherited from Mark 13. He has Jesus deliver it from within the temple precincts, and he organizes Jesus' prophecies so that they concern three discrete temporal stages. The first events concern the tribulations to be experienced by his followers. These Luke shows to have been literally fulfilled by the events he himself relates in Acts 1—8. The second events concern the destruction of the city by the Romans and the beginning of the time of the Gentiles. For Luke's first readers, these predictions—still fresh in memory—would also have been proven true. The verification of the first two sets of predictions makes Jesus' prophecies concerning the last days and the return of the Son of man all the more reliable.

These brief observations show how several different lines of evidence converge within Luke's narrative to create the image of Jesus as prophet: the explicit use of the title; stereotypical language associated with Moses; direct literary links drawn to Moses, Elijah, and Elisha; the construction of scenes based on stories involving these figures; the characteristic actions and speeches of Jesus as recounted in the Gospel; and the two-stage structure of the entire composition, modeled by the story of Moses as found in the Stephen Speech of Acts.

These elements enable the reading of Luke's narrative as the story of the "Prophet and the People": Jesus is sent a first time to the people Israel for their salvation, but the people do not recognize the time of their visitation and reject him. He is killed but rises from the dead and is exalted at the right hand of God. He sends his Spirit on his disciples, who continue his prophetic mission among the people, offering them a second chance at salvation—that is, at being included in the restored people God is creating around the prophet Jesus. Although the leaders of the people continue to reject the message, many thousands in Jerusalem accept this second visitation. They embody within historic Israel the restored people of God, defined in terms of possession of the prophetic Spirit, so that when the message is extended to the Gentiles, as God had desired from the first, it represents not the replacement of the Jews but rather a growth of the *laos* to include all the nations of the earth.

Telling the story this way serves Luke's rhetorical purposes, showing how God proved faithful to the promises made to Abraham, and that therefore the faith of the Gentiles such as Theophilus is secure. God is not a God who fails to keep a promise or who abandons a people. Thus, the image of Jesus and the argument made by the composition reinforce each other.

TESTING THE PROPHETIC IMAGE

I suggested above that the operative premise for investigating the Christology of Luke-Acts is that the author had considerable, though not absolute, control over his materials. Some elements in Luke's portrayal of Jesus came to him from his sources. One way of testing the adequacy of the prophetic hypothesis, then, is to ask whether and to what extent Luke's other images and themes attaching to Jesus confirm or detract from his presentation as a prophet. There is not space to do a complete account here, but I comment on three aspects of Luke's text that are not obviously part of the presentation of Jesus as prophet.

Son of Man. Luke takes over this designation from Mark and does not substantially alter its applications to Jesus as the one who has present power, who will suffer, and who will come in glory. We do notice, however, that Luke's description of Jesus setting "his face to go to Jerusalem" in 9:51 echoes the "Son of man" logion of Ezekiel and thus accentuates the prophetic and divisive character of his path toward his suffering. Luke is also the only evangelist to use the title "Son of man" in the empty-tomb account (24:7), thereby confirming that Jesus' prophecy concerning his resurrection had come true. Finally, Luke reports Stephen's vision in the moment before his execution: "But filled with the Holy Spirit, he gazed into heaven and saw the glory of God and Jesus standing at the right hand of God. 'Look,' he said, 'I see the heavens opened and the Son of Man standing at the right hand of God'" (Acts 7:55). The prophet Stephen thus confirms Jesus' statement to the Sanhedrin: "But from now on the Son of Man will be seated at the right hand of the power of God" (Luke 22:69). In short, Luke's use of the title "Son of man" is complementary to his presentation of Jesus as the prophet whom God has raised up.

Savior. Salvation is a fundamental theme in Luke-Acts in a manner not found in Mark and only very partially in John (see John 3:17; 4:22; 5:34; 10:9; 11:12; 12:47) and Matthew (see Matt. 1:21; 8:25). Like Matthew and Mark, Luke uses *sozein* for the healings of Jesus, but he amplifies the Markan theme that faith saves (see Mark 5:34; Matt. 9:22/Luke 8:48) by adding it to the accounts in 7:50; 8:12; 8:50; 17:19; and 18:42. More pertinent, Luke expands the notion of being "saved" from that of physical healing to inclusion in the people (see 9:24; 13:23; 19:10). Thus, in response to the threefold taunt at the cross challenging his capacity to save himself although he had saved others, Jesus promises the *lestes* (thief) that he would be with Jesus that day in paradise (23:43). Jesus saves not only by healing but by including within God's restored people.

Salvation in Luke-Acts, as I have demonstrated elsewhere, has a social meaning and is directly connected to the theme of the prophet and the people. Remember that in Stephen's speech Moses "visited" his people a first time (Acts 7:23), but they did not understand "that God through him was rescuing them" (7:25). In the same fashion, Zechariah praises God at the birth of John because God's visiting his people involved raising up "a mighty savior [Greek, 'a horn for salvation'] for us in the house of his servant David" (Luke 1:68–69) in order that his people "would be saved from our enemies" (1:71) and in order to "give knowledge of salvation to his people" (1:77). In Mary's proclamation of praise, she designates God as "Savior" (1:47) because God has "helped his servant Israel" (1:54). The agent through whom God would work his saving of the people is called Savior at his birth (2:11), and when Simeon receives the child Jesus in his arms, he praises God because "my eyes have seen your salvation" (2:30).

In this framing, Luke's portrayal in chapters 9—19 of Jesus as the prophet making his way toward his death in Jerusalem and forming a people around himself while on that path, a people that is "saved by faith"— that becomes part of God's people by committing themselves to the message and person of this prophet—reaches its culmination in the "visitation" of the house of the chief tax collector Zacchaeus: "Today salvation has come to this house, because he [Zacchaeus] too is a son of Abraham. For the Son of Man came to seek out and to save the lost" (19:9–10).

The social dimension of salvation is obvious in the first part of Acts, when to be "saved" means specifically to join the people that is forming around the proclamation of the prophet whom God raised up as Lord and Messiah (Acts 2:36)—and Savior (5:31)! All those who call on that name would be saved from the crooked generation that had rejected the prophet and would be joined to God's restored Israel (see Acts 2:21, 40, 47; 4:9, 12; 13:26). The inclusion of the Gentiles in God's people is likewise characterized in terms of salvation. Luke extended the Isaiah citation in his Gospel (3:6) to include the promise that "all flesh shall see the salvation of God." The conversion of Cornelius is seen as "salvation for you and your whole household" (Acts 11:14). Paul's mission to the Gentiles is covered by the citation from Isaiah 49:6, "you may bring salvation to the ends of the earth" (Acts 13:47). His message concerns the "way of salvation" (16:17), and those who hear it and respond in faith are saved by joining this people (14:9; 16:31). The final prophecy in the narrative is uttered by Paul, who declares, "Let it be known to you then that this salvation of God has been sent to the Gentiles; they will listen" (28:28). Luke's understanding of Jesus as savior and of his work as salvation, in short, fits perfectly within his presentation of him as the prophet around whom God was forming the restored Israel.

Son of David/King. It is not too great a stretch for the image of prophet and king to coalesce, since they combine in the profile of Moses in Hellenistic Judaism. Are they linked as well in Luke-Acts? The answer must take Luke's treatment of David into account as well, especially in view of Gabriel's opening announcement that God would give Mary's child "the throne of his ancestor [father] David. He will reign over the house of Jacob forever, and of his kingdom there will be no end" (Luke 1:32–33) and of Zechariah's characterization of God's visitation of the people as raising up "a mighty savior [Greek, 'a horn of salvation'] for us in the house of his servant David" (1:69). Although Luke stresses Jesus' descent from David, however (1:27, 69; 2:11; 3:31), and carries forward the identification of Jesus as "son of David" (6:3; 18:38–39), the rule the Lukan Jesus proclaims is not one over a Jewish state but the *basileia tou theou* (kingdom of God).

Jesus stresses his obligation (*dei*) to proclaim the good news of God's rule (4:43) immediately after his self-designation as a prophetic Messiah in 4:16–18. And the prophet who was to announce good news to the poor (4:18) does so by announcing, "Blessed are you who are poor, for yours is the kingdom of God" (6:20). The prophet who is filled with the Holy Spirit (4:14) and speaks the "word of God" (8:11, 21) does so by preaching the good news of the rule of God (8:1) and revealing its mysteries in parabolic discourse (8:10). Those he sends as his emissaries likewise proclaim God's rule, even as they continue to work the same signs of healings that Jesus performs (9:2; 10:9, 11). Jesus' opposition consists not of the local political bosses or even of the empire but of the powers of Satan, who controls all the kingdoms of the known world (4:5). Jesus' triumph over these demonic forces signifies the arrival of God's rule (11:20).

As the prophet Jesus moves toward Jerusalem, his proclamation of God's kingdom intensifies (11:18; 12:31–32; 13:18, 20, 28, 29; 14:15; 16:16; 17:20; 18:16–17, 24–25, 29). It is because many among the people heed his prophetic challenge and join him on his way to Jerusalem that Jesus can tell the Pharisees that "the kingdom of God is among you" (17:21). Luke's "kingship parable" in 19:11–27 serves to focus and interpret this progression. Jesus is the one who will be proclaimed as a king by the populace (19:38) and identified as a king by the Roman prefect who executes him (23:38). Before his arrest, he will bestow *basileia* (kingdom) on the Twelve (22:29–30). Mocked on the cross as a king who cannot save himself (22:37), he extends a welcome to the criminal who asks of him a place when he enters into his kingdom (23:42).

The paradoxical character of Jesus' kingly rule is indicated by the way in which he is both identified with and distinguished from his ancestor David. Luke takes over from Mark 12:35–37 the pericope that claims, through the use of LXX Psalm 109:1, that the Messiah is not David's son but David's Lord (Luke 20:41–44). But Luke makes the point even more emphatically by invoking the same verse in Acts 2:33 for the resurrection of Jesus as an enthronement at God's right hand. It is as the prophet whom God raised up (Acts 3:22) that Jesus receives "the throne of his ancestor David" (Luke 1:32), and therefore "of his kingdom (*basileia*) there will be no end" (Luke 1:33). In Acts, David appears mostly as a prophet who, by the power of the Holy Spirit, foretold the truth about the Messiah Jesus (Acts 1:16; 2:25; 4:25). And the truth is that although David was also a prophet (Acts 2:30), he died and his tomb was still among them (2:29). David did not ascend into heaven (2:34), and his words about the Lord saying to my Lord therefore referred to the resurrected Jesus, whom God had made both Lord and Christ (2:36).

The subtlety of Luke's language can be seen in Paul's account of Israel's history in Acts 13:16–41. He declares that God raised up David to be a king (13:22), but it was of his seed that God brought—some manuscripts read "raised"—Jesus as savior for Israel (13:23). David once more serves as the source of prophecy (13:33–35) and the point of comparison for Jesus: "For

David, after he had served the purpose of God in his own generation, died [Greek, 'fell asleep'], was laid beside his ancestors, and experienced corruption; but he whom God raised up experienced no corruption" (13:36–37).

The continued proclamation of the kingdom of God throughout Acts (1:3; 8:12; 14:22; 19:8; 20:25; 28:23, 31), therefore, is explicitly distinguished from a political restoration of *basileia* (kingdom) to Israel (1:6). Although the *basileia* exercised by the risen Jesus through his prophetic representatives is a real one and is over the "house of Jacob" that is the restored Israel gathered into the Jerusalem church, it extends to all humans as that "salvation" which is equivalent to inclusion in God's prophetic people. Thus Luke has James say of the inclusion of Gentiles: "This agrees with the words of the prophets, as it is written: 'After this I will return, and I will rebuild the dwelling of David, which has fallen; from its ruins I will rebuild it, and I will set it up, so that all other peoples may seek the Lord—even all the Gentiles over whom my name has been called'" (Acts 15:15–17).

CONCLUSION

The position that Luke's Jesus is fundamentally a prophetic figure is supported not only by multiple and converging lines of literary evidence but also by the way in which other important Lukan themes connected to Jesus are at least consonant and in most cases positively complementary to that prophetic presentation.

NOTES

1. Counting only his books, see Jack Dean Kingsbury, *Matthew: Structure, Christology, Kingdom* (Philadelphia: Fortress Press, 1975); *Jesus Christ in Matthew, Mark, and Luke* (Philadelphia: Fortress Press, 1981); *The Christology of Mark's Gospel* (Philadelphia: Fortress Press, 1983); *Matthew*, 2d ed. (Philadelphia: Fortress Press, 1986); *Conflict in Mark: Jesus, Authorities, Disciples* (Philadelphia: Fortress Press, 1989); *Conflict in Luke: Jesus, Authorities, Disciples* (Minneapolis: Fortress Press, 1991).

2. See Luke Timothy Johnson, *The Literary Function of Possessions in Luke-Acts*, Society of Biblical Literature Dissertation Series 39 (Missoula, Mont.: Scholars Press, 1977); *The Gospel of Luke*, Sacra Pagina 3 (Collegeville, Minn.: Liturgical Press, 1991); *The Acts of the Apostles*, Sacra Pagina 5 (Collegeville, Minn.: Liturgical Press, 1992).

3. As classically demonstrated by O. Cullman, *The Christology of the New Testament*, rev. ed., trans. S. C. Guthrie and C. A. M. Hall (Philadelphia: Westminster Press, 1963).

4. See J. Wanke, *Die Emmauserzaehlung*, Erfurter Theologische Studien 31 (Leipzig: St. Benno-Verlag, 1973), 61, 64.

5. As with J. A. T. Robinson, "The Most Primitive Christology of All?" *Journal of Theological Studies* 7 (1956): 177–89.

6. As in R. E. Brown, *The Birth of the Messiah: A Commentary on the Infancy Narratives in Matthew and Luke* (Garden City, N.Y.: Doubleday & Co., 1979), 29–32, 311–15.

7. H. Conzelmann, *The Theology of St. Luke,* trans. G. Buswell (New York: Harper & Row, 1961), 24, 48–49, 75, 172, 188; for the decisive argument against Conzelmann on this point, see P. Minear, "Luke's Use of the Birth Stories," in *Studies in Luke-Acts,* ed. L. Keck and J. L. Martyn (Nashville: Abingdon Press, 1966), 111–30.

8. C. F. D. Moule, "The Christology of Acts," in Keck and Martyn, eds. *Studies in Luke-Acts,* 159–85.

9. The case was made first and most convincingly by H. J. Cadbury, *The Making of Luke-Acts* (New York: Macmillan Co., 1927).

10. My commentaries in the Sacra Pagina series (see note 2, above) are, as far as I know, still the only major commentary on both volumes written by the same scholar in the same series. Not in the form of a commentary but of major importance is R. C. Tannehill, *The Narrative Unity of Luke-Acts: A Literary Interpretation,* 2 vols. (Philadelphia and Minneapolis: Fortress Press, 1986 and 1990).

11. See M. C. Parsons and R. I. Pervo, *Rethinking the Unity of Luke and Acts* (Minneapolis: Fortress Press, 1993).

12. See Parsons and Pervo, *Rethinking,* 8–13; and B. S. Childs, *The New Testament as Canon: An Introduction* (Philadelphia: Fortress Press, 1984), 218–40.

13. See R. I. Pervo, *Profit with Delight: The Literary Genre of the Acts of the Apostles* (Philadelphia: Fortress Press, 1987).

14. D. L. Brown and J. L. Wentling, "The Conventions of Classical Biography and the Genre of Luke-Acts: A Preliminary Study," in *Luke-Acts: New Perspectives from the Society of Biblical Literature,* ed. C. H. Talbert (New York: Crossroad, 1984).

15. See especially G. E. Sterling, *Historiography and Self-Definition: Josephus, Luke-Acts, and Apologetic Historiography,* Novum Testamentum Supplements 64 (Leiden: E. J. Brill, 1992); and J. T. Squires, *The Plan of God in Luke-Acts,* Society for New Testament Studies Monograph Series 76 (Cambridge: Cambridge University Press, 1993).

16. For fuller discussion, see Johnson, *Gospel of Luke,* 9–10.

17. See S. G. Wilson, *The Gentiles and the Gentile Mission in Luke-Acts,* Society for New Testament Studies Monograph Series 23 (Cambridge: Cambridge University Press, 1973); J. Dupont, "The Salvation of the Gentiles and the Theological Significance of Acts," in *The Salvation of the Gentiles,* trans. J. Eating (New York: Paulist Press, 1979), 11–33.

18. Johnson, *Gospel of Luke,* 9–10.

19. See J. Meagher, *Clumsy Construction in Mark's Gospel: A Critique of Form and Redaktionsgeschichte* (Lewiston, N.Y.: Edwin Mellen Press, 1979).
20. Still unsurpassed on this point is J. Dupont, *The Sources of the Acts,* trans. K. Pond (New York: Herder & Herder, 1964).
21. Johnson, *Literary Function,* 13–28.
22. See L. T. Johnson, "Luke-Acts," in *Anchor Bible Dictionary* 4:405.
23. See R. J. Dillon, "Previewing Luke's Program from his Prologue," *Catholic Biblical Quarterly* 43 (1981): 205–27.
24. See W. S. Kurz, *Reading Luke-Acts: Dynamics of Biblical Narrative* (Louisville, Ky.: Westminster/John Knox Press, 1993).
25. For the construction of character in Luke-Acts, see J. A. Darr, *On Character-Building: The Reader and the Rhetoric of Characterization in Luke-Acts* (Louisville, Ky.: Westminster/John Knox Press, 1992); and W. H. Shepherd, *The Narrative Function of the Holy Spirit as a Character in Luke-Acts,* Society of Biblical Literature Dissertation Series 147 (Atlanta: Scholars Press, 1994).
26. In addition to Johnson, *Literary Function,* 38–126, see, for the profile of the prophet, P. Schubert, "The Structure and Significance of Luke 24," in *Neutestamentliche Studien für Rudolf Bultmann,* Beihefte zur Zeitschrift für die neutestamentliche Wissenschaft 21 (Berlin: A. Töpelmann, 1954), 165–86; J. Dupont, *Les Béatitudes,* vol. 3: *Les Évangélistes* (Paris: J. Gabalda, 1973); P. Minear, *To Heal and to Reveal: The Prophetic Vocation according to Luke* (New York: Seabury Press, 1976); D. Tiede, *Prophecy and History in Luke-Acts* (Philadelphia: Fortress Press, 1980); R. Dillon, *From Eyewitnesses to Ministers of the Word,* Analecta biblica 82 (Rome: Pontifical Biblical Institute Press, 1978); D. Moessner, "Luke 9:1–50: Luke's Preview of the Journey of the Prophet like Moses of Deuteronomy," *Journal of Biblical Literature* 102 (1983): 575–605.
27. See Mark 6:4, 15; 8:28; Matt. 13:57; 16:14; 21:11, 46; John 4:19, 44; 6:14; 7:40, 52; 9:17. Compare Luke 4:24; 7:16, 39; 9:8, 19; 13:33–34; 24:19; Acts 3:22; 7:37.
28. For Luke's distinctive rendering of John, see L. T. Johnson, "John the Baptist: Prophet of the Great Reversal," *Bible Today* 34 (1996): 295–99.
29. See Johnson, *Gospel of Luke,* 116–26.
30. Ibid., 161–71, 386–91.
31. Johnson, *Acts of the Apostles,* 21–32.

THE CHRISTOLOGY OF
THE JOHANNINE WRITINGS

R. Alan Culpepper

John is the most overtly theological of the Gospels, and Christology is its central focus. Nevertheless, to speak of Christology is to bring to bear on the Gospel a systematization of thought and an abstraction of theological categories that had not yet developed in the history of Christian thought. In the Gospel of John memory has passed into tradition, and tradition has been rendered into a narrative that tells the story of Jesus for a particular community. This narrative has clear implications for the community's debates about the person and work of Jesus, but those debates are still carried on in the medium of narrative rather than in doctrine or dogma. First John moves one step further in that it interprets the community's debates by making judgments about christological claims apart from the Gospel's narrative context.

Typically, Johannine Christology has been approached through a survey of christological titles, through efforts to reconstruct various stages in the development of the Johannine community and its thought, or through some combination of the two. The survey of Johannine Christology in this chapter shows that these approaches are not easily compatible or complementary. On the contrary, the conceptual relationships within the Gospel of John make it very difficult to sort out stages in the development of Johannine Christology. I survey briefly both some leading reconstructions of the development of John's Christology and the ways in which John uses some of the christological titles. This survey calls attention to relationships between various strands of John's Christology so that one can see, in rough outline at least, the difficulty of harmonizing theories regarding how the

Gospel's Christology developed historically and how the Gospel develops its Christology.

HOW THE GOSPEL'S CHRISTOLOGY DEVELOPED

Because the prevailing view is that the Gospel of John was composed over a period of time in a process that probably involved the testimony of the beloved disciple, materials shaped within the Johannine community, perhaps two editions of the Gospel, and the work of a redactor, various interpreters have sought to show how Johannine Christology developed in the course of this process. The writers I survey here developed their views independently, but they form an interesting lineage in American Johannine scholarship. Robert Fortna was a student of J. Louis Martyn shortly before Martyn published his *History and Theology in the Fourth Gospel* (1968). Raymond Brown and J. Louis Martyn both taught at Union Theological Seminary in New York, and Martinus de Boer studied with them.

Robert Fortna recast Rudolf Bultmann's hypothesis of a signs source, advancing the study of Johannine sources methodologically and identifying the contours of an early signs Gospel.[1] Fortna subsequently developed his earlier work on the signs Gospel by showing how the evangelist edited it into the present form of the Gospel.[2] The function of the signs Gospel, which probably included a passion narrative, was simply to present Jesus as the Messiah. The signs were "demonstrations of his messiahship," and belief was "the paradigmatic response."[3] The signs Gospel's account of Jesus' death is apologetic, showing that Jesus suffered and died in order to fulfill the scriptures. Accordingly, there is little theological reflection on the soteriological significance of Jesus' death. The fourth evangelist reaffirmed the source's Christology, changed it, and deepened and enhanced it. Christology remains central, however. The presentation of Jesus' ministry revolves around the signs, but the fourth evangelist drops the report "We have found Elijah," which probably stood at 1:43, in order to defend the claim in John 3:13 that "no one has ascended into heaven except the one who descended from heaven, the Son of Man." Jesus is the one "sent by the Father," and John the Baptist is solely a witness to him. Similarly, Jesus is a "new Moses," like him but greater, for through Jesus came not the law but grace and truth (1:17).

The fourth evangelist enhances the Christology of the signs Gospel by adding the discourses in which Jesus speaks revelatory words. The christological titles, which were all subsumed under Jesus' messiahship in the source, are now differentiated and their significance deepened. The title "Son of man" appears in material added to the source, and Jesus speaks as one from heaven. Jesus declares what the Father has given him to say. He knows what is in the hearts of others; he uses the divine "I am"; and he lays down his life and takes it up again. In short, he reveals the divine glory. The fourth Gospel's Christology of the incarnation, therefore, transforms the Jewish, messianic view of the source into "a cosmic christology."[4]

J. Louis Martyn and Raymond E. Brown have set the framework for understanding the development of the Johannine community and its Christology. Their work is well known and hardly needs to be summarized again. Of particular interest for our survey of Johannine Christology, however, is the way in which each of these interpreters views the development of John's Logos Christology. Both affirm that the conflict with the synagogue was in a sense christological and related, either before or after the fact, to the move from a lower (messianic miracle worker) to a higher (otherworldly Logos) Christology. Martyn contends that during the early period, while the Johannine believers were still within the synagogue, they preached Jesus as a miracle worker, "the Mosaic prophet, the eschatological Elijah, the expected Messiah."[5] The success of this preaching eventually led the authorities to take radical steps to control the problem of conversions and dissension within the synagogue. During the middle period, after the expulsion of believers from the synagogue, the socially dislocated believers increasingly conceived of Jesus as "a numinous and somewhat other-worldly figure."[6] Martyn therefore assigns the Logos hymn to this period of the Johannine community's history.[7]

Raymond Brown, in contrast, posits the entrance into the community of a "second group" of antitemple Jews who also brought in Samaritan converts. This group served as a catalyst for the development of the preexistence Christology, which in turn precipitated the expulsion of the Johannine Christians from the synagogue. As support for this reconstruction, Brown appeals to three elements in the text of John: (1) the conversion of Samaritans in John 4:4–42, which occurs prior to the conflict with "the Jews" in chapter 5; (2) the antitemple attitude expressed in John 4:21; and (3) the new title "Savior of the world" in John 4:42.[8]

In short, Brown and Martyn differ over the causal relationship between the development of a higher Christology and the expulsion of believers from the synagogue, with Brown contending that the development of such a Christology led to the expulsion and Martyn contending that the development of the higher, otherworldly Christology followed the expulsion. Nevertheless, both agree that the Johannine believers moved from a lower to a higher Christology and that the Johannine Logos Christology developed prior to the entrance of Gentiles into the Johannine community.

Martinus C. de Boer has proposed a similar developmental approach to the Christology of John by uncovering a series of stages in the christological perspectives on the death of Jesus in the Gospel of John.[9] Building on the work of Brown and Martyn, de Boer identifies three crises in the history of the Johannine community: (1) expulsion from the synagogue, (2) execution of Johannine Christians for making the claim that Jesus was one with God, and (3) schism within the community (reflected in 1 and 2 John). The three crises divide the development of the Johannine community into four periods. Correspondingly, de Boer identifies four stages in the composition history of the Gospel, with each stage formulating a different understanding of Jesus' death.

John I (the Gospel of the first period) was a collection of miracle stories. Its "miracle-working prophet-messiah" (a term de Boer borrowed from D. Moody Smith)[10] performed "signs" reminiscent of Elijah and Elisha, fulfilling the contemporary expectations of the "prophet like Moses" who was to come. This presentation of Jesus sought to convince Jewish readers that Jesus, not John the Baptist, was the Messiah. Jesus' death was an embarrassment, but one that was deflected by demonstrating that it fulfilled the scriptures. It also served as a prelude to the climactic sign (his resurrection).[11]

The argument with the Jews culminated in the expulsion of Johannine believers from the synagogue, and this separation from the synagogue prompted a major revision of the Gospel (John II). Believers were challenged for professing that Jesus was the Messiah, and the question of Jesus' authority centered on the issue of where he was from. Did he not come from Galilee, and did they not know his family? How then could he have divine authority? In response, John II affirms that Jesus is the Son of God, the one sent by the Father. Hence he bears divine authority and can even use God's name, "I am."[12] John II also presents an appeal to those believers who remained in the synagogue to declare their faith publicly and depart with the other believers. Consequently, John II develops the importance of Jesus' departure to the Father. Following Brown, de Boer argues that John 20:17 requires the reader to understand that the exaltation to the Father has already occurred in the resurrection. The focus on the departure of the Son to the Father in John II means that the death of Jesus is still subordinate in significance to the resurrection/exaltation/departure of Jesus.[13]

John III, produced after the persecution of Johannine believers, sought to vindicate Jesus and his followers while condemning their persecutors ("the Jews") as those who were controlled by the murderous "ruler of this world."[14] To this end, the designation "the Son of man" was introduced into discourses that had already been framed in John II, and the emphasis was on the departure or exaltation of the Son of man rather than on his coming. The "lifting up" sayings precipitate a striking change in perspective: "The ascension of Jesus to heaven is newly interpreted as a hidden reference to the sort of death Jesus had died (3:13–15, 12:32–33)."[15] The crucifixion, then, served as an outward sign of its own significance: the exaltation of Jesus. As a result of this reinterpretation, references to Jesus' glorification have in view not merely his resurrection/ascension but also his death.[16] Jesus' death can therefore serve as a paradigm in the Gospel's two-level drama for the martyrdom of his followers, who also glorify God through their deaths. As in the case of Jesus' death, their deaths will bear fruit also.[17]

The final period in the history of the Johannine tradition is marked by the division of the community and the departure of a group of Johannine believers who held to different beliefs regarding the significance of Jesus' life and death. In response, the elder, the author of the Johannine epistles, reasserted the salvific, expiatory significance of Jesus' death by emphasizing that Jesus was the Christ who had come in flesh and that the Johannine believers were cleansed by water and by blood. The giving of Jesus' flesh and blood is related to the significance of his death (John 6:51–56), and the foot washing is a demonstration of its cleansing effect. The final redactor of the Gospel weaves this late understanding of Jesus' death into the Gospel through the account of the water and blood flowing from Jesus' side (John 19:34–35). Through this masterful analysis, de Boer shows not one but many Christologies in the Johannine writings, that the various Christologies can be distinguished and related to events in the history of the Johannine community, and that while Jesus' death was not important in the two early stages, it grew in importance in the latter two stages.

The strength of such a careful and comprehensive developmental approach to Johannine Christology is that it provides a rationale for the various christological perspectives in the Gospel by relating them to a reconstruction of the history of the community in which the Gospel was produced. Fascinating and persuasive as its results may be, the developmental approach nevertheless suffers from three weaknesses: (1) It must rely on a reconstruction of the history of the community that is itself uncertain; (2) it distinguishes and separates christological emphases within the Gospel so that they no longer stand in tension, balance, or harmony with one another; and (3) it does not sufficiently account for the ways in which these various Christologies are related to each other and function in the Gospel as we have it. The solution is not to cease to explore either the variety of christological perspectives in the Gospel or the history of the Johannine community but to bring the historical and literary approaches to Johannine Christology into dialogue with each other.

This survey of developmental approaches to the Christology of John has focused on several closely related proposals that in a sense represent the work of American Johannine scholarship. A more representative survey would consider other approaches to the history of the Johannine tradition as well. One basic line of development would remain constant, however, even in a broader survey of developmental theories: Johannine Christology appears to have developed from an early stage in which Jesus was viewed as a miracle-working Messiah who fulfilled the scriptures to a later stage in which this Messiah was viewed as the Logos who had become flesh. This means that the Johannine signs stem from an early period, while the Gospel's Logos Christology, which is most clearly present in the prologue, represents the mature development of Johannine thought. Paradoxically, when one reads the Gospel, one begins with the prologue and then reads all the rest of the Gospel narrative in the light of its Logos Christology. To a degree not sufficiently recognized, the leading strands of John's Christology are also tied to this late, Logos Christology.

HOW THE GOSPEL
DEVELOPS ITS CHRISTOLOGY

Although the christological titles provide important avenues for understanding John's Christology, care must be taken to treat these titles in their Johannine contexts because the Gospel of John uses the titles in distinctive ways, fills them with new meanings, and relates them to one another and to important Johannine themes in ways that give them unique meanings and functions in this Gospel. Closely related to the titles are the Johannine "I am" sayings, and these too need to be interpreted in their narrative context in the Gospel. Similarly, the "signs" that Jesus does point to his identity: He turns water to wine (2:1–11), heals the official's son (4:46–54), heals the man at the pool of Bethesda (5:1–18), feeds a multitude (6:1–15), walks on water (6:16–21), gives sight to a man born blind (9:1–7), and raises Lazarus from the tomb (11:38–44). Other actions, if not actual signs, also fulfill an interpretive function in the Gospel: Jesus drives the merchants out of the temple (2:13–22), enters Jerusalem riding on a donkey (12:12–19), washes his disciples' feet (13:1–11), and directs the disciples to a great catch of fish (21:1–14). Jesus' debates with the religious leaders place his ministry in a trial-like setting and clarify the charges against Jesus and the basis of his authority. Throughout, Old Testament quotations, allusions, and imagery set Jesus' ministry in the larger sweep of Moses and the prophets in Israel's past and its hopes for the future. From among this at times overwhelming multiplicity of ways in which the Gospel interprets Jesus, a few dominant emphases rise above the others: Jesus is the one sent from above to reveal the Father, take away the sin of the world, and give life to those who receive him.

Logos Christology and the Wisdom Tradition

Since the publication of Brown's commentary on John, consensus has grown that John's Logos Christology developed against the background of the Jewish wisdom tradition. The wisdom writings served as fertile soil for christological reflection, and from the Gospel itself one familiar with the wisdom tradition can see numerous points of contact. As early as Proverbs 8, the figure of Wisdom was being personified. Wisdom was identified with God's word and therefore was God's agent in the creation (Prov. 3:19). Wisdom was thus created first (Prov. 8:22). Wisdom is received by her children (Prov. 8:32), and she prepares a table of bread and wine for them (Prov. 9:5). With Sirach (190 B.C.E.), Wisdom was identified with keeping the Torah (Sir. 15:1; 19:20; compare Bar. 4:1). The place of the Torah was being elevated, and sages began to claim that it, too, was preexistent. Wisdom, like Torah, provided "the bread of learning" and "the water of wisdom" (Sir. 15:3). She could therefore tell of her "glory" (Sir. 24:2). Wisdom "came forth from the mouth of the Most High" (Sir. 24:3) in the beginning (24:9) and made her dwelling place with Israel (24:8; see also Bar. 3:37). The praise of Wisdom continues with the Wisdom of Solomon. All things were created by God's word (*logos;* Wisd. Sol. 9:1), and Wisdom is unique (*monogenēs;* Wisd. Sol. 7:22). Wisdom, moreover, was present with Israel throughout its history (Wisd. Sol. 10–11), and the people were saved by Wisdom (Wisd. Sol. 9:18; 10:4).

On this foundation, the evangelist was able to articulate a Christology in which Jesus is identified as the fulfillment of the Torah revealed to Moses, the creative Logos that was in the beginning with God, and the Wisdom of God that tabernacled with Israel and makes its dwelling place among God's people. This constellation of themes drawn from the wisdom tradition explains the development of seemingly diverse elements in John. Like Wisdom, the Johannine Logos was God's agent in the creation, but unlike the praise of Wisdom in Proverbs and Sirach, the evangelist indicates that the Logos was not created first but was with God in the beginning. The Logos enjoyed "glory" with God before the creation of the world (John 17:5). Then Jesus, as the Word become flesh, can claim that before Abraham was "I am" (John 8:58; compare 8:56) and that Isaiah saw his glory and spoke about him (John 12:41). As the creative Logos, Jesus continues to exercise sovereign and creative power. He can change water to wine, walk on water, and raise the dead. Like Wisdom, Jesus calls to the children of God and feeds them the bread of life and living water. In this respect, the influence of the wisdom tradition on John's Christology is evident not only in the prologue but throughout the Gospel. It is integral to both the actions and the sayings that characterize Jesus in the body of the Gospel.

Son of God

The confession that Jesus is the Son of God functions as a christological climax in the Gospel of Mark. Quite intentionally, according to Mark it is neither the miracles that Jesus does nor the teachings of Jesus that reveal his identity as the Son of God but only his death. The passion of Jesus in Mark is thereby emphasized over his power; the interpretations of Jesus as wisdom teacher and thaumaturge are subordinated to the gospel of his death and resurrection; and the revelatory function of Jesus' death is underscored. In Matthew and Luke, the confession that Jesus is the Son of God is given a literal rather than a metaphorical sense, and the virgin birth accounts serve to defend and explain the literal sense of the confession.

John, by contrast, omits any account of Jesus' birth, thereby opening the way to alternative understandings of the confession that Jesus was the Son of God. Simultaneously, John extends the significance of this confession and gives a much greater role to the Father–Son terminology. Rather than explaining or justifying the confession "Son of God," John treats it as an outgrowth of Wisdom/Logos Christology. To put the matter sharply, Jesus did not become the Son of God by means of the virgin birth; he always was the Son of God. The Johannine Jesus can therefore pray, "Father, glorify me in your own presence with the glory that I had in your presence before the world existed" (17:5). The Synoptic Jesus never makes any such claim, and could not, given the Synoptics' more literal, physical grounding of Jesus' Sonship in the birth narratives. This transition allows John to present Jesus as the one who was sent by the Father, sent from above, because he is the preexistent Wisdom/Logos that became flesh in Jesus. He is the one who is in the Father's bosom (1:18), who was sent to reveal the Father. Indeed, he and the Father are one (10:30), yet all that he does and says has been given to him by the Father (5:19, 36; 8:28).

Whereas the centurion's confession that Jesus is the Son of God stands in a climactic position in Mark, in the Gospel of John both John the Baptist (1:34) and Nathanael (1:49) confess that Jesus is the Son of God. Because these confessions come so early in the Gospel, they establish Jesus' Sonship as the standard by which other responses to him will be measured. John the Baptist was sent from God to bear witness to Jesus (1:6–8, 15, 19–20), and Nathanael was "an Israelite in whom there is no deceit" (1:47). The Gospel therefore explicitly certifies both John and Nathanael as authoritative witnesses to Jesus.

The next set of references to the Son of God in John further clarifies his role. The Father sent the Son into the world so that those who would believe in him might have life (3:16, 36; see below the exploration of the giving of life in John's Christology). Jesus is the only, or unique, Son. John speaks of "children of God" (1:12; 11:52), but there is no other Son, and none like him.[18]

John 3:17 for the first time in the Gospel speaks explicitly of Jesus as the one sent by the Father. John uses both the verb *apostellein* (seventeen times) and the verb *pempein* (twenty-five times) when referring to Jesus as the one sent. Some of these sayings are cryptic ("him whom he has sent," 5:38; 6:29) while others are explicit ("the Father has sent me," 5:36). Recognizing that Jesus is the one sent by God, however, is virtually synonymous with believing in Jesus (see 11:42; 17:3, 8, 21, 23, 25). Although the Jewish concept of the emissary (*shaliah*) charged with the authority of the sender no doubt lies in the background, it is noteworthy that in John the language of sending is closely tied to the portrayal of Jesus as the Son. It is the Father who sends the Son. Accordingly, it is not surprising that Jesus rarely speaks of himself in the Synoptic Gospels as the one sent (see, however, Matt. 10:40; Mark 9:37; Luke 4:18, 43; 9:48; 10:16; 20:13). While the role of Jesus as the one sent has roots in Jewish and early Christian tradition, in John sending is closely related to the Father–Son paradigm in its distinctive Johannine expression.

Because the Son was sent by the Father, the Son can do nothing on his own authority (5:19). Nevertheless, the Son does what the Father has given him to do. Like an apprentice, the Son does what he sees the Father doing, even raising the dead and giving life. A few verses later, the Son (that is, Son of God) assumes the role of the expected Son of man, judging the nations and raising the dead (5:25–27). Likewise, the Son says what the Father has given him to say (8:28).

The latter part of John 8 is a virtual paternity suit in which Jesus and the Jewish religious leaders each contest the other's claims. The Jews say their father is Abraham, while there is uncertainty about who Jesus' father is.

Jesus replies that if the Jews were children of Abraham, they would do what Abraham did. On the contrary, however, their efforts to kill Jesus show that their father is not Abraham, who rejoiced when he saw Jesus' day (8:56), but the devil, who has always been a murderer. Jesus does the will of his Father, and the Father glorifies him (8:54). The Father knows the Son (10:15), loves the Son (10:17), sanctifies the Son (10:36), and sends the Son to do his works (10:36). Indeed, the Father and the Son are one (10:30), and the Father is in the Son and the Son in the Father (10:38). Nevertheless, the one revealed is greater than the revealer, the sender greater than the one sent: The Father is greater than the Son (14:28). The Father will therefore be glorified by the death of the Son (14:13; 17:1). Because the Son has revealed the Father as only the Son could, and because he has been sent to give life, the Gospel was written to lead those who read it to believe that Jesus is "the Christ [NRSV, 'Messiah'], the Son of God," and through believing to have eternal life (20:30–31).

The Gospel of John has therefore tied the title "Son of God" to the Gospel's Wisdom/Logos Christology. Although the title "Son of God" circulated elsewhere in early Christianity quite separate from the wisdom tradition and Logos Christology, John portrays a Son who was with the Father from the beginning and who does and says what the Father who sent him into the world gave him to do and say. It would be very difficult to conceive of such a characterization of the "Son of God" apart from John's Logos Christology.

Son of Man

A similar situation prevails in relation to the confession that Jesus is the Son of man. John uses the same terminology that we find in the other Gospels, but in a very distinctive way. The Synoptic Son of man sayings are traditionally divided into three categories: (1) the Son of man as a glorious figure who will come in the future to judge humanity (Matt. 16:27); (2) the earthly, suffering Son of man (Mark 8:31); and (3) the earthly Son of man apart from his suffering (Matt. 8:20; 11:19; Mark 2:10, 28; Luke 19:10; 22:48). The distinctive feature of the thirteen references to the Son of man in John is that they consistently deal with his descent to earth and his ascent to heaven (3:13; 6:62), his exaltation (3:14; 8:28; 12:34), and his glorification (12:23; 13:31). These are not unrelated; John presents a consistent picture of the Son of man that is another facet of the Christology we have found expressed by the Son of God sayings and the Wisdom/Logos Christology.

John reverses the sequence of the Synoptic Son of man scheme, in which Jesus will be raised, ascend, and then return in glory. In John, Jesus has come from above (descent) and will return to his Father (ascent). The Johannine Son of man sayings, therefore, speak not of Jesus' return to earth as judge in the future but of his return to heaven. For John, the all-important affirmation is not the "second coming" but the confession that the expected Judge and Messiah has already come: "And this is the judgment, that the light has come into the world, and people loved darkness rather than light" (3:19).

If John is familiar with the tradition of the Son of man sayings preserved in the Synoptics, then, characteristically, he does not use the Synoptics as a source for his Son of man sayings. John 5:27, which claims that the Son has been given "authority to execute judgment, because he is the Son of Man," echoes the first category of the Synoptic sayings, those that speak of the coming Son of man, endowed with authority to judge. The difference is that John perceives that the earthly Jesus was already the authorized Judge, and the judgment was occurring in individual responses to Jesus.

Similarly, the ascension of Jesus is not, for John, the prelude to Jesus' future authority, as it is in the Synoptics (see Matt. 28:18). Instead, Jesus' exaltation is the completion of his mission to reveal the Father. Three sayings that speak of the exaltation of the Son of man form a subgroup. These sayings all use the distinctive verb *to lift up* (*hypsoun;* 3:14; 8:28; 12:32). The "lifting up" of the Son of man does not occur after his humiliation on the cross, as in the Pauline confession in Philippians 2:5–11. Instead, the cross is the first step in his exaltation. When John speaks of Jesus' being lifted up, therefore, he invites the reader to reflect on the paradox that the lifting up of Jesus on the cross marked Jesus' ascent to the Father. The ascension, after all, is not narrated as a separate event in John. The result is that the Son of man sayings that predict Jesus' exaltation are the Johannine counterpart to the Synoptic passion predictions, the second group of the Synoptic Son of man sayings. The third group of the Synoptic Son of man sayings—the earthly Son of man apart from his suffering—does not have direct parallels in John.[19] John, therefore, has not drawn his concept of Jesus as Son of man from the Synoptics but rather has reinterpreted the Son of man concept in light of the wisdom/Logos tradition in its distinctive Johannine development.[20]

Moving from one reference to another, one can see that John progressively defines the role of the Son of man. In response to acclamations from his first disciples, Jesus announces that they will see the angels of God ascending and descending on the Son of man (1:51). Since this announcement recalls Jacob's dream vision of a ladder reaching to heaven, with angels ascending and descending on it (Gen. 28:12), the implication is that Jesus is the new Bethel, the new meeting place between heaven and earth. Jesus' role as heavenly revealer is secure because only the Son of man has descended from heaven, and no one else has ascended to heaven (3:13). There will be something paradoxical about this ascension, however. The Son of man must be lifted up like the serpent in the wilderness (3:14). When Moses prayed that the people of Israel might be delivered from a plague of fiery serpents, the Lord commanded that he set a bronze serpent on a pole. If a serpent bit one of the Israelites, the victim could look to the bronze serpent and live (Num. 21:3–9). Similarly, Jesus' exaltation would provide life for those who looked to him in faith.

The next reference explains that the Son has not only the power to give life but also the authority to judge—the role of the Son of man that is emphasized in the Synoptic Gospels. Because Jesus has descended from above, like the personification of Wisdom, he can invite those who accept him to drink living water and eat the bread of life (6:27). The bread and drink he gives, however, are his own body and blood (6:53). Unless one eats his body and drinks his blood, one can have no part in him. The insight that holds this obscure reasoning together is that the revelation Jesus embodies in himself and gives to those who will receive it nourishes one's life in the spirit as surely as bread nourishes our physical bodies. The language is eucharistic, but the declaration has christological, soteriological, and ecclesiological significance. For the original readers of the Gospel, Jesus' pronouncement probably meant that those who would not break from the synagogue, make a public declaration of faith in Jesus, and join with the Christian community in its worship had no hope of life in Christ. The other side of the scandal is that the Son of man who gives himself to provide life for others will ascend again to the Father (6:52).

A verse from Isaiah unifies important Johannine themes: "See, my servant shall prosper, he shall be exalted and lifted up, and shall be very high" (Isa. 52:13). But only when the Son of man has been lifted up will his identity and divine authority be evident (8:28). When Jesus asks, "Do you believe in the Son of Man?" (9:35), the blind man to whom he has given sight asks who the Son of man is. With delightful wit, Jesus says to the man born blind, "You have seen him!" When the Greeks come and ask to see Jesus, he realizes that the hour has come for him to be glorified. He can no longer remain a provincial messiah (12:23). It is now time for him to be lifted up so that he can draw all people to himself (12:32). Although Jesus has not mentioned the Son of man in this immediate context, the Son of man was referred to in the first two lifting-up sayings (3:14; 8:28), so the crowd responds by asking the identity of the Son of man. The hour has come, and quickly the events that will lead to Jesus' death are set in motion. When Judas goes out to betray him, Jesus announces, "Now the Son of Man has been glorified, and God has been glorified in him" (13:31). For John, that is the essential truth about Jesus. The Son of man has already come. He has been lifted up and glorified, and the judgment is determined by how we respond to his revelation of the Father.[21]

John's portrayal of Jesus as the Logos incarnate, against the background of the wisdom tradition, has therefore also had a profound impact on John's interpretation of Jesus as the Son of man. Although the Gospel uses the title "Son of man," the Son of man concept functions quite differently in John than it does in the Jewish sources or the Synoptic Gospels. The brief survey here supports Moody Smith's conclusion:

> Apparently, the meaning and function of the Son of Man title in John stands closer to Johannine christology generally than to the several uses of the term in the Synoptic Gospels. Thus it would be difficult to speak of a Son of Man christology in the Gospel of John that stands out distinctly from a Son of God christology.[22]

The Gospel of John has recast the Son of man concept in light of the Gospel's interpretation of Jesus as the Son of God sent from above, who is the Logos incarnate. The emphasis has shifted from the future role of the Son of man to Jesus' present fulfillment of traditional eschatological expectations. Jesus' authority as the Son of man, moreover, is derived from his identity as the Son of God and the Logos. Again, it would be hard to understand this recasting of the Son of man apart from John's Logos Christology.

The One in Whom There Is Life

One of the first affirmations that John makes about the Logos is "What has come into being in him was life" (1:3–4), and this motif runs throughout the Gospel. The end result of the work of the one who is Wisdom/Logos, the Son of God, and the Son of man is not "salvation" (which occurs only once in John; 4:22) or "justification" (*dikaiosynē* occurs only twice in John; 16:8, 10, and then in the sense of "righteousness" rather than "justification") but "life" (which occurs thirty-six times in John, seventeen of which are in the phrase "eternal life"). Moreover, John's understanding of eternal life is also distinctive. Characteristically, John does not regard eternal life as something believers will receive in the future. Those who believe already have eternal life. They have crossed over from death into life (5:24; 1 John 3:14). The dominant reality of eternal life is not quantitative but qualitative: "And this is eternal life, that they may know you, the only true God, and Jesus Christ whom you have sent" (John 17:3). The purpose of the Gospel, therefore, is an extension of the work of the Revealer: "Now Jesus did many other signs in the presence of his disciples, which are not written in this book. But these are written so that you may come to believe that Jesus is the Messiah, the Son of God, and that through believing you may have life in his name" (20:30–31).

The characterization of Jesus as the giver of life is one of the themes that unifies John 2—4. Jesus' first public act is the changing of water to wine at the wedding at Cana. The imagery of a wedding and the symbolism of wine both suggest that in the provision of the best wine at the end, Jesus is fulfilling the Old Testament visions of the end time (Isa. 25:6–8; Zech. 10:6–7; Joel 2:19, 24; Rev. 19:7–9). Jesus not only provides the good wine; he is the bridegroom (John 3:29).

The scene in the temple in John 2:14–22 differs from the Synoptic parallels in that Jesus' act of overturning the tables and driving out the money changers serves to set up his pronouncement "Destroy this temple, and in three days I will raise it up" (2:19). This saying occurs elsewhere, at the trial of Jesus and at the mockery at the cross, but in none of the other accounts of the demonstration in the temple. John interprets this saying as a reference to the death and resurrection of Jesus and adds that after his resurrection the disciples remembered that he had made this claim (2:22). Through his resurrection, therefore, Jesus provides a new place in which the glory of God can dwell on earth.

In John 3, Jesus declares that no one can enter the kingdom of God unless he or she is born from above (3:3; compare Matt. 18:3). Nicodemus misunderstands because he fails to recognize that Jesus is the one through whom a person can receive this new life from above. He is the Son of man who has descended from above (3:13), and when he is lifted up, whoever believes in him may have eternal life, just as the act of looking to the serpent that Moses lifted up in the wilderness gave life to the dying Israelites (3:14–15). The Father's purpose in sending the Son was that he might give eternal life to all who believe in him (3:16, 36).

In the conversation with the woman at the well in Samaria, Jesus again offers life, this time in the image of living water (4:14). Water is a necessity for life, especially in an arid region, and like wine, "living water" had become a symbol for the eschatological fulfillment of blessing for God's people, both in the prophetic writings (Zech. 14:8; Ezek. 47:1–2) and in the writings of Qumran (CD 3:16–17; 19:34). The hymns of the community at Qumran praise the Teacher of Righteousness as the source of streams of living water that water the plantation in the wilderness (1QH 16 (=8):4, 6–7a, 13b–14a, 16). Whether in direct relationship to the claims for the Teacher of Righteousness or not, John appropriates this claim for Jesus: Jesus is the source of living water for all who thirst (John 4:14; 7:37–38).

As if to underscore the validity of this claim, the next act in the Gospel narrative shows Jesus giving life to an official's son (4:46–54). After an introduction in which death is imminent (4:47, 49), three references to believing (4:48, 50, 54) are followed by three references to living (4:50, 51, 53).

The greatest concentration of references to Jesus as the giver of life is in John 5 and 6. After the healing of the man at the pool, Jesus claims that those who believe in him have eternal life. They have "passed from death to life" (5:24). The Son has life in himself (5:26), but his opponents refuse to accept life from him (5:39–40). In the discourse that follows and interprets the feeding of the multitude, Jesus tells the people to strive for the food that endures to eternal life, the food that the Son of man will give them (6:27). Jesus is himself the bread of life, given by the Father, and all who eat of his flesh and drink of his blood have life in him. References to life occur twelve times in this discourse (6:27–68). With wonderful subtlety, therefore, the rhetoric of the discourse sets up Peter's confession at the end of the discourse. In contrast to the Synoptic accounts, Peter does not claim that Jesus is the Christ. Instead he says, "You have the words of eternal life. . . . You are the Holy One of God" (6:68).

As the good shepherd, Jesus has come that his sheep might have life (10:10, 28) "and have it abundantly" (10:10). The images of abundance in the Gospel underscore this claim. Jesus supplies wine in abundance, points to springs of living water and fields white for harvest. He multiplies loaves and fish so that there is more than enough for all. Rivers of living water flow from him, and in John 21 he directs the disciples to a bountiful catch of fish.

Gathering up all the previous references to the giving of life, the raising of Lazarus paints a narrative portrait of Jesus as the giver of life. Earlier Jesus had announced that the dead would come forth from their tombs (5:28–29). Now, as a sign that Jesus is the one in whom all hopes for the future are fulfilled, now and in the future, Jesus raises Lazarus from the dead and calls him out from his tomb.

Like a seed falling into the ground, Jesus must die if he is going to give life (12:24–25). The remainder of the Gospel focuses on the preparations for Jesus' death and the meaning of his death and resurrection. He is "the way, and the truth, and the life" (14:6), and eternal life is defined as knowing God through Jesus (17:3). The Gospel, therefore, is written in order that its readers might have life (20:31).

The Gospel of John has no distinctive title for Jesus as the giver of life, but this theme is articulated in the prologue and then provides a unifying perspective from which to understand the end result of Jesus' mission as the one who reveals the Father and takes away the sin of the world. Moreover, because the theme is introduced in the Logos hymn at the beginning of the Gospel, readers interpret all subsequent allusions to Jesus' life-giving role in light of its connection with the work of the Logos.

The "I Am" Sayings in Context

Jesus' messianic identity is a secret in the Gospel of Mark, and much of Mark's plot turns on how those around Jesus learn of his identity. Jesus makes no explicit messianic claims (at least not until his trial; Mark 14:62), and neither his teachings nor his miracles disclose his divinity. Only at his death does anyone exclaim, "Truly this man was God's Son!" (Mark 15:39). In sharp contrast, the first disciples use a whole series of christological titles for Jesus in the first chapter of John, and Jesus makes repeated claims regarding his messianic identity in the form of "I am" sayings. Complementing Jesus' use of titles, "I am" sayings, and aphoristic sayings, the Gospel's narration of Jesus' actions adds a further layer of christological interpretation.

The "I am" sayings in John can be divided into three groups: (1) sayings in which the phrase occurs in common speech, such as "I am he" or "It is I" (4:26; 6:20; 18:5, 6, 8; compare 9:9); (2) sayings in which the phrase is used in an absolute sense as a solemn formula of revelation, echoing Exodus 3:14 (8:24, 28, 58; 13:19); and (3) sayings in which "I am" is followed by one of seven different complements:

1. "I am the bread of life" (6:35, 48)
   or "the living bread" (6:51)
   or "the bread that came down from heaven" (6:51)
2. "I am the light of the world" (8:12)
3. "I am the gate" (10:7, 9)
4. "I am the good shepherd" (10:11, 14)
5. "I am the resurrection and the life" (11:25)
6. "I am the way, and the truth, and the life" (14:6)
7. "I am the true vine" (15:1, 5)

Further attention needs to be given to the ways in which the "I am" sayings are related to their narrative contexts in the Gospel. The first two "I am" sayings in the Gospel use the phrase in ordinary speech, but in a context of self-disclosure. In the conversation with the woman at the well, which revolves around the woman's progressive recognition of Jesus' identity, Jesus responds to the woman's reference to the messiah by saying, "I am he, the one who is speaking to you" (4:26). Jesus' response is tantamount to saying, "I am the Christ." The second "I am" saying, which is also generally interpreted as an instance of ordinary speech, occurs in the context of Jesus' walking on the water—which is treated as a divine epiphany.[23] The occurrence of the "I am" saying here has a parallel in the Markan account of the walking on the water (Mark 6:50), which shows that the usage probably predates John and is drawn from early Christian tradition. Rudolf Schnackenburg plausibly suggests that the use of "I am" in this context suggested the idiom to John.[24] If so, the occurrence of this "I am" saying in the context of Jesus' dramatic act of self-disclosure leads to the absolute use of "I am" in John 8:24, 28, and 58 and to the first of the uses of "I am" with a complement, which occurs in the discourse on the bread from heaven that follows in the rest of John 6 (compare verses 35, 48, and 51).

Some years ago, Franklin Young observed that the Gospel of John has numerous contacts with the book of Isaiah.[25] In Deutero-Isaiah, "I am" is used virtually as a name for God; for instance, Isaiah 43:10–11; 43:25 (where the LXX uses *Egō eimi*); 51:12; 52:6. The Johannine Jesus, therefore, speaks in the same idiom in which Yahweh speaks in Deutero-Isaiah. One instance in the Synoptics approaches the absolute use of "I am" in Deutero-Isaiah and John (Mark 13:6; Luke 21:8): "Many will come in my name and say, 'I am he!' and they will lead many astray." This saying is important because it provides a parallel for the use of the formula to sum up Jesus' messianic identity and authority.

The first of the absolute "I am" sayings (8:24) occurs after Jesus' claim that he is going away, an allusion to his death and return to the Father (8:21; cf. 7:33–35; 13:33). The connection between Jesus' claim to divinity through the use of this idiom and his exaltation as the Son of man becomes explicit a few verses later: "When you have lifted up the Son of Man, then you will realize that I am he, and that I do nothing on my own, but I speak these things as the Father instructed me" (John 8:28). As we have seen, the lifting-up sayings serve much the same function as the passion predictions in the Synoptics, and the Son of man sayings typically address Jesus' exaltation. When Jesus is lifted up, the people will know that "I am he," and he will draw all people to himself (12:32) so that whoever believes might have eternal life (3:14–16). Jesus is both one with the Father (10:30) and absolutely dependent on the Father (8:28–14:28). John 8:28, therefore, is both christological and soteriological; life comes only by believing in Jesus as the one who can say, "I am," in the absolute sense.

In the wisdom tradition, Wisdom often speaks in the first person, but the figure of Wisdom does not use the "I am" formula. Nevertheless, the wisdom tradition helps explain the use of the "I am" formula in John. When Jesus claims, "Very truly, I tell you, before Abraham was, I am" (John 8:58), the use of "I am" in the absolute sense has merged with the claim of preexistence in the prologue that arose from the influence of the wisdom tradition on John's Logos Christology. Readers of the Gospel, therefore, read the "I am" saying in John 8:58 in light of the frame of reference set by the prologue.

In addition to the absolute "I am" sayings, John contains a series of "I am" sayings with complements. Most of the complements are drawn from the Old Testament, where they are often used as images for Israel. In the Gospel, these complements provide rudimentary images that further interpret Jesus' identity and functions. None of the Synoptic parables appears in John, and the Johannine Jesus does not use parables to describe any reality beyond himself. Instead, the imagery of the Gospel serves a christological function also. Jesus is the good shepherd, the seed falling into the ground, and the true vine.

The "I am" sayings with complements are also closely related to their narrative contexts and often function to crystallize in a single assertion the image that is being developed in that section of the Gospel. The first of these sayings, "I am the bread of life" (6:35), follows the feeding of the five thousand and the "I am" saying in the context of the walking on the water (see above). Jesus has entered into a dialogue with the crowd that found him again the next day, looking for another free meal. He challenges them to seek instead to fulfill their deeper needs (6:27). They challenge Jesus with the quotation from Exodus 16:4 and 16:15 in verse 31, and Jesus begins to interpret this text in relation to himself. "He" was not Moses but God, who gave bread to their ancestors. The bread, moreover, is not the manna but ultimately Jesus himself. The "I am" saying serves, therefore, to crystallize this narrative movement into a single memorable and emphatic pronouncement. If one does not eat the bread, one has no part in Jesus. Although the Gospel of John does not contain the words of institution at the Last Supper, this section suggests that the Johannine community knew and observed the Lord's Supper. These words, too, have christological, soteriological, and sociological significance. Unless one broke from the synagogue, publicly declared faith in Jesus as the Messiah, and joined the Christian community in its worship, one had no life in Christ.

The pattern of crystallizing narrative imagery in an "I am" saying is evident with the remaining "I am" sayings with complements. The prologue affirms, "What has come into being in him was life, and the life was the light of all people" (1:3–4). In John 8:12, before the giving of sight to the blind man, Jesus says, "I am the light of the world . . . the light of life." The claim that Jesus is the light of the world captures the revelatory significance of the incarnation. In a sense, we are all born blind, and we all need to come to sight. Otherwise, we love darkness and find ourselves following those who go out into the night with torches to arrest the light of the world.

The allegory of the sheep and the shepherd gives rise to two "I am" sayings. Much of John 10 is devoted to identifying the sheep, the hirelings, the door, and the shepherd. The background of this chapter is probably to be found in the references to sheep and shepherds in the imagery of the Old Testament (especially Ezekiel 34). Israel is pictured as a flock of sheep, and her leaders are the shepherds. The issue is then raised of who the true shepherds are, and who the hirelings are. In the verse after Jesus' claim that he has come to give life to his sheep, he says, "I am the good shepherd" (10:11, 14). The good shepherd lays down his life for the sheep. The saying functions as another Johannine passion prediction, but Jesus will later tell Peter that he, too, will lay down his life as a shepherd (13:37–38; compare 21:15–19).

Jesus is also the good shepherd because he knows his sheep and his sheep know him (10:14). This part of the allegory describes the intimate union between the believer and Jesus that Jesus will speak of in the Farewell Discourse, where he invites the disciples to abide in him and he will abide in them. Knowing the truth means the full and open reception of God's revelation in Jesus.

In John 11, just before the raising of Lazarus, Jesus says to Martha, "I am the resurrection and the life" (11:25). The raising of Lazarus then dramatically animates John's claim that Jesus has come to give life. (See the discussion of this theme above.) The two "I am" sayings in the Farewell Discourse seem to serve to articulate themes that will be developed in the next verses. In John 14:6, Jesus says, "I am the way, and the truth, and the life." Following the typical pattern of Johannine misunderstandings, Jesus has introduced an ambiguous reference, in this case preparing a place for the disciples, and Thomas has confessed that they do not understand what Jesus is talking about. The "I am" saying is meant to clarify, at least for the reader, that Jesus himself is the means, the process, and the goal. He is the giver of life; but the disciples still do not understand, as Philip's request in the next verses shows.

Jesus' claim that he is the true vine (15:1, 5) again employs an image that the Old Testament uses for Israel (Isa. 5:1–7; Ps. 80:8–13). The children of God (John 1:12; 11:52) abide in Jesus and draw their life from him. They are one, just as he and the Father are one.

Our brief review of the Johannine "I am" sayings that have a complement suggests that these sayings function as aphoristic summaries of the narrative pictures John paints of Jesus. These sayings are generally tied to their narrative context and crystallize in vivid aphorisms elements of John's christological imagery. Many of these sayings, moreover, are related to John's portrayal of Jesus as the giver of life, his preexistence, or his divinity. When the Johannine Jesus says, "I am," therefore, the reader of the Gospel understands that it is the Logos who has become flesh who is able to speak in this way.

CONCLUSION

We have surveyed the two dominant approaches to Johannine Christology: proposals regarding the stages in its development and the range of christological titles John uses. Neither, however, adequately captures the nuances of John's Christology. Developmental theories typically offer persuasive accounts of the history of the Johannine community and illuminating explanations regarding how Johannine Christology provoked or responded to each new crisis in the community. As illuminating as some of these theories are, they stop short of explaining how the various stages or strands of thought are now related in what we know as the Gospel of John. Similarly, descriptions of Johannine Christology that survey the christological titles in John often treat each title as a static entity that can be extracted from its narrative contexts and understood in detached isolation. Our survey, however, suggests that the christological titles are intertwined in the Gospel. No one title can be understood apart from its narrative contexts and its conceptual relationship to other titles and to the presentation of Jesus in the Gospel as a whole. In particular, the Gospel's Logos Christology, which is generally regarded as a late stage in the development of Johannine thought, exerts a controlling influence on the Gospel's portrayal of Jesus from the prologue on. The "Son of God" or "Son" (of the Father) is John's dominant title for Jesus, but it is grounded in the Logos concept in important ways. The Son of God is the one sent to reveal the Father, take away the sin of the world, and bring life. The Son of man sayings are related, in turn, to the Son of God and Son sayings.

If these observations about John's Christology are valid, advances in our understanding of John's Christology will depend on our ability to interpret the Gospel's thought holistically, as a construct of the Gospel as a whole, and to perceive more clearly the interrelationships between concepts we have typically kept separate and compartmentalized. Even so, John's Word will continue to elude our grasp. The light shines on in the darkness, but the darkness cannot comprehend it.

NOTES

1. Robert T. Fortna, *The Gospel of Signs: A Reconstruction of the Narrative Source Underlying the Fourth Gospel,* Society of New Testament Studies Monograph Series 11 (Cambridge: Cambridge University Press, 1970).
2. Robert T. Fortna, *The Fourth Gospel and Its Predecessor: From Narrative Source to Present Gospel* (Philadelphia: Fortress Press, 1988).
3. Ibid., 226.
4. Ibid., 232–34.
5. J. Louis Martyn, *The Gospel of John in Christian History* (New York: Paulist Press, 1978), 96.
6. Ibid., 104.
7. Ibid., 105.
8. Raymond E. Brown, *The Community of the Beloved Disciple* (New York: Paulist Press, 1979), 36–40.
9. Martinus C. de Boer, *Johannine Perspectives on the Death of Jesus,* Contributions to Biblical Exegesis and Theology 17 (Kampen, the Netherlands: Kok Pharos, 1996).
10. Ibid., 88, citing D. Moody Smith, "The Milieu of the Johannine Miracle Source," in *Johannine Christianity: Essays on Its Setting, Sources, and Theology* (Columbia: University of South Carolina Press, 1984), 77.
11. de Boer, *Johannine Perspectives on the Death of Jesus,* 93.
12. Ibid., 115.
13. Ibid., 144.
14. Ibid., 156.
15. Ibid., 171.
16. Ibid., 189.
17. Ibid., 192.
18. See Dale Moody, "God's Only Son: The Translation of Jn 3,16 in the R.S.V.," *Journal of Biblical Literature* 72 (1953): 213–19.
19. Rudolf Schnackenburg, "The 'Son of Man' in the Fourth Gospel," in *The Gospel according to St. John,* trans. Kevin Smyth (New York: Herder & Herder, 1968), 1:536.
20. Ibid., 1:541.
21. See further ibid., 1:529–42.

22. D. Moody Smith, *The Theology of the Gospel of John* (Cambridge: Cambridge University Press, 1995), 132.

23. See Gail O'Day, "John 6:15–21: Jesus Walking on Water as Narrative Embodiment of Johannine Christology," in *Critical Readings of John 6*, ed. R. Alan Culpepper (Leiden: E. J. Brill, 1997), 149–59.

24. Rudolf Schnackenburg, *The Gospel according to St. John* (New York: Seabury Press, 1980), 2:87.

25. Franklin W. Young, "A Study of the Relation of Isaiah to the Fourth Gospel," *Zeitschrift für die neutestamentliche Wissenschaft* 46 (1955): 215–33.

CHRISTOLOGY OF THE PAULINE EPISTLES

Marion L. Soards

Prominent among the many significant contributions that Jack Dean Kingsbury has made to the study of the New Testament witnesses are an emphasis on the narrative (or story) dimensions of texts and a careful analysis of the christological convictions, concerns, and purposes of various documents in the corpus of scripture. One thinks of these important aspects of Kingsbury's work primarily in relation to the Gospels and their source materials (Q and pre-Gospels traditions), but these same incisive angles of interpretation may be brought to the study of the letters of Paul in order to gain insight into the apostle's complete understanding and appreciation of Jesus Christ.

This chapter ventures to identify and assess the story of Jesus Christ that Paul presents through his writings. That story is not a narrative per se; rather, crucial narrative elements appear in Paul's writings, and these items inform his thinking and teaching in specific letters in relation to specific congregational circumstances. The interpreter is required first to identify these narrative materials amid the larger set of statements that comprise Paul's letters. After discerning the aspects of the "christological" story that Paul preserves in his letters, this chapter lists these narrative elements in the order of their canonical occurrence, without regard for their probable chronological sequence. The chapter then reconstructs a version of the general story from these particular facets in such a way that the overall story becomes intelligible. Finally, this investigation identifies and distinguishes the character of the different components of the story of Jesus Christ that Paul preserves in and through the remarks in his letters. Having set out the story of Jesus Christ as one may discern it from Paul's statements in his letters, and having sought to be aware of the differences among the particular parts of that overall narrative, this reconstruction asks about Paul's knowledge and beliefs concerning Jesus Christ.[1]

To summarize in other words: From the story that Paul tells of Jesus Christ, what do his readers see that he knew? What kinds of things did Paul know (as seen in the letters)? And what difference does the story told of Jesus Christ make for Paul, the congregations to which he wrote, and even for Christian faith and practice today? The use of Paul's story of Jesus Christ and its significance for reflection on the life of the church today is, of course, a hermeneutical endeavor, but appropriate for a work intended to express appreciation for Jack Dean Kingsbury, whose scholarship has always been offered as a service to Christ and his people.

PERUSING PERTINENT PASSAGES IN PAUL

From time to time and in one place and another, Paul makes explicit statements about Jesus Christ that show his knowledge of a larger story of which the particular remarks are but smaller parts.[2] In Romans 1:3, Paul writes of the human existence and heritage of Jesus Christ, saying, "[He] was descended from David according to the flesh." This reference to the life and lineage of Jesus Christ is coupled with another statement related to a moment in the story that seems far removed from birth and ancestry: He "was declared to be Son of God with power according to the spirit of holiness by resurrection from the dead" (Rom. 1:4). This striking remark seems to presuppose other, unstated narrative materials, at least a statement and more likely an account of the death of Jesus Christ. Indeed, the movement from conception or birth to resurrection after death is a tremendous shift that requires further information, a larger story, if these references in Romans 1:3–4 are to stand as anything other than bookends with nothing in between. Knowing "the facts" of Jesus Christ's birth, lineage, (death?) and resurrection, and divinely founded identity requires that one know other elements of the story in order that these important items have a coherent context in which to exist and find meaning. In his letters Paul gives other data that he knows from the story of Jesus Christ, and taken together these details ultimately form a larger narrative (in which Paul's sometimes isolated statements about Jesus Christ make sense). A reading of Paul's letters locates the following statements about Jesus Christ:[3]

- Jesus Christ is God's Son (Rom. 1:3–4,[4] 9; 5:10; 8:3, 14, 19, 29, 32; 1 Cor. 1:9; 15:28; 2 Cor. 1:19; Gal. 1:16; 2:20; 4:4, 6; 1 Thess. 1:10).
- Jesus Christ was descended from David (Rom. 1:3).
- Jesus Christ was declared God's Son in "power according to the spirit of holiness by resurrection from the dead" (Rom. 1:4; compare 2 Cor. 13:4); thus, readers know that Jesus Christ was raised from the dead (Rom. 4:24; 6:4–5, 9; 7:4; 8:11, 34; 10:9; 14:9; 1 Cor. 6:14; 15:4, 12–17, 20–21; 2 Cor. 4:14; 5:15; Gal. 1:1; Phil. 3:10; 1 Thess. 1:10). (Such statements, of course, assume and imply that Jesus Christ died.)
- Jesus Christ is Lord, specifically of the community of believers who experience the grace of this resurrected One (Rom. 1:4–7; 1 Cor. 1:2–3; 2 Cor. 1:2–3; Gal. 1:3; Phil. 1:2; 1 Thess. 1:1–3; Philemon 3—see esp. Rom. 10:9; 1 Cor. 12:3; 2 Cor. 4:5–6).
- Jesus Christ died, Paul declares, for the ungodly or sinners, among whom Paul numbers himself and those to whom he writes (Rom. 4:25; 5:6, 8, 10; 6:3; 8:34; 14:9; 1 Cor. 15:3; 2 Cor. 5:14–15; 1 Thess. 4:14; 5:10).
- The death of Jesus Christ, for Paul and those to whom he writes, means "justification" (Rom. 5:9), "reconciliation" (Rom. 5:10–11; 2 Cor. 5:16–21),[5] and "being saved" from the wrath of God (Rom. 5:9). In turn, this justification means new "life" and ultimately "resurrection from the dead" (Rom. 5:15–19; 6:4, 5–11; 1 Cor. 15; 2 Cor. 5:15, 17).
- Jesus Christ was buried (Rom. 6:4; 1 Cor. 15:2).
- Jesus Christ's death (and resurrection) amounted to a "rescue" or "delivery" (Rom. 7:24; Gal. 1:4; 1 Thess. 1:10).
- God sent forth the Son in human form (Rom. 8:3–4; Gal. 4:4).
- Jesus Christ, who died and was raised, is in a position of power to condemn, at the right hand of God, but there he intercedes for Paul and those to whom Paul writes (Rom. 8:32–35).
- Jesus Christ was a Jew (Rom. 9:5).
- Jesus Christ is the end of the law (Rom. 10:4).
- The visible results of the saving reconciliation or rescue effected by Jesus Christ's death are seen, at least in part, in the assembly of persons who "are one body in Christ, and individually . . . members one of another" (Rom. 12:5; 1 Cor. 12:27).
- In his life Jesus Christ had a ministry among the Jews that ful-

filled God's promises to the ancestors of Israel and that extended God's mercy to the Gentiles (Rom. 15:8–9).

- Jesus Christ (the Lord) *will be revealed* at a future time or *he will come* (1 Cor. 1:7; 4:5; 15:23–28; 1 Thess. 4:13–18; 5:1–11, 23).
- The time of Jesus Christ's coming is "the day of [the] Lord Jesus" (1 Cor. 1:8) or "the day of the Lord" (1 Cor. 5:5; 1 Thess. 5:2), "the day of Jesus Christ" (Phil. 1:6) or "the day of Christ" (Phil. 1:10; 2:16 — see also 1 Thess. 5:23).
- Jesus Christ was crucified on a cross (1 Cor. 1:17, 23; 2:2; Gal. 3:1; 5:11; 6:14; Phil. 2:8; 3:18).
- Jesus Christ is God's power and God's wisdom (1 Cor. 1:24).
- "The Lord of glory" was crucified by "the rulers of this age," who were without understanding of God's "wisdom" (1 Cor. 2:8).
- Jesus Christ is the foundation of the church (1 Cor. 3:11).
- The Lord Jesus is present in power in the assembling of the church (1 Cor. 5:4).
- Christ the paschal lamb was sacrificed (1 Cor. 5:7).
- Through the Lord Jesus Christ are all things, especially the church (1 Cor. 8:6).
- Jesus Christ had a family; named in particular are "the brothers of the Lord" (1 Cor. 9:5).
- Christ was present in the wilderness with the Israelites during the exodus as "the spiritual rock" from whom/which the Israelites drank (1 Cor. 10:4).
- Christ is "the head of every man . . . and God is the head of Christ" (1 Cor. 11:3).
- Jesus Christ was betrayed at night (1 Cor. 11:23).
- Jesus Christ instituted the Lord's Supper with statements about his body and the new covenant in his blood that were made over a loaf of bread and the cup (1 Cor. 11:23–25).
- Jesus Christ appeared after his resurrection to identifiable individuals and groups (1 Cor. 15:5–8).
- The coming of Christ is associated with "the end," when he will hand over the kingdom (a picture of cosmic hegemony) to God the Father after having ruled and subordinated all powers and his enemies (1 Cor. 15:24–26).
- After achieving victory and handing the kingdom over to God, Christ himself will be placed in subjection to God (1 Cor. 15:27–28).
- Christ Jesus the Lord is the last Adam, the second man from heaven, the heavenly man (1 Cor. 15:31, 45, 47–48).

- Jesus Christ was rich, yet for the sake of humans he became poor, so that by his poverty they might become rich (2 Cor. 8:9).
- Jesus Christ, who gave himself for the sins of humanity, did so to deliver humanity "from the present evil age" (Gal. 1:4; also Gal. 2:20).
- Jesus Christ acted according to God's will (Gal. 1:4).
- God's resurrected Son, Jesus Christ, was revealed to Paul through divine revelation (Gal. 1:12, 15–16).
- One of Jesus' brothers was named James (Gal. 1:19).
- Jesus Christ became himself cursed by the law in order to redeem humanity from the curse of the law (Gal. 3:13).
- Jesus Christ's activity in behalf of humanity was/is "to redeem" (Gal. 3:13; 4:5; similarly Paul tells the Corinthians, "You are not your own . . . you were bought with a price" [1 Cor. 6:19–20]).
- Jesus Christ was the "seed" (offspring or heir) of Abraham and the fulfillment of the promise of God to Abraham (Gal. 3:16–18).
- Jesus Christ, God's Son, was born of a woman (Gal. 4:4).
- Jesus Christ was born under the law (Gal. 4:4).
- Jesus Christ "set free" Paul and those to whom Paul wrote (Gal. 5:1).
- Christ Jesus was in the form of God, an equality that he did not exploit (Phil. 2:6).
- Jesus Christ emptied himself, taking the form of a slave, born in human likeness (Phil. 2:7).
- In human form Jesus Christ humbled himself to be obedient and died on a cross (Phil. 2:8).
- Jesus Christ has been exalted by God and given a name above every other so that "at the name of Jesus" every knee should bend in heaven, on earth, and under the earth; and every tongue should confess that "Jesus Christ is Lord" to the glory of God his Father (Phil. 2:9–11).
- From heaven, Paul and those to whom he wrote expected "a Savior, the Lord Jesus Christ" (Phil. 3:20; also 1 Thess. 1:10).
- At the time of the coming of "the Lord," Jesus Christ will descend from heaven and "the dead in Christ" will rise, and then the living will be caught up in the clouds with them to meet the Lord (1 Thess. 4:16–17).
- "Through [the] Lord Jesus Christ," God destined Paul and those to whom he wrote "for obtaining salvation" rather than for wrath (1 Thess. 5:9).

- Throughout the letters, Paul tells of the living resurrected Jesus Christ, *through* whom (Rom. 1:8; 2:16; 5:1–2) and *in* whom (Rom. 3:24; 6:11) he and other believers live and communicate with one another and God. Conversely, it is possible for the members of the church to "sin against Christ" (1 Cor. 8:12).

On the whole, this list amounts to a jumble of declarations that only partly makes sense. Yet, as should be evident from examining this list of assertions, Paul sometimes makes a series of statements that are themselves, when taken in the order of their occurrence, concentrated narratives. For example, in both 1 Corinthians 11:23–25 and 15:5–8, Paul briefly and pointedly makes a series of statements that have a chronological relationship and that concisely narrate a particular incident or sequence of related occasions. One finds other instances of such succinct narration at 1 Corinthians 15:24–28; Galatians 4:4; Philippians 2:6–11; 1 Thessalonians 4:16–17; and perhaps Romans 8:3–4. These mini-narratives demonstrate that Paul was familiar with story materials about Jesus Christ and not merely isolated statements. Yet at no place in Paul's preserved letters do readers encounter a complete story that tells all that Paul knows about Jesus Christ.[6] Instead, readers encounter isolated statements and occasional, brief series of statements that appear to be related to a coherent story that Paul does not present as a unified composition.

SEEKING THE STORY
BEHIND THE STATEMENTS

Recognizing that certain statements that Paul makes may have been simple statements that never belonged in a narrative context, it is still possible to take the collection of statements concerning Jesus Christ and to assemble (or reassemble?) them into a basically congruent account. Also, while recognizing that particular items of information might be fitted into a constructive synthetic narrative at different points, one may nevertheless acknowledge the importance of chronology in sensible narrative and use temporal sequence to fashion the following (or a similar) story. (At this point, to facilitate the compact presentation of these items in the next section of this chapter, each of the "story elements" is being numbered.)

1. Jesus Christ is God's Son (Rom. 1:3–4, 9; 5:10; 8:3, 14, 19, 29, 32; 1 Cor. 1:9; 15:28; 2 Cor. 1:19; Gal. 1:16; 2:20; 4:4, 6; 1 Thess. 1:10).[7]

2. Jesus Christ is God's power and God's wisdom.[8] (1 Cor. 1:24).
3. Through the Lord Jesus Christ are all things, especially the church (1 Cor. 8:6).
4. Christ Jesus was in the form of God, an equality that he did not exploit (Phil. 2:6).
5. Jesus Christ was rich, yet for the sake of humans he became poor, so that by his poverty they might become rich (2 Cor. 8:9).
6. Christ was present in the wilderness with the Israelites during the exodus as "the spiritual rock" from whom/which the Israelites drank (1 Cor. 10:4).
7. God sent forth the Son in human form (Rom. 8:3–4; Gal. 4:4).[9]
8. Jesus Christ acted according to God's will (Gal. 1:4).
9. Jesus Christ emptied himself, taking the form of a slave, born in human likeness (Phil. 2:7).
10. Christ Jesus the Lord is the last Adam, the second man from heaven, the heavenly man (1 Cor. 15:31, 45, 47–48).[10]
11. Jesus Christ, God's Son, was born of a woman (Gal. 4:4).
12. Jesus Christ was a Jew (Rom. 9:5).
13. Jesus Christ was born under the law (Gal. 4:4).
14. Jesus Christ was the "seed" (offspring or heir) of Abraham and the fulfillment of the promise of God to Abraham (Gal. 3:16–18).
15. Jesus Christ was descended from David (Rom. 1:3).
16. Jesus Christ had a family; named in particular are "the brothers of the Lord" (1 Cor. 9:5).
17. One of Jesus' brothers was named James (Gal. 1:19).
18. In his life Jesus Christ had a ministry among the Jews that fulfilled God's promises to the ancestors of Israel and that extended God's mercy to the Gentiles (Rom. 15:8–9).
19. Jesus Christ instituted the Lord's Supper with statements about his body and the new covenant in his blood that were made over a loaf of bread and the cup (1 Cor. 11:23–25).
20. Jesus Christ was betrayed at night (1 Cor. 11:23).
21. Jesus Christ was crucified on a cross (1 Cor. 1:17, 23; 2:2; Gal. 3:1; 5:11; 6:14; Phil. 2:8; 3:18).[11]
22. The "Lord of glory" was crucified by "the rulers of this

age," who were without understanding of God's "wisdom" (1 Cor. 2:8).

23. In human form Jesus Christ humbled himself to be obedient and died on a cross (Phil. 2:8).

24. Christ the paschal lamb was sacrificed (1 Cor. 5:7).[12]

25. Jesus Christ became himself cursed by the law in order to redeem[13] humanity from the curse of the law (Gal. 3:13).

26. Jesus Christ is the end of the law (Rom. 10:4).

27. Jesus Christ died, Paul declares, for the ungodly or sinners, among whom Paul numbers himself and those to whom he writes (Rom. 4:25; 5:6, 8, 10; 6:3; 8:34; 14:9; 1 Cor. 15:3; 2 Cor. 5:14–15; 1 Thess. 4:14; 5:10).

28. Jesus Christ, who gave himself for the sins of humanity, did so to deliver humanity "from the present evil age" (Gal. 1:4; also Gal. 2:20).

29. The death of Jesus Christ, for Paul and those to whom he writes, means "justification" (Rom. 5:9), "reconciliation" (Rom. 5:10–11; 2 Cor. 5:16–21), and "being saved" from the wrath of God (Rom. 5:9). In turn, this justification means new "life" and ultimately "resurrection from the dead" (Rom. 5:15–19; 6:4, 5–11; 1 Cor. 15; 2 Cor. 5:15, 17).

30. Jesus Christ's death (and resurrection) amounted to a "rescue" or "delivery" (Rom. 7:24; Gal. 1:4; 1 Thess. 1:10).[14]

31. Jesus Christ was buried (Rom. 6:4; 1 Cor. 15:2).

32. Jesus Christ was declared God's Son in "power according to the spirit of holiness by resurrection from the dead" (Rom. 1:4; compare 2 Cor. 13:4); thus, readers know that he was raised from the dead (Rom. 4:24; 6:4–5, 9; 7:4; 8:11, 34; 10:9; 14:9; 1 Cor. 6:14; 15:4, 12–17, 20–21; 2 Cor. 4:14; 5:15; Gal. 1:1; Phil. 3:10; 1 Thess. 1:10).

33. Jesus Christ appeared after his resurrection to identifiable individuals and groups (1 Cor. 15:5–8).

34. God's resurrected Son, Jesus Christ, was revealed to Paul through divine revelation (Gal. 1:12, 15–16).

35. Jesus Christ has been exalted by God and given a name above every other so that "at the name of Jesus" every knee should bend in heaven, on earth, and under the earth; and every tongue should confess that "Jesus Christ is Lord" to the glory of God his Father (Phil. 2:9–11).

36. Jesus Christ, who died and was raised, is in a position of

power to condemn, at the right hand of God, but there he intercedes for Paul and those to whom Paul writes (Rom. 8:32–35).

38. Jesus Christ is the foundation of the church (1 Cor. 3:11).

39. Jesus Christ is Lord, specifically of the community of believers who experience the grace of this resurrected One (Rom. 1:4–7; 1 Cor. 1:2–3; 2 Cor. 1:2–3; Gal. 1:3; Phil. 1:2; 1 Thess. 1:1–3; Philemon 3 — see esp. Rom. 10:9; 1 Cor. 12:3; 2 Cor. 4:5–6).

40. "Through [the] Lord Jesus Christ," God destined Paul and those to whom he wrote "for obtaining salvation" rather than for wrath (1 Thess. 5:9).

41. Jesus Christ's activity in behalf of humanity was/is "to redeem" (Gal. 3:13; 4:5); similarly Paul tells the Corinthians, "You are not your own . . . you were bought with a price" (1 Cor. 6:19–20).

42. Jesus Christ "set free" Paul and those to whom Paul wrote (Gal. 5:1).

43. The visible results of the saving reconciliation or rescue effected by Jesus Christ's death are seen, at least in part, in the assembly of persons who "are one body in Christ, and individually . . . members one of another" (Rom. 12:5; 1 Cor. 12:27).

44. The Lord Jesus is present in power in the assembling of the church (1 Cor. 5:4).

45. Christ is "the head of every man . . . and God is the head of Christ" (1 Cor. 11:3).

46. Throughout the letters, Paul tells of the living resurrected Jesus Christ, *through* whom (for example, Rom. 1:8; 2:16; 5:1–2) and *in* whom (for example, Rom. 3:24; 6:11) he and other believers live and communicate with one another and God. Conversely, it is possible for the members of the church to "sin against Christ" (1 Cor. 8:12).

47. Jesus Christ (the Lord) *will be revealed* at a future time or *he will come* (1 Cor. 1:7; 4:5; 15:23–28; 1 Thess. 4:13–18; 5:1–11, 23).

48. From heaven, Paul and those to whom he wrote expected "a Savior, the Lord Jesus Christ" (Phil. 3:20; also 1 Thess. 1:10).

49. At the time of the coming of "the Lord," Jesus Christ will

descend from heaven and "the dead in Christ" will rise, and then the living will be caught up in the clouds with them to meet the Lord (1 Thess. 4:16–17).

50. The time of Jesus Christ's coming is "the day of [the] Lord Jesus" (1 Cor. 1:8) or "the day of the Lord" (1 Cor. 5:5; 1 Thess. 5:2), "the day of Jesus Christ" (Phil. 1:6) or "the day of Christ" (Phil. 1:10; 2:16—see also 1 Thess. 5:23).

51. The coming of Christ is associated with "the end," when he will hand over the kingdom (a picture of cosmic hegemony) to God the Father after having ruled and subordinated all powers and his enemies (1 Cor. 15:24–26).

52. After achieving victory and handing the kingdom over to God, Christ himself will be placed in subjection to God (1 Cor. 15:27–28).

The assembling of this account enables the reader to reflect on matters that might not be apparent from the normal encounter(s) with Paul's statements in their epistolary settings. Viewing this chronicle as a synthetic narrative, while recognizing its artificiality, one is still able to begin to appreciate such issues of narrative interpretation as *character, plot, time,* and *mode of narration*.[15] Briefly considered, readers may note the following observations as starting points for further consideration of Paul's christological materials that extends beyond the parameters of the present chapter.

Characters. Paul's story of Jesus Christ includes a complex, though briefly presented, cast of characters. First, there is *Jesus Christ* himself. Paul names him in a number of ways. "Christ" is itself a title, and Paul uses this designation both independently and in conjunction with the proper name Jesus (before and after the name: Christ Jesus and Jesus Christ).[16] Paul also names this character God's Son, the spiritual rock, the Lord (Lord, the Lord, the Lord of glory, Lord Jesus, Lord Jesus Christ), and Savior. Beyond this obvious "main character," Paul includes the following in his account of Jesus:

> *God*—called the Father of Jesus Christ, according to whose will Jesus Christ was sent, God raised Jesus Christ from the dead and exalted him into heaven, where God brings every enemy into submission to him, and will receive the kingdom and submission from the victorious Jesus Christ.
> *Humanity*—called the ungodly by Paul, these characters appear as variously disposed toward Jesus Christ and God's work in and through him.

The ancestors of Israel—these figures are present with Moses in the wilderness, where their rebelliousness produces divine judgment; they are also those to whom Christ the Rock came.

A woman—this is obviously Jesus' mother, of whom he was born.

Abraham—he received (and believed) God's promise of an heir, who ultimately is Jesus Christ.

David—the prophet-king from whose lineage Jesus Christ was born.

The brothers of the Lord, especially James—these are apparently the biological family of Jesus, who were later part of the church; at least, James encountered the resurrected Jesus Christ.

The Gentiles—the group comprises those persons brought into the experience of the fulfillment in Jesus Christ of God's promises of grace for all humanity.

The rulers of this age—this refers to those who crucified Jesus Christ.

Paul's assumed audience—it would consist of those to whom Paul tells of Jesus Christ, themselves drawn into the narrative by the way in which Paul writes of their relationship to Jesus Christ; this group comprises the members of the church and would include both the dead in Christ and the living addressees.

Spirit of holiness—this is possibly, even probably, a Semitic form referring to the Holy Spirit.

Cephas, the Twelve, five hundred brethren (adelphoi), *the apostles, Paul*—all such are references to those to whom the resurrected Jesus Christ appeared.

All those attached to "every knee" in heaven, on earth, and under the earth—this is a cosmic, apparently universal, way of designating all those who recognize the lordship of Jesus Christ.

Plot. The story focuses on Jesus Christ.[17] Initially, as the story is told, the readers find the main character of the story associated with God in a way that does not specify place or time or suggest anything resembling a plot. The first incident in the story that gives a concrete sense of time, space, and story line is the reference to Jesus Christ as the spiritual rock who was present with the Israelites in the wilderness. This striking note seems to anticipate the subsequent development in the plot, as God sends Jesus Christ, the Son, into the context of human existence. In turn, Paul connects his story specifically with the historical life of Jesus. Readers follow the major moments and developments in Jesus Christ's life as he is born, associated with his family, ministers among the Jews, initiates the Lord's Supper, is betrayed, is crucified, dies, is buried, is raised from the dead, appears after his resurrection, is exalted, reigns and intercedes in heaven, is present in the life of the church, comes to consummate the kingdom, and finally subjects himself to God.

Time. In relation to the main character of the story, Jesus Christ, are apparently three (perhaps four) distinguishable periods of time.[18] First is the unspecified time that is seemingly prior to the human life of Jesus Christ. Second is the temporally defined time of Jesus Christ's human life, from birth to death. Third is the time of Jesus Christ's resurrection and exaltation; readers might conclude there are two distinct periods in this third time of the narrative: (1) after the resurrection and prior to the exaltation and (2) after the exaltation. Furthermore, readers might conclude that the story depicts yet a fourth time in the future, the time of Jesus Christ's coming and the completion of the story that Paul tells.

Mode of Narration. Paul takes at least two distinct stances as the narrator of the story of Jesus Christ. On the one hand, he stands outside the account and acts as an omniscient storyteller, though the reader would never understand that Paul was anyone other than himself. In this role, Paul speaks knowingly of Jesus Christ, never suggesting the possibility of his own fallibility, subjectivity, or lack of authority as proclaimer of Jesus Christ. Indeed, in this mode Paul explicitly states that his message is from God, not humanity (Gal. 1:11–12, 20). On the other hand, Paul takes his stance within the account, particularly in telling of Jesus Christ's appearance to him. Remarkably, at this exact point Paul declares his human limitations, noting that his flaws were revealed as the revelation of Jesus Christ exposed the error of his opposition to Jesus Christ and the members of the church. Paul's disclosure and confession of this earlier significant limitation or fallacious behavior in no way undermines Paul's assumption of an omniscient stance as narrator in other portions of the story of Jesus Christ. Indeed, this striking confession of the transformation of Paul's behavior from opponent to proponent of Jesus Christ seems to function to enhance Paul's authority as an espouser of Jesus Christ's story (Gal. 1:13–24).

PONDERING THE NATURE OF
PAUL'S PRESENTATION OF JESUS CHRIST

On reflection, alert readers of Paul's materials about Jesus Christ may notice that all the data are not the same kind of information. For example, the statement that Jesus Christ was *born of a woman* makes a different sort of claim than one that says he was *the offspring* (*literally*, "*seed*") *of Abraham who fulfilled God's promises to that ancestor or to Israel.* The declarations that he was *in the form of God,* that he was *God's Son,* and that *God sent him forth into the world in human form* are quite different still. How are readers to understand the rich mixture of statements, assertions, and declarations offered by Paul as he tells his readers about Jesus Christ?

One reasonable way to assess Paul's materials is to consider their constitution and to classify the statements in terms of the apparent nature of the declarations. Insight concerning what *kind* of element is being presented at particular points in the story helps readers discern the possible sources of the information. In the analysis that follows, a large factor in assessing the christological remarks is the exercise of common sense. An endless number of labels could be devised to distinguish among Paul's comments, but in fact, four independent, though sometimes combined, descriptions are adequate to explicate Paul's materials about Jesus Christ for clear comprehension of their character. The four rubrics or descriptive designations employed here are *historical remarks, mythic reports, metaphorical statements,* and *theological assertions.*[19] To apply these descriptions to the specific statements of Paul's letters, the interpreter must recognize (1) the plain sense of the text(s), (2) the literary mode of expression(s), and (3) possible parallels to other writings that Paul himself may have known. A brief explanation of the sense in which this terminology is understood in relation to Paul's written materials is required:

> *Historical remark*—refers to concrete memories of events in the context of human affairs. One might call such statements "factual," since they are related to *facts.*
>
> *Mythic report*—designates information drawn from, related to, or expressed in nonhistorical categories or language. Mythic does not mean fictional or false but describes statements made in a quite definite fashion that are still not flat historical declarations. One might call such statements "traditional," since they are related to *traditions.*
>
> *Metaphorical statement*—means that Paul uses colorful but

concrete language in a symbolic manner to communicate information for which plain words were apparently inadequate. One might call such statements "pictorial," since they are made in *picture language*.

Theological assertion—describes statements that assert ideas, values, contentions, or assessments related to God that cannot be demonstrated beyond debate. One might call such statements "belief-full," since they are related to *beliefs*.

Application of Categories to the Materials in the Story

With these designations in mind, the christological information in Paul's letters may be viewed in categories. At times, statements seem to exhibit or express more nuances than one of the possible designations. In the summary that follows, an example appears under each of the headings. Then a series of numbers refer to the particular items that were numbered above in the synthesized form of the Pauline story of Jesus Christ.

Historical Remarks. The first unambiguous historical point is item 12, that Jesus Christ was a Jew. Such information has theological meaning or significance, since Judaism is a religious faith and practice; but this report is made as a flat statement of fact that imparts specific information to the reader. Historical points include items 11, 12, 13, 16, 17, 19, 20, 21, 31, 33, and probably 15 and 34.

Mythic Reports. Several statements communicate mythic elements to the readers of Paul's letters, though no statement made in a mythic fashion can be understood as anything other than a theological assertion. The mythic idea that "Christ Jesus was in the form of God" is itself a theological belief that Paul immediately expands by appending that it was an equality that he did not exploit (item 4). The notion of the preexistence of Christ appears to be present in the statement about Christ's "form," but Paul is not so much trying to communicate that idea as he is aiming to explain the profundity of Christ's humility, a contention that registers an important theological persuasion. Paul does not communicate tradition for the sake of the tradition or its communication; rather, he employs mythic elements in making theological assertions while simultaneously bonding such assertions to the historical figure of Jesus Christ. Thus, it seems impossible to designate any one of the statements as purely mythic. This crucial component of Paul's materials about Jesus Christ serves as a vehicle for the communication of theological convictions.

Metaphorical Statements. Metaphor, like mythic expression, functions as a means of communicating theological beliefs and contentions. The simple, straightforward statement that Jesus Christ is God's Son (item 1) forms a metaphor, using family language to register the intimate, even unique relationship between God and Jesus Christ. One might argue a historical dimension to this claim, since Jesus Christ is himself a historical figure. While this contention is correct in one way, the same position could be taken in relation to all the statements in Paul's story of Jesus Christ, since every statement relates to the complete picture of Jesus Christ that has a historical character at its core. Yet in this declaration, as in the others where metaphor occurs, the symbolic statement serves primarily to register or to explicate some deeply held belief that seems to elude or to transcend banal prose. Thus, the readers find that metaphor is at least a means of communicating a theological conviction or expressing a theological belief.

Theological Assertions. Readers encounter theological matters in combination with historical, mythic, and metaphorical statements; but Paul also makes overt theological assertions that seem independent of these other modes of expression. For example, Paul declares that "[Jesus] Christ is the end of the law" (item 26) and that Jesus Christ died for the ungodly (item 27). Such statements incorporate factual references or materials, but they actually stand as pure theological declarations that are only consequentially related to history, seemingly free of metaphor, and insufficiently traditional to be considered mythic. Such theological assertions include items 8, 26, 27, 29, 36, 37, 39, 40, 41, 43, 45, 46, 47, and perhaps 25.

History and Theological Assertion. Paul makes historical statements that are so heavily theological in character that readers cannot view them as mere reports of historical fact. At root level these statements make factual declarations, but the fact(s) presented are so meshed with interpretation that readers encounter historical remarks and theological assertions at the same time. Item 18 is a clear example of such a combination: Paul reports the fact of Jesus Christ's historical ministry among the Jews; in the same statement, however, he declares that this ministry was the fulfillment of God's promises to Israel and the reason for the Gentiles' praise of God's mercy. Other instances that should be regarded as a mixture of history and theology include 22, 23, 32, 38, and possibly 25 and 34.[20]

History and Metaphor. Item 24 may appear to belong in the category that follows this one, "theological assertion and metaphor," but in fact, this declaration is a combination of metaphor and history that functions theologically. This reference to the death of Jesus in relation to the paschal lamb is striking not only in its form but also in its further historical associations with the Passover and God's deliverance of Israel from bondage in the exodus events. Paul relates one historical event to another by means of metaphor in order to register theological information.

Theological Assertion and Metaphor. The discussion above noted how statements such as item 1 are a combination of theology and metaphor; the theological assertions occur in the form of metaphorical statements. Other items that seem to fall into this combined category include items 2, 5, 6, 9, 10, 14, 28, 30, 42, 44, and perhaps 15; possibly even 11 and 19 contain explicitly metaphorical elements, though they are not necessarily or primarily metaphorical statements.

Among the items in this grouping, item 6 merits further explanation. In speaking to the Corinthians, Paul forms an analogy between the exodus experience of the children of Israel and the congregational life of the Corinthian Christians. As he elaborates that creative comparison, he offers an image and commentary that may not make sense to readers at the turn of the twenty-first century; he writes, "For they all drank from the spiritual rock that followed them, and the rock was Christ." Clearly, Paul has the story from Exodus 17 in mind, and he may have combined that account with Numbers 21:16–18 (or perhaps he inherited an already amalgamated version of the story) before making his own creative use of the element from the exodus narrative: "The rock was Christ." This claim strikes the reader of today as fantastic, although such connections were not considered odd or inappropriate in Paul's day. Targumic writings (*t. Sukk.* 3:11; *Tg. Onq.* Num. 21:16–20), Philo of Alexandria, and Pseudo-Philo all make similar and equally creative interpretations of the same Old Testament account. Philo, a contemporary of Paul, interpreted the water-giving rock of the exodus story as the presence of preexistent Wisdom among the wandering Israelites (*Allegorical Interpretation* 2.86); so Paul's christological re-reading of the story is but one interpretation of the "identity" of God's saving presence among the Israelites. Paul may simply be "Christianizing" a standard theme of Jewish wisdom teaching, or he may be appropriating images and ideas from developed wisdom traditions in his own creative reflection. In any case, the exodus story has become an allegory that also operates at the metaphorical level to make a crucial theological assertion in relation to the particular situation that existed in Corinth.

Theological Assertion and Myth. In discussing mythic reports, we saw that the statement "Christ Jesus was in the form of God" (item 4) illustrated the kind of nonhistorical information that Paul includes in his telling about Jesus Christ. This mythic report, like the others found in Paul's statements, is not made as a mere factual proposition but functions to express a clear theological conviction that is important for Paul and for those to whom he writes. Mythic reports consistently occur in Paul's telling of Jesus Christ in order to communicate theological beliefs that move beyond the realm of mere history. Other such combinations appear in items 3, 7, 35, 48, 49, 50, 51, and possibly 9.

Item 7 is a remarkable element of Paul's overall story of Jesus Christ. Interpreters have long recognized the marked parallels between the statements in Romans 8:3–4 and Galatians 4:4 and other writings from Hellenistic Judaism. In these passages Paul writes in reference to the time of God's sending of Jesus Christ, God's Son. He crafts his argument in a fashion that is particularly powerful. In general, the idea of God's sending a divine emissary for the purpose of saving humanity is not unique or unprecedented. The idea also occurs outside the corpus of Paul's letters. Thus, it seems that Paul employs a motif from Hellenistic Judaism of God's sending a savior for the sake of humanity. Outside the Old Testament, in the Jewish writings of the Hellenistic period, one sees in Philo, *Dreams* 1.69; Sirach 24; Baruch 3; and Wisdom of Solomon 9 the idea that *God acted by sending a savior in order to bring salvation,* although in these places the texts declare that God sent Wisdom or the Logos as the agent of salvation. Paul appears to take up the framework and content of this abstract, mythical theme and make it concrete: "God acted for the salvation of humanity by sending a savior" = *God sent God's Son, Jesus Christ, to redeem humanity so that humans might receive adoption as children of God.* As Paul develops this mythic theological assertion, the once-hopeful thought is declared to be a *reality;* the mythical figures Wisdom and Logos are simply replaced by the humanly born, real "Son of God, Jesus Christ." Paul transforms a pattern of wishful mythic expression into a vehicle for declaring the reality of the gospel of God's salvation in Jesus Christ brought into being in the context of actual human existence.

DRAWING TOGETHER
THE LINES OF STUDY

Through often independent, often brief statements, Paul provides a surprisingly full portrait of Jesus Christ in the assortment of christological comments throughout his letters. When the elements of his christological teaching are pieced together in a plausible chronological series, the predominantly independent statements generally cohere. Yet readers find that Paul brings a striking array of materials related to Jesus Christ into his letters. First is *history,* telling of the life of Jesus. Second is *religious tradi-*

tion, telling of Jesus Christ both through references and allusions to the sacred writings of Judaism and in information that Paul plainly states was passed on to him by those who were before him in the life of the church. Third are *firm theological convictions,* telling of the significance of God's work through Jesus Christ—some of these declarations are obviously related to and drawn from Judaism and earlier Christianity, but others are not so clearly identified with respect to a particular background. This finding should come as no surprise to careful readers of Paul's letters, for in Galatians 1 he insists that his message came to him from God through *revelation.* Whatever a modern skeptic makes of this claim, Paul unambiguously indicates his own understanding of the revelatory nature of important portions of his message concerning Jesus Christ. Of course, no precise measure can be taken of the amount of Paul's total christological teaching that is to be understood as coming to him through revelation. Nevertheless, readers should expect to find information without precedent or parallel in earlier religious writings and traditions, for Paul insists that his message was imparted directly by God and was not, therefore, merely human knowledge or religious tradition.

Still further insight may be gained into the christological materials in Paul's letters by correlating the earlier findings regarding the narrative dimensions of Paul's story of Jesus Christ and the reflections on the nature of those materials that he communicates. First, note that Paul tells of (at least) three different but related times:

1. *The time before God's sending the Son and Jesus Christ's birth as a human.* Here readers find God, Jesus Christ, Adam, and the Israelites during the exodus. The characters and the story evoke a sense of origins—divine, human, and religious. Paul tells of this "first time" in items 1–10, though already in item 7 is an anticipation of the next time in the story, the time of Jesus Christ's life. In telling of this time, Paul employs theological assertions mixed with mythic references and metaphors. No full-fledged historical remarks appear in the telling of this initial time.

2. *The time of Jesus Christ's life in the context of human existence.* God and Jesus Christ, now with the Spirit of holiness, along with a number of specific humans—Jesus' mother, Abraham, David, Jesus' brothers, James, the rulers of this age, Cephas and the others whom Paul names to whom the risen Jesus Christ appeared, including himself—make up the characters in this segment of the materials. By contrast to the storytelling related to the first time, the dominant element in the telling of this "second time" is historical reporting (found in items 11–34). Thus, the appearance of the large cast of human characters along with the divine is appropriate.

Nevertheless, while the materials are highly historical in character, a rich mixture of theological assertion and metaphor is present in this portion of the materials. The mythic dimensions of expression, however, are noticeably absent from the second time of the story of Jesus Christ.

3. *The time(s) after Jesus Christ's resurrection and of his exaltation.* In telling of the "third time," Paul again moves beyond the communication of historical information. Jesus Christ himself is the dominant figure alongside God. Humanity appears, but either in the cosmic drama of the end or as the members of the church in Christ. Historical remarks are lacking; readers encounter theological assertions that are often blended with mythic reports and metaphor.

From the earth-bound, time-bound, human point of view, the heart of Paul's story of Jesus Christ is history. Paul writes *factually* about Jesus Christ, who was born and died. Among the facts, the significance of Jesus Christ's birth requires brief commentary through metaphor and the explanation of scripture (item 14). Moreover, Paul's telling of the historical ministry of Jesus Christ elicits interpretive theological assertion (item 18). Above all, however, the memory of Jesus Christ's death by crucifixion produces a significant set of theological assertions and vivid metaphors with references to the Old Testament. Nine items offer interpretation of the death (items 22–30). The density of this material creates emphasis and shows Paul's concern with the cross and its significance. Finally and strikingly, the reality of the resurrection is told only in theological assertion, although in conjunction with the declaration of Jesus Christ's resurrection Paul offers historical reports of a series of appearances by the risen Jesus Christ to specific individuals and groups who are historical figures.

In a sense, the nature of the statements in relation to the three narrative times shows that God, God's will, and God's actions prior to the birth of Jesus Christ were theological "truths" that could only be asserted and find mythic or metaphorical expression. Yet in Jesus Christ, from his birth through his death and in the experience of his resurrection, the earlier declarations about God are made *real and historical.* Moreover, after the historical period from the birth to the death and the appearances of the resurrected Jesus Christ, Paul again talks of God's future in nonhistorical terms; but now the future and the hope of the future as God's time of triumph over evil find a firm foundation on the historical reality of Jesus Christ. Thus, as Paul tells this story, the origins and destiny of creation and creature alike are intimately tied to the historical revelation of God in and through God's Son, Jesus Christ.

What might this story say to the church of Jesus Christ today? As Paul refers to the story of Jesus Christ, many important facets shine and draw the readers' attention, but in its essence—in both content and manner of expression—Paul's account emphasizes the crucial role and authority of Jesus Christ for comprehending God and for living as Christians. Jesus Christ is the one

through whom all things are,
who humbled himself in obedience to God's will and died on a cross,
who now as the raised and exalted Lord is bringing to completion God's
    victory over all opposition.

Jesus Christ: the Power and Wisdom of God,
                the humble and faithful crucified Christ,
                the foundation of the church,
                the victorious Son of God.[21]

This is the one of whom Paul writes and into whose communion Paul calls others. In telling the story of Jesus Christ, Paul beckons other humans to join him in reverent and joyous obedience to the Lord Jesus Christ, that through Jesus Christ in the end God may be all to all. The message, its meaning, and its purpose have not changed.

NOTES

1. This chapter does not follow the path of many important earlier studies in treating Paul's Christology by examining or reflecting on "christological titles," though some awareness of these titles, their occurrence, and their significance necessarily informs the analysis of Paul's story of Jesus Christ. Important examples of reflection on Paul's Christology through titles may be found in R. Bultmann, *Theology of the New Testament,* 2 vols. (New York: Charles Scribner's Sons, 1951 and 1955), 1:121–33; F. Hahn, *The Titles of Jesus in Christology: Their History in Early Christianity* (Cleveland and New York: World Publishing Co., 1969); and G. O'Collins, *Christology: A Biblical, Historical, and Systematic Study of Jesus* (Oxford: Oxford University Press, 1995).

2. For a concise summary and treatment of what Paul knew about Jesus Christ, see L. E. Keck's discussion "Paul and the Traditions of the Pivotal Event," in *Paul and His Letters,* 2d rev. ed. (Philadelphia: Fortress Press, 1988), 38–43.

3. The verses given for the statements listed below are illustrative of the statements, not exhaustive listings of all instances where such statements are made.

4. On this important passage, see G. D. Fee's discussion of the phrase "spirit

of holiness" in *God's Empowering Presence: The Holy Spirit in the Letters of Paul* (Peabody, Mass.: Hendrickson Publishers, 1994), 478–84.

5. Concerning the eloquent text in 2 Corinthians, see the insightful essay by J. L. Martyn, "Epistemology at the Turn of the Ages: 2 Corinthians 5:16," in *Christian History and Interpretation: Studies Presented to John Knox*, ed. W. R. Farmer, C. F. D. Moule, and R. R. Niebuhr (Cambridge: Cambridge University Press, 1967), 269–87, now also available in a revised form in Martyn's collected essays on Paul, *Theological Issues in the Letters of Paul* (Nashville: Abingdon Press, 1997), 89–110.

6. Keck writes about the "shape" of the pivotal events of the Christ event; in part he seems to mean to refer to the "story"—plot and content—of Paul's christological materials (*Paul*, 43–48).

7. On Jesus Christ as God's Son, see J. D. G. Dunn, *Christology in the Making: An Inquiry into the Origins of the Doctrine of the Incarnation*, 2d ed. (London: SCM Press, 1989), 12–64, esp. 33–46.

8. See Dunn for a thorough discussion of "Wisdom" in relation to christological thinking in early Christianity (*Christology*, 168–212).

9. Regarding this item of information, as well as the statement in item 4 that "Christ Jesus was in the form of God": The vast majority of scholars conclude that these elements of Paul's account of Jesus are indications that Paul believed (perhaps he assumed) that Jesus Christ was preexistent. Yet a minority of scholars, including Dunn (*Christology*, 113–28), follow the logic of J. Murphy-O'Connor, who contends that Paul's point in this statement is not that Christ was preexistent but that he was "sent forth" by God as he "came forth" in human terms, as had Adam and the prophets of Israel. See J. Murphy-O'Connor, "Christological Anthropology in Phil. 2.6–11," *Revue biblique* 83 (1976): 25–50. Dunn makes much of the Adam connection at this point.

10. Dunn presents a lengthy discussion on the connections between Adam and Christ, which he develops in two parts: "Adam and Humanity" and "Adam and Christ" (*Christology*, 98–128); but compare Keck's interpretation (*Paul*, 43–45).

11. On the significance of the crucifixion of Jesus the Messiah, see the important and provocative essay by N. A. Dahl, "The Crucified Messiah," in *Jesus the Christ: The Historical Origins of Christological Doctrine*, ed. D. H. Juel (Minneapolis: Fortress Press, 1991), 27–47.

12. E. Käsemann engages in tricky exegesis in handling 1 Corinthians 5:7, apparently allowing a Lutheran/Catholic doctrinal issue to make him force this text not to say what it seems plainly to say, that Jesus' death was a sacrifice; nevertheless, his general treatment of the salvific meaning of Jesus' death is an important examination of Paul's references to the crucifixion of Jesus. See "The Saving Significance of the Death of Jesus in Paul," in *Perspectives on Paul* (Philadelphia: Fortress Press, 1971), 32–59.

13. Extensive essays on Jesus as "redeemer" are in the work of O'Collins ("Redeemer," in *Christology,* 279–95; "Universal Redeemer," in *Christology,* 296–305).

14. J. A. Fitzmyer offers a succinct discussion of the interpretations of the significance of Jesus' death that treats all the ideas listed in items 24–30. See "Effects of the Christ-Event," in *Paul and His Theology: A Brief Sketch,* 2d ed. (Englewood Cliffs, N.J.: Prentice-Hall, 1989), 59–71.

15. Another way of summarizing the christological dimensions that also draws conclusions after surveying the individual Pauline letters is offered by E. Richard, "Paul's Creed: Christ Crucified," in *Jesus: One and Many. The Christological Concept of New Testament Authors* (Wilmington, Del.: Michael Glazier, 1988), 321–32.

16. For a careful study of the relationship of "Jesus" and "Christ," see Dahl, "The Messiahship of Jesus in Paul," in Juel, ed., *Jesus,* 15–25.

17. Keck's discussion of the "shape" of Paul's account of Jesus Christ is helpful in giving nuance to understanding the movement of the plot in conceptual terms, not merely temporal categories; he follows the story through three conceptual movements: preexistence, incarnation, postexistence (note 6, above).

18. Remarkably, G. B. Caird and L. D. Hurst treat the overall New Testament account of Jesus Christ in terms of three periods: an accomplished fact, an experience continuing in the present, and a consummation still to come ("Three Tenses of Salvation," in *New Testament Theology* [Oxford: Clarendon Press, 1994], 118–35). Apparently, in this view, the first and second times discussed in this chapter are conflated into a single period, but the third time in this chapter is divided into two parts. Thus, some may insist that the story of Jesus Christ in Paul's letters encompasses four times.

19. A major discussion of the concerns addressed in this section appears in Dahl's "Sources of Christological Language," in Juel, ed., *Jesus,* 113–36.

20. J. Becker writes about the important combination of history and theology in a discussion titled "The Gospel of Jesus Christ," in *Paul: Apostle to the Gentiles* (Louisville, Ky.: Westminster/John Knox Press, 1993), 399–411.

21. See 1 Cor. 8:6; Phil. 2:9, 1 Cor. 1:24. Two quite different but classic discussions of the aspect of "victory" in relation to Paul's Christology are those of G. Aulen, *Christus Victor: An Historical Study of the Three Main Types of the Idea of the Atonement* (New York: Macmillan Co., 1969); and J. C. Beker, *Paul the Apostle: The Triumph of God in Life and Thought* (Philadelphia: Fortress Press, 1980).

THE CHRISTOLOGY
OF HEBREWS

C. K. Barrett

A study of the Christology of Hebrews may be given direction and precision by a hypothesis concerning the background and origin of the epistle. If the resultant Christology is convincing the hypothesis may at the same time be to some extent confirmed.

Long ago William Manson[1] argued that there was a close relation, both historical and theological, between Hebrews and Stephen, for whom Manson regarded the material in Acts 6 and 7 as trustworthy historical evidence. He made much of a community of eschatological belief and saw Stephen and his fellow Christian diaspora Jews as initiating a Gentile mission responsible, among other things, for the spread of Christianity not only to Antioch (Acts 11:19–26) but also to Alexandria and to Rome. At the time when Hebrews was written, the Roman church (if in those early stages the word *ekklēsia* is appropriate for it) was still a section of the synagogue and overemphasized the Jewish element in Christianity. It needed to be made aware of the wider horizons and deeper implications of the new faith.[2] Hebrews was addressed to them[3] with this aim. In achieving this, the author showed something of the influence of Alexandrian Hellenism.

We may affirm a great deal of this, even if we rate the evidence of Acts somewhat less highly than Manson did. Luke seems, in fact, to distinguish less clearly than is desirable between Pauline and non-Pauline missions to the Gentile world. He knows, or wishes to tell, nothing of the unhappy event at Antioch (Gal. 2:11–21) and represents the dispute over circumcision as quickly settled. He represents Paul as an agent of the church of Antioch; so, perhaps, at first he was, but in the period of the latter part of Acts he was acting as an apostle "neither by human commission nor from human authorities" (cf. Gal. 1:1). There was a non-Pauline mission (there may have been more than one), and the Seven of Acts (6; 7; 21:8) and the church at Antioch played parts in it. This mission, though ready to address Gentiles, was less critical of the law than was Paul (or perhaps we should say, less critical than the critical element in Paul's thought, less affirmative than the affirmative element) and was probably responsible for the Decree of Acts 15:29.[4] Pioneer mission work in Alexandria and Rome is an interesting possibility to keep in mind, but is unlikely to contribute much to our present task. More relevant is the hypothesis that the speeches of Acts 7 (attributed to Stephen) and Acts 17 (attributed to Paul) originated with this group of Christians.[5]

The most striking feature of both speeches is their extremely slight Christian content. The greater part of Stephen's speech is devoted to a review of Old Testament history, beginning with Abraham and the patriarchs, continuing with Moses and the exodus, and going as far as Solomon, his temple, and some prophetic comments on the temple. Notwithstanding repeated emphasis on the power of God to overcome suffering and apparent defeat, and to bring positive good out of them, for example in the story of Joseph (Acts 7:9–16), a theme which it would have been easy to apply to the crucifixion and resurrection of Jesus, and the application to Moses of terms (e.g., *ruler* and *redeemer,* 7:25) which, on the lips of a Christian preacher, might have seemed more appropriately applied to Jesus, no attempt is made to relate the Old Testament material directly to the Christian story. The law was "living oracles" (7:38); there is no suggestion of any sense in which a Christian might be "dead to the law" (e.g., Galatians 2:19). The temple, however, was a mistake; God was more at home in a moving tent; he had no wish for a house. The lesson of Jeremiah 7 had been learnt; God sought obedience to his word rather than cultus. It is only in the last few lines that Jesus is alluded to (not by name), and this allusion does not involve any positive value that his life and teaching might have contained; Jesus provided the final example of the failure of God's people to hear and obey God's word. If we omit the seven words of 7:52b (*hou nun humeis prodotai kai phoneis egenesthe;* "of whom you have now become betrayers and murderers"), the speech could have been delivered by a Jew in any diaspora synagogue. Some might have disapproved the disparagement of the temple (though it is based on scripture); all would have approved the praise of Moses and the law; some might have been moved to penitence for their neglect of God's word in Torah and resolved to be more faithful members of God's people. It is an attractive hypothesis that this was, in fact, the origin of the speech. If the original speaker became a Christian, there was no reason why it should not be preached in a Christian context; it needed only a hint at the end to give it a new point.

In many respects the Areopagus speech of Acts 17 is different. It contains no allusion to the history of Israel. There is however a striking resemblance in the slight Christian touch with which the speech ends. That God intends to judge the whole of mankind is not a uniquely Christian belief; it is not specifically Jewish. There are Greek parallels. Again we have what could have originated as a lightly Christianized version of a synagogue sermon. The body of the sermon is indeed different from that of Acts 7, but it is equally suitable for synagogue use. The speaker treads the border line between Old Testament prophecy and Greek religious philosophy, showing how close they are to each other. Each is opposed to idolatry, knowing that God is not to be represented by human art working on wood or stone. Each knows that God is close to his human creatures; in him we live and move and have our being. He is not in need of our gifts; on the contrary, he not only gives us all that we need but controls history, and appoints to the various races periods of authority and areas for residence. The speaker declares that he is about to inform the Areopagites of what they do not know as they worship an unknown God, but most of what he says would be familiar enough in the Stoa Poikile or the Garden of Epicurus, or both. To rehearse it, however, might persuade a tolerant Greek of the virtue of Judaism and encourage a doubting and hellenizing Jew to remain loyal to the faith of his fathers.

The diaspora Jews who began their preaching in these ways became, when converted to Christianity, in some respects the most influential group of early Christians.[6] Luke, who was a good enough historian to recognize the importance of Paul, seems nevertheless to have confused the two Gentile missions, that of Paul and that of the Seven. He probably thought of Paul as deeply influenced by Stephen and as continuing his work (Acts 7:58; 8:1–3; 22:20). The Areopagus speech was theirs, not his (he had a different approach, without "wisdom," concentrating on the cross: 1 Cor. 2:1–5); the Decree of Acts 15:29 was theirs, not his (and not James's). Authors of the Decree, they controlled and directed the great Gentile expansion of the church in the 70s, 80s, and 90s C.E. They lacked the theological sharpness and profundity of Paul; this may to some extent have accounted for their success. But there were gaps in their statement of the Christian case. It is easy to name two. One was the temple. There was in the diaspora no single view of the temple.[7] Some, because of its inaccessibility, valued it the more, but there must have been some who reflected, "We have to practice and do practice Judaism without the temple; therefore the temple is not indispensable." The destruction of the temple in 70 C.E. must have made this thought bite. Yet the temple was—until, and in a different sense after its destruction—a major part of the Israelite inheritance. Though prophetic passages that are critical of the temple do exist, prophetic books were also full of the hope of its reconstruction, and a considerable part of the law itself was given up to instructions for the conduct of the temple's sacrificial system. The Mishnah tractate *Middot* recalls (perhaps here and there invents) countless details of temple procedures and dimensions which there was little point in memorizing apart from the hope that they might someday be put again to practical use. The Temple and the sacrifices (many would think) cannot have counted for nothing in God's call and guidance of his people; and now (so at least a few would think) that we are Christians we must believe that the true meaning of the Temple has been fulfilled in Christ—an article of faith which those to whom the temple was something of an embarrassment[8] might welcome with relief.

This observation points immediately to the second gap in the Christian diaspora group's theological system. It was (if we may judge by Acts 7 and 17) sadly deficient in Christology. Jesus had marked the unhappy climax in the story of Israel's disobedience, its readiness to neglect the Word of God in the interests of its religious institutions, and the moment when God chose to announce the final judgment of humankind and to indicate the ground and principle of judgment by appointing the last and greatest prophet as Judge, demonstrating his status by raising him from death. This was true as far as it went; but it did not go very far, and the author of Hebrews was on hand to supply what was lacking. Theology, like nature, abhors a vacuum, and a vacuum was waiting to be filled.

The two outstanding characteristic themes of Hebrews are the work of atonement in the heavenly temple and Christ as its priestly officiant. Consideration of these themes prompts a further, more speculative, observation. If the Areopagus speech gives a fair and representative insight into Hellenistic Jewish use of Greek philosophy, this was, on the whole, limited to Stoicism and Epicureanism.[9] This is a large assumption, and we must not build too heavy a structure on it, but it may at least permit the suggestion that these two practical lines of philosophy were being practiced to the neglect of more speculative Platonism, which thus remained as a field waiting to be explored. It may be no accident that the author of Hebrews makes use of a popular Platonism—not unrelated to apocalyptic,[10] as Stoicism and Epicureanism were not unrelated to prophecy—as his means of developing at the same time an interpretation of the temple and its practices and an advanced Christology.

So much by way of introduction. It remains to examine the data of the epistle itself, considering its christological statements in the light of its quasi-Platonic interpretation of the temple and its cultus. Within the compass of this chapter it will be possible to examine, and that briefly, only some of the most important passages.

HEBREWS 1:1–4

It is consistent with these observations that the epistle begins with a very emphatic assertion of a high Christology, which both fulfills and antiquates the Old Testament. God had indeed spoken in the past to the fathers of the Jewish people, but he had done so *polumerōs* (in many parts) and *polutropōs* (in various ways). God's message had been delivered through a number of prophets, piecemeal and with no consistent formulation. This partial communication of truth belongs to the past, from which the present is distinguished as the *eschaton tōn hēmerōn*—a LXX expression[11] which often means little more than *finally, now at last*, but here can hardly mean less than a claim that the author is writing in the closing period of human history. There can therefore be no further revelation beyond that which is now given *en huiōi* (in a Son), that is, in one who in his essential nature is a son and thus a member of the divine family. To affirm this at the outset will not prevent the author from recognizing the true humanity of the incarnate Son, but it does make clear what he is in himself. The Father–Son relationship will be taken up in verse 5. Its roots are in belief about the king (including the supreme, final King) of Israel; it is messianic terminology, though as the next lines show, it goes far beyond conventional messianic belief. It appears too that the Son is also the Word (though the word *logos* is not used here).[12] The prologue of Hebrews is not without resemblance to the prologue of John.

The status of the new agent of revelation is emphasized in a sequence of honorific clauses, which lay down an initial framework and standard for the Christology of Hebrews. The surprising order (final inheritance coming before creation) is probably determined by the association of creation with the allusions and images to come in verse 3, though eschatology will return in verse 4. The result is a chiastic structure. At the beginning, when the Son was the agent of creation, God had already planned that he should in the end be the Lord of creation. He would be the first and the last (cf. Rev. 1:17; 2:8; 22:13). The spanning of creation and consummation is characteristic of the more advanced christological passages in the New Testament (John 1:1–18; Phil. 2:6–11; Col. 1:15–20).

The Son is thus the Word throughout history, God's self-communication from the beginning to the end of time. To describe his being and its significance the author picks up another concept but, surprisingly, does not use its key word. It is hard to doubt that the word *apaugasma* (effulgence) in verse 3 points to the figure of Wisdom (see especially Wisdom of Solomon 7:26). Wisdom (*sophia*) is God's agent in creation (Prov. 8:30) and continues to uphold that which is made.

Almost every word in verse 3 is heavy with meaning. It would be anachronistic to read into *hypostasis* (NRSV, "being") the meaning (or meanings) it acquired in the christological debates of the fourth and fifth centuries, but it points to the underlying being of God, as *apaugasma* (effulgence) and *charaktēr* (imprint) point to what is visible in light and shape. The Son is God in his audibility (v. 1) and also in his visibility. The two channels of revelation are combined here as they are in John,[13] though there is no ground for positing a literary relation between the two works.

There is no immediate contiguity between creation and consummation; there must intervene God's way of dealing with the human sin that has perverted creation. Here, too, the Son/Word/Wisdom is the agent of divine action. He effects purgation of sins: how he did this will receive so much attention later in the epistle that at this point we may be content to pass it by as a simple affirmation. The ascent and heavenly session of the Son (v. 3d) may also be considered later, though we should note the contact here with the important Jewish question: Who (if anyone) may share God's throne in heaven?

HEBREWS 1:5–14

At this point a new theme, which will fill the rest of the chapter, is introduced. He who is Son, Word, and Wisdom is contrasted with angels; the contrast is developed by means of Old Testament quotations from verse 4 to the end of the chapter. The Son is better (*kreittōn*) than the angels, as he has inherited (from his Father?) a more excellent (*diaphorōteron*) name; he is distinctive as a son, begotten by the Father; the angels are to worship him; they are ministering spirits, whereas he shares the throne of God; he laid the foundations of the earth, and when all else changes he will remain unchanged; God invited him to sit at his right hand with his enemies beneath his feet.

In all this there is nothing with which any New Testament writer would be likely to disagree, but one wonders why it was necessary to lay so much weight on the Son's superiority to angels. The thought springs to mind that the author wished to discredit a Christology that portrayed Jesus as an angel appearing in the form of a man. One can easily imagine the development of such a Christology, no doubt arising out of excellent motives. It might seem to be a suitable way of defining the person of one who was certainly understood to be greater than human beings; he must have been an angel taking the form of man. The difficulty is that there seems to be no evidence for such an angel-christology in the first century or soon afterward. At most, a few passages in the Shepherd of Hermas[14] might be relevant; the Elchesaites claimed[15] that revelation had been given by an angel of enormous size who was the Son of God; Justin Martyr[16] applies to Christ the title of Isaiah 9:5 (LXX), *megalēs boulēs angelos* (angel of great counsel), but he can hardly be said to make a Christology out of it—and even if he did, it would not be properly called an angel-christology but simply one that rested on (supposed) messianic titles in the Old Testament. All this material is in any case too late to provide a background for Hebrews. The heavily underlined contrast in Hebrews 1 must have an internal explanation, and there is no need to look further than Hebrews 2:2–4. Angels mediated a law that had to be observed (compare Acts 7:53), but Christ was the bringer of the gospel. The fact that the Son of God was so greatly superior to angels serves also to emphasize his voluntary and gracious humility in accepting a position lower than theirs.

HEBREWS 2

Hebrews 2:1–4 uses the comparison between the Son and angels in an exhortation to give heed to the Christian message, no angelic word, important as that could be, but one spoken by the Lord himself and passed on with the confirmation of signs and portents and spiritual gifts by those who heard him.

This warning leads to a fundamental statement of the theme to which it draws attention. This is expressed, we must observe, not in Platonic but in eschatological terms. What we are speaking about is the world (*oikoumenē*) to come. As we proceed, however, it will appear that this is a term that holds the door open to a measure of Platonic, or quasi-Platonic, interpretation, for that which to us is the world to come is the world that already exists in heaven, where it may be seen by those who are willing to be guided by the Christian revelation.[17] We may, therefore, speak about the world to come though we live in the present world, which, if it is in any sense a copy of the heavenly world, is a defaced copy, awaiting cleansing.

The opening verse of the new paragraph (2:5) contains its own problems, though on the whole these are cleared up as we follow the argument. Who, we may ask, is the subject of *hypetaxen?* For the present it is sufficient to observe that the subject of *hypetaxas* is undoubtedly God; no one else could, in the psalm, be addressed as *Thou.* And why should the world to come be subjected to anyone? Perhaps it is a position which that world would itself choose to occupy. It has not been subjected to angels; if not to them, to whom? The answer sometimes given, based on the quotation of Psalm 8 that follows in 2:6–8, is, it is subject to the human race. This answer is, I think, mistaken. The figure who stands over against angels is, as chapter 1 makes unmistakably clear, not humanity in general but the Son of God; it is to him that the world to come is made subject. He is here described as Son of man (*huios anthrōpou*); modern readers of the Psalms are, of course, familiar with parallelism as the fundamental form of Hebrew verse and recognize that *anthrōpos* in verse 6b and *huios anthrōpou* in verse 6c are in synonymous parallelism, and that both refer to human beings (collectively). But the use of parallelism in Hebrew poetry was first recognized by Robert Lowth (1710–1787) and, whatever the psalmist may have meant, we have no right to suppose that the author of Hebrews took *huios anthrōpou* to mean merely *man.* He had a clear pointer in a different direction. Psalm 8:7 (quoted in 2:8) concludes with the affirmation "Thou hast put all things in subjection under his feet" (author's translation). This cannot fail to call to mind the similar affirmation of Psalm 110:1, quoted in Hebrews 1:13, where God addresses his Son, who shares his throne, sitting at God's right hand, and promises that his enemies shall be set as a footstool for his feet. It is the same person to whom all things, including his enemies, are put under his feet, and he is the Son of God and the Son of man.[18]

Out of Psalm 8 we learn the story of the Son of God/Son of man. It is in three stages: (1) God made him for a little while[19] lower than the angels — an extraordinary paradox in view of what is said about the angels in chapter 1, where their inferiority to the Son is repeatedly emphasized. To be made lower than the angels is to be made man; the reference is to the incarnation of the Son of God. (2) God crowned him with glory and honor. In view of what follows (v. 9), we may say that his humiliation, suffering, and death are presupposed. Because of his voluntary acceptance of these, he is highly exalted. The reference is clearly to the resurrection (to which Hebrews refers explicitly only once) and to the ascension (which, of course, presupposes the resurrection) of Jesus. (3) As the final stage of his exaltation, when the history of humankind has run its course, all things are put in subjection to him.

These three points, with their interpretation, are set out clearly in verses

8 and 9. We see Jesus made lower than the angels (for he becomes a man), suffering death, and crowned, in resurrection and ascension, with glory and honor. It is, however, recognized explicitly that we do not yet see all things set in subjection under him; the story is not complete. The final state of universal sovereignty belongs to the world to come, of which we are speaking (2:5).

The paradoxical element in this story, to which many will have instinctively objected, is that it involves one who might seem to be nothing less than immortal in suffering and death. The justification for this begins with a plain, and unsupported, affirmation. It pleased God (*eprepen autōi* [God]) in bringing many children into glory to perfect their leader into salvation through suffering. For the present this must remain unexplained, except insofar as there is an explanation in the very word *leader* (*archēgos*): If he is to lead the way he must start where the human race is. For them, the way is bound to lead through suffering, including the suffering of death; if he is to lead them, he too must tread that path. Another way of putting this is to say that he is brother to the human race (v. 11); that he who is sanctified and they that are sanctified are of the same human origin. So if they are partakers of blood and flesh, so must he be; and blood and flesh mean suffering and death. By his voluntary experience of suffering and death, however, he will overcome the devil, who held the power of death, and thus set humankind free from bondage and fear. His own suffering and death are the means of liberation for those whom he has accepted as brothers. It is at this point that Hebrews' distinctive designation of Jesus as high priest enters the exposition. It is his readiness to be made in all respects identical with his brothers, his readiness therefore to accept with them the experience of suffering and death, that qualifies him to act as a merciful and faithful high priest (2:17). Because of his unique relationship with God (which his relationship with humanity does not destroy), he can act in relation to God and can expiate (*hilaskesthai*) the sins of his people. Having been tested by suffering, he can help those who are tried; it is not angels but the seed of Abraham[20] whom he helps.

The figure of the high priest, reached at the end of chapter 2, is set on hold for two chapters while two related matters are developed. One is directly christological. The Son, who has already been shown to be greater than angels, is now seen to occupy a higher position than Moses. Moses was a faithful servant in God's household; Christ, as God's Son, is over the household (3:5). This would seem to be too obvious to be worth saying, were it not that priesthood is bound up with covenant and law—theological themes that will occur later; and Moses is the brother of Aaron, first high priest and head of the whole priestly operation. A further connection will appear shortly.

The second matter is only indirectly christological. It will be recalled that Psalm 8, quoted in Hebrews 2:6–8, sets out a timetable for the work of the Son of God/Son of Man: He will be made lower than the angels; he will be crowned with glory and honor; all things will be set under his feet. The first two stages have already been accomplished; the third has not. This means that the Christians are living in the final, eschatological period of history. Part of God's plan has already been completed; part has not. Human beings are thus confronted with the final outworking of God's purpose and are thereby challenged to accept their place in it. This situation is analogous to that contained in the story of Moses and the exodus, especially as this is set out in Psalm 96 (quoted in Heb. 3:7–11). There remains, as yet unachieved, a "rest," a *katapausis,* for the people of God;[21] the old story shows that it is possible, by disobedience and lack of faith, to miss this rest. The new, Christian, story shows that human beings are still subject to the same decision of faith, and this decision has to be made in relation to the person of Christ.

HEBREWS 5

Chapters 3 and 4 contain other themes that are not unrelated to Christology, but a decisive step is taken at the end of chapter 4 and in chapter 5. The theme of high priesthood is taken up at 4:14 with a general emphasis on its importance, on the ability of the Son of God as high priest to sympathize with our weaknesses, and with the parenthetical and, at this point, unexplained statement that he "passed through the heavens." In the opening verse of chapter 5, the theme begins to be developed. At first there are general propositions about the functions and office of a high priest. His work is done in matters relating to God; he has to make sacrifices for sins; he offers for himself as well as for others. He does not seize the office for himself but must be called and appointed by God. At this point (5:5–6) the author returns to Psalm 2, which speaks of the divine begetting that constitutes the Son of God ("Thou art my Son, this day have I begotten thee," author's translation), and to Psalm 110, which contains the divine appointment which makes the Son of God high priest ("Thou art a priest forever in the order of Melchizedek").

The latter passage provides a fresh point of departure for the treatment of high priesthood[22] in Hebrews. The first point of departure is Psalm 8, in the representative role of the Son of man. This may or may not appear as a piece of Hebrew parallelism; in scripture it is a theological factor. It is a

familiar observation that in Daniel 7, the Son of man vision is interpreted
as a representation of the people of the saints of the Most High; if he receives a kingdom, that means that the people do. If this means that in any
sense or at any stage he is identified with the Messiah, the same interpretation applies, for the king is the representative of the people; in their king
the people as a whole experience defeat or victory. In the Gospels the Son
of man (whatever precisely the term may mean) acts representatively for
the people; he gives his life a *lutron anti pollōn* ("a ransom for many,"
Mark 10:45). In the Pauline literature the curious expression *ho huios tou
anthrōpou* (the Son of man) does not occur, but (in better Greek) Jesus is
the new Adam, the second representative man, and "as all die in Adam, so
all will be made alive in Christ" (1 Cor. 15:22). Of this representative function the high priest is a specialized figure; the high priest acts, sacrifices,
on behalf of the people as a whole. When the term *high priest* is first used
in Hebrews 2:17, this is the background against which it has to be understood. Now, however, Psalm 8 leads to Psalm 110, connected by way of the
picture of universal sovereignty, and the triumphant figure — all things set
under his feet — is said to be a priest forever in the order of Melchizedek. This
is another great figure: greater than Abraham, as the epistle points out at
7:4–10, greater than Levi, and, one might add, greater than Moses and his
brother Aaron, the first high priest. The important thing about the Aaronic
high priest is precisely that he is Aaronic; that is, he is from the beginning in-
tegrated into the structure of the people on whose behalf he is to act. Aaron
himself is the brother of Moses, and from their time *Torah* and *Abodah*, law
and temple worship, are brothers, together constituting the life of God's people.[23] It is true that Jesus stands a little aside from this pattern because he does
not belong to the tribe of Levi, but as we shall see, his actions duplicate precisely (though on a different level) those of the Aaronic high priest. The
essence of Melchizedek is that all this is what he is not: he has no country,
no father, no mother, no beginning, no end. Scripture has made him like the
Son of God (Heb. 7:3). He appears suddenly on the biblical stage and is seen
for a moment as its supreme figure, recognized as such even by Abraham.
The two high priests provide an illustration of J. L. Leuba's theme in *L' Institution et l'Événement*.[24] Jesus fulfills the Aaronic high priestly institution
but fulfills it in a quite unexpectedly radical way, because he does so as the
non-Aaronic, non-Israelite, non-institutional Melchizedek.

At the end of Hebrews 5, the argument of the epistle breaks off (5:11),
and the author exhorts his readers. They must press on, giving careful heed
to what he writes, and show ceaseless vigilance, lest they become sluggish
and lose the hope that has been set before them.

HEBREWS 7

With chapter 7 the author returns to Melchizedek, emphasizing his greatness and importance. Much of the material in this chapter I have anticipated; but the exaltation of Melchizedek leads to criticism of the alternative, the Levitical priesthood. If this priesthood had led to perfection (*teleiōsis*), there would have been no need and no room for another priesthood, and God would not have supplied one (7:11). It is here that the family connection between the priesthood and Moses the lawgiver—if it may be so described—becomes important. It is on the basis of the Levitical priesthood that the people *nenomothetētai* (NRSV, "received the law," 7:11). It is not easy to find a precise rendering for this verb, especially when its somewhat different use in 8:6 is borne in mind. "To constitute legally" or "to give a legal constitution to" will do perhaps as well as any. The word has the importance of bringing together the Levitical priestly system and the law; also (from 8:6) the covenant. At the same time, it means that if the Melchizedekian high priest is substituted for the Levitical high priest, the law and the covenant must be radically changed. In this way the deficiencies of the old Jewish Christian diaspora are on the way to being dealt with. Christology, which was lacking, is introduced by the entry of a new high priestly figure, already appearing in the roles of Son, Word, and Wisdom, and not a functionary (as was the Levitical high priest) of the old law. The new high priest means a new legal enactment, a change in the legal basis of the people. And with the new law is bound up a new covenant, replacing the old legal basis.

Again we are anticipating material, with which we shall catch up in chapter 8. For the present, it is important to note the distinctiveness of the new high priest, though this proves to be inseparable from the question of the law. The old high priest was established by a law consisting of a fleshly commandment, the new priest by the power of an indissoluble life (7:16). This leads to a statement about the law that is as radical as anything written by Paul, though the language is completely different: "There is, on the one hand, the abrogation of an earlier commandment because it was weak and ineffectual (for the law made nothing perfect); there is, on the other hand, the introduction of a better hope, through which we approach God" (7:18–19). Appointed by the divine oath of Psalm 110:4, Jesus is the surety of a better covenant; and he was appointed forever, unlike the many successive Levitical priests appointed by the law who offered sacrifice after sacrifice. He is able to save forever (or completely) those who approach God through him (7:20–28).

HEBREWS 8

The operations of the new high priest are thus hinted at and will be developed in more detail later, but the writer now proceeds in chapter 8 to point out the *kephalaion,* the summary or main point (there is something of each sense in the word) of the whole argument. This begins with the contrast between those priests who serve what is but the image and shadow of the true tabernacle and the ministrant of the Holy Place and true tabernacle, which the Lord pitched, not man. The basis of the exposition, however, is not a Platonic figure of ideal and phenomenal but biblical eschatology and its fulfillment. Inevitably the paragraph is cast in terms of covenant, not simply because it includes a long quotation from the new covenant prophecy in Jeremiah 31 but because covenant means the relation between two parties, here God and human beings, and this is at the heart both of the Christian message and in particular of the work of a high priest. When scripture speaks of a new covenant, it has antiquated the old one; and that which is antiquated and growing old is near to disappearing (8:13).

From this point what may be called the eschatological Platonism of the epistle is developed. I discussed this briefly long ago[25] and must here consider it only from the point of view of Christology. The raw material of which it is composed is the Old Testament account of the Levitical high priest and his activity, especially on the Day of Atonement; the mysterious figure of Melchizedek; and the hint, recorded especially in Exodus 25:39–40, of a heavenly antitype of the earthly tabernacle. We must trace its development in the concluding chapters of the epistle.

HEBREWS 9

Hebrews 9 contains an account of the actions of the earthly priests in the earthly tabernacle, with hints, and more than hints, of a better liturgy in a better sanctuary. An account of the tabernacle and the way it was used (9:1–10) leads to a devastating criticism (descended from the polemic against the temple contained in Stephen's speech?) of material sacrifices. Such gifts can never perfect the worshipers in their conscience and merely relate to foods and drinks and washings. Their value is that they point forward to a time when something better will be provided. This paragraph is followed by 9:11–14, in which the thought of the epistle is summarized. It begins inevitably, and verbally, with Christ. He is defined by his role as High Priest, and he is set in historical and theological terms as the High Priest of the good things that have now come into being, not with the blood of bulls and goats but with his own blood, and in quasi-Platonic terms as one who has entered into the holy place—the holy place of the tent not made with hands, the holy place that is not of this creation (9:11–12). Because this High Priest has thus acted in this place, he has found for us a redemption that is eternal. If animal blood can convey an external purification, how much more will the blood of Christ cleanse our conscience from dead works! The rest of the chapter justifies, amplifies, and applies the image.

HEBREWS 10

Chapter 10 begins with a sharp but speedily qualified reassertion of Platonic terminology: The law has a shadow of good things but not their very image (*autēn tēn eikona*), the three-dimensional representation of the actual realities. The shadow sacrifices are repeated again and again—the repetition itself a proof of their inadequacy and inefficiency. If they really achieved their object in cleansing the worshiper, they would have ceased to be offered; why should they be repeated if their work was done? We may pass the bad logic of this argument—new sins were committed year by year, requiring the annual ceremony of the Day of Atonement. For the annual sacrifice had at least the virtue of reminding the worshiper that sin exists and that sin needs to be forgiven; the virtue also of providing terminology suitable for use in speaking of the one effective sacrifice. But material sacrifices create rather than deal with "conscience of sins" (*suneidēsis hamartiōn,* 10:2). It is conscience, an inward thing, that needs cleansing. The blood of bulls and goats belongs to a different category of existence, and a sacrifice must be sought that operates in the sphere of the conscience. Here the writer is able to pick up an important Old Testament passage, critical of the operations of the old, earthly sanctuary.[26] Sacrifices are commanded in the law (*kata nomon,* 10:8), but at this point the law has to be not merely criticized but plainly contradicted. "Sacrifice and offering thou didst not desire, but thou didst prepare for me a body; whole-burnt-offerings and sin-offerings did not please thee. Then I said, 'Behold, I have come (in the roll of the book it is written about me) to do thy will O God'" (Ps. 40:6–8; Heb. 10:5–7). This is so important that the writer repeats it and states its meaning in the baldest terms. He (the one who is speaking in scripture, the representative of God—it is, of course, Christ who is meant) takes away the first-named matters (sacrifices as performed *kata nomon*) in order that he may establish the second-named (the doing of God's will). The goal is still (but in a profounder sense) sanctification, and two words, offering and will, are taken up from the quotation, defining each other. By the will of God, accepted and completely performed by the Son, we have been sanctified through the offering (not of the blood of bulls and goats but) of the body of Jesus Christ, which was devoted without remainder to the will of God.

In 10:1, the law and the sacrifices it commanded are described by the quasi-Platonic "shadow." It would be easy to conclude that in the offering made by Jesus Christ we have the true, ideal parallel to the earthly, phenomenal, high priest and his work in the earthly, phenomenal, tabernacle. The matter, however, is not so simple. The work of Christ is inseparable from material and historical circumstances. The conscience itself is an inward spiritual entity, but the sins by which it is defiled are earthly enough. The devotion of Jesus to the Father's will is an inward spiritual entity, but our author is careful to select and quote an Old Testament passage that insists upon his body.[27] The sacrifice is that of a completely obedient will, but it finds concrete historical expression in a death as real as that of any bull or goat offered in the temple. There is in fact a threefold set of relationships within which the work of Jesus, which is the core of the Gospel, operates. It operates on a simple historical level, in the crucifixion of Jesus, an act in history. Second, this crucifixion is a moral act, in which Jesus offered to God his completely obedient will, a moral act which had the effect, third, of cleansing the defiled consciences of those who had not seen fit to offer their wills in obedience to God but had used them in pursuit of their own self-centered ends. These three operations are bound together by a fourth dimension, which is related at once to history, to the Old Testament temple and the regulations that governed it, and to what may be called a Platonic way of conceiving reality. This is most simply set out in the form of a table, summarizing, on the one hand, the account in Leviticus 16 (with help from the Mishnah tractate *Yoma*) of the events, especially the actions of the high priest, on the Day of Atonement[28] and, on the other hand, the acts ascribed to Jesus in the story of the cross.

Leviticus 16 (Yoma):
1. Sacrifice publicly carried out, outside the shrine, visible to all.
2. Entry of the high priest into the Holy Place, with blood, the visible and effective evidence that sacrifice has been offered.
3. Intercession and atonement made by the high priest within the Holy Place, where he alone may enter. He represents the people before God.
4. Return of the high priest to the waiting public, outside the Holy Place. He is able to tell them that their sins are forgiven.

Hebrews:

1. Christ suffered publicly, in an act visible to all mankind (13:12), offering his obedient will expressed through his body, obedient to death (10:10). This was a once-for-all act (9:13–14)—historically, the crucifixion.

2. After his death Christ ascended into heaven, with his own blood, the sign of his sacrificial death. Hebrews scarcely refers to the resurrection, though the author certainly believed in it (13:20). It is the ascension that matters, because this is the Son's entry into the heavenly sanctuary.

3. In the heavenly sanctuary Christ makes an act of atonement. This is eternal (7:25), in the sense that the atonement effected is eternal in its application and results (10:14) and in the simple chronological sense that until his return Christ is continuously in heaven.

4. Like the returning high priest, Christ will appear *ek deuterou* (a second time, 9:28). The second coming is *eis sōtērian* (for salvation)—to complete and apply the results of atonement. These are already anticipated in access to God and in the enjoyment of the powers of the age to come (6:5).

All this may be said to retain of Plato's famous cave only the stage set and the stage machinery.[29] The whole is rotated from a horizontal to a vertical position—not "inside the cave and outside the cave" but "below and above." And we have not objects standing or moving outside and casting shadows on the wall within but one being who acts both outside and within, moving from the visible world of historical event to the interior hiddenness of heaven, dying a human death and from this death going to plead the cause of his fellow human beings (for he is one of them, though much else also) with his Father in heaven. It is the temple and the law that are shadows, indicating as it were the shape of reality, but—though this introduces a new factor into the imagery—they are shadows that disappear as the new day of the new covenant dawns.

There is a further sense in which the historical event, recognizable to us in this world as the crucifixion of Jesus, has a double interpretation. It is an event that belongs at once to the realms of the visible and the invisible, of the phenomenal and the ideal; it also belongs to both time and eternity. It is of its nature that it happened once; its effects persist. By one offering he has perfected forever those who are sanctified (10:14). The Son, after the sacrifice of himself, has no more to do in the visible world until his return. He makes intercession (7:25) and waits until all his foes are subjected to him (10:12–13).

Having reached this conclusion, the author has little more Christology to offer; he draws practical consequences and exhorts his readers to live the life of faith, running with endurance the race that is set before them, their eyes fixed on Jesus. Into the details of this exhortation we cannot follow him; it has not been possible to go into the details of his appropriation of the sacrificial system of the Old Testament. The author of Hebrews has drawn on an aspect of the Old Testament neglected in most of the New, on traditional eschatology, and on his knowledge of Greek thought, to make up any deficiency there may have been in the Christology of his predecessors.

NOTES

1. W. Manson, *The Epistle to the Hebrews: An Historical and Theological Reconsideration* (London: Hodder & Stoughton, 1951).

2. One wonders what they may have made of Romans.

3. The destination of Hebrews is a notable puzzle. Rome, or somewhere in Italy, may well be correct; other possibilities are Corinth, Ephesus, the Lycus valley, Antioch, Cyprus, Jerusalem or elsewhere in Palestine. See Werner Georg Kümmel, *Introduction to the New Testament,* rev. ed. (Nashville: Abingdon Press, 1975), 398–401.

4. See C. K. Barrett, "Christocentricity at Antioch," in *Jesus Christus als die Mitte der Schrift: Studien zur Hermeneutik des Evangeliums,* ed. Christof Landmesser, Hans-Jochim Eckstein, and Hermann Lichtenberger; Beihefte zur Zeitschrift für die neutestamentliche Wissenschaft und die Kunde der älteren Kirche 86 (Berlin and New York: Walter de Gruyter, 1997), 338. See also C. K. Barrett, "Acts and Christian Consensus," in *Context: Essays in Honour of Peder Johan Borgen,* ed. P. W. Børkman and R. E. Kristiansen (Trondheim: TAPIR, 1987), 19–33.

5. See C. K. Barrett, *The Acts of the Apostles,* International Critical Commentary, 2 vols. (Edinburgh: T. & T. Clark, 1994 and 1998), 1:334–340; 2:civ, 825–26.

6. See C. K. Barrett, "What Minorities?" in *Mighty Minorities? Minorities in Early Christianity: Essays Presented to Jacob Jervell on His Seventieth Birthday 21 May 1995,* ed. D. Hellholm, H. Moxnes, and T. K. Seim (Oslo: Scandinavian, 1995), 8–9.

7. See C. K. Barrett, "Attitudes to the Temple in Acts," in *Templum Amicitiae: Essays on the Second Temple Presented to Ernst Bammel,* ed. W. Horbury, Journal for the Study of the New Testament Supplement Series 48 (Sheffield: JSOT, 1991): 357–62.

8. See Barrett, "Attitudes to the Temple," 359–60.

9. See C. K. Barrett, "Paul's Speech on the Areopagus," in *New Testament Christianity for Africa and the World: Essays in Honour of Harry Sawyerr,* ed. M. E. Glasswell and E. W. Fasholé-Luke (London: SPCK, 1974), 72–77.

10. See C. K. Barrett, "The Eschatology of the Epistle to the Hebrews," in *The Background of the New Testament and Its Eschatology: In Honour of C. H. Dodd,* ed. W. D. Davies and D. Daube (Cambridge: Cambridge University Press, 1956), 363–93.
11. It renders *bĕ'ahărît hayyāmîm.*
12. See Hebrews 4:2, 12.
13. The use of the word *logos,* especially in the Prologue, for audibility; for visibility, 14:9.
14. Notably, Hermas, *Similitude* 9.12.7–8.
15. See Hippolytus, *Philosophumena* 9.13.
16. Justin Martyr, *Trypho* 76, 126; Hebrew, *pele' yō 'ēṣ.* See also *1 Apology* 63; *Trypho* 56, 58, 59.
17. For the background of this, see especially C. Rowland, *The Open Heaven: A Study of Apocalyptic in Judaism and Early Christianity* (New York: Crossroad, 1982).
18. Psalms 8 and 110 are similarly combined in 1 Cor. 15:25, 27.
19. It would be possible to translate the words *brachu ti,* "a little (lower)," but this is less suitable to the context.
20. However the "seed of Abraham" may be constituted. Cf. Galatians 3:29.
21. On this, see O. Hofius, *Katapausis: Die Vorstellung vom endzeitlichen Ruheort im Hebräerbrief,* Wissenschaftliche Untersuchungen zum Neuen Testament 11 (Tübingen: J. C. B. Mohr [Paul Siebeck], 1970).
22. There seems to be no difference in Hebrews between "priest" and "high priest." The use of *priest* is probably dependent on the Melchizedek passage in Psalm 110.
23. Compare *Aboth* 1.2; also Romans 9:4.
24. J. L. Leuba, *L'Institution et l'Événement* (Paris, Neuchâtel, 1950). Unfortunately, the author offers no discussion of Hebrews in this important book.
25. See Barrett, "Eschatology of the Epistle to the Hebrews," 363–93. See also *Scottish Journal of Theology* 6 (1953): 136–55, 225–43.
26. We may recall once more Stephen's criticism of the temple.
27. The Hebrew text differs: *'oznayîm kārîtā lî* for LXX *ōtia de katērtisō moi.* So Rahlfs, but for *ōtia* (G a), B S A have *sōma.* There can be little doubt that our author found *sōma* in his text.
28. Our author finds no use for the scapegoat, sent away bearing sins to Azazel. He does not freely create doctrine by allegorizing the Old Testament text; priority is with doctrine.
29. Plato, *Republic* 7.514a–517a.

CHRISTOLOGY OF JAMES

John Reumann

To be assigned the epistle of James in a book on Christology is a bit like the task several Catholic friends undertook, after Vatican II, to honor a colleague on his appointment to a traditional office. They presented him with a monograph on "The Scriptural Origins of the Office of Domestic Prelate"—an elegant title page and ninety-eight blank sheets!

The problem for this chapter is the paucity of obvious references in the primary document. Jack Dean Kingsbury's stock-in-trade excellencies on narrative features—plot, characters, and so forth—do not match well with this grab bag of paraenetic topics, a Jacobean *Stromata,* where, as Martin Luther put it, "One minute he talks of clothes, the next of anger."

The title of this book recalls for me one published some thirty years ago by the Division for Theological Studies of the Lutheran Council in the U.S.A., *Who Can This Be?*[1] In those days of bright hopes for Lutheran unity, ecumenism, and emergence of many a wunderkind out of the Lutheran Church–Missouri Synod, this rather popularly written résumé on Christology caused a storm of protest in the Missouri Synod. It is a reminder that biblical theologians must expect battles. James waxed vehement on the responsibility of teachers, the tongue, and truth in society and world.[2] Perhaps 4:4, "friendship with the world is enmity with God," poses most sharply "the fundamental choice."[3] Life is a struggle but also offers occasions like this to salute a colleague.

Of all the matters of introduction and research that we might discuss here,[4] we must note two. First, the shift from an early date and Palestinian origin has continued, in favor of a later date and diaspora setting. Scholars now most often cite Hellenistic sources, not Semitic ones, to explain details.[5]

In the history of interpretation,[6] the second matter of introduction and research is this: Students of James single out Luther not only as significant but unfortunately as influential. Johnson manages to pin on Luther what (to him) is the pejorative label of "historical-critical"[7]—perhaps prematurely, depending on how we define and date "historical criticism." A careful reading of the quoted material will show that humanists like Erasmus and catholics like Cajetanus shared most of Luther's opinions on the origins of James. Indeed, much of Luther's criticism about content had been voiced by others long before 1520. Luther's theological principle did not, surprisingly, have to do with justification but with Christology. Built on straw, not silver or gold (cf. 1 Cor. 3:12), the epistle of James simply does not placard Christ before us (Gal 3:1).

That tin can tied to the tail of James has echoed over the centuries. Still, in German ecumenical scholarship, new notes have been heard, reopening the Christology question. This is evident, for example, in the commentary of Franz Mussner[8] and in articles by Martin Karrer[9] and Christof Burchard,[10] as Hubert Frankemölle[11] has pointed out. But what kind of Christology, and on what basis?

THE LIMITED CHRISTOLOGICAL DATA IN JAMES

The following passages have, to one degree or another, been claimed over the years as teaching on the work and person of Christ. It is possible to maximize or minimize each one. Some of the clearest instances have been called interpolations into an originally Jewish document; but if so, they are the more important for the final text. I will discuss passages in the sequence in which a reader of the canonical document encounters them, even if that requires occasional cross-referencing.

James 1:1 ("James, a servant of God and of *the Lord Jesus Christ [theou kai kyriou Iēsou Christou doulos].*")

Servant (better, *slave*) is also used at Romans 1:1, Titus 1:1, Philippians 1:1 (plural), and by Jude and 2 Peter. In three of these instances the *intitulatio* continues with the words "of Jesus Christ" or "of Christ Jesus." In all these instances, *Christos* is probably a name rather than a title. The title *kyrios* ("Lord") appears here only in all these salutations. In James, *kyrios* can be used of God[12] or of Jesus[13] (so Joseph Fitzmyer, who traces early Christian development of the title, especially in light of use in the Dead Sea Scrolls of *mareh,* as well as *kyrios* in Greek, for Yahweh).[14]

Those who have argued for a Jewish *Vorlage* wish to excise *kai kyriou*

Iēsou Christou ("and the Lord Jesus Christ"), but there is no manuscript evidence for such omissions, and today the full description is generally read.[15] François Vouga heightened James's Christology by interpreting "servant of Jesus Christ, God and Lord."[16] He cites in support of this 1:27 (where NRSV's "before God, the Father" is literally *toi theoi kai patri*) and 3:9 ("the Lord and Father"), plus Pseudo-Andrew of Crete. Johnson terms it "forced"[17] (similarly Burchard).[18] Calling Jesus "God" is rare in the New Testament. But Johnson adds, "The Greeting . . . works effectively to construct a compositional world"; it "also deftly sketches the symbolic world shared by the implied readers and author." This world, from the outset of the letter, is that of "God and the Lord Jesus Christ."[19] Burchard adds "exalted Lord," since the author makes no connection with the earthly Lord Jesus.[20]

> *James 1:18* ("In fulfillment of his own purpose [the Father of lights]
> gave us *birth by the word of truth,* so that we would become a
> kind of first fruits of his creatures.")

Is this statement about the divine initiative in the (new) birth a christological reference, akin to 1 Peter 1:23 ("You have been born anew . . . through the living and enduring word of God")? The first hurdle is whether the "birth" that is mentioned refers to Christian baptism,[21] to creation,[22] or to the formation of Israel.[23] Martin Dibelius (as revised by H. Greeven) opted for the rebirth as "conversion to Christianity"; then the "word of truth" denotes the gospel.[24] If "begetting" means creation, the appeal must be to Philo,[25] not the Old Testament. The context about "the Father of lights" suggests creation, but Sophie Laws allows that "the language of sonship and birth" was at the time of James "so entrenched as the language of Christian conversion that this is inevitably brought to mind."[26] Johnson surfaces all these possibilities[27] and settles on "word of truth" in the sense of the gospel as "most likely" (though *euangelion* never occurs in James): not what God uttered at Genesis 1:26–30 (reflected at James 3:9 in the phrase "the likeness of God"), not Sinai (Ps. 119:43, "word of truth" of the Torah), but the gospel (Col. 1:5 [hope = word of truth = gospel]; Col. 1:27 [*Christ,* the hope of glory]; Eph. 1:13). So the passage is tenuously christological, assuming "word of truth" as a title or symbol for Christ. This word effects regeneration (conversion, perhaps baptism) or may have had a role cosmologically in creation of "us" as first fruits of God's creatures—or both.

> *James 1:21* ("Welcome with meekness *the implanted word*
> that has the power to save your souls.")

This second example of word/gospel adds a soteriological aspect: power to save people. The word is described as *emphytos,* which here means "implanted" or "deep-rooted"; the Stoic sense of the term as "innate" or "natural" (as a reflection of cosmic Reason) does not fit the context. Johnson, who couples "power" with Romans 1:16, "saving" with 1 Corinthians 1:18, and "word" and "power" with 2 Corinthians 6:7, speaks of how passages in James "emphatically assert the *extra nos* character of salvation."[28] The verse is christological to the extent that "word" and "gospel" are. Sophie Laws buttresses the point by appeal to the way in which James 1:21 (as well as 1:18) and 1 Peter 1:23–2:2 "are strikingly similar in sequence and language": birth by the word, renunciation of wickedness, and a deep interest in the call to live the life of the word. First Peter is far more overt about Jesus Christ (2:5–8), but behind both may be baptismal experience. The now almost forgotten works by P. Carrington[29] and E. G. Selwyn[30] made James 1:18, 21 part of the evidence for baptismal paraenesis, along with parallels in clearer passages in Paul or the Catholic epistles (for example, "baptism into [Christ's] death," Rom. 6:4–5).

James 2:1 ("My brothers and sisters, do you with your acts of favoritism really believe in *our glorious Lord Jesus Christ* [NRSV note, 'hold the faith of our glorious Lord Jesus Christ without acts of favoritism']?")

As at 1:1, the title "Lord Jesus Christ" (*kyrios Iēsous Christos*) is used, but this time with the modifiers *hēmōn* (our) and *tēs doxēs* (here rendered "glorious"). The latter genitive, from the noun *glory,* has been variously construed:[31]

1. Some take it as an objective genitive with *pistis* (faith): "faith in the glory of our Lord Jesus Christ." But *tēs doxēs* is separated from *pistin* by five words.

2. Others take it as an objective genitive with *prosōpolēmpsiais* (acts of favoritism): "actions of favoritism which accord with external splendor."[32] But this requires hyperbaton (misplacement of a word instead of natural order)[33] and raises the issue of what the writer intended by such an alteration—an emphasis on *tēs doxēs?*

3. Still others have construed it as a subjective genitive, with *doxa* given its classical sense of "opinion": "acts of favoritism based on opinion" (so Erasmus and Calvin, but followed by no one anymore).[34]

4. It has been taken as a genitive of quality, describing something; but what? Interpreters have argued for "glorious faith in Christ," or "Messiah of Glory" (but can one separate "Christ" from "Jesus"?), or "our Lord, Jesus

Christ the glorious," or "our lord of glory, Jesus Christ" (cf. 1 Cor. 2:8),[35] or, with all five preceding words, "our glorious Lord Jesus Christ" (the NRSV translation cited above).[36] Even given that translation, there are questions. Johnson (who translates the NRSV margin: "the faith of Jesus Christ our glorious Lord") nevertheless takes the latter six words of that phrase as subjective, as a reference to faith that might be attributed to Jesus Christ our glorious Lord. Johnson thus relates the phrase to " 'the faith of Jesus in God as reflected in his teaching' or perhaps 'the faith that is from Jesus Christ,' in the sense 'declared by Jesus.' " But does the Jacobean Jesus speak thus?[37]

5. J. A. Bengel suggests yet another option, taking *tēs doxēs* (glorious) in apposition: "Jesus Christ, the Glory." It becomes a title like "the Truth" or "the Life."[38] Others have taken "glory" at 2:1 as the equivalent of "the Shekinah" in Israel. Thus, Laws explores christological overtones to theophany as "the presence of God."[39] It is this concept of Christ, the Glory, that makes the sort of discrimination described in 2:1–6 so flagrant.[40]

With the NRSV text, I take 2:1 as affirming real belief in the Lord Jesus Christ, who is given the unusual title "the Glory." Burchard[41] suggested that both the glory of Jesus—earthly,[42] exalted,[43] and coming[44]—and glory as a future gift connected with salvation[45] are involved, the latter clearly eschatological.[46]

James 2:7 ("Is it not they who blaspheme *the excellent name* that was invoked over you?")

This verse against "the rich" who "oppress you" and "drag you into court" was brought forth by Dibelius-Greeven as evidence against theories of origin for James as a Jewish document.[47] The "honorable name" (*kalon onoma*) has *not* been invoked over these rich people. If only Jews were involved, rich and poor, then "the name" (of God) would stand over all of them.[48] But here "the name" is that of the Lord Jesus Christ, invoked over the poor at baptism but blasphemed by (Gentile) opponents. This may involve going to court over debts and property issues, slander, or persecution over religion.[49] Disputes between baptized slaves and heads of households might be in the picture. As Laws states, "The name of Jesus has replaced the name of Yahweh." Dibelius-Greeven takes all this as evidence that James "originated in Christian circles,"[50] with, we may add, a certain amount of expressed "name christology."[51]

James 2:14–26 (On Faith and Works)

It can be argued that this section of the epistle "is not conceivable prior to Paul" and so "is a sign of Christian formulation."[52] The passage, however, is about not Christology but "faith" (as more than intellectual belief in monotheism) and "works" (not "works of the law" as in Paul).[53] James writes to correct what Paulinists have wrongly concluded from the apostle's teaching. The absence of Paul's phrase *pistis Iēsou Christou* ("faith in Jesus Christ") is striking.

James 5:6 ("You have condemned and murdered *the righteous one*, who does not resist you.")

In this scathing attack on the rich who live in luxury but exploit the laborers in their fields, the climax comes in their martyring "the righteous one" (*ton dikaion*). Is there a reference—it would be the only one in James—to the death of Jesus?[54] The initial background seems to be that of "the righteous sufferer" in Old Testament and Jewish thought.[55] Others have seen "the Christian righteous," specifically Stephen (Acts 7) and James the brother of the Lord.[56] Frankemölle,[57] building on the tradition of the brother of Jesus as "James the just,"[58] argues (in light of the combination of individual and collective in "the righteous sufferer" tradition) that the reference at 5:6 would have been understood by readers to be the author referred to in 1:1. Mussner[59] felt Jesus was "not to be excluded," and the church fathers often took 5:6 christologically.[60] But many interpreters have come to Mayor's more cautious judgment: The reference is generic or a "representative figure,"[61] not Christ.[62]

The last clause ("who does not resist you" in NRSV) has sometimes been taken as a clue that Christ is meant.[63] Others would punctuate it as a question ("Does he not resist you?")[64] and so refer it to the vengeance of the Just One par excellence;[65] thus Johnson, who supplies "God" as the subject.[66] But little of this encourages support of a christological interpretation of "the righteous one."

James 5:7–11 ("Be patient, therefore, beloved, until *the coming of the Lord.* . . . Strengthen your hearts, for *the coming of the Lord* is near. . . . See, *the Judge* is standing at the doors! . . . You have heard of the endurance of Job, and you have seen *the purpose of the Lord* [*to telos kyriou*], how *the Lord* is compassionate and merciful.")

While *kyrios* can be used of God,[67] *parousia* (coming) was so consistently used of Christ's future coming that most interpreters give the first two uses of the word here (in verses 7 and 8) a christological reference.[68] Feuillet[69] attempted to see here[70] an appearance of Christ for "a *historical* judgment of the Jewish people"[71] who mistreat the poor and who murdered Jesus. This is very doubtful—the destruction of Jerusalem in 70 C.E. was not "the end of the age"![72]

The verb *ēggiken* ("is near") in verse 8 strengthens the eschatological sense.[73] But how near is the Parousia? Its nature is that Jesus comes as the Judge.[74] Burchard's exegesis[75] focuses on the "until" clauses in verse 7: "until the parousia . . . until (the earth or the farmer) receives the early and the late rains." That a half year is involved between the two rainy seasons does not fit the "suddenness" associated with the Parousia. Instead, a "sowing–harvesting" sequence of fruits is involved:[76] The reference is to future blessings from heaven, for the righteous. On this reading, Jesus may also be viewed as the Lord who will grant glory (2:1), the "crown of life" (1:12, where NRSV supplies "Lord"), "the kingdom" (2:5), and so forth. But Frankemölle[77] reads all this as applying to God, not to Christ; the "purpose (*telos*) of the Lord" in verse 11 is not the death of Jesus (Augustine, Bede) or his parousia but has a "theocentric context."[78] Likewise with the reference to the Lord as "compassionate and merciful": Taking this as descriptive of Jesus is "out of the question."[79] Karrer saw "mercy" (v. 11) shaping the word's power to save.

In my opinion, the relatively clear references to Jesus' parousia in 5:7 and 5:8 and to his role as judge in 5:9 cast a christological possibility over 5:6 (discussed above) and 5:11 as well, though few are committed on this.

James 5:14–15 ("They should call for the elders of the church and have
  them pray over them, anointing them with oil *in the name of the Lord.*
The prayer of faith will save the sick, and *the Lord* will raise them up.")

While references to the *kyrios* in this section on anointing with oil can be referred to God,[80] a reference to Christ has been understood by many.[81] Frankemölle,[82] recalling his excurses on "Anthropologie und Theologie"[83] and "Christologie,"[84] terms the "God or Christ debate" in James a false alternative. The verse expresses "name" theology (compare 2:7, above). There are ample Gospel stories about Jesus as the agent in raising a person from a sickbed,[85] and Acts 3:16 and 4:10–12 connect later raisings with Jesus' being "raised up." The "prayer of faith" in verse 15 could then be to Jesus (as agent? compare Acts 4:30). The passage suggests the Lord Jesus' present activity in contrast to future gifts.[86]

Teaching Material from Jesus in James

The amount of material in James that parallels the teaching of Jesus is extensive, more than in "any other book in the New Testament apart from the

Gospels."[87] See, for example, 1:5 (Matt. 7:7); 1:22–25 (Matt. 7:24–27); 5:12 (compare Matt. 5:33–37).[88] For our interests, two points stand out: None of the "Jesus material" makes christological claims, and never is it actually attributed to Jesus. What seems *to us* to come from Jesus is presented, like other topics, as *teaching of the letter and its author*. Never does "Jesus said" occur, as in the *Gospel of Thomas,* nor is there any narrative about Jesus or any Son of man sayings, as in Q. Teaching is important, but nothing is earmarked as coming from Jesus the teacher. One cannot claim for James even the sort of Christology to be seen in *Thomas* or reconstructed for Q.

WHAT KIND OF CHRISTOLOGY?

The evidence above finds Jesus Christ in James to be exalted Lord and "Glory" (1:1; 2:1), reigning over us (in a community with teachers, elders, assemblies). By a "word of truth" (1:18) and the "implanted word" (1:21), birth is brought about among the "first fruits" of God's creatures, the word having power to save.[89] His "excellent name" was invoked over those converted (2:7, baptism?), and in this Lord's name prayers are offered for the sick, whom the Lord will raise up (5:14–15). The Parousia of the Lord as the Judge (5:7–9) points to fruits as blessings to be given to the righteous faithful. Perhaps all this allows a reference to the Lord's death as righteous one or as a judge who opposes rich exploiters (5:6).

James demands we rethink our categories of Christology. His is not a "kerygmatic Christology" about the meaning of Jesus' death and resurrection. Nor does it allow a "salvation history" view; even if creation is included (1:18) and the terminus is the Parousia, the letter indicates little of events in history. If for Paul "justification" was his "functional Christology," the same cannot be said of James, for what 2:14–26 says about believing God and being reckoned righteous is not connected with Christ.

We cannot claim that James is christologically deficient because Spirit-centered and enthusiast.[90] God is emphasized, but even Morris, who is normally very strong on seeing the Deity in New Testament writers, finds relatively little to point out.[91] Clearly, what James presents is in the wisdom mode. But Jesus is not Sophia. James has come into new prominence nowadays because of the social-ethical concerns voiced for the poor, though without Jesus as Liberator. James saw the Lord as shaping faith and ethical activity in his people in the testing ground of the world.

Where and why such a Christology grew up scholars are wary to say. That it was long around is hard to establish. But what we can grasp of this

Christology in its single literary monument reminds us of how varied are the images that Jesus Christ has cast, and indeed had cast already in the first century.

NOTES

1. *Who Can This Be?* (New York: Division for Theological Studies of the Lutheran Council in the U.S.A., 1968).
2. James 3:1–12; 5:1–6.
3. Luke Timothy Johnson, *The Letter of James,* Anchor Bible 37A (New York: Doubleday, 1995), 205.
4. John Reumann, *Variety and Unity in New Testament Thought,* Oxford Bible Series (New York: Oxford University Press, 1991), 189–202, commentaries cited on 304.
5. Johnson in *Letter of James* uses Greco-Roman hortatory literature. Note also that Christof Burchard and others take 5:7, "the early and the late rains," long regarded as a sign of Palestinian provenance, as early and later fruits. See Christof Burchard, "Zu einigen chistologischen Stellen des Jakobusbriefes," in *Anfänge der Christologie: Festschrift für Ferdinand Hahn zum 65. Geburtstag,* ed. Cilliers Breytenbach and Henning Paulsen (Göttingen: Vandenhoeck & Ruprecht, 1991), 361–62.
6. Johnson, *Letter of James,* 124–61; Hubert Frankemölle, *Der Brief des Jakobus. Ökumenischer Taschenbuchkommentar zum Neuen Testament,* vols. 17, nos. 1, 2 (Gütersloh: Gütersloher Verlagshaus Gerd Mohn; Würzburg: Echter, 1994), 93–118.
7. Johnson, *Letter of James,* 124–26, 140–43.
8. Franz Mussner, *Der Jakobusbrief. Herders theologischer Kommentar zum Neuen Testament,* ed. Alfred Wikenhauser and Anton Vögtle, vol. 13, no. 1, 3d ed. (Freiburg: Herder, 1975), 250–54.
9. M. Karrer, "Christus der Herr und die Welt als Stätte der Prüfung. Zur Theologie des Jakobusbrief," *Kerygma und Dogma* 35 (1989): 166–88.
10. Burchard, "Zu einigen christologischen Stellen."
11. Frankemölle, *Der Brief des Jakobus,* 376–87.
12. James 3:9; 4:10, 15; 5:4, 11a, b.
13. James 1:1, 7; 2:1; 5:7, 8, 14, 15.
14. Joseph Fitzmyer, *"Kyrios,"* in *Exegetical Dictionary of the New Testament,* ed. Horst Balz and Gerhard Schneider, vol. 2 (Grand Rapids: Wm. B. Eerdmans Publishing Co., 1981), 330–31.
15. Martin Dibelius, *James,* rev. H. Greeven, trans. M. A. Williams, Hermeneia (Philadelphia: Fortress Press, 1976), 66 (author hereafter given as Dibelius-Greeven); Johnson, *Letter of James,* 168.
16. François Vouga, *L'Épître de Saint Jacques,* Commentaire du Nouveau Testament, deuxiéme série 13a (Geneva: Labor et Fides, 1984), 35.

17. Johnson, *Letter of James,* 168.
18. Burchard, "Zu einigen christologischen Stellen," 359.
19. Johnson, *Letter of James,* 171.
20. Burchard, "Zu einigen christologischen Stellen," 360.
21. So Bede. Regeneration in Joseph B. Mayor, *The Epistle of James* (London: Macmillan & Co., 1897), 59.
22. This is primary in Sophie Laws, *The Epistle of James,* Harper's New Testament Commentaries (San Francisco: Harper & Row, 1980), 75–78.
23. Hosea 11:1; Deuteronomy 32:18.
24. Dibelius-Greeven, *James,* 105.
25. Philo, *De Ebviatate,* 30.
26. Laws, *Epistle of James,* 78.
27. Johnson, *Letter of James,* 197–98, 205.
28. Ibid., 202.
29. P. Carrington, *The Primitive Christian Catechism* (New York: Cambridge University Press, 1940).
30. E. G. Selwyn, *The First Epistle of St. Peter* (London: Macmillan Co., 1946), 363–466, esp. 388.
31. Burchard, "Lu einigen christologischen Stellen," 354–59.
32. Michaelis, cited in Mayor, *Epistle of James,* 76.
33. Friedrich Blass, *A Greek Grammar of the New Testament and Other Early Christian Literature,* rev. Albert Debrunner, ed. and trans. Robert Funk (Chicago: University of Chicago Press, 1961), 447, 1.
34. Burchard, "Zu einigen christologischen Stellen," 356, n. 16.
35. Ceslas Spicq, *Theological Lexicon of the New Testament,* ed. and trans. James D. Ernest (Peabody, Mass.: Hendrickson, 1994), 1:370n. 49.
36. So Dibelius-Greeven, *James,* 128. Details in Mayor, *Epistle of James,* 76–77.
37. See comments on the teaching material of Jesus, below.
38. *D. Joh. Alberti Bengeli Gnomon Novi Testamentum,* 3rd ed., 2 vols. (Tübingen: L. F. Fues, 1850), 2.492. Compare Ephesians 1:17 ("the Father of glory"); Colossians 1:27; 1 Peter 4:14; and 2 Peter 1:17, God as Majestic Glory.
39. Laws, *Epistle of James,* 94–97.
40. Mayor, *Epistle of James,* 77–79; Laws, *Epistle of James.*
41. Burchard, "Zu einigen christologischen Stellen," 358.
42. John 1:14; 2 Peter 1:17.
43. Luke 24:26; 2 Cor. 4:4, 6.
44. Mark 10:37; 13:26.
45. See on James 5:7–8, below.
46. An object of faith and hope, as in Colossians 1:27 and Hebrews 6:12; 11:1.
47. Dibelius-Greeven, *James,* 23.
48. Deuteronomy 28:10; Isaiah 43:7; 2 Chronicles 7:14.
49. Laws, *Epistle of James,* 105–6.

50. Dibelius-Greeven, *James*, 141.
51. Burchard, "Zu einigen christologischen Stellen," 363–64, with "name of God" as possible background.
52. Dibelius-Greeven, *James*, 23; compare 174–80.
53. For fuller treatment, see John Reumann, "Righteousness, New Testament," *Anchor Bible Dictionary*, ed. David Noel Freedman (New York: Doubleday), 5: 745–73, esp. 769.
54. Cf. Mayor, *Epistle of James*, 155.
55. Isaiah 3:10; Amos 5:12; Psalm 37:14, 32; esp. Wisdom of Solomon 2:12, 20.
56. Josephus, *Antiquities* 20.200 = 20.9.1, assuming pseudonymity; Dibelius-Greeven, *James*, 240n. 58.
57. Frankemölle, *Der Brief des Jakobus*, 663–66.
58. For example, Hippolytus in Eusebius 2.23.4, 7.
59. Mussner, *Jakobusbrief*, 199.
60. Oecumenicus, Cassiodorus, Bede. Compare Matthew 27:4; 1 Peter 3:14. On the title, see Laws, *Epistle of James*, 205–6.
61. Laws, *Epistle of James*, 205; Johnson, *Letter of James*, 304.
62. Burchard, "Zu einigen christologischen Stellen," 354n. 5.
63. Compare Acts 8:32–35 = Isaiah 53:7–8; 1 Peter 2:21–25.
64. So Brooke Foss Westcott and Fenton Hort.
65. A. Feuillet, "Le Sens du mot Parousie dans l'évangile de Matthieu. Comparaison entre Matth. xxiv et Jac. v. 1–11," in *The Background of the New Testament and Its Eschatology: In Honor of C. H. Dodd*, ed. W. D. Davies and D. Daube (New York: Cambridge, 1954), 276.
66. Johnson, *Letter of James*, 305.
67. See comments on 1:1, above; 5:4; cf. 2:5, 5:10–11.
68. So Leon Morris, *New Testament Theology* (Grand Rapids: Zondervan, 1986), 312; Burchard, "Zu einigen christologischen Stellen," 360n. 36; Frankemölle, *Der Brief des Jakobus*, 679.
69. Feuillet, "Les Sens du mot Parousie," 272–78.
70. Also in Matthew 24:3, 27, 37–39, in contrast to "the end of the age."
71. Feuillet, "Le Sens du mot Parousie," 278.
72. Dibelius-Greeven, *James*, 243n. 5; compare J. D. Kingsbury, *Matthew: Structure, Christology, Kingdom* (Philadelphia: Fortress Press, 1975), 29n. 119.
73. Laws, *Epistle of James*, 209–10.
74. Johnson, *Letter of James*, 313–14, admitting that this strengthens the case of a reference to Jesus in 5:6.
75. Burchard, "Zu einigen christologischen Stellen," 360–62.
76. Frankemölle, *Der Brief des Jakobus*, 681.
77. Ibid., 685–704.
78. Ibid., 695.
79. Dibelius-Greeven, *James*, 247; Burchard, "Zu einigen christologischen Stellen," 354n. 5.

80. Compare 5:10; Frankemölle, *Der Brief des Jakobus*, 711.
81. Mayor, *Epistle of James*, 168; Dibelius-Greeven, *James*, 253; Laws, *Epistle of James*, 228. Compare Mark 6:13 (disciples anoint with oil); 16:17; Luke 10:17; Acts 3:6, 16; 4:10; 16:18.
82. Frankemölle, *Der Brief des Jakobus*, 711–13.
83. Ibid., 305–20.
84. Ibid., 376–87.
85. Mark 1:31; 2:9; 3:3; 9:27; Luke 5:23–24; Acts 3:7; 9:34, 41.
86. Burchard, "Zu einigen christologischen Stellen," 364 and n. 61
87. Morris, *New Testament Theology*, 312n. 1.
88. See Reumann, *Variety and Unity*, 191–92; Mayor, *Epistle of James*, lxxxiv–lxxxvi; F. Mussner, "'Direkte' und 'indirekte' Christologie im Jakobusbrief," *Catholica* 24 (1970): 111–17. Johnson, *Letter of James*, 55–58; Andrew Chester, "The Theology of James," in *The Theology of the Letters of James, Peter, and Jude*, New Testament Theology (New York: Cambridge University Press, 1994), 5–8; Klaus Berger, *Theologiegeschichte des Urchristentums: Theologie des Neuen Testament*, 2d ed. (Tübingen and Basel: Francke, 1995), 191–92.
89. Berger, *Theologiegeschichte*, 192–93, sees here a Johannine sense.
90. Laws, *Epistle of James*, 33. The prophets mentioned are figures of the past.
91. Morris, *New Testament Theology*, 312–13.

THE CHRISTOLOGY OF 1 PETER: SOME REFLECTIONS

Paul J. Achtemeier

It is a pleasure and privilege to pay tribute to my colleague of more than two decades and my friend of more than three on the occasion of his sixty-fifth birthday. I acknowledge by this chapter the high esteem in which I hold him as friend, colleague, and scholar and pay tribute to his many contributions to the better theological understanding of the New Testament, particularly the Gospels.

I

As in most New Testament letters, the Christology of 1 Peter is better conceived as a series of images than as a coherent disquisition on the nature of Christ.[1] With one or two exceptions, its Christology is quite routine, which is not surprising considering that the letter reflects so many early Christian traditions. The presence of such traditions led a number of scholars in decades past to propose that 1 Peter was an adaptation of an original baptismal homily, turned into a letter with the addition of a letter opening and the material after 4:11. More recent studies, however, have concluded that the letter is in fact a literary unity,[2] and that such references to baptism as are present are the result—as they are, for example in Romans 6—of the content of the discussion and the use of early traditions to make the point in that discussion.[3]

The general outline of New Testament Christology is also evident in this letter. The Christ who, though innocent of any sin (1:19b) or political offense, suffered (2:21) and died (2:24) on the cross;[4] was subsequently raised from the dead by God (1:21; 2:3; 3:21b; compare 2:4); and ascended into heaven to assume a position of power at God's right hand after all other powers were subjected to him (3:22)—all this is in accordance with God's plan established before the creation of the world (1:20). All is exploited, as in other early traditions, to make the point that Christ's death was for our sins (3:18), his resurrection for our salvation (1:21),[5] and his ascension to God's right hand the guarantee of our eventual deliverance from the evil forces operating within this present sinful world (4:13; 5:10; compare 5:6).

The author of 1 Peter uses a number of figures to illustrate these christological points, and a cursory examination of them will point us to one of the major characteristics of the letter and thus of its Christology. One way in which the author chooses to speak of the benefit of Christ's innocent suffering and crucifixion for sinful human beings, itself a commonplace of early Christian tradition (Acts 20:28; Rom. 3:24–25; Eph. 1:7; Heb. 9:12), is to speak of that death in terms of the redemptive significance of a sacrificial "lamb without spot or blemish." Such a figure, drawn evidently from the cultic language of Israel,[6] points to the background out of which our author is operating, namely, that of Israel as God's chosen people rather than that of Greco-Roman cultic ideas. The assumption underlying such a reference, neither identified explicitly nor given further explanation, is all the more remarkable since the readers were almost certainly not Jewish Christians but people who had a pagan background, a point evident from the language of 1:18–19, which indicates their redemption was from a formerly pagan rather than Jewish lifestyle.[7] It points to a substantial characteristic of this letter, to which we must return in more detail below.

The same derivation holds for one of the figures the author uses to describe the risen Christ, namely, that of "living stone" (2:4). As the subsequent verses show (vv. 6–8) and as the author explicitly states ("it stands in scripture," v. 6), that figure of a stone precious in God's sight though rejected by human beings is drawn from Isaiah (8:14; 28:16) and from LXX Psalm 117:22. While these verses are also used by Paul in Romans 9:33 and by Matthew in 21:42, thus indicating that the figure of a stone was already a part of Christian tradition, the author's reference to "scripture" at the beginning of their citation indicates that if he is drawing on early Christian tradition, he is aware that the material does come from the sacred writings of the Jewish people. The author's awareness and deliberate use of Hebrew scripture is thus evident.

That Christ is the reigning Lord whose return will benefit those who are faithful to him is described, in addition to more traditional language (3:22;

4:13), by means of the rare term *chief shepherd* (*archipoimēn;* e.g., 5:4).[8] The earlier reference to Christ as "shepherd" in 2:25 shows that this concept belonged to the regular christological terminology of our author, and its further derivation from the Hebrew scriptures, where "shepherd" is a regular designation for God,[9] indicates not only the source for such a figure but also the willingness of our author to apply to Jesus a term usually applied to God. While there is obviously no indication here of later Trinitarian thought, the author's willingness to do this points to the inevitability of the kind of reflection that became sedimented in the later Trinitarian confessions.

II

While 1 Peter thus shares in the general christological approach and outlook of the New Testament, other aspects of this letter and its view of Christ are singular and more characteristic of its own outlook than of the larger outlook of early Christian traditions. To gain a perspective on that singular outlook, it is necessary to take a closer and more detailed look at the role played in the thought and language of 1 Peter by the language and traditions of Hebrew scripture.

In common with the rest of the New Testament, 1 Peter draws significantly on the Old Testament for the language and concepts it uses to describe the Christian community. From the kind of figures used to describe Jesus and his career, discussed above; to such passing references as the one to Sarah, who is understood as the model for a Christian wife (3:6), and the word *flock* to describe the local congregation (5:2); to its more extensive use of verses from Isaiah 53 to describe Jesus' suffering and death on the cross (2:22, 24–25) and its use of Psalm 34 to describe conduct within the community of faith (3:10–12), 1 Peter displays its reliance on Old Testament traditions.[10]

Such common reliance on Old Testament figures and concepts does not exhaust the way in which the author of 1 Peter has taken over the language of Israel. More than seeing in Israel the forerunner of or even the model for the nascent Christian community as chosen people, our author has, in a way singular among Christian canonical writings, appropriated without remainder the language of Israel for the church.[11] That appropriation has occurred in such a way that Israel in its totality has become for this letter virtually synonymous in the author's mind with the Christian communities to which he is writing. Israel has become in 1 Peter, one may say, the controlling metaphor in terms of which not only its Christology but indeed its entire theology is expressed.

A comparison with Paul will make the point more vivid. In his appropriation of various Old Testament traditions and passages of scripture, Paul finds a continuing place for Israel in God's plan of salvation. Indeed, so important is that question for Paul that he makes it thematic for major segments of his letter to the Christians in Rome (chapters 4, 9—11). First Peter, in contrast, makes no specific reference to Israel or its history; for example, there is no discussion of the place of the Jewish law in the life of the Christians. Indeed, the word for "law" (*nomos*) does not even occur in 1 Peter. No references whatsoever appear to Israel as an independent entity or even as an elect people, either before or after the appearance of Jesus of Nazareth. While covenantal language does occur (*dikaiosynē*), the word for "covenant" (*diathēkē*) does not, so that there is no hint of Israel understood as the forerunner to a more perfect covenant realized through Jesus Christ, as is the case in Hebrews.[12]

In sum, in 1 Peter the language and reality of Israel pass without remainder into the language and therefore the reality of the Christian community, who now constitute the new people of God.[13] What this means is that the language of Israel is foundational and constitutive for the Christian community. It therefore functions as something far more than illustrative, a point that has not always been acknowledged by those scholars who have studied this epistle.[14]

The significance for this appropriation of the language of Israel for the Christian community is indicated in 2:9–10, verses that conclude the body opening of 1 Peter.[15] After explaining the foundation of the Christian community in terms of Christ as the living stone, framed in terms of passages from Isaiah and the Psalms, the author turns to a concluding description of the Christian community. In what can only be seen as a programmatic statement, that community is described in terms taken from the Old Testament that there described the unique role Israel understood itself to have in its relationship to God and the role it was given to play in God's redemptive plan.

The first term, *elect generation* (*genos eklekton*), drawn from Isaiah 43:20, points to the unique covenant relationship between God and Israel. The second term, *royal priesthood* (*basileion hierateuma*), drawn from Exodus 19:6; 23:22, again within the context of the covenant, points to the mediatorial role Israel was to play in God's dealings with the other peoples. The third term, *holy nation* (*ethnos hagion*), taken from Isaiah 43:21, points to the ethical responsibility that goes with being God's chosen people and is thus exploited elsewhere in 1 Peter (1:14–17). The final term, *people for peculiar possession* (*laos eis peripoiēsin*), once more drawn from Isaiah 43:21, serves as a summary to describe the unique relationship between Israel and God in its all encompassing ramifications. In that way, our author understands the election of Israel to have passed without remainder into the Christian community, and language appropriate to a description of Israel in the past has now been appropriated to describe the new chosen people, those chosen in Christ who is himself the elect and precious cornerstone.

The next verse, 2:10, a quotation from Hosea 2:23 (MT 2:25; see also Hos. 1:6, 9; 2:3) originally used by the prophet to describe the reconstitution of Israel into a renewed people of God, is here applied to the Christian community. This verse from Hosea is also used by Paul in Romans 9:25, where again it is used to demonstrate the inclusion of Gentiles in the people of God, but there at least it appears within the context of a discussion of Israel as the historic people of God. No such reference to Israel appears here, where the verse is applied exclusively to the new people of God. Thus 1 Peter 2:10 makes explicit what had surely been implied in 2:9, namely, that those who now make up the Christian community are called to play the role of God's people that was once played by Israel. This does not mean Jews are to be excluded from God's new people; there is no anti-Semitism evident in this letter.[16] But it does mean that the role Israel once played has now been assumed without remainder by this new people of God.[17]

III

Such a position vis-à-vis Israel poses a further question: On what basis did the author of 1 Peter feel justified in so appropriating the language of Israel for the new community based on Christ? The answer to that question lies in the verses that conclude the *prooumium* (introduction) of the letter, namely, 1:10–12. It is there that our author's understanding of the nature and origin of the Old Testament materials comes clear. The immediate purpose of 1:10–12 is to show that the salvation which the Christians await is truly based on the intention of God as revealed in Christ, since that intention was announced by the prophets.

That prophetic oracles spoke about end times is not a Christian invention; it was already a familiar theme in Jewish apocalyptic writings. The phrase "searched and inquired" (1:10; *exedzētēsan kai exēreunēsai*) reflects 1 Maccabees 9:26. The prophetic desire to know the time of God's salvation (1:11; *tina hē poion kairon*) is also familiar in apocalyptic speculation (Dan. 12:6–13; 2 Esd. 4:33–5:13; 1QpHab)[18] and is contained in a saying of Jesus

(Matt. 13:17; Luke 10:24).[19] The idea that the point of what was said by the prophets had a significance not only for their contemporaries but also for Christians (1:12) is reflected in Paul (Rom. 4:23–24; 15:41; 1 Cor. 9:10; 10:11). To what the "grace" mentioned in 1:10 is specifically intended to refer—whether to the admission of Gentiles into the Christian community or not—is not clear.[20] What is clear is that the passage points to the continuity of God's purpose, and hence to the unity contained in the witness of the Old Testament and the Christian community.[21]

The same line of argument is continued in 1:11, but a variety of problems obscure the specific intention of the verse. Among those problems, and their suggested resolutions, are the following: (1) The phrase *tina hē poion kairon* is probably to be rendered "which or what kind of time"[22] rather than "what person or time."[23] (2) The verb *edēlou* ("was indicating") is probably to be construed with *eis tina . . .* as its object[24] rather than *ta eis christon . . . doxas.*[25] (3) In the phrase *pneuma christou,* the latter word is probably to be understood as epexegetical ("the Spirit that was Christ")[26] rather than as an objective genitive ("the Spirit that informed about Christ").[27] (4) The phrase *ta eis christon kathēmata* is probably to be understood as "the suffering to be visited upon Christ" (compare the parallel *tēs eis hymas choritos* ["the grace coming to you"] in 1:10), and hence as referring to Christ's passion[28] rather than as "the suffering for Christ," in which case it would refer to the suffering of those who followed Christ.[29] (5) In the author's mind, "Christ" here probably refers to Jesus of Nazareth[30] rather than to "messiah" in a more general sense,[31] since the next word, *doxas* (glories), appears to refer to Christ's resurrection and exaltation (compare Luke 24:26).[32] By way of summary, I argue that in this verse our author intends to convey that the prophets, illumined by Christ's Spirit, in fact witnessed beforehand (*promartyromenon*) to the passion of Jesus of Nazareth.

The final verse in our passage, 1:12, continues to comment on the function and importance of those prophets. Once more, the point is emphasized that the prophets' purpose can be fully known only in terms of the events surrounding Jesus of Nazareth. Such emphasis occurs in two ways: The prophets themselves realized their service was for a generation other than their own, and the time to which they pointed was so important that it piqued the interest of the angels. We limit ourselves to a discussion of the first of these two points.[33]

Passages in the Old Testament had already hinted at the fact that the prophets did not serve their own generation,[34] and that idea became a regular feature in Jewish apocalyptic.[35] It is probably from these sources that such an idea passed into the Christian tradition and then found expression both in the Gospels (Matt. 13:17; Luke 10:24; John 8:56; 12:41) and in the epistles (Rom. 4:23–24; 15:4; 1 Cor. 1:9–10; 10:11; Heb. 11:13–16). That is the tradition on which the author of 1 Peter drew in the first part of 1:12. The emphasis on the fact that the divine Spirit lies behind the announcement of the gospel to the Christians has led to the inference that our author had in mind here the Spirit's descent at Pentecost.[36] While one cannot rule out such a reference, since in Acts it underlies the entire Spirit-empowered mission of the early church, it is, I think, doubtful that this was the event our author had primarily in mind.[37] More likely, in my view, is a reference to the fact that those who brought the gospel to the readers of 1 Peter did so at the impulse and with the accompaniment of divine power. Here our author does have the same emphasis on Spirit-empowered proclamation as is typical of Acts. Reference to the Spirit[38] further serves to show that the announcement that the events had taken place had the same divine power behind it as did the foretelling of those events, with the implication that as a result, those events not only are securely in divine hands and reflect the divine intention but also reflect the activity of the preincarnate Christ.

A further problem is associated with the understanding of these verses, namely, the identity of the "prophets" here referred to: Are they to be understood as Old Testament prophets, or does the word refer to prophets who operated within the Christian community? That the prophets referred to here are to be understood in the latter category, that is, as Christian prophets, was argued vigorously by E. G. Selwyn in his commentary on this letter.[39] He based his argument principally on two points.

The first was the use in 1:10 of the verb *edzēreunēsan* (searched), which Selwyn felt implied a search of written scriptures. Yet such activity does not correspond to how Old Testament prophets are described as functioning; nor would it refer to how contemporary Jewish thought understood them. As a result, Selwyn felt that by using such a verb, our author must have intended to refer to Christian prophets who searched the writings of the Old Testament prophets in an attempt to find references there to the gospel about Jesus of Nazareth.[40]

The second piece of evidence to which Selwyn pointed to justify his contention that these were Christian prophets was the phrase *ta eis christon pathēmata* in 1:11, which, in his judgment, could not mean "Christ's suffering" but rather meant "Christward suffering," referring to the "sufferings of the Christward road," which Christian prophets would have announced to the Christians in Asia.[41]

Selwyn's arguments have remained unpersuasive. While (*ex)ereunnaō* can refer to the act of searching scripture (John 5:39; 7:52 = *ereunnaō*), it is also used in LXX Psalm 119:2 (= (*ex*)*ereunnaō*) to describe seeking the testimonies of the Lord, even to seeking out the Lord himself.[42] Further, the phrase *ta tou christou pathēmata* can mean "Christ's suffering," as one can see from the phrase *tēs eis hymas charitos* in 1:10, which has the same structure and which in its context clearly means "the grace coming to you" (that is, "your grace"). All this makes it reasonable to suppose that 1 Peter shared the common early Christian view, reflected in the New Testament, that the Old Testament was prophetic of Christ,[43] and as a result we may see in the reference to the prophets in 1:10 an acknowledgment of the activity of the Hebrew prophets.[44]

IV

If, then, we find in 1 Peter a theological justification for the appropriation of the language of Israel for the Christian community, we would expect that to work itself out in the way in which the author formulates his Christology. I urge that we find just such a formulation in the description of Christ in terms of the figure of the Suffering Servant found in 1 Peter 2:21–25.

It is remarkable how little Isaiah 52:13–53:12, and particularly 53:3–9, was used in early Christian tradition, particularly in relation to accounts of Jesus' passion. Such references to the material as are found tend to be oblique (Mark 10:45; Heb. 9:28)[45] or highly fragmentary (Rom. 4:25a). When a longer portion of Isaiah is quoted, it remains unexploited in relation to the passion of Jesus (Matt. 8:17; Luke 22:37). The fullest citation is found in Acts 8:32–33, and while it is understood to refer to Jesus, it receives no further explication. When Luke does come to describe the Passion, he ignores the Isaianic material.

For our author, in contrast, the Isaianic material plays a key role in this important passage for understanding the Christology of 1 Peter, because the suffering Christ here described plays a central role in discerning how Christians are to conduct themselves in the midst of a fundamentally hostile society.[46] First Peter 2:21–25 constitutes part of a social code that extends from 2:13 to 3:12; these verses are specifically addressed to household slaves, as 2:18 makes clear. There is good reason to suspect, however, that the two groups to whom the author of 1 Peter has given most attention (slaves, wives of non-Christian husbands) were selected to serve metaphorically for the powerless status of all Christians in the larger structure of the Roman Empire.[47] The passage displays its importance, therefore, by serving as the christological basis for the conduct of Christians when they are confronted by threatening neighbors or by the hostile power structures of the Roman Empire.

Not all scholars, however, have agreed that our author has used material from Isaiah 53 in this passage. Some have argued that the reminiscences of an eyewitness are reflected in this passage rather than material drawn from Isaiah 53,[48] a view that the majority of scholars has failed to find persuasive.[49] Again, some have argued that the kind of traditions one finds in the passion account in the Gospels, particularly in Mark,[50] underlies this passage in 1 Peter, rather than certain verses of Isaiah 53, but most scholars have remained unconvinced of that proposition also. To be sure, the account in Mark does reflect material drawn from the Old Testament, but from Psalm 22 rather than from Isaiah 53.[51]

By contrast, I would urge, even a cursory reading makes apparent the extent to which our author depended directly on the material from Isaiah 53:4–9 in this passage. First Peter 2:22 is taken directly from Isaiah 53:9,[52] the only changes being the addition of the relative pronoun *hos* ("who" [NRSV, "he"]) and the substitution, probably under the influence of Christian tradition about the sinlessness of Christ,[53] of *hamartian* (sin) for the less common *anomian* (lawlessness).[54] There is no direct quotation of Isaiah 53 in verse 23,[55] but the silence of the Servant in Isaiah 53:7 is surely reflected there.[56] That silence is combined in this verse, I argue, with the tradition of the silence of Jesus before his accusers at the time of his trial; the latter tradition has had a strong influence on the language of this verse.[57] In 1 Peter 2:24a, with its reference to "bearing our sins," we find the language of Isaiah 53 reflected once more, the phrase taken either from 53:4 or 53:12.[58] Some have found in the use of the word *anapherō* in 1 Peter 2:24a an additional influence from the Levitical sin offering,[59] particularly with respect to the scapegoat,[60] but the notion of presenting sin on an altar as sacrifice renders such an allusion problematic.[61] First Peter 2:24b returns once more to the language of Isaiah 53:5d,[62] though the person of the verb is changed from first to second, a change in person then continued in the next verse. That verse, 2:25, also reflects in its opening words the language of Isaiah 53:6a[63] and is used here to introduce in 2:25b a typically Petrine contrast between the readers' (evil) past and (salutary) present. Here, I urge, we find the point of the entire quotation from Isaiah 53, that is, the deliverance of the Christians from such a past by the redemptive act of the cross into a present in which former sins have been forgiven.

In this way, because of his understanding that the Spirit of Christ was present with the prophets in Israel, the author of 1 Peter could exploit for Christian purposes the material from Isaiah 53 that to that time had not found such detailed application in describing Christ's passion.[64] In addition, it was our author's insight that the Spirit of Christ was present with and informed the prophets that opened the way for later Christian writers to exploit other Old Testament traditions in the explication of the meaning of Christ. The Christ-centered reading of the Old Testament was thus the contribution of our author's Christology to later Christian theological reflection.

NOTES

1. I take 1 Peter to be a pseudonymous writing of the last decades of the first century, written as a coherent letter by followers of Peter the apostle. For a more detailed discussion of these points, see Paul J. Achtemeier, *1 Peter,* Hermeneia (Minneapolis: Fortress Press, 1996), 1–75.

2. Ernest Best, *1 Peter,* New Century Bible (London: Oliphants, 1971), 27; William Joseph Dalton, *Christ's Proclamation to the Spirits: A Study of 1 Peter 3:18–4:6* (Rome: Pontifical Biblical Institute, 1965), 68; J. Ramsey Michaels, *1 Peter,* Word Biblical Commentary 49 (Waco, Tex.: Word, 1988), xxxix; Earl Richard, "The Functional Christology of 1 Peter," in C. H. Talbert, ed., *Perspectives on 1 Peter,* National Association of Baptist Professors of Religion Special Studies 9 (Macon, Ga.: Mercer University Press, 1986), 124; Norbert Brox, *Der erste Petrusbrief,* Evangelisch-Katholischer Kommentar zum New Testament (Zurich: Benziger Verlag, 1979), 18, 22.

3. Frederick W. Danker ("1 Peter 1:23–2:17 — A Consolatory Pericope," *Zeitschrift für die neuetestamentliche Wissenschaft* 58 [1967]: 101) points to Romans 6:1–4; Galatians 3:27; Ephesians 4:24; Colossians 2:12; D. Hill ("On Suffering and Baptism in 1 Peter," *Novum Testamentum* 18 [1976]: 181) adds Hebrews 6. See also David W. Kendall, "The Literary and Theological Function of 1 Peter 1:3–12," in Talbert, ed., *Perspectives on 1 Peter,* 118.

4. Interestingly, the word for "cross" or "crucify" does not occur in 1 Peter, although it is evident from the reference to Christ bearing our sins on the "tree" (*zylon,* 2:24) that our author knew of the crucifixion. It is one more bit of evidence that this letter is not dominated by Pauline influence; on that point, see Achtemeier *1 Peter,* 15–19.

5. Typically, 1 Peter speaks of such redemption in terms of "new birth" (1:3), which is indicative not so much of baptism, as was once thought, but of the new situation faced by Christians within the Roman world, from which their behavior has now distanced them and made them subject to ridicule, if not persecution (3:15b–16; 4:3–4, 12, 14).

6. While some have argued this points to the Passover lamb, context and language argue rather that it comes from the general cultic language of Israel. For more on this point, see Achtemeier, *1 Peter,* 128–29.

7. For more on this, see Achtemeier, *1 Peter,* 127–28, esp. notes 52–55 and the references given there.

8. Its only other known non-Christian use is on a mummy case of an Egyptian peasant; see Achtemeier, *1 Peter,* 329n. 114.

9. See Numbers 27:17; 1 Kings 22:17; Psalms 23; 119:176; Isaiah 40:11; Jeremiah 23:1–4; Ezekiel 34:11–15; compare Zechariah 11:7.

10. See William L. Schutter, *Hermeneutic and Composition in 1 Peter,* Wissenschaftliche Untersuchungen zum Neuen Testament 2, Reihe, 30 (Tübingen: J. C. B. Mohr [Paul Siebeck], 1989), 35–43, for a cataloging of the variety of ways in which the author of 1 Peter draws on the Old Testament.

11. The case of *Barnabas* 5.2 is quite different. There, in using the language of Isaiah 53, the author sees such language referring partly to Israel, partly to Christians. Such an implication is absent from 1 Peter.

12. On the absence of all reference to historic Israel, see also Albert Vanhoye, S.J., "1 Pierre au Carrefour des théologies du nouveau testament," in C. Perrot, ed., *Études sur la première lettre de Pierre,* Lectio divina 102 (Paris: Editions du Cerf, 1980), 112.

13. In agreement with, among others, Norbert Brox, "'Sara zum Beispiel . . .' Israel im 1. Petrusbrief," in *Kontinuität und Einheit. Festschrift Franz Mussner* (Freiburg: Herder, 1981), 490, 492; see also F. H. Chase, "Peter, First Epistle," in *Dictionary of the Bible,* ed. J. Hastings (Edinburgh: T. & T. Clark, 1900), 3:794; J. N. D. Kelly, *A Commentary on the Epistles of Peter and of Jude,* Harper's New Testament Commentaries (New York: Harper & Row, 1969), 26. A. R. Jonsen ("The Moral Theology of the First Epistle of St. Peter," *Sciences Ecclésiastiques* 16 [1964]: 102) wrongly narrows the scope in limiting the purpose of such appropriation of rhetoric to the idea of a "new temple"; see also Schutter, *Hermeneutic,* 176.

14. More common is the identification of some aspect of the history of Israel as underlying the appropriation of Old Testament language: (1) *The exodus:* O. S. Brooks, "1 Peter 3:21—The Clue to the Literary Structure of the Epistle," *Novum Testamentum* 16 (1974): 297; see also Paul E. Deterding, "Exodus Motifs in First Peter," *Concordia Journal* 7 (1981): passim. (2) *The exile:* J. Ramsey Michaels, *1 Peter,* Word Biblical Commentary 49 (Waco, Tex.: Word, 1988), xlv; see also John Hall Elliott, *A Home for the Homeless: A Sociological Exegesis of 1 Peter, Its Situation and Strategy* (Philadelphia: Fortress Press, 1981), 131, 226. (3) *Election/covenant:* Eugene A. LaVerdiere, "Covenant Theology in 1 Peter 1:1–2:10," *Bible Today* 42 (1969): 2914; see also Victor Paul Furnish, "Elect Sojourners in Christ: An Approach to the Theology of 1 Peter," *Perkins School of Theology Journal* 28 (1975): 3. (4) *Exodus, election, restoration:* Heinrich Schlier, "Eine Adhortatio aus Rom. Die Botschaft des Ersten Petrusbriefes," *Strukturen Christlicher Existenz. Festgabe F. Wulf,* ed. H. Schlier (Würzburg: Echter Verlag, 1968), 60–61, 68. (5) *Exodus, Suffering Servant, scapegoat:* Randy Hall, "For to This You Have Been Called: The

Cross and Suffering in 1 Peter," *Restoration Quarterly* 19 (1976): 140–41. Because all such elements, and more, are present in 1 Peter, it is better to speak of Israel in its totality as the controlling metaphor, rather than simply trying to identify isolated examples.

15. I am assuming here the structure of the letter proposed and explained in Achtemeier, *1 Peter*, 73–74, namely, that the letter in broad outline consists of an epistolary opening (1:1–2), *prooumium* (1:3–12), body opening (1:13–2:10), body middle (2:11–4:11), body closing (4:12–5:11), and epistolary closing (5:12–14).

16. Unlike Paul, the author of 1 Peter sees no "Jewish problem" in the fact that Jews have not in fact become members of the Christian community in any significant numbers. It is simply the case that, for our author, the language describing the significance of the people of God has passed without remainder into the vocabulary of the Christian community.

17. That the passages cited in 1 Peter 2:9–10 were familiar already to Christian tradition does not detract from their importance here. The choice of Old Testament materials already used in the early Christian community is as significant for displaying the viewpoint of the author as original citations drawn from the Old Testament would be; so also Furnish, "Elect Sojourners," 2.

18. I am indebted for these references to Kelly, *Commentary*, 60.

19. A point also noted by John Calvin, *Commentaries on the Catholic Epistles*, trans. J. Owen (Grand Rapids: Wm. B. Eerdmans Publishing Co., 1948), 38.

20. Dalton argues that it was (*Christ's Proclamation*, 49), Best that it was not (*1 Peter*, 81).

21. So Brox, *Der erste Petrusbrief*, 70; Kelly, *Commentary*, 62; Jean-Claude Margot, *Les Épîtres de Pierre* (Geneva: Labor et Fides, 1960), 25.

22. With Michaels, *1 Peter*, 41; J. W. C. Wand, *The General Epistles of St. Peter and St. Jude*, Westminster Commentaries (London: Methuen & Co., 1934), 50.

23. As in Best, *1 Peter*, 81.

24. With J. H. A. Hart, "The First Epistle General of Peter," in *The Expositor's Greek Testament*, 5 vols., ed. W. R. Nicoll (Grand Rapids: Wm. B. Eerdmans Publishing Co., 1974), 5:46.

25. As in F. J. A. Hort, *The First Epistle of St. Peter: I.1–II.17: The Greek Text with Introductory Lecture, Commentary, and Additional Notes* (London: Macmillan & Co., 1898), 50.

26. With Charles A. Bigg, *Critical and Exegetical Commentary on the Epistles of St. Peter and St. Jude*, International Critical Commentary (New York: Charles Scribner's Sons, 1901), 109; Karl Hermann Schelkle, *Die Petrusbriefe, der Judasbrief*, 3d ed., Herders Theologischer Kommentar zum Neuen Testament (Freiburg: Herder, 1970), 41.

27. As argued by Margot, *Les Épîtres de Pierre*, 25.

28. In agreement with Best, *1 Peter*, 81; C. E. B. Cranfield, *I and II Peter and Jude: Introduction and Commentary*, Torch Bible Commentaries (London:

SCM Press, 1960), 44; Michaels (*1 Peter*, 44) finds that this form reflects the standpoint of the past; when the standpoint is the present, the author uses instead *ta tou christou pathēmata* (4:13; 5:1); Wand thinks this is a Hebraism: "that belongs to Christ" (*General Epistles of St. Peter and St. Jude*, 50).

29. As in Calvin, *Commentaries on the Catholic Epistles*, 40; Martin Luther, *D. Martin Luthers Epistel-Auslegung*, trans. H. Guenther and E. Volk (Göttingen: Vandenhoeck & Ruprecht, 1983), 197.

30. With Hart, "First Epistle General of Peter," 46; Michaels, *1 Peter*, 44; Schelkle, *Die Petrusbriefe, der Judasbrief*, 40.

31. As in Hort, *First Epistle of St. Peter*, 54.

32. With Schelkle, *Die Petrusbriefe, der Judasbrief*, 40; Ceslas Spicq, *Les Épîtres de Saint Pierre*, Sources Bibliques (Paris: Libraire Lecoffre, 1966), 56.

33. For a discussion of the second, see Achtemeier, *1 Peter*, 111–13.

34. See Numbers 24:17; Deuteronomy 18:15; Habakkuk 2:1–3; 2 Esdras 4:51–52: I owe these references to Kelly, *Commentary* 62; Leonhard Goppelt (*Der erste Petrusbrief*, Kritische-exegetischer über das Neuen Testament, ed. F. Hahn [Göttingen: Vandenhoeck & Ruprecht, 1978]) adds Daniel 9:3, 22–27; 12:6–13 and argues that these passages from Daniel are the origin of such an idea.

35. The beginning of *1 Enoch* displays its typical form: "I look not for this generation but for the distant one that is coming" (1:2); it was also then taken up at Qumran, 1QpHab 7:1–8 (I owe this reference to Goppelt, *Der erste Petrusbrief*, 108).

36. For example, Wand, *General Epistles of St. Peter and St. Jude*, 52.

37. In agreement with Kelly, *Commentary*, 63; Spicq, *Les Épîtres de Saint Pierre*, 57.

38. Since the agents of that proclamation are identified by the *dia*, the *en pneumati hagiō* is probably not an instrumental dative. Closer to the mark is Michaels (*1 Peter*, 47), who finds that it is an "associative dative, or accompanying circumstances and manner"; see also Hort, *First Epistle of St. Peter*, 61.

39. Ernest Gordon Selwyn, *The First Epistle of St. Peter* (London: Macmillan & Co., 1955).

40. Selwyn, *First Epistle of St. Peter*, 134; see also 260.

41. Ibid., 263, 265, respectively.

42. I owe these references to Michaels, *1 Peter*, 40.

43. See Cranfield, *I and II Peter*, 43, with mention of specific New Testament passages.

44. Best, *1 Peter*, 83–84, specifically refuting Selwyn; see also Francis W. Beare, *The First Epistle of Peter* (Oxford: Basil Blackwell, 1958), 90; Kelly, *Commentary*, 59; Eduard Schweizer, *Der erste Petrusbrief*, 3d ed.

Zürcher Biblekommentare (Zurich: Theologischer Verlag, 1972), 27. The list could be greatly extended.

45. In my judgment, N. T. Wright (*Jesus and the Victory of God* [Minneapolis: Fortress Press, 1996], 588–91) overstates the influence of the Servant Songs on the Gospel accounts, and hence also on Jesus' own understanding of himself and his mission.

46. The thrust of the passage is surely to be seen more in the notion of following than imitating Christ, as the *hapax* ("once [for all]") in 3:18 makes clear. Because Christ's suffering took away sins, it is essentially inimitable. Our conduct follows his in the manner of suffering, that is, mildly and without rebuke, but not in the effects of that suffering, that is, the removal of sin.

47. This idea of the representative nature of slaves and wives of non-Christian husbands was proposed as early as Calvin, *Commentaries,* 89; see also Goppelt, *Der erste Petrusbrief,* 204–5; Jacques Schlosser, "Ancien Testament et christologie dans la prima Petri," *Études sur la première Lettre de Pierre,* ed. C. Perrot, Lectio divina 102 (Paris: Éditions du Cerf, 1980), 84; Schutter, *Hermeneutic,* 141.

48. See Bigg, *Critical and Exegetical Commentary,* 146; Cranfield, *I and II Peter,* 85; James Moffatt, *The General Epistles: James, Peter and Jude,* Moffatt New Testament Commentary (Garden City, N.Y.: Doubleday, Doran & Co., 1928), 127.

49. See Best, *1 Peter,* 119–20; Hans Windisch (*Die katholischen Briefe,* 3d. ed., rev. and ed. H. Preisker, Handbuch zum Neuen Testament [Tübingen: J. C. B. Mohr (Paul Siebeck), 1951], 65) notes Peter's absence during the time period reflected in these verses. Cranfield's positing of dependence partly on eyewitness, partly on Isaiah 53 remains similarly unpersuasive (*I and II Peter,* 85).

50. So Goppelt, *Der erste Petrusbrief,* 208, citing Mark 14:65; 15:17–20, 29–32; see also Windisch, *Die katholischen Briefe,* 65.

51. See Eduard Lohse, "Parenesis and Kerygma in 1 Peter," trans. John Steely, in Talbert, ed., *Perspectives on 1 Peter* 57; Schlosser, "Ancien Testament," 82.

52. T. P. Osborne ("L'Utilisation des citations de l'Ancien Testament dans la première épître de Pierre," *Revue théologique de Louvain* 12 [1981]: 71) notes that it follows the LXX, which contrasts with the MT, particularly with the LXX addition of the verb *heurethē.*

53. Goppelt (*Der erste Petrusbrief,* 207) argues it was changed by the tradition the author is following. Thomas P. Osborne ("Guide Lines for Christian Suffering: A Source-Critical and Theological Study of 1 Peter 2,21–25," *Biblica* 64 [1983]: 394) suggests, rightly I think, that it was made by the author of the letter.

54. This has often been observed, e.g., Michaels, *1 Peter,* 145; Schlosser, "Ancien Testament," 83.

55. Such absence of quotation from Isaiah led Cranfield to find here, wrongly I think, an "eye-witness memory" of events (*I and II Peter*, 85). It has led Michaels (*1 Peter*, 145) to posit, again wrongly I think, that this verse is simply a commentary on verse 22. The reflection of the thought of Isaiah 53:7 is too strong for such a conclusion.

56. So also Schlosser, "Ancien Testament," 87. Best (*1 Peter*, 121), on the basis of a common use of the verb *paradidōmi*, sees here a reflection of Isaiah 53:12.

57. So Cranfield, *I and II Peter*, 85; Goppelt, *Der erste Petrusbrief*, 208. This is the extent of the validity of the argument of such scholars as Julian Price Love ("The First Epistle of Peter," *Interpretation* 8 [1954]: 72) and F. H. Chase ("Peter, First Epistle," in *Dictionary of the Bible*, ed. J. Hastings [Edinburgh: T. & T. Clark, 1900], 3:787) that this verse represents the language of an eyewitness; as Windisch (*Die katholischen Briefe*, 65) points out, Peter was not present to witness these events according to the Gospel narratives.

58. If one puts more emphasis on "*our* sins," the reflection is from 53:4, where that pronoun also occurs; in 53:12 it is the sins "of *many*." If one puts more emphasis on the "bore . . . *upon*," the reflection is from 53:12, where that verb (*anēnegken*) occurs; in 53:4 the verb is the simple *bears* (*pherei*); so D. Edmond Hiebert, "Following Christ's Example: An Exposition of 1 Peter 2:21–25," *Biblica Sacra* 139 (1982): 40. It is a difficult point to decide. Some have also found a reflection of Deuteronomy 21:23 in 1 Peter's reference to "his body upon the tree" (lit., "wood"); so Osborne, "Guide Lines," 398–99.

59. See Bigg, *Critical and Exegetical Commentary*, 147; Schelkle, *Die Petrusbriefe, der Judasbrief*, 85; Spicq, *Les Épîtres*, 112.

60. See Wand, *General Epistles of St. Peter and St. Jude*, 83; Windisch, *Die katholischen Briefe*, 65–66.

61. One suspects no Jew ever thought of sin itself being laid on the altar, as Selwyn (*First Epistle of St. Peter*, 180) notes. Those who argue for such a notion of sacrifice must, as a result, interpret the *hamartias* of 1 Peter 2:24 not as "sins" but as "sin offering." I therefore urge that the true source is Isaiah 53.

62. Gerhard Delling ("Der Bezug der christlichen Existenz auf das Heilshandeln Gottes nach den ersten Petrusbrief," in *Neues Testament und christliche Existenz*, ed. H. D. Betz and L. Schottroff [Tübingen: J. C. B. Mohr (Paul Siebeck), 1973], 102) argues, correctly I think, that the reference is to Jesus' death rather than to his whipping by the Roman soldiers.

63. This is generally recognized, e.g., Bigg, *Critical and Exegetical Commentary*, 149; Hiebert, "Following Christ's Example," 42; Selwyn, *First Epistle of St. Peter*, 181.

64. The long quotation of Isaiah 53 in *1 Clement* 16.3–14 shows its increasing popularity after its appearance in 1 Peter. See Brox, *Der erste Petrusbrief*, 136; E. Norman Hillyer, "The Servant of God," *Evangelical Quarterly* 41 (1969): 159–60; Best, *1 Peter*, 120; also Osborne, "Guide Lines," 385.

CHRIST IN JUDE
AND 2 PETER

Pheme Perkins

Perhaps no other writings in the New Testament come closer to demonstrating what Jack Dean Kingsbury calls "christological fatigue" than Jude and 2 Peter. In his pioneering work on Mark, Kingsbury demonstrated that, when combined with the Gospel's narrative focus on the cross, christological titles such as "Son of God" play a central role in the evangelist's Christology.[1] Such a rescue operation is difficult to perform for Jude and 2 Peter. Though "Son of God" is familiar from the transfiguration account (2 Peter 1:17), it plays no role in the epistle. The preferred christological titles, "Lord" and "Savior," are largely honorific designations due the divine benefactor to whom Christians must remain loyal. The cross plays no significant role at all.[2] Jude may represent a development of Jewish Christianity that retains a monotheistic emphasis. Jesus is the agent through whom Gentiles are called to obedience.[3] Christian faith and conduct are formulated not in light of the cross but in anticipation of divine judgment. Though similar to Paul's formula in 1 Thessalonians 1:9–10, Jude lacks any sense of suffering as participation in the cross of Christ.

For Jude, one might conclude that lack of reflection on the cross results from either the epistle's brevity or the tradition from which it comes. One cannot make the same suggestion for 2 Peter. Not only has 2 Peter incorporated substantial portions of Jude into its counterargument that divine judgment has been active from ancient times,[4] but it also reflects knowledge of both the Synoptic Gospels and the Pauline epistles.[5] Though Kingsbury has shown that Mark's presentation of the transfiguration anticipates the glory of resurrection that follows on the cross,[6] 2 Peter shows no awareness of that connection. Even if one concludes that the argument in 2 Peter dictates a selective reference to the transfiguration as probable proof for the Parousia,[7] the lack of any reference to the cross and resurrection of Jesus as the center of Christian life and practice remains unusual.

Second Peter refers to knowledge of the Lord Jesus as the key to piety. Such knowledge embraces both conversion from the immorality of one's past life and ongoing moral conversion. Yet neither the life of Jesus nor his death and resurrection play any role in the exhortation.[8] Thus Jude and 2 Peter raise the possibility that by the end of the New Testament period, Jesus is perceived as Lord, recipient of divine power, and future judge. Ethical progress and fidelity to an inherited apostolic tradition define one's relationship to the Lord, whose judgment will determine the believer's final destiny. Analysis of the christological references in the individual epistles demonstrates the limitations of this vision.

JUDE

Emphasis on the use of rhetorical *topoi* in Jude and 2 Peter has introduced caution in treating divisions between the author and opponents as evidence for specific teaching. The author needs to present the alleged facts in a way that will lead the audience to adopt his point of view.[9] Thus, one finds the key christological charge in Jude 4 that the opponents deny the Lord and Master, Jesus Christ, correlated with rebellion against all forms of authority: the powers of heaven (v. 8), apostles (vv. 17–18), the law (vv. 8–16). Immorality is generally associated with rejection of authority.[10] What is the rhetorical agenda behind this depiction? The author seeks a sharp separation between the audience and persons who are depicted as intruders into the communal *agapē* (v. 12). The example of the wilderness generation (v. 5) provides evidence that a sharp separation within the community of faith is required by God. To win his audience to this position, the author praises them by making clear that none of them is among those being vilified as opponents.[11]

In this context, the christological titles "Lord" and "Master" remind the audience of the disgrace attached to rejecting a divine benefactor. Jesus is the one through whom God saves (vv. 24–25).[12] In addition, "Lord" picks up the constant references to God as "Lord" in the *exempla* of divine judgment. Verbally, the links between Lord (*kyrios*) and judgment (*krima*) are established by sounding these terms repeatedly in close proximity to each other (vv. 4, 5–6, 9, 14–15). Whether it refers to God or to Jesus, *kyrios* resounds throughout the letter (vv. 4, 5, 9, 14, 17, 21, 25).[13] Thus, both at the level of concept and imagery and at the level of verbal association, Jude hammers home the message that to deny Jesus is to come under the irreversible condemnation of divine judgment.[14]

The judgment *exempla* focus one's attention on God as source of condemnation. They support the apostolic prophecy concerning the fate of such Christians (v. 17). But the author does not direct these woes against his audience. For his hearers, the primary function of Jesus as Lord is to rescue those who remain obedient from such a fate (v. 21). Jude frames the condemnation of his Christian audience's opponents with positive statements about the power of God and Jesus to keep believers safe in the judgment (vv. 1, 24–25).[15]

This strong focus on blessing even leads some interpreters to challenge the assumption that Jude is formulated as a tract against heretical teachers. By insisting that charges of infiltration are rhetorical commonplaces, Lauri Thurén concludes that Jude is directed entirely at maintaining the faith of a believing audience and does not refer to heretics at all.[16] Since Jude has transposed the dualism from believers against outsiders to various divisions within an apparently elect community, I cannot accept this conclusion. There must be some persons within the local Christian fellowship who are to be identified as opponents.

I do agree that the christological affirmations in Jude as found in the greeting and final benediction are aimed to promote attachment to salvation that has been received.[17] Salvation has a strongly monotheistic orientation. Believers have become "beloved" of God through the agency of Jesus Christ.[18] Protection forms the central category in Christian experience. It is not oriented toward their present experience as much as toward that end-time judgment. Even though a reference to apostles predicting the appearance of end-time apostates indicates that the audience knows some details concerning the life of Jesus (v. 17), the Jesus of this epistle is the one who comes as Judge (compare 1 Thess. 5:23).[19] This eschatological emphasis makes it unnecessary for Jude to indicate what prior actions of Christ established the believers as "beloved" of God. Some hints are implied by the terms in v. 4 that are not repeated in the epistle: *Master* and *deny*.[20] Christ is the Master of believers. In conventional terms, Jesus has purchased believers as household slaves. Since Jewish authors usually use *Master* (*despotēs*) of God, this term invests Jesus with divine authority.[21] Those who turn against their Master are charged with converting God's grace into impiety. The adjective *only*, typically used for conversion to monotheism from paganism, now appears in conjunction with Jesus as Master. Rhetorically, the author may imply that such opposition involves

return to serving pagan gods. Denial of God's Lordship provides the unifying image in the Old Testament *exempla* that follow.[22]

After so describing the opponents, Jude returns to encourage the audience to be built up in faith (v. 20). In this formulation, God rather than Jesus
is connected with keeping the believers. Remaining in the love of God
anticipates mercy to be received from Jesus as eschatological judge. Its end
result is eternal life. This development provides the positive side to the
judgment motif that was introduced in castigating the opponents (vv. 5–7,
10, 13–15).[23] As in the earlier transposition of "master" terminology from
God to Jesus in depicting the opposition, so another set of terms usually
connected with God, *mercy* and *judgment,* has been transposed to Jesus.[24]
While God's wrath against impiety perceived as rebellion against a divine
Master formed the central part of the letter, its conclusion takes a new turn.
Without explicating the reasons for this christological shift, faithful Chris-
tians receive mercy from Jesus. He now functions as end-time judge.

The combination of God's power and Jesus' divine status as the one
through whom Christians experience salvation appears in the final benediction. Who is responsible for preserving the holiness that the faithful require in the judgment (v. 24)? One might conclude that, rhetorically, the
pronoun attaches to Jesus Christ from verse 21.[25] But the addition of "to
the only God" in verse 25 implies that God is the referent. The title "Savior" is being applied to God.[26] Jesus served as God's agent in bringing
faithful believers to stand rejoicing in God's presence. Thus, the benediction looks beyond judgment to salvation in the presence of God. The attributes of eternal glory, majesty, power, and authority belong to God in
this formulation. The monotheistic orientation that scholars have noted in
this epistle returns in its depiction of the destiny of believers. They are to
rejoice forever in God's presence.

2 PETER

Though the conclusion of Jude made it clear that divine glory remains associated with the Father and that those divine attributes ascribed to Jesus are
in view of his function in bringing the faithful to eternal life with God, 2 Peter does not exhibit the same restraint. Ambiguities in the phrasing of both
the letter's opening (2 Peter 1:1–2) and its conclusion (2 Peter 3:18) exhibit
a much stronger tendency to speak of the Savior Jesus as God.[27] Comparison of its doxology (3:18) with Jude 25 makes the shift to honoring Jesus
as God evident.[28] This shift does not determine the more complex problem
of how to read the parallel phrases in 2 Peter 1:1–2. Though verse 1 appears

to call Jesus God, verse 2 distinguishes Jesus from the Father in referring to the work of salvation. Therefore, the distinction should be read back into the more ambiguous phrasing of verse 1.[29] The debate between 2 Peter and false teachers did not require christological precision. As Jerome Neyrey has shown, typical Epicurean arguments against divine providence provide a coherent structure for the attack on Christian belief in the Parousia that elicited 2 Peter. He identifies four typical arguments that 2 Peter refutes: (1) The universe originated by chance. (2) Without Providence, prophecy or other claims to know the future will be wrong. (3) Providence would destroy human freedom. (4) The delay in punishing wickedness is cited as evidence against divine providence.[30] The opponents' charge that Christians who believe in the Parousia have been deceived by foolish myths about the gods fits this line of argument (2 Peter 1:16). Several counterarguments may be aimed at Epicurean *topoi*. Apostolic testimony to the glory that Christ will possess at the Parousia is followed immediately by a defense of prophecy (2 Peter 1:19–21). The opponents' claims of freedom are merely renewed slavery to the passions (2:19).[31]

Commentators remain divided over the referent of 2 Peter 1:3–4. Who is responsible for calling believers to the divine glory and excellence? Unlike the apocalyptic conclusion in Jude, participation in divine glory no longer denotes participation in the heavenly praise of God. Second Peter links divine glory to incorporation into divine nature. Those commentators who see Jesus as the subject of these verses, since he was mentioned last in 1:2, can avoid the philosophical dilemma posed by that shift.[32] However, one would anticipate some indication that 2 Peter holds to an "image of the Son" soteriology to describe the believer's final transformation. Such a perspective never emerges. Knowledge of Christ as Lord is associated with salvation (2 Peter 1:8; 2:20; 3:18). But moral perfection is connected with freedom from contamination by passions, another element in the epistle's philosophizing polemic. It does not even point to Christ as example (contrast 1 Peter 2:21–22; 3:17–18; 4:1).[33] Therefore, it seems likely that God, rather than Jesus, is the subject of 2 Peter 1:3–4. The section praises God's power as benefactor. God even grants believers a share in the divine nature.[34]

If the passages, which some interpreters see as speaking about Jesus as though he were God, in fact refer to God as divine benefactor, then this epistle's connection between Christology and the moral life of believers is more like that found in Jude. The "knowledge" of Jesus designates conversion. Fidelity to Jesus as Lord will guarantee inclusion in his kingdom (2 Peter 1:8, 11).[35] In this case, there has been a shift in terminology. Ordinarily the kingdom is described as "of God," while here the eschatological conclusion of the opening section emphasizes the eternity of the kingdom of Jesus Christ.[36] As a preliminary to the argument against opponents' denial of the Parousia, the assertion that Jesus' kingdom is eternal contradicts the argument that the world as we know it is eternal. Second Peter concludes with a vision of the new heaven and earth (3:11–13).[37]

Just as the kingdom has shifted from God to Jesus, so the knowledge of the Lord that designates both conversion and the moral reform that follows can refer to either God or Christ (2 Peter 1:3, 8). The letter assumes that the connection between such knowledge and virtue is evident to its audience. The connection between knowledge and virtue is not spelled out. Those who see "knowledge" (*epignōsis*) primarily as conversion conclude that it is the prior condition necessary to produce the virtues as its fruit.[38] Those who see knowledge of God or of Jesus Christ as the goal of Christian life understand knowledge as the consequence of faithful practice of the virtues that constitute a godly life.[39] Use of the term *gnōsis* in the chain of verses 5–7 highlights the role of knowledge in the moral life rather than at the point of conversion (vv. 3, 8).[40] Without specifying what is the peculiarly Christian element to this moral conversion, 2 Peter appears to engage the philosophical objections of its opponents. Only a particular knowledge of Christian teaching will generate the virtues necessary to participation in the divine life.[41]

Second Peter shifts to the testament genre to establish its authority as the teacher of such knowledge. Since the opponents contest prophetic and revealed authority, the author treats his knowledge of his impending death as revealed by Jesus Christ (2 Peter 1:14).[42] With this introduction, the teaching in the epistle becomes a normative statement that can replace the loss of the apostolic generation. Though the Lord Jesus has made a direct revelation to the apostle, no such connection exists between the risen Lord and Christians after the death of the apostles. For them, "knowledge of the Lord" implies fidelity to inherited teaching about Christian life and practice. Second Peter 2:20–22 castigates the opposition as persons whose false teaching about freedom makes their present state worse than before their conversion.[43] Thus, the language associated with the Lord Jesus Christ conveys little knowledge about him. It serves as a call for loyalty to a particular understanding of the apostolic tradition.

If loyalty is to be rewarded by inclusion in the eternal kingdom, then 2 Peter has to defend the traditional view that Jesus' kingdom is to be established at the Parousia, the point of contention in the letter. Exegetes agree that while 1:16–18 refers to the transfiguration scene, it is not a direct citation from one of the Synoptics (Mark 9:2–8; Luke 9:28–36; Matt.

17:1–18).[44] Unlike its Synoptic antecedents, the Christology implied by voice in "my Son, my Beloved" plays no role in 2 Peter.[45] Nor does 2 Peter evoke the Synoptic meaning of the transfiguration in connection with Jesus' turn toward Jerusalem and the cross. The author's argument has only one point to make. The divine glory conferred on Jesus at the transfiguration is evidence for the truth of apostolic teaching about his second coming in power (Matt. 24:30; Mark 9:1; 13:26; Luke 21:27). Therefore, 2 Peter pursues a new exegetical reading of the story: The divine glory evident at the Parousia was witnessed there. Both Matthew and Luke have exploited the suggestion of dazzling garments and divine presence in the cloud to imply such glory. Matthew 17:2 reformulates the clothes and face with light imagery. Luke 9:32 notes that on awakening, Peter and the others see the glory of Jesus and his companions.[46] This transfer of divine glory and majesty to Jesus is not treated as a christological revelation in the argument of 2 Peter, as though the apostles were witnesses to an unveiling of his divine nature.[47] The opening of the letter makes it clear that Jesus merits divine honor as Lord and Savior. That viewpoint is even more strongly advanced in the final doxology, where the praise given to God is directly applied to Jesus (3:18), an unusual move in a New Testament doxology.[48] The glory of the Parousia and the honor and praise due Jesus are reflections of true, divine eternity in 2 Peter. Consequently, the day in 3:18 is not the day of judgment but the "day of eternity." The Parousia has become the day on which the eternal kingdom of Jesus is inaugurated.

CONCLUSION

Christology does not play a central role in either Jude or 2 Peter. Both presume a traditional way of speaking about Jesus as Lord and Savior, who is responsible for the benefits of salvation to be enjoyed by loyal believers. Both assume that such loyalty is expressed in a life of godliness, of moral reform. But neither epistle incorporates the figure of Christ into Christian exhortation. For Jude, Christ is assimilated to God as the Judge from whom faithful Christians will receive mercy and eternal life in God's presence. Though 2 Peter responds to an explicit challenge to Christian belief in the Parousia, the epistle uses very different language to describe the believers' destiny. Believers are not being preserved in light of an impending judgment but are practicing for a share in the divine nature and an eternal kingdom whenever it appears. The judgment language inherited from Jude serves to highlight the severe punishment that awaits false teachers. They are not merely dogs and pigs following traits of nature; they are examples of the corruption that follows from rejecting apostolic teaching. In both cases, the predominant image of Jesus is that of a powerful, distant, and benevolent master known to the addressees only through his agents. There is no ambiguity in what is required: loyalty to the community, holiness, moral perfection, and adherence to tradition. As in the human analogy of powerful benefactors and their clients, so in the divine, when the Lord and Master comes, he punishes the unfaithful harshly and rewards loyal followers with a share in what belongs to him.

NOTES

1. Jack Dean Kingsbury, *The Christology of Mark's Gospel* (Philadelphia: Fortress Press, 1983), ix–xi.
2. Pheme Perkins, *First and Second Peter, James and Jude* (Louisville, Ky.: Westminster John Knox Press, 1995), 142–44, 148.
3. Jean Cantinat, *Les Épîtres de Saint Jacques et de Saint Jude,* Sources Bibliques (Paris: J. Gabalda, 1973), 278.
4. 2 Peter 2:1–18, 3:1–3; and Jude 4–13, 16–18; Richard J. Bauckham, *Jude, 2 Peter,* Word Biblical Commentary 50 (Waco, Tex.: Word, 1983), 141–43; on the rhetorical use of this material, see Duane Frederick Watson, *Invention, Arrangement, and Style: Rhetorical Criticism of Jude and 2 Peter,* Society of Biblical Literature Dissertation Series 104 (Atlanta: Scholars Press, 1988), 106–26, 162–87.
5. Neither are cited as texts. For the Synoptics, see the reference to the transfiguration episode in 2 Peter 1:16–18 (Mark 9:2–8; Matt. 17:1–8; Luke 9:28–36) and a possible allusion to Matthew 12:45b in 2 Peter 2:20. Interpretation of the Pauline epistles has caused controversy among Christians (2 Peter 3:15–16). Despite that turmoil, the letters are treated as among the scriptures (Watson, *Invention,* 137).
6. Kingsbury, *Christology,* 99.
7. Watson, *Invention,* 102–3.
8. Perkins, *First and Second Peter,* 163–64.
9. Stephan J. Joubert, "Persuasion in the Letter of Jude," *Journal for the Study of the New Testament* 58 (1995): 78–79.
10. Ibid., 79.
11. Ibid., 82.
12. Jerome H. Neyrey, *2 Peter, Jude,* Anchor Bible 37C (New York: Doubleday, 1993), 24–25.
13. J. Daryl Charles, "Literary Artifice in the Epistle of Jude," *Zeitschrift für die neutestamentliche Wissenschaft* 82 (1991): 111–12. The brevity of the letter makes such repetitions all the more effective.
14. Ibid., 121.
15. Joubert ("Persuasion," 87) reads the correlation between the letter's greet-

ing and its closing as evidence that Jude focuses attention on God's eschatological blessing.

16. Lauri Thurén, "Hey Jude! Asking for the Original Situation and Message of a Catholic Epistle," *New Testament Studies* 43 (1997): 451–65.
17. Cantinat, *Les Épîtres,* 267.
18. Ibid., 278.
19. See Eric Fuchs and Pierre Reymond, *La Deuxième Épître de Saint Pierre. L'Épître de Saint Jude,* Commentaire du Nouveau Testament Deuxième Série 14, 6 (Neuchatel: Delachaux & Niestlé, 1980), 155; Fred Craddock, *First and Second Peter and Jude* (Louisville, Ky.: Westminster John Knox Press, 1995), 130. Simon J. Kistemaker (*New Testament Commentary: Exposition of James, Epistles of John, Peter and Jude* [Grand Rapids: Baker Book House, 1996], 367) also points to the theme of protection in John 17:15. In that context, it has been divorced from the apocalyptic imagery of divine judgment, which is the focus of this motif in Jude.
20. Thurén, "Hey Jude!" 463.
21. Bauckham, *Jude, 2 Peter,* 39–40.
22. Neyrey (*2 Peter, Jude,* 37–40) treats impiety as the theme of the entire letter. He does not qualify the rhetorical charges of the author but treats them all as real descriptions of the antinomianism of the opposing teachers.
23. Cantinat, *Les Épîtres,* 331.
24. Bauckham (*Jude, 2 Peter,* 114) cites the following examples of mercy and eschatological judgment: 2 Maccabees 2:7; *Psalm of Solomon* 7:10; 8:27, 28; 104:17; *1 Enoch* 1:8; 5:6; *2 Baruch* 78:7. Also see Fuchs and Reymond, *La Deuxième Épître,* 185.
25. So Thurén, "Hey Jude!" 464.
26. Bauckham, *Jude, 2 Peter,* 120–22. Bauckham notes the similarity between this doxology and Romans 16:25.
27. Ibid., 168–70; Fuchs and Reymond, *La Deuxième Épître,* 45. Divine characteristics are attributed to Jesus in association with the christological titles "Lord" and "Savior."
28. Neyrey, *2 Peter, Jude,* 110.
29. So Perkins, *First and Second Peter,* 167; Neyrey, *2 Peter, Jude,* 148. Bauckham (*Jude, 2 Peter,* 168) invokes the parallelism between the two verses to reach the opposite conclusion. Ability to make the distinction clearly in verse 2 implies that 2 Peter did not wish to do so in verse 1.
30. Neyrey, *2 Peter, Jude,* 122–23.
31. Ibid., 127.
32. Fuchs and Reymond, *La Deuxième Épître,* 51; Bauckham (*Jude, 2 Peter,* 177) concludes that Jesus is the referent but admits that God is usually the subject of such expressions of praise.
33. On the striking contrast between the two epistles in their references to Christ, see Fuchs and Reymond, *La Deuxième Épître,* 31, 45.

34. On God as subject of the section, see Kistemaker, *New Testament Commentary,* 245–47; on the benefactor ethos of the whole section, see Fred W. Danker, "2 Peter 1: A Solemn Decree," *Catholic Biblical Quarterly* 40 (1978): 62–83; Bauckham (*Jude, 2 Peter,* 174) agrees that the passage refers to God but doubts that the author has modeled it on discourses in praise of a benefactor, since much of the terminology that Danker finds in such decrees is lacking in 2 Peter.

35. Bauckham, *Jude, 2 Peter,* 191; Fuchs and Reymond, *La Deuxième Épître,* 59.

36. Bauckham, *Jude, 2 Peter,* 191; Fuchs and Reymond, *La Deuxième Épître,* 59.

37. Bauckham, *Jude, 2 Peter,* 191. This reference to the eternity of Jesus' kingdom forms another striking contrast to the Pauline eschatology, in which the Parousia is marked by Christ delivering the kingdom to the Father (1 Cor. 15:24–28).

38. Ibid., 189.

39. So Ceslas Spicq, *Les Épîtres de Saint Pierre,* Sources Bibliques (Paris: J. Gabalda, 1966), 214; against dividing the two possible implications, see Kistemaker, *New Testament Commentary,* 253.

40. Bauckham (*Jude, 2 Peter,* 169–70) argues for a strong semantic distinction between *epignōsis,* as the knowledge associated with conversion, and *gnōsis.*

41. Though commentators point to Jewish sources such as Wisdom of Solomon 2:23 as evidence that immortality is the referent of participation in the divine nature, a Gentile audience would probably hear this claim as an adaptation of a typical Stoic or Platonic position (see Fuchs and Reymond, *La Deuxième Épître,* 51). On the various possible meanings of participating in the divine nature see Bauckham, *Jude, 2 Peter,* 177.

42. Neyrey, *2 Peter, Jude,* 164–67. It is unclear whether 2 Peter is familiar with the tradition of a prophetic word from Jesus to Peter concerning the latter's death, as in John 21:19. The testament genre presumes that the dying figure possesses the ability to foresee the future of those left behind.

43. Bauckham (*Jude, 2 Peter,* 277) points to *Testament of Benjamin* 8:3 as a Jewish parallel to the need for freedom from the pollution of the world. The link between moral pedagogy and knowledge of God is common in Jewish sources (Prov. 2:1; 6:23; 19:6; Eccl. 8:5). Though 2:20c is sometimes seen as an allusion to the Gospel (Matt. 12:45 = Luke 11:26), 2 Peter apparently sees it as a piece of proverbial wisdom associated with the proverb about the dog and the sow cited in verse 22 (Prov. 26:11).

44. Inclusion of "well pleased" suggests closer proximity to Matthew 17:1–8 (see Bauckham, *Jude, 2 Peter,* 209). The reference to "my Beloved" is treated by some commentators as an allusion to LXX Isaiah 42:1 (so Bauckham, *Jude, 2 Peter,* 208; Kistemaker, *New Testament Commentary,* 267). But it may represent a conflation of the transfiguration and the baptism of Jesus (so Neyrey, *2 Peter, Jude,* 173).

45. The letter's use of *beloved* to designate the addressees (3:1, 8, 14) stems from the testament genre and reflects the authoritative claim of the dying apostle on their loyalty to his teaching. It is not connected with their relationship to Jesus as adopted children or to his relationship with the Father.

46. Neyrey, *2 Peter, Jude,* 173.

47. See the discussion in Bauckham, *Jude, 2 Peter,* 217–18. This interpretation does not mean that 2 Peter would reject claims for the divinity of Jesus.

48. Kistemaker, *New Testament Commentary,* 348; Neyrey, *2 Peter, Jude,* 110; Bauckham (*Jude, 2 Peter,* 338) notes that the only other doxology applied to Jesus directly appears in Revelation 1:5–6.

THE CHRISTOLOGY
OF THE APOCALYPSE

Charles H. Talbert

It is true that the Revelation to John does not present a complete[1] and or-dered[2] account of the nature and work of Christ. It is also true that there are relatively few major studies of the Christology of the Apocalypse.[3] The former should not preclude our pursuit of the seer's distinctive picture of Christ; the latter should encourage it. The purpose of this chapter is to at-tempt to describe John's portrait of Christ and to discern how it would have been heard by ancient auditors. The argument will follow a progression from *names* to *titles* to *functions* to *faces* to *contexts*.

NAMES

The one about whom we are writing is spoken of by John the seer using the name Jesus (1:9; 12:17; 14:12; 17:6; 19:10; 20:4; 22:16; 22:20; 22:21) or Jesus Christ (1:1, 2, 5), with Christ functioning in these references without an article as a second name rather than as a title.

TITLES

Numerous titles are given to this one in Revelation.[4] A list includes at least the following:

- *Lord* (11:8; 14:13?; 22:20, 21). This traditional Christian title for Jesus (Rom. 10:9; Phil. 2:11; Acts 2:36) was used in Israel's scriptures for God (Isa. 45:3 LXX).[5]

- *The Christ/Messiah* (11:15; 12:10; 20:4, 6). Again, this is a traditional Christian title for Jesus (Mark 8:29; John 20:31; Acts 2:36). It was used in the scriptures of Israel for a coming anointed ruler of God's people (Dan. 9:25–26).
- *The Son of God* (2:18). Once again, this is a traditional Christian title for Jesus (John 20:31; 1 John 3:8; 4:15; 5:13). Evidence at Qumran suggests that "Son of God" was occasionally used as a messianic title in at least some circles of ancient Judaism (4QFlor 10–14).
- *The faithful witness/martyr* (1:5; 3:14; 19:11). The idea behind the title is found in Christian sources in 1 Timothy 6:13. References to one who is a "faithful witness" in the LXX are to humans in a court setting (Prov. 14:5, 25) and to God in a similar milieu (Jer. 49:5). Obviously, the Christian title emerged from Jesus' behavior in a situation where martyrdom was a possibility and in which he remained faithful to God in spite of the consequences. This was how, according to Eusebius, *Church History* 5.2.3, the Christian martyrs in Gaul took it. They refused to be called martyrs, yielding that title to Christ alone, "the faithful witness, the firstborn of the dead."[6]
- *The firstborn of the dead* (1:5). The title has common Christian roots (Rom. 8:29; 1 Cor. 15:20; Col. 1:18; Heb. 12:23).
- *The ruler of the kings of the earth* (1:5; 3:14?; 19:16). Third Maccabees 5:35 and *1 Enoch* 9:4 show that this was a traditional title for God in ancient Judaism. Such a title is sometimes taken to be a counter to the claims of the Roman emperors.[7]
- *The first and the last* (1:17; 2:8; 22:13). Isaiah 44:6 and 48:12–13 use this expression of God.
- *The living one* (1:18; 2:8). In Revelation 4:9–10; 7:2; 10:6; 15:7, God is spoken of in these terms. The roots of this type of language for God are in the scriptures of Israel (Deut. 5:26; Josh. 3:10; Isa. 37:4).
- *The holy one* (3:7). God is spoken of in these terms in Israel's scriptures (Isa. 1:4; 5:24; Hab. 1:2), in postbiblical Judaism (*1 Enoch* 1:2), and in Revelation 6:10. In Mark 1:24 such language is used for Jesus.
- *The true one* (3:7; 19:11). Again, this language is used for God in Israel's scriptures (Ex. 34:6; Isa. 65:16) and in Revelation 6:10. In John 14:6 it is used for Jesus.
- *The one who has the key of David* (3:7). Just as Eliakim carried

the keys of the house of David in the court of Hezekiah, that is, controlled entry into the king's house (Isa. 22:22), so does Christ in the kingdom of God.

- *The Amen* (3:14). The background of this title is doubtless in the thought expressed in 2 Corinthians 1:20. For Christ to be the Amen is for God's promises to be fulfilled in him.
- *The* archē (*origin*) *of God's creation* (3:14). The meaning of *archē* is problematic. Three serious possibilities exist: (1) the first created (as in Job 40:19; Prov. 8:22; and Justin, *1 Apology* 1.21); (2) the first cause or creator (as in Josephus, *Against Apion* 2.190);[8] and (3) ruler (as in Neh. 9:17). Of the three possible meanings, the first is problematic because in Revelation, Christ is not a creature (1:17; 2:8; 22:13; also, worship of him is regarded as legitimate, something that is due God only— 19:10; 22:8–9). The second is problematic because in Revelation, God is called the creator (4:11; 21:5). The third is the best option, for two reasons. First, ruling is the predominant role of Christ in the Apocalypse (12:5; 19:15; 20:4). Second, the progression of thought in 3:14 is from faithful martyr to ruler, as it is in Revelation 5:6–14. Hence, in 3:14 *archē* should probably be translated "ruler of God's creation."
- *The beginning and the end* (22:13). The label is used for God in Josephus, *Antiquities* 8.11.2 + 280, and in Revelation 21:6. Implied is preexistence.
- *The Alpha and the Omega* (22:13). In Revelation 1:8 and 21:6, the title is used for God. Again, preexistence is implied.
- *The Lion of the tribe of Judah* (5:5). The roots of the title are doubtless in Genesis 49:9 and were developed in 2 Esdras 12:31–32. It is, of course, a reference to the Davidic messiah.
- *The Root of David* (5:5). Again, the origins are in Israel's scriptures (Isa. 11:10; Sir. 47:22). The language is known at Qumran (4QapGen av). Such usage was taken over by early Christians (Rom. 15:12). The title refers to the Davidic messiah.
- *The Lamb* (5:6, 8, 12, 13; 6:1, 16; 7:9, 10, 14, 17; 12:11; 13:8; 14:1, 4, 10; 15:3; 17:14; 19:7, 9; 21:9, 14, 22, 23, 27; 23:1, 3). This is the dominant title used for Jesus in Revelation. The Lamb is redeemer (5:6, 9–10; 13:8), who sets in motion God's will on the earth (5:6–7; 6:1). At the end of history, he defeats God's enemies (17:14). In the new age beyond the resurrection, he is the bridegroom of the church (19:7, 9; 21:9), the temple of the heavenly

city (21:22) and its light (21:23). Both within history (7:17) and in the new creation (22:1, 3), he sits on the throne of God. The roots of this title are complex. On the one hand, the redeemer role of the Lamb most likely reflects the Passover lamb. The links are numerous: Both are said to be slain (Ex. 12:6; Rev. 5:6, 9, 12); reference is made to the blood of each (Ex. 12:7, 13, 22; Rev. 5:9); both result in a kingdom of priests (Ex. 19:6; Rev. 5:10); both are connected with the Song of Moses (Ex. 15:1–18; Rev. 15:3); both involve exodus typology (locusts—Ex. 10:12–15, Rev. 9:1–11; hail—Ex. 9:22–23, Rev. 8:7; darkness—Ex. 10:21–23, Rev. 8:12). Also, the Passover lamb is called an *arēn* (in Revelation, the diminutive *arnion*), not *amnos* (as in Isa. 53:7). On the other hand, the conquering Lamb most likely reflects the apocalyptic lamb/ram of *1 Enoch* 89—90 (*arēn*) and the *Testament of Joseph* 19:8. These two roots do not exhaust all the dimensions of the Lamb in the Apocalypse of John, but they furnish categories for the two most important functions of the Lamb. Because of its frequency, the title "Lamb" is often taken to be the centerpiece of John the seer's Christology.[9]

• *The Word of God* (19:13; however, in 1:2, 9; 6:9; 20:4, the "word of God" is not likely a title of Jesus but rather a reference to the prophetic word). The roots of the conquering, judging Word of God are probably in the Wisdom of Solomon 18:15–16, where the word is an extension of God, whose functions are described in terms of the angel of the Lord. This is a bit different from the use of the Word in John 1, where the Word is Creator and incarnate One.

• *The bright morning star* (22:16). Numbers 24:17 is likely the source of the star imagery for the Messiah. In the early second century C.E., Bar Kokhba (son of a star) used "star" as a messianic title.

• *The one who has the sharp, two-edged sword* (1:16; 2:12; 19:15). The closest thing to this title is the description of the word of God who leaps from God's throne with a two-edged sword in Wisdom of Solomon 18:15–16. It is an image of conquest and judgment.

From this list of titles used for Jesus in Revelation, one can draw several conclusions. First, these titles are sometimes carryovers of earlier titles (for example, Lord, Christ, Son of God) but sometimes are created by the author of Revelation from descriptions of God (for example, living one, true one) or of other figures (for example, Lamb, bright morning star) in ancient Judaism.[10] Second, of the titles applied to Christ in Revelation, some are taken from language by which God is referred to in Israel's scriptures and in postbiblical Judaism (for example, Lord, ruler of kings of the earth); some are taken from language used by scripture and later tradition to describe the messiah or some other vice-regent of God (for example, Lion of tribe of Judah, the Root of David, the one who has the key of David); some are used to refer to one who is faithful to God in whatever circumstances (for example, the faithful witness/martyr). Third, while some titles are used for a specific trait or function of Christ (for example, the beginning and the end, the Alpha and the Omega), others encompass multiple functions (for example, Lamb). Finally, it becomes clear from working with the titles of Jesus in Revelation that from these data alone one will not be able to answer the questions with which we began. This recognition leads us to the next logical step: functions of Christ in the Apocalypse.

FUNCTIONS

The Revelation to John portrays Christ as carrying out a number of functions, among which are:

- *Revealer*. The Apocalypse opens with Christ depicted as a revealer (1:1, 12–20; 2:1, 8, 12, 18; 3:1, 7, 14). The document ends on the same note (22:16).
- *Redeemer*. In Revelation, Christ is also described as a redeemer. He has freed us from our sins by his blood (1:5–6; 5:9; 14:4). He has made us a kingdom of priests (1:5–6; 5:10; 20:6). We are enabled to conquer by the blood of the Lamb (12:11; 15:3). He is mediator of salvation (3:7). Before the foundation of the world our names were written in the Lamb's book of life (13:8).
- *Ruler*. John the seer also portrays Christ as a heavenly ruler, God's vice-regent. He is the one who is to rule all nations (2:27; 12:5; 19:15). Within history, he sits on his Father's throne (3:21; 12:5). He receives worship (5:14; 7:10). He sets in motion God's will on the earth (5:5, 7; 6:1–8:1). At the end of history, he is returning Lord (1:7; 16:15; 22:7, 12, 20). He defeats God's enemies (19:11–21) and executes wrath or judges (6:16–17; 19:11, 15). During the millennium, he reigns for one thousand years (20:4).

In the new heavens and earth, he sits on the Father's throne (7:17; 22:1, 3). He is the bridegroom of the church (19:7; 21:9), the temple of the heavenly city (21:22) and its light (21:23).

From this survey of the functions of Christ in the Apocalypse, it is clear that the focus is on the exalted Christ. What attention is paid to Jesus' death is used to establish his credentials for his exalted reign. Such observations lead naturally into a discussion of the faces of Christ in Revelation.

FACES

John the seer presents Christ with two faces: human and heavenly.[11] We begin with the human face of Jesus. Christ in his human history was Jewish (12:1). He was descended from the tribe of Judah, of the family of David (5:5; 22:16). His birth took place in hostile circumstances (12:1–5). A number of sayings of the earthly Jesus are echoed in the sayings of the risen Lord (Rev. 1:3; compare Luke 11:28; Rev. 1:7; compare Matt. 24:30; Rev. 3:2–3; compare Matt. 24:42–44; Rev. 3:5; compare Matt. 10:32; Rev. 3:20; compare Luke 12:36–37; Rev. 3:21; compare Luke 22:28–30; Rev. 13:10; compare Matt. 26:52).[12] He had apostles who function as the foundations of the church (21:14). His death (1:5, 18; 5:6, 9) was in Jerusalem by crucifixion (11:8). He was raised from the dead (1:5, 18).

The heavenly face of Christ, however, is Revelation's focus. For one thing, his preexistence is assumed. The titles "the beginning and the end" (22:13) and "the Alpha and the Omega" (22:13) attest it. Note, these are titles used for God (1:8; 21:6, Alpha and Omega; 21:6, beginning and end). In 13:8 the reference to the writing of the names of the elect in the Lamb's book of life "before the foundation of the world" confirms it.

In addition, his heavenly nature is affirmed. First, throughout Revelation many of the titles applied to Christ are those used elsewhere for God. For example, besides those just mentioned above, see (1) Lord—for Christ in Revelation 11:8; 22:20–21; for God in Isaiah 45:3; Revelation 11:17; (2) ruler of the kings of the earth—for Christ in Revelation 1:5; 17:14; 19:16; for God in 3 Maccabees 5:35; *1 Enoch* 9:4; (3) the holy one—for Christ in Revelation 3:7; for God in *1 Enoch* 1:2; Isaiah 1:4; 5:24; Revelation 6:10; (4) the true one—for Christ in Revelation 3:7; 19:11; for God in Exodus 34:6; Revelation 6:10. Second, he sits on the throne of God (3:21; 7:17; 22:1, 3). Third, above all, he is a legitimate object of worship (5:14; 7:10; 22:3).[13] In Revelation angels, as creatures, resist worship (19:10; 22:8–9), knowing that worship belongs to God alone.[14] Fourth, mention of God and

Christ together is sometimes followed by a singular verb (11:15) or by singular pronouns (6:17; 22:3–4).

These data confirm that in Revelation, Christ is portrayed with two faces: human and heavenly. How the two faces are related does not seem to be a matter of concern for John the seer, as it is in the Johannine epistles and the fourth Gospel.[15] Eugene Boring puts it precisely: "As the agent of God, Christ came into history—we do not speculate about how—as the man Jesus."[16] Having paid attention to names, titles, functions, and faces of Christ in Revelation, it remains to ask about the contexts in which one would hear these data.

CONTEXTS

The contexts are two. On the one hand, we must set the names, titles, functions, and faces of Christ in the context of the story assumed by the Revelation to John. Such an approach has been taken in the study of Pauline theology of late.[17] It has also been used in the study of the Christology of the Apocalypse.[18] Boring asks: What is the narrative presupposed by Revelation? His answer is that it is a drama involving three acts: the past activity of Christ, the present activity, and the future activity.[19] A sketch of his proposal looks like this:

1. The past activity of Christ
   a. Protological acts at or before creation (1:17–18; 13:8)
   b. Acts of the historical Jesus (12:1–5, birth; 21:4, apostles; 1:3; 2:7; 3:3 and 16:15; 13:11; 18:24; 19:7, sayings of the earthly Jesus; 1:18, death/resurrection)
2. The present activity of Christ (that is, from the resurrection of Jesus to his parousia)
   a. Exalted ruler of the universe who is worshiped in heaven and who shares the throne of God (3:21; 5:7–14; 7:9–17)
   b. Lord of potentially hostile powers (1:16; 2:1)
   c. The one in charge of death (1:18)
   d. The one whose shed blood is effective in the present (12:11)
   e. The one who is present and speaks in the churches (1:1, 13; 2:1, 7, 24; 3:20; 4:1; 16:15; 22:6, 20)
3. The future activity of Christ: the coming one (19:11–21; 22:7, 20)

In the setting in which Revelation would have been heard, the auditors would have known this story. As the plot of the Apocalypse unfolded, the auditors would have been able unconsciously to sort out and fit the various names, titles, functions, and faces of Christ into the underlying narrative. This would have given coherence to the various pieces of John the seer's Christology. The diverse components would make sense in the context of Revelation's story of salvation, past, present, and future.

Nevertheless, the picture of Christ that results from reading Revelation in terms of its presupposed narrative must be set in the context of ancient Mediterranean assumptions and beliefs. How would ancient auditors have heard it? First, what is the picture? John assumes a preexistent, heavenly being who enters the human world as Jesus or Jesus Christ, who dies as a faithful martyr and is raised/exalted to share God's throne and to act as God's vice-regent in history, at the end of history, and beyond history, when he will dwell forever with God's people.

How would this portrait of Christ have been heard by ancient Mediterranean auditors of the Revelation to John? The thesis of this chapter is that the thought world of the Christology of Revelation is to be found in reflections about the divine throne in ancient Judaism, especially among those that mention a figure apart from the throne who is said to be in human or angelic form.

Numerous references to the divine throne in ancient Jewish sources do not involve any such second figure. Without trying to be exhaustive, one may mention 1 Kings 22:19; Isaiah 6:1–6;[20] *1 Enoch* 14; *2 Enoch* 20—21; *Testament of Levi* 2—3, 5; *Life of Adam and Eve* 25; 4Q405, especially fragments 20, 21, 22; 4Q385 4; and 4Q286.

In some references to the throne of God in heaven, however, a second figure is implicitly or explicitly present. Again, without trying to be exhaustive, we may mention the following:

1. In Ezekiel 1:26–28 is a vision of the throne of glory with the likeness of the form of a man above it. In 8:2 the prophet sees the likeness of a man who delivers a revelation to Ezekiel. The description of this figure makes clear that he is the one spoken of in 1:26–28 (for example, "loins like fire"). The separation of the divine glory in chapter 8 from the throne chariot in chapter 1 enables it to function as a quasi-angelic mediator.[21]

2. Daniel 7:9–10, 13–14 MT[22] tells of one that was "Ancient of Days" (an old man) taking his seat on a fiery throne and then having one like a son of man (an angelic figure) presented to him. To this one like a son of man everlasting dominion was given. In Daniel 10:5, the seer has a vision of an angelic being who is described in verse 16 as "like a son of man." This one gives Daniel a revelation. There is reason to think that this is the same figure mentioned in chapter 7 and possibly 8:13.[23]

3. Ezekiel the Tragedian's *Exagōgē* contains a section in which Moses has a dream that his father-in-law interprets. Moses sees a throne on which is seated a man with a scepter. He beckons Moses to stand before the throne. Then "he handed o'er the scepter and he bade me mount the throne, and gave to me the crown; then he withdrew from off the throne" (74–76).[24] Here the second figure is not an angelic being but a human who is set on God's throne.

4. The Wisdom of Solomon 9 speaks of wisdom (also called "word," v. 1, and "holy spirit," v. 17) as a divine agent. Petition is made to God: "Send her forth from the holy heavens, and from the throne of your glory send her" (v. 10). Wisdom of Solomon 18 narrates the events of the exodus. Regarding the slaying of the firstborn in Egypt, verse 15 says: "Your all-powerful word leaped from heaven, from the royal throne, into the midst of the land that was doomed, a stern warrior carrying the sharp sword of your authentic command, and stood and filled all things with death, and touched heaven while standing on the earth." Here the divine agent is God's word, depicted as the angel of death.

5. The *Testament of Moses* 10 describes the end of history and the judgment meted out on the wicked. It is described in three stages. First we are told, "Then his kingdom will appear throughout his whole creation" (v. 1). This presumably refers to God's kingdom. Second we read:

> Then will be filled the hands of the messenger,
>   who is in the highest place appointed. (v. 2)
> For the Heavenly One will arise from his kingly throne.
> Yea, he will go forth from his holy habitation
>   with indignation and wrath on behalf of his sons. (v. 3)

This may be taken in one of two ways. Either the entire segment refers to the angel of judgment or verse 2 refers to the angel and verse 3 to God himself. Third, verse 7 says that "God Most High will surge forth, the Eternal One alone. In full view he will come to work vengeance on the nations." Regardless of how one takes verses 2 and 3, the chapter as a whole speaks about God and his angel intervening for judgment. They are spoken of in such a way that they seem virtually interchangeable.

6. *First Enoch* 37—71 has a number of throne visions, some of which involve a second figure variously described as the Elect One, the Son of man, and the Messiah (48:10). *First Enoch* 45:3 says that the Elect One sits on the seat of glory at judgment time, while *1 Enoch* 51:3 says that in those days (the last days) the Elect One will sit on God's throne. *First Enoch* 55:4 has the Lord say: "See my Elect One, how he sits in the throne of glory and

judges." In *1 Enoch* 61:8, God places the Elect One on the throne of glory to carry out judgment. In *1 Enoch* 69:29, the Son of man has appeared and has seated himself on the throne of his glory and is ready to judge. In chapter 70, Enoch is taken up into the presence of the Son of man and the Lord. The correct reading of the text in chapter 71 seems to have Enoch become the Son of man. This Elect One or Son of man in *1 Enoch* 37—71 is pre-existent (48:2–3, 6; 62:7). He is worshiped (62:9). He will dwell with the righteous in a transformed earth (45:4–5; 62:15). Here, the traditions of an angelic and a human figure merge, with the human figure being identified with the heavenly one.

7. The Magharians were a pre-Christian ascetic Jewish group whose views influenced those of the Christian heretic Arius. They held that God created an angel who then created the world; that this angel revealed the law; that he is the subject of all anthropomorphic expressions about God in Israel's scriptures, including those about the throne of glory; and that he was sent down in the form of man to represent God.[25]

8. The *Apocalypse of Abraham* 9—19 contains a vision of the throne of glory in chapter 18. The context involves the eternal God saying to Abraham, "I am your protector" (9:4). Then God sends the angel Yaoel (a variant of Yahweh) in the likeness of a man, through the mediation of the ineffable name, to care for Abraham (10:3); that is, God's name is in Yaoel (10:8). This angel's hair is white like snow (11:2). Yaoel shows Abraham how to offer a sacrifice to God. In 17:2 the angel kneels down and worships with Abraham; in 17:7 he recites the song with Abraham. It is a song of praise to the "Eternal One, Mighty One, Holy El . . . , self-originate, incorruptible . . . , unbegotten . . . , without mother, without father, ungenerated . . . most glorious EL . . . , Yaoel, you are he my soul has loved, my protector." In the *Apocalypse of Abraham*, then, the angel has God's name (Yahweh) and God's appearance (like sapphire—Ezek. 1:26; white hair—Dan. 7:9) and performs God's functions (protection). Moreover, God is praised in terms of the name Yaoel. Most interesting is the end of the song. Abraham sings: "Accept the sacrifice which you yourself made to yourself through me as I searched for you" (17:20). It is as though Yaoel's part in offering the sacrifice to God is God's offering it to himself, through Abraham. The angel and God are virtually interchangeable.[26]

9. *Third Enoch* brings our cursory survey to an end. In this Hekalot document[27] one encounters Metatron, the prince of the divine presence (1:4, 9; 3:1). He is more exalted than all the angels (4:1), being the prince and ruler over angels in heavenly places (4:9; 16:1). He serves the throne of glory (7:1; 15:1). He sits[28] on a second throne, like the throne of glory

(10:1; 16:1). Whatever he says to anyone in God's name, that one must do (10:5). Anyone who has anything to say to God must go before Metatron and speak to him (10:4). He wears a crown and is called by God "the Lesser Yahweh" (12:5).[29] Nevertheless, he is not equal to God (chapter 16).[30] He is, however, identified with Enoch, who was appointed as a prince and ruler among the ministering angels (chapter 4).

Sources such as those just mentioned have been the object of serious study in recent years.[31] Opinions still vary widely. The views expressed here represent my path through the thicket. The nine sources mentioned above cover a time period from the second century B.C.E. to the third century C.E. or later. Some seem to be interrelated: for example, Ezekiel, Daniel, *1 Enoch, 3 Enoch*. Some seem to reflect independent strands of Jewish life: Ezekiel the Tragedian, the *Testament of Moses,* the Magharians, the Wisdom of Solomon. Essentially, the literature presents two views. On the one hand, some sources seem to reflect the old *malek Yahweh* tradition, where the second figure is but an extension of God. On the other hand, others seem to think of a distinct second figure, either heavenly (for example, *1 Enoch,* Magharians, *3 Enoch*) or earthly (for example, *1 Enoch,* Ezekiel the Tragedian). Variety reigns. Nevertheless, in all the sources discussed above, God's actions are associated with a second figure.

Scholarly resistance to such evidence comes from a recognition of the monotheistic character of ancient Judaism.[32] Monotheism, so the argument goes, was part of Jewish self-perception. Israel's scriptures affirmed it: for example, Deuteronomy 6:4; Isaiah 45:20–25. Philo (*Decalogue* 65) says:

> Let us, then, engrave deep in our hearts this as the first and most sacred of commandments, to acknowledge and honor one God who is above all, and let the idea that gods are many never even reach the ears of the man whose rule of life is to seek for truth in purity and goodness. (Loeb Classical Library)

Josephus (*Antiquities* 5.1.27 + 112) claims "to recognize God as one is common to all the Hebrews." Jesus in Mark 12:29–30 reflects the same perspective. Outsiders so viewed the Jewish people (so Celsus in Origen, *Against Celsus* 1.23–24).

If the sources understand the second figure as the *malek Yahweh,* however, there is no violation of monotheism. In numerous passages in Israel's scriptures appears an angel figure who is regarded as an extension of God (Gen. 16:7, 9, 10, 11; 19:1, 15, 16; 21:17; 22:11, 15; 24:40; 31:11; 48:15–16 [the God, the angel]; Ex. 3:2–6; 4:24; 14:19; 23:20–21, 23 [angel in whom God's name dwells]; 32:34; 33:2; Num. 20:16; Judg. 2:1, 4;

5:23; 6:11–12; 13:3, 9, 13; Zech. 12:8). How ancient Jews probably viewed this figure is reflected in Justin's *Dialogue with Trypho* 128.3. Justin says some Jews[33] contend that the angel who appeared to Abraham, Jacob, and Moses

> is indivisible and inseparable from the Father, just as they say that the light of the sun on earth is indivisible and inseparable from the sun in the heavens . . . so the Father, when He chooses, say they, causes His power to spring forth, and when He chooses, He makes it return to Himself. In this way, they teach, He made the angels.[34]

Such an understanding of the ontology of the angel avoids any threat to Jewish monotheism.

At the same time, certain Jews, like the Magharians, regarded the second figure as a creation of God (an angelic creature) who then created all of the rest of the creation. In the case of Enoch and Moses, a human figure from the legendary past (a creature) is regarded as elevated to the position of sharing God's throne. In the case of *1 Enoch,* Enoch is transformed into the Son of man (a heavenly preexistent being); in *3 Enoch,* Enoch becomes an angelic figure;[35] in Ezekiel the Tragedian, Moses is granted a seat on the throne of glory, which is vacated by God. Recognition of the diversity of ancient Judaism allows for such stances, which are so different from later rabbinic orthodoxy.[36] The tendency to speak of a second figure, God's vice-regent, could reflect the monotheism of the *malek Yahweh* tradition or a position against which the rabbis would later polemicize.[37] The position against which the rabbis contended was one that assumed a second figure who was numerically distinct from God, who was a creature and so ontologically differentiated from God, but who functioned as an extension of the divine will or purpose.

Messianists such as Justin represented yet a third view of the ontology of the second figure in ancient Judaism. In his *Dialogue* 128 he clarifies his understanding of the ontology of the *malek Yahweh*/Christ. Rather than being a projection of God, the Word/Angel is numerically distinct from the Father. Yet, he was not begotten from the Father by abscission (cutting off), as if the essence of the Father were divided. Rather, it is like a fire being kindled from a fire: distinct from it but leaving the original not less but the same. The Word/Angel can be a legitimate object of worship because he is God. His ontology is understood differently from either Jewish option presented above because, on the one hand, he is not a projection of the Father and, on the other, he is not a creature created by the Father.

If ancient auditors heard the Revelation to John read, how would they have understood John's Christology? The Revelation talks about an eternal, preexistent figure who becomes identified with Jesus in history; is born from the Jewish people; dies a martyr's death; is exalted to the throne of God, where he is a legitimate object of worship; and acts as God's vice-regent in history, at history's end, and in the new world where he dwells forever with his people.[38] A person who was aware of the tradition of second figures associated with God in dealings with humans would have felt no significant discontinuity. The idea of a human becoming identified with a heavenly being would have been familiar. The notion of such a one sharing the throne of God would have been known. The expectation that such a one would carry out the last judgment would have been traditional. That this one would dwell with God's righteous ones beyond the resurrection would have been expected. Of all the particular sources of the idea of a second figure associated with the throne of God, *1 Enoch* 37–71[39] is the closest to Revelation. Here, the preexistence of the Elect One/Son of man/Messiah is assumed; a human, Enoch, is identified with this heavenly one; he sits on the throne of glory; he functions for God at the last judgment; he dwells with God's people forever thereafter. An auditor would have sensed that Revelation was speaking about Christ in these terms.[40]

Of course, the Christian depiction of Christ in Revelation does not fit the cultural pattern perfectly. In the Apocalypse, Christ dies before he is taken up. His death has soteriological significance, both for him and for others. The facts of the Christian story obviously call for adjustments to the pattern. The pattern, however, functions as one way in which early Christians could speak about the significance of Jesus Christ. Revelation does not call Jesus an angel, but it does talk about him in ways that echo the larger tradition. By speaking of Jesus Christ as eternal (the first and last) and by depicting him as a legitimate object of worship, the author of the Apocalypse clearly locates him on the side of Deity rather than on the side of creatures. When Revelation's story of Jesus is read against the background of Justin's statement of his understanding of the ontology of the Word/Angel, it makes good "Christian" sense. If some Jews regarded the *malek Yahweh* as "projected," and others viewed angels as "made," early Messianists like Justin (and John the seer?) believed the second figure to be "begotten." If the *pattern* of John the seer's Christology is that of the Jewish myth of a second figure associated with the throne, the *ontology* seems to be that verbalized by Justin. It is in these terms, I propose, that ancient auditors would have heard the christological data in Revelation.

If the thesis proposed in this chapter is tenable, then it casts light on other issues. First, it enables us to see continuity between Revelation's Christology in the 90s and that in the *Ascension of Isaiah,* the Shepherd of Hermas, and Justin Martyr in the first part of the second century.[41] Second, it encourages us to reread other New Testament documents with fresh eyes. Perhaps Jude 5–7 should be understood as a reference to Christ as the *malek Yahweh;* perhaps the Synoptic Son of man Christology comes out of the same context.[42] If so, then rather than angelomorphic Christology being a second-century innovation, it becomes a first-century phenomenon that carries into the second century and later. The Christology of Revelation becomes part of a trajectory whose outlines can be traced over several centuries.

NOTES

1. Donald Guthrie, "The Christology of Revelation," in *Jesus of Nazareth: Lord and Christ,* ed. Joel B. Green and Max Turner (Grand Rapids: Wm. B. Eerdmans Publishing Co., 1994), 397.

2. D. M. Beck, "The Christology of the Apocalypse of John," in *New Testament Studies,* ed. E. P. Booth (Nashville: Abingdon-Cokesbury Press, 1942), 275.

3. Chief among the studies are Donald E. Cook, "The Christology of the Apocalypse" (Ph.D. diss., Duke University, 1962), summarized in "Christology of the Apocalypse," *The Outlook* 16 (1967): 3–9; J. Comblin, *Le Christ dans l'Apocalypse,* Biblique de theologie, Theologie biblique 3, 6 (Paris: Descleé de Brouwer, 1965); Traugott Holtz, *Die Christologie der Apokalypse des Johannes,* 2d ed., Texte und Untersuchungen 85 (Berlin: Akademie-Verlag, 1971); Hans-Ruedi Weber, *The Way of the Lamb: Christ in the Apocalypse* (Geneva: WCC Publications, 1988). Richard Bauckham, *The Theology of the Book of Revelation* (Cambridge: Cambridge University Press, 1993), offers two insightful chapters: chapter 3, "The Lamb on the Throne," and chapter 4, "The Victory of the Lamb and His Followers." See also Loren Stuckenbruck, *Angel Veneration and Christology: A Study in Early Judaism and in the Christology of the Apocalypse of John,* Wissenschaftliche Untersuchungen zum Neuen Testament 2, 70 (Tübingen: J. C. B. Mohr [Paul Siebeck], 1995).

4. Comblin, *Le Christ dans l'Apocalypse,* focuses on titles: Lamb, the coming one (Son of man, Word of God, ruler, Wisdom), witness, Christ, the living one.

5. Joseph A. Fitzmyer, "The Contribution of Qumran Aramaic to the Study of the New Testament," *New Testament Studies* 20 (1974): 386–91, points out the absolute use of *Mara* for God in the Qumran *Targum of Job.*

6. M. G. Reddish, "Martyr Christology in the Apocalypse," *Journal for the Study of the New Testament* 33 (1988): 85–95, contends that Revelation depicts Christ as the supreme martyr who conquers through his martyrdom as an encouragement to the readers to imitate Jesus. "His followers are to

follow in his path, being willing to suffer and die on account of their witness. Jesus, the faithful witness, is their example" (91).

7. Ernest P. Janzen, "The Jesus of the Apocalypse Wears the Emperor's Clothes," *Society of Biblical Literature 1994 Seminar Papers,* ed. E. H. Lovering Jr. (Atlanta: Scholars Press, 1994), 637–61. After all the literary and numismatic evidence is sifted, it is astonishing how few parallels emerge between the way in which Jesus is depicted in the Revelation and the symbols associated with the imperial household.

8. William F. Arndt, F. Wilbur Gingrich, and Frederick Danker, *A Greek-English Lexicon of the New Testament,* 2d ed. (Chicago: University of Chicago Press, 1979), 112, prefer "first cause" but grant that "first created" is linguistically possible as well.

9. Robert H. Mounce, "The Christology of the Apocalypse," *Foundations* 11 (1969): 42–51, says: "In Revelation Jesus is supremely the Lamb" (42); see also Norman Hillyer, "The Lamb in the Apocalypse," *Evangelical Quarterly* 39 (1967): 228–36.

10. If this practice of creating titles out of functional descriptions of figures is to be taken as characteristic of early Christians generally, one can see how "one like a son of man" in apocalyptic could become, in messianist writings, a title, "the Son of man."

11. The categories are taken from Weber's *Way of the Lamb.*

12. Louis A. Vos, *The Synoptic Traditions in the Apocalypse* (Kampen, the Netherlands: Kok Pharos, 1965).

13. Richard Bauckham, "The Worship of Jesus in Apocalyptic Christianity," *New Testament Studies* 27 (1980–1981): 322–41; R. T. France, "The Worship of Jesus: A Neglected Factor in Christological Debate," in *Christ the Lord,* ed. H. H. Rowden (Downer's Grove, Ill.: Inter-Varsity Press, 1982), 17–36.

14. Loren T. Stuckenbruck, "An Angelic Refusal of Worship: The Tradition and Its Function in the Apocalypse of John," *Society of Biblical Literature 1994 Seminar Papers,* ed. E. H. Lovering Jr. (Atlanta: Scholars Press, 1994), 679–96.

15. On the issue of the incarnation in the Johannine epistles and fourth Gospel, see Charles H. Talbert, *Reading John* (New York: Crossroad, 1992), 44–47, 66–79; and idem, "And the Word Became Flesh: When?" in *The Future of Christology,* ed. A. J. Malherbe and W. A. Meeks (Minneapolis: Fortress Press, 1993), 43–52. Guthrie, "Christology of Revelation," 403, says rightly that the Apocalypse presents little evidence for an incarnational Christology.

16. M. Eugene Boring, "Narrative Christology in the Apocalypse," *Catholic Biblical Quarterly* 54 (1992): 719.

17. Ben Witherington III, *Paul's Narrative Thought World* (Louisville, Ky.: Westminster John Knox Press, 1994).

18. Boring, "Narrative Christology in the Apocalypse," 702–23.

19. This is a bit different from the approach of Holtz, *Die Christologie der Apokalypse des Johannes*. Holtz organizes his book around the present of Christ and the future of Christ. These are merely logical categories; they do not arise out of a presupposed narrative.

20. Of course, the *Targum on Isaiah* has the prophet say in 6:5 that he had seen "the glory of the Shekinah of the King of the ages" and in 6:1 that he saw "the glory of the Lord." Some Jews took "the glory" as a reference to a second figure (John 12:41).

21. Christopher Rowland, "The Vision of the Risen Christ in Revelation 1:13ff.: The Debt of an Early Christology to an Aspect of Jewish Angelology," *Journal of Theological Studies* 31 (1980): 1–11.

22. The LXX tradition tends to coalesce the figures of Daniel 7:9 and 7:13: "He came as Son of Man and was presented as Ancient of Days." Stuckenbruck, *Angel Veneration and Christology,* 213–18, says this is most likely not an error but a translation interpretation. His view is supported by the same tendency elsewhere in the LXX. Ecclesiastes 5:6 LXX has "do not say in the presence of God" whereas the MT has "do not say before the angel." Isaiah 63:9 LXX has "not a messenger nor an angel but He himself saved them" whereas the MT has "the angel of his presence saved them."

23. Christopher Rowland, "A Man Clothed in Linen: Daniel 10:6ff and Jewish Angelology," *Journal for the Study of the New Testament* 24 (1985): 99–110.

24. Pieter W. van der Horst, "Moses' Throne Vision in Ezekiel the Dramatist," *Journal of Jewish Studies* 34 (1983): 21–29. The translation is from James H. Charlesworth, ed., *The Old Testament Pseudepigrapha* (Garden City, N.Y.: Doubleday, 1985), 2:812.

25. H. A. Wolfson, "The Pre-existent Angel of the Magharians and al-Nahawandi," *Jewish Quarterly Review* 51 (1960–1961): 89–106; Norman Golb, "Who Were the Magariya?" *Journal of the American Oriental Society* 80 (1960): 347–59.

26. C. R. A. Morray-Jones, "Transformational Mysticism in the Apocalyptic-Merkabah Tradition," *Journal of Jewish Studies* 43 (1992): 1–31.

27. For a discussion of all the Hekalot materials, including *3 Enoch (Sefer Hekalot)*, see part 2 of Ithamar Gruenwald, *Apocalyptic and Merkavah Mysticism,* Arbeiten zur Geschichtes des antiken Judentums und des Urchristentums 14 (Leiden: E. J. Brill, 1980). For the texts of the Hekalot writings, see Peter Schafer, *Synopse zur Hekhalot-Literatur* (Tübingen: J. C. B. Mohr [Paul Siebeck], 1981); and idem, *Geniza-Fragmente zur Hekhalot-Literatur* (Tübingen: J. C. B. Mohr [Paul Siebeck], 1984).

28. *B. Ḥag* 15a says that no one is allowed to sit in heaven except God.

29. *B. Sanh.* 38b has Rab Idit apply the name Yahweh to Metatron, whose name is like his master's.

30. The similarities between Metatron and Jesus are so great that Almo

Murtonen, "The Figure of Metatron," *Vetus Testamentum* 3 (1953): 409–14, argues wrongly that Jesus was the prototype for Metatron.

31. Martin Werner, *The Formation of Christian Dogma,* trans. S. G. F. Brandon (New York: Harper & Brothers, 1957; German original, 1941), argued that angel Christology was the oldest Christology of the church, developing from the Son of man figure of *1 Enoch.* A critique of his thesis was offered immediately by W. Michaelis, *Zur Engelchristologie im Urchristentum: Abbau der Konstruktion Martin Werners* (Basel: Heinrich Majer, 1942). J. Barbel, *Christos Angelos* (1941; reprint, Bonn: Peter Hanstein, 1964), focused on the patristic evidence and concluded that some of the fathers interpreted Christ in terms of the *malek Yahweh* of the Old Testament. Until recently, research stood with the assertion that there was an angel Christology in the fathers but not in the New Testament. A series of studies has, of late, revised the earlier consensus: Jarl E. Fossum, *The Name of God and the Angel of the Lord,* Wissenschaftliche Untersuchungen zum Neuen Testament 1, 36 (Tübingen: J. C. B. Mohr [Paul Siebeck], 1985); Alan F. Segal, *Two Powers in Heaven,* Studies in Judaism in Late Antiquity 25 (Leiden: E. J. Brill, 1978); Christopher Rowland, *The Open Heaven: A Study of Apocalyptic in Judaism and Early Christianity* (London: SPCK, 1982); Margaret Barker, *The Great Angel: A Study of Israel's Second God* (Louisville, Ky.: Westminster/John Knox Press, 1992). These volumes suffered from the excesses of attempting to establish a new position. They were critiqued by the like of James D. G. Dunn, *Christology in the Making* (Philadelphia: Westminster Press, 1980) and Larry W. Hurtado, *One God One Lord* (Philadelphia: Fortress Press, 1988). As the result of an ongoing dialogue, however, one finds an emerging consensus that some type of angel Christology was traditional in the first century. See Stuckenbruck, *Angel Veneration and Christology,* who concludes: Why use angelic language for Christ in Revelation? It was a retention of tradition (272). Alan F. Segal, "Heavenly Ascent in Hellenistic Judaism, Early Christianity and Their Environment," *Aufstieg und Niedergang der Römischen Welt* II.23.2, 1371, says: "It is probable that Jesus' identity was very early associated with the angel of YHWH who is superior to all angels in that he represents God's name on earth." Nils A. Dahl, "Sources of Christological Language," in *Jesus the Christ* (Minneapolis: Fortress Press, 1991), 113–36, especially 120–21, concludes that "there seems to be increasing agreement that angelology is one source of christological language." Werner, in essentials, has been vindicated.

32. Rowland, "Man Clothed in Linen," proposes the term *angelomorphic* in order to avoid categorizing Christ as a creature instead of deity, in contrast to *angelic,* implying creatureliness.

33. Daniel Abrams, "The Boundaries of Divine Ontology: The Inclusion and Exclusion of Metatron in the Godhead," *Harvard Theological Review* 87

(1994): 291–321, accepts Justin's claim as a true reflection of how some Jews would have thought in antiquity.

34. Translation from *The Ante-Nicene Fathers,* ed. A. Roberts and J. Donaldson (Grand Rapids: Wm. B. Eerdmans Publishing Co., 1979), 1:264.

35. A human's becoming an angelic deliverer or judge is found elsewhere in ancient Jewish sources: (1) Melchizedek in 11QMelch—Was he taken up without dying?—as well as Melchizedek in *2 Enoch* 91 and following. (2) Abel in the *Testament of Abraham* 12–13—Was he taken up after death? (3) Joshua in the *Sibylline Oracles* 5.256–59—Was he taken up after death? (Is this a Jewish reference to Joshua or a Christian reference to Jesus?) The phenomenon was not without analogies in pagan circles. Compare Romulus's being taken up and becoming the god Quirinus (Plutarch, "Romulus," *Lives,* 28.2–3; Cicero, *The Republic* 1.41).

36. Peter Hayman, "Monotheism—A Misused Word in Jewish Studies," *Journal of Jewish Studies* 42 (1991): 1–15. Hayman contends that there is always a prominent number two in the heavenly hierarchy to whom Israel relates. This pattern is inherited from biblical times. So until Christians tried to fit the Holy Spirit into the picture, they did not deviate as far as one might think from a well-established pattern in Judaism.

37. Judah Goldin, "Not by Means of an Angel and Not by Means of a Messenger," in *Religions in Antiquity,* ed. J. Neusner (Leiden: E. J. Brill, 1968), 412–24, points out how the rabbis objected to some concepts of divine mediators and to the redemptive role of angels.

38. This type of approach works on an entirely different level from those studies of Revelation that inquire of three passages in the Apocalypse as to whether or not Jesus is portrayed as an angel in them: Revelation 1:12–20, where Christ is portrayed in terms derived from Daniel 10 and other apocalyptic visions (probably depicted in terms of a vision of an angel); 10:1–3 (probably not a reference to Christ); and 14:14 (probably not a reference to Christ).

39. A consensus seems to have formed for a dating of the *Similitudes* in the first part of the first century C.E. Compare David Winston Suter, "Weighed in the Balance: The Similitudes of Enoch in Recent Discussion," *Religious Studies Review* 7 (1981): 217–21 (*1 Enoch* 37–71 is first-century Jewish and 71:14 identifies Enoch as "that Son of Man"); Craig A. Evans, *Noncanonical Writings and New Testament Interpretation* (Peabody, Mass.: Hendrickson Publishers, 1992), 23.

40. I do not claim that Revelation is indebted to *1 Enoch* 37–71; I suggest only that it reflects the type of thought of which *1 Enoch* 37–71 is the closest extant early example.

41. Jean Danielou, *The Theology of Jewish Christianity,* trans. J. A. Baker (London: Darton, Longman & Todd, 1964), chaps. 4 and 5, offers a survey of second-century developments.

42. Two articles by Barnabas Lindars are suggestive: "Re-enter the Apocalyptic Son of Man," *New Testament Studies* 22 (1975): 52–72; "The Apocalyptic Myth and the Death of Christ," *Bulletin of the John Rylands Library* 57 (1975): 366–87. With a much more limited focus, see D. R. Catchpole, "The Angelic Son of Man in Luke 12:8," *Novum Testamentum* 24 (1982): 255–65, who contends that the Son of man in Luke 12:8 is an angelic figure, just as in Daniel 7.

CHRISTOLOGY OF THE NEW TESTAMENT: WHAT, THEN, IS NEW TESTAMENT CHRISTOLOGY?

Leander E. Keck

The editors of this book provided the title of this chapter; I have added a subtitle. The Contents for the book shows that, on the one hand, each of the first eleven contributions discusses the Christology of a specific text or cluster of texts, thereby implying that each has a distinct Christology that should be seen on its own terms; accordingly, one might use "New Testament Christologies," because the singular noun skews the subject matter. This view, in fact, has become the accepted wisdom of the scholars' guild. On the other hand, the last four chapters listed in this volume's Contents retain the singular, implying that when one turns to the "significance" of the subject matter for systematic theology, ethics, ministry, or preaching, it suddenly becomes legitimate (necessary?) to revert to "New Testament Christology" after all. Putting this chapter between the two parts of the anthology implies that the subject matter needs to be redefined if the discipline is to be clear about its task and if its work is to be available for the church—both results being wholly in accord with the distinguished career of the honoree.[1]

Redefining the subject matter implies dissatisfaction with the ways in which historical scholarship has already dealt with it, for it is this legacy that makes the question inevitable and the answer essential. First, however, it is useful to remind ourselves briefly of the ways in which Christology appears in the New Testament.

THE PHENOMENON OF CHRISTOLOGY
IN THE NEW TESTAMENT

Since Christology expresses the identity and significance of Jesus Christ, it permeates the whole New Testament, though not in equal measure throughout. One first observes that explicit christological statements are embedded in passages concerned with moral and pastoral matters, for which they provide warrants for the author's counsel. For instance, the extended christological passage in Philippians 2:6–11 is adduced as a warrant for a mode of behavior, and even Hebrews, while dominated by a particular Christology, is essentially a paraenetic book. This feature has three significant consequences: (1) At no point do we have the author's full Christology, only those aspects of it that he deemed pertinent to the issue at hand. The rest is assumed. (2) It is precarious to convert this silence into evidence of the author's ignorance or disinterest, as the discussions of Paul's knowledge of the Jesus traditions show. (3) These diverse, incomplete christological passages cannot be assembled into a single "Christology of the New Testament," as if they were scattered pieces of a jigsaw puzzle that various authors used as they saw fit.

Second, the Christology is expressed in quite diverse literary forms: titles, assertions, arguments, parables, poetry, vision reports, kerygmatic appeals, allegories, and narratives ranging from brief accounts to entire Gospels. The Gospels themselves are complex bearers of Christology, for not only do they contain many of the aforementioned forms but they also build Christology into their narrative structures, thereby creating a "show and tell" Christology. Moreover, the Gospels contain both the narrator's christological assertions and Jesus' self-interpretations.

Third, the New Testament's christological materials are derived from diverse religious/cultural concepts and modes of thought, each with its own complex history. One finds Jewish apocalyptic and midrash, as well as Gentile (Stoic) formulas (1 Cor. 8:6 refers to Christ "through whom are all things and through whom we exist"), as well as concepts and motifs used in hellenized Judaism. Especially important is the role of the synagogue's scripture, cited in Greek (LXX).

Fourth, not to be overlooked is the persistent polemical character of many passages. According to Matthew 24:4–5, Jesus himself warns against deceivers ("false Christs" in 24:24) who will come in his name saying "I am the Christ." Paul mentions those who "proclaim another Jesus" (2 Cor. 11:4), and 1 John does not hesitate to label those with the wrong view of Jesus as "antichrists" (1 John 2:18–25)—to cite but the best known of such passages. In other words, the New Testament comes with a warning: "The wrong Christology can be dangerous to your health!"

Finally, Jesus is related to the same topic in quite different ways. For example, Paul, John, and Hebrews clearly understand Jesus to be the incarnation of the preexistent Son of God,[2] but in Matthew and Luke he is Son of God from conception onward. The former offer a three-stage Christology (preexistence, existence, postexistence), the latter a two-stage one (existence, postexistence). Another difference pertains to Jesus' relation to the law. According to Matthew 5:17–21, Jesus came to fulfill it completely, but according to Hebrews, as the priest like Melchizedek (that is, Christ did not become a priest through lineage but "through the power of an indestructible life") he set aside the "earlier commandment" because it "made nothing perfect" (Heb. 7:15–19). A third difference concerns the relation of the believer to Christ: Whereas the Synoptics emphasize discipleship, following Jesus and taking up one's own cross, Paul writes of being "in Christ" and of being baptized "into [Christ's] death" (Rom. 6:3); *disciple* is not part of Paul's vocabulary, and participation in Christ is absent from the Synoptics. To be sure, these are not flat contradictions (mutually exclusive assertions) but perspectives that often can be correlated by taking them up into a more comprehensive conceptuality (such as "the Christian life"), thereby making each view, adequate in its own context, a contributor to something not found in, or necessarily required by, the texts themselves. But is this what one means by "New Testament Christology"? That is precisely the view that historical criticism rejected. But is its own treatment of the subject matter any better?

HISTORICAL CRITICISM
AND NEW TESTAMENT CHRISTOLOGY

Historical criticism, determined to overcome the habit of quarrying scripture for passages adduced to support the loci of Christian doctrine, undertook to reconstruct the history of early Christian thought so that each author, text, or idea could be explained *in situ*. Thereby the texts became sources of information about "Christian origins," whose shaping factor was said to be the hellenization of the originally Jewish Christian faith, the adjustments made to accommodate the unfulfilled apocalyptic hope of the Parousia, the rise of institutional "early catholicism," or some combination of such trends. To reconstruct this history, the New Testament alone does not suffice; all early Christian literature, and pertinent non-Christian texts as well, must be taken into account.

With the rise of the "history of religions" approach in the closing decades of the nineteenth century, the scope and task were broadened to place early Christianity more precisely in the context of the history of religious belief and practice, especially cultic, in antiquity. Inevitably, historical-critical study of early Christian belief and practice concentrated more and more on non-Christian parallels that could be regarded as antecedents to, and influences on, early Christianity, which in turn was regarded as a particular instance of ancient religiosity. Thus, the formative factor was no longer located in the church's scripture but in the beliefs, myths, and rituals of the ancient Near Eastern and Greek religions.

Among New Testament scholars, no one grasped more fully the import of this paradigm for the study of New Testament theology or advocated its consequences more vigorously than William Wrede (1859–1906), whose famous "The Task and Methods of 'New Testament Theology'" clearly pertains to Christology as well.[3] Noting that many of the epistles are too brief to provide "doctrinal positions," and that most of the New Testament is "practical advice" in which creedal statements "are touched on in passing or presupposed, rather than consciously developed," he accuses New Testament theology of making "doctrine out of what in itself is not doctrine" (75). Moreover, since rigorous historical study cannot be limited to canonical texts, "the name New Testament theology is wrong in both its terms," for the subject matter is "the history of early Christian religion and theology" (116), understood as "what was believed, thought, taught, hoped, required and *striven for* . . . not what certain writings say about faith, doctrine, hope, etc." (84–85).

Wrede would have little patience with the Contents of this volume, for he contended that the thoughts of individual writings and authors (apart from Paul and John) are secondary; what matters are "connections and effects. Where does this come from? How did this happen? What conditioned it? . . . Every historical datum is only made comprehensible so far as we are able to set it in the context out of which it has grown" (96). To find what was historically decisive, "we must go for the dominant features" (101). Because "Paul signifies the very wide distance from Jesus," it is necessary to "measure the distance between them and, so far as one can, to explain it" (108) and to detect the "after-effects of Paul" as well.[4] Given the focus of his essay, Wrede said little about the relation of the emerging Christian religion to other religions of the time; he did, however, point out that "Judaism, not the Old Testament, is the basis of Christianity in the history of religion," and that "Greco-Roman paganism" must be considered as well, meaning "the typical outlook of the man in the street," not the philosophers (114–15).

What Wrede "prophesied" was largely "fulfilled" in Wilhelm Bousset's (1865–1920) magisterial *Kyrios Christos: A History of the Belief in Christ from the Beginnings of Christianity to Irenaeus,* in which hellenization is the decisive factor.[5] Like Wrede and other champions of this approach, he insisted that early Christianity "has nothing, nothing at all, to do with the truly philosophical literature of the educated circles" (15); hellenization came through the influence of the mystery religions and Gnosticism, the latter understood as a pre-Christian phenomenon, not merely a Christian heresy. Bousset located the pivotal turn to Hellenism in the Gentile Christian worship of Jesus the Lord (*Kyrios*) who was present in the enthusiastic cult. It was Paul who turned Christianity into "a 'redemption' religion in the supernatural sense" (182, 258) in which Jesus is the redeemed redeemer, similar to the myth of the dying and rising gods. Thereby "the Jewish primitive Christian eschatology is finally overcome" (198). Christ mysticism was developed differently in John, where Jesus appears as "the mystagogue who with his marvelous words leads his people to the goal" (228); he is the Son of God, or God, "sojourning on the earth" (217), though still retaining "the little bit of humanity" (217, 220). Bousset writes so vividly and empathetically of the religious experience of Paul that one scarcely notices that he makes almost no mention of the law in relation to God's righteousness and human justification. In the post-apostolic era, we hear only echoes of Paul's language, as the office replaced the Spirit; what endured was Christianity as a "cultic society" in which the frequent references to Christ's death, atonement, and person are "thankful confessions of a believing community to the Kyrios who has done so much for his own," but these are "no real theology"—and hence, no real Christology either (318).

The (Wrede-)Bousset legacy turned out to be especially influential for one dimension of the study of early Christian Christology—its relation to Jesus. After the Great War, Rudolf Bultmann used Bousset's grand portrayal of hellenization to distinguish earlier Palestinian items in the Jesus tradition from later Hellenistic accretions. Wrede had already shown that Mark's Jesus story, basic to both Matthew and Luke, was not history but a narrative in which the dogma of Jesus' secret messiahship was imposed on the tradition of a nonmessianic Jesus,[6] thus severing the link between Jesus' self-interpretation and that of Christian faith in him. Now Bultmann's detailed form-critical analysis of each item in the Jesus tradition reinforced this by claiming to show how little of the tradition actually went back to Jesus.[7] Like Mark, the other Synoptists were neither historians nor theologians but compilers and editors of the hellenized Jesus traditions.[8]

Were it not for the impact of redaction criticism, which flourished for several decades after the Second World War, it is doubtful whether this book would include essays devoted to the Christology of each of the Synoptics, for it is by analyzing in great detail exactly how the Synoptic evangelists structured and modified their materials that redaction critics exposed each Gospel's distinctive theological views. However, redaction criticism was not limited to the Gospels, for virtually every New Testament text was subjected to this type of analysis. Furthermore, scholars did not hesitate to locate the excavated traditions, and the inferred communities that allegedly formed and used them, on the map of early Christianity. Steadily it became evident that early Christianity was a highly diverse phenomenon. In other words, while redaction criticism made it possible to speak of the theology of each Gospel, it also had the effect of fragmenting the picture of early Christianity and its thought. The method itself made this result inevitable, for in order to locate and delineate a piece of tradition thought to be used in an existing text, one emphasized as much as possible the difference between tradition and redaction. Indeed, it was not unusual to read that the author's own view differed so much from the tradition that he cited the latter only to correct it.

Three important factors have made the results of this intensive work ever more hypothetical: (1) Frequently, scholars have been unable to achieve a consensus about the traditions' actual scope and wording; the same is true of alleged aggregates of traditions (for example, Q, the signs source used in John, the antecedents of the Sermon on the Mount). In some cases, even the existence of such antecedent materials has been vigorously contested. (2) The explicit christological traditions that have been recovered usually consist of a few lines, a formulaic phrase or two, or a motif—hardly enough evidence from which to infer discrete communities and their Christologies. (3) The task of assembling the disparate pieces into a coherent, convincing history of early Christianity has had to proceed with no controls other than the historical reasoning—and often the lively imagination—of the critic, who inevitably produced an account of what might have been if communities had adhered to a single Christology and if their historical development had been in a straight line. Early Christianity indeed was far more diverse and conflicted than had generally been surmised,[9] but the sources simply do not permit one to tell the whole story accurately. Understandably, in recent years many New Testament students have turned to nonhistorical literary ways of reading the texts, to rhetorical analyses or to synchronic sociological/anthropological modes of inquiry.

But by no means all; to the contrary, many have intensified precisely their diachronic—that is, historical—study of earliest Christology in the quest of the origins of various christological ideas, motifs, and titles. Once the keystone of Bousset's grand history disintegrated, namely, his claim that it was the Hellenistic (that is, predominantly Gentile) Christians who first hailed Jesus as Lord (*Kyrios*), it became natural to look to Palestinian Judaism and to Jewish literature of the second temple era generally for the roots of earliest Christology, especially after the Dead Sea Scrolls (and Scraps) began to be known. Above all, there were renewed efforts to trace the earliest Christology to the self-interpretation of Jesus in order to overcome the alleged historical hiatus between Jesus and the earliest church.[10] However one evaluates the results, the overall outcome supports the wise word of Marinus de Jonge, who views New Testament Christology as responses to Jesus: "Jesus is at the center of all early (and later) Christology. This presupposes some degree of continuity between what he said and did and people's reactions. It also presupposes some continuity between the situation of his followers before Jesus' cross and resurrection and their situation after these events." Difficult as it is to get back to Jesus, "we *have* to speak of Jesus' own teaching, including his teaching about himself, if we want to do justice to the early Christian message about him."[11]

Despite the vast and undeniably significant increase in our knowledge of both Jesus and early Christianity, and their roots in the religious and cultural environment of the time, for the study of Christology in the New Testament the record of scholarship hardly constitutes a grand success story. This is largely because the preoccupation with historical questions—especially the quest for the origins of christological concepts and titles—has obscured the subject matter itself. One has the suspicion that George Berkeley's quip, doubtless made in a quite different context, is appropriate here: We "first raised a dust and then complained that we cannot see."[12] Perhaps a new start is possible, one that neither ignores nor repudiates historical inquiry but that understands the subject matter differently, one that does not simply use the New Testament as source material for the first chapter in the history of Christian thought. Such a new beginning entails going back to the point where the study of Christology in the New Testament was absorbed into the study of early Christian religion.

WREDE REVISITED

Wrede's programmatic piece rested on three basic convictions, which he stated at the outset (69–73): (1) Analyzing the New Testament writings for their theology (read: Christology) "does considerable violence" to their occasioned, practical character, whereas (he implied) using them as evidence for the history of early Christian religion does not. (2) There is no demonstrable reason for treating these writings as a special group because "where the doctrine of inspiration has been discarded, it is impossible to maintain the dogmatic conception of the canon." Consequently, since "no New Testament writing was born with the predicate 'canonical' attached," these texts are to be seen "simply as early Christian writings." (3) A strictly historical account of early Christian religion is "guided by a pure disinterested concern for knowledge," and the result will be "totally indifferent to all dogma and systematic theology. What could dogmatics offer it?"

Appropriate as Wrede's convictions may be for an unprejudiced study of early Christian history, they cannot inhibit a fresh approach to the study of Christology in the New Testament, because they pertain to another mode of inquiry. To begin with, his call for an unbridgeable gulf between the reconstruction of early Christian religion and theology simply cannot be transferred to the study of Christology (in the latter sense), because by definition Christology is part of systematic theology. Isolating Christology from the study of New Testament Christology would be like insulating the study of Plato from philosophy. To the contrary, just as a grasp of the rhetoric and logic of philosophy alerts one to what to look for in Plato, so a grasp of the rhetoric and inner logic of Christology identifies what is to be looked for in the New Testament's Christology. Likewise, Wrede's first point too does not preclude studying the New Testament for its Christology because if one knows what to look for, one need not do "considerable violence" to the New Testament's character. Because Christology is a distinct mode of discourse with its own "grammar" (to be sketched shortly), there is no need to replace New Testament Christology with the history of early Christian religion in order to respect the nature of the New Testament writings; for history and Christology are two distinct, though related, undertakings that look for different things in the same material. The one is as legitimate as the other. Indeed, an overall view of early Christian history is necessary if one is not to portray the New Testament's Christology in an ahistorical way for ahistorical readers. Finally, Wrede's second conviction—that without a doctrine of inspiration one has no warrant for limiting the inquiry to the New Testament—is also valid for the study of Christian origins but not for the study of Christology in the New Testament. It is no more arbitrary to deal only with the New Testament than it is to restrict one's study to any other intelligible body of materials. In fact, one can say that for precisely historical reasons it is less arbitrary, because the New Testament canon is a historical fact, and its writings have been influential precisely because they were canonized. By contrast, "early Christian writings" as such never existed, for this is but a convenient, necessary, modern label for distinguishing one body of texts from another, and its boundaries are both elastic and porous.[13] These writings can, of course, be studied for their Christology—if one knows what to look for.

THE RHETORIC OF CHRISTOLOGY

Christology is a coherent statement of Christ's identity and significance— in traditional language, the person and work of Christ. ("Christ" is used to indicate that the subject matter exceeds Jesus of Nazareth, though he remains its historical center.) Were it not for his significance there would be no need to speak of his identity. Thus, we may say that Christology is the discourse by means of which Christians account for what they believe they have experienced, and will experience, through Jesus Christ (liberation, new life, forgiveness), customarily understood as "salvation" (Greek, *sōtēria*). Consequently, one can also say that in a coherent Christology the understanding of salvation (soteriology, the work of Christ) implies the identity (the person of Christ) as its ground, and that his person, or identity, implies soteriology as its significance or work. Because each implies the other, one may enter the discourse at either point, for a full-orbed Christology embraces both.

This initial consideration has two important consequences. First, Christology, even when it focuses attention on the person of Christ, never concerns Christ alone, like a Kantian *Ding an sich,* but always understands him in specific relationships or correlations. Second, the coherence of Christology refers to the requirement that the correlations be appropriate, that they make sense conceptually. Since the cure must fit the disease, the salvation effected by Jesus Christ must be correlated appropriately with the understanding of the human condition. In other words, the soteriological correlate implies an anthropology, and vice versa. Thus, if the human condition is essentially ignorance and folly, what is needed is instruction and wisdom. There is then no need of forgiveness—unless, of course, ignorance and folly are understood as sin against God. But then more is required than instruction and wisdom.

It is precisely at this point that the construal of Christ's significance or work becomes decisive, because if it is to have an adequate ground, there must be a basis in Christ for what he does to remedy the human condition. Since "the human condition" refers at its deepest level to the relation to God, the coherence of christological discourse requires that the person of Christ be related rightly to God and that the question "Who, then, is he really?" be answered properly. Thus, if Jesus is really a sage who deals effectively and sufficiently with the human condition by imparting wisdom to those who will receive it, his relation to God is adequately accounted for by saying that he was inspired or endowed by God with divine wisdom. But if his work is to free us from the tyranny of death and mortality, he must be related to God quite differently, for an inspired sage might liberate us from misconceptions of death and mortality but could not free us from death itself. In short, the deeper the problem, the "higher" the Christology needed to deal with it definitively. Accordingly, for instance, were it not for the prologue of John, the claims of the Johannine Jesus would be preposterous, arrogant assertions without a grounding in reality. It is the identification of Jesus as the Logos enfleshed that makes the Johannine Jesus intelligible and credible — if one believes the prologue.

This formal correlation between the person and the work of Christ would leave Christology totally vulnerable to the human propensity to make of Christ whatever legitimates a congenial view of salvation or "religious experience," were it not for the fact that the person in view was a particular historical individual who was executed on the cross. The historicity of Jesus, when taken with full seriousness, resists making him into a construct completely deduced from Christian experience. At this point, therefore, another element in the grammar of Christology comes into play — the solution discloses the plight. The Christ event is a given that exposes dimensions of the human condition that otherwise would be overlooked or suppressed. In this light, one may paraphrase de Jonge's observation (that Christology is response to Jesus): Christology is *ex post facto* reasoning about Christ.

This formal understanding of the grammar of Christology (how it "works") reflects the long history of reflection and debate about the subject matter, whose beginnings are in the New Testament. None of its writings or authors studied the rules or followed this script deliberately. Rather, in construing the identity and significance of Christ for their communities, they intuitively created the grammar of christological discourse, because the logic of the situation required them to do so. Nonetheless, it is as legitimate to use the developed rationale of Christology to analyze the Christology in their writings as it is to use musicology to study folk music created by persons with no inkling of music theory or composition.

NEW TESTAMENT CHRISTOLOGY REVISITED

The definition itself is quite simple and straightforward; the implications are more subtle. First of all, New Testament Christology is Christology as it appears in the New Testament texts. They are the only thing that exists; all else is inference. And not even a correct inference is evidence. Reconstructing, insofar as possible, the Christology of groups (Hellenistic Jewish Christians in Antioch) or of traditions and sources used in the texts (for example, Q or the signs source allegedly used by John) is essential for tracing the history of early Christology as the context of the Christology of New Testament texts. But the Christology of inferred sources and traditions exists only as an element in the Christology of existing texts. What concerns the student of the Christology of the present text is the role of the received material in the Christology that results from using it. For example, it is quite likely that John 1:1–18 is the result of incorporating and modifying several earlier traditions. Identifying these as precisely as possible can contribute to the history of Christology; but even if the resulting reconstruction were beyond reasonable question, it would not be the Christology of the existing prologue, for here, too, the whole is greater than the sum of the parts. And even if the prologue were added relatively late to an earlier version of the fourth Gospel, as is sometimes argued, the fact that it is a prologue and not an epilogue requires one to treat it as the key signature for the whole Gospel and not as an afterthought.

Given the occasional character of the writings, it is not surprising that the Christology of a text will be focused and logically incomplete, or that the anthropological correlate will appear separately from what is said elsewhere about Christ. Thus, for Paul's Christology in Romans, for example, it does not matter that the construal of the human condition in chapters 1—3 and chapter 7 lacks references to Christ, or that the explicit references to Christ do not always refer explicitly to the anthropological passages, for being alert to the nature of Christology enables one to correlate the material according to the grammar of Christology. To do so is not to impose an alien Christology on the text but to make explicit what is logically implicit.

The fact that the New Testament contains seven—and some would say more than seven—letters from one author, Paul, is no reason to be deflected from this understanding of the subject matter; the effect of having this corpus is rather to provide a much richer context in which to read the Christology of each writing. For one thing, using the whole corpus to get a more complete picture of Paul's views of Christ and his significance enables one to see the Christology of 1 Thessalonians, for example, in light of the whole, to position his thinking more precisely in emerging Christianity, and so forth—but the results belong more to the history of Paul and of early Christology than to the Christology of the letter itself. The focus or emphasis of that particular Christology is, in turn, illumined by what can be inferred about Paul's reading of the situation in the Thessalonian church. Moreover, seeing as best one can Paul's understanding of Christ as a whole can illumine the Christology of a particular passage or letter because it helps one see how Paul thinks,[14] not only about Christ but also about the connections he makes with his view of Christ. Still, by not letting the study of the Christology of Paul's letters simply lapse into the study of the Christology of Paul, one guards against trying to understand the subject matter by recourse to the psychology of his "conversion."

The Christology of the text cannot be grasped by concentrating on christological titles used in it. Most texts use several titles, with no evident concern to show how they are related to one another. More important, "Christ" largely lost its original "messianic" meaning and became virtually a proper name, no longer capable of expressing both the *theo*logical and the soteriological/anthropological correlate implied in its (Hebrew) etymology-shaped meaning (God's anointed, through whom God's reign was made effective in the people of God); consequently, like Son or Son of God, it derives its actual meaning from its usage. This is hardly surprising, since in general "meaning" is conveyed not by single words but by sentences and paragraphs and by the tissue of the whole text, for it is in these larger linguistic constructions that the relationship of persons, things, and concepts is expressed. This is especially true of extended narratives like the Gospels and of discourses. Accordingly, in Romans the significance of Jesus for the disclosure of God's righteousness is neither expressed nor implied in any christological title but requires Paul's argument; similarly, in John the whole narrative interprets the "Son." Further, because titles that accent Jesus' identity in terms of his relation to God (for instance, Logos, Son, Son of man) can be used in connection with various views of his significance, concentrating on the titles tends to rupture the inherent nature of Christology as bipolar discourse, in which person and work must be thought together.[15]

Above all, one would grossly misread the New Testament were one to assume that the historical figure of Jesus was merely the passive recipient of sundry christological titles; for not only do the titles identify him but he also redefines them. Otherwise, they do not really "fit" Jesus, especially in light of his decision to go to Jerusalem, where he would end up on a cross. This is precisely the point of the Markan story of Jesus' response to Peter's "confession" at Caesarea Philippi. Indeed, it underlies the whole Markan insistence that the disciples, having heard Peter use the "right" title for Jesus, nonetheless fail to grasp who he really is.

Since the New Testament indeed presents numerous Christologies, the continued use of the customary singular noun requires justification. At the most rudimentary level, it simply identifies the texts in view, without necessarily implying anything significant about the New Testament's content or its canonical standing. The phrase becomes problematic when it is construed to mean that the New Testament contains a single, coherent Christology, sufficiently unified conceptually that it can be treated as a single voice; at that point, like a lightning rod, it attracts all the energies generated by the stormy debates over the unity of the New Testament. But *unity* is too ambiguous a term, and it readily seduces one to look for the wrong things.

More promising is the effort to identify the persistent features, the common traits, that mark Christology in the New Testament, even if they are not found exclusively in the canonical texts. In fact, it would be quite unfortunate if these traits were found only in the New Testament; were that the case, its Christology not only would be sundered from its roots in early Christianity but would also have forfeited its influence. It is the canonical status of the New Testament that gives special standing to the shared features of these Christologies. Whereas the contents of the Christologies in the New Testament canon are understandings that can be repudiated only by rupturing the continuity of the church's teaching, their persistent traits serve as guidelines or as channel markers that help safeguard the integrity of continuing christological thought.

Since channel markers indicate where the dangerous water begins, it is appropriate to formulate the traits of these Christologies negatively. Five are especially crucial: (1) Consistently, the New Testament canon does not integrate Jesus into an open-ended series; rather, Jesus the Christ is the event in which God acted decisively and definitively to overcome what had gone awry. Because the consummation of what was begun in Christ is not contingent on the arrival of another, none of the New Testament Christologies abandons completely the "return" of Christ himself. (2) No matter how "high" the Christology, Christ never competes with or replaces God; to the contrary, the high exaltation of Christ is precisely "to the glory of God the Father," as Philippians 2:11 puts it. Christian monotheism may be Christomorphic, but it is not Christocentric. (3) Christ never becomes a Christ-figure, a symbol of something else, such as an idea or a process, but retains his particularity as a being who once, as a human, bore a personal name in a particular place and time. (4) Although Christ's relation to Israel and the Old Testament is portrayed in quite different ways, the relation is stubbornly positive. By no means is this a matter of integrating Christ into an alleged salvation history (*Heilsgeschichte*)—a modern invention—nor is the synagogue's scripture (LXX) to be absorbed into "second temple literature" (the Jewish equivalent to "early Christian literature") in order to expand the range of material to be scoured for the "background" of christological concepts, motifs, and titles, essential as such sources may be for the history of early Christology and its vocabulary. It is rather a matter of taking seriously the actual New Testament exegesis of LXX as an essential part of the Christology of the text. (5) The Spirit (the immediate presence of the Divine) never displaces Jesus Christ; consequently, no religious experience, however "meaningful," makes Christology irrelevant. To the contrary, it is the mode in which Christ is present to the believer in the community.

Taken together, these characteristics of the New Testament's several Christologies provide a profile of Christology sufficient for measuring the faithfulness and the adequacy of subsequent Christologies, including those of our own day. The New Testament's Christologies do not simply provide "answers" made obligatory by its canonical status; they also pose questions that summon its interpreters to think as theologians.

The essential thing, therefore, is to see that the study of Christology in the New Testament will find its vitality and relevance renewed if it is reconceived as a theological discipline with historical horizons. Wrede's question "What can dogmatics offer it?" albeit posed with reference to the study of history, can be asked appropriately also here, and the answer is not arcane: It can define and focus the subject matter so that the Christologies of the New Testament can be studied as Christology, not as something else.[16]

NOTES

1. I want to record my appreciation of Professor Jack Dean Kingsbury's multifaceted contribution to the study of the New Testament's Christology. Our interests overlap at many points, despite our long-standing disagreement over the significance of christological titles; indeed, our disagreements have prompted me to reconsider many matters and have deepened our collegiality and friendship.

2. This is to be maintained despite Dunn's attempt to show that Paul's Christology does not include preexistence. See James D. G. Dunn, *Christology in the Making* (Philadelphia: Westminster Press, 1980).

3. The quotation marks around "New Testament theology" replace the German *sogenannte* (so-called). This essay, expanding a series of lectures to pastors in 1897, is available in Robert Morgan, *The Nature of New Testament Theology,* Studies in Biblical Theology, 2d series, 25 (Naperville, Ill.: Alec R. Allenson, 1973), 68–116. The book also includes Adolf Schlatter's "The Theology of the New Testament and Dogmatics," as well as Morgan's valuable introduction (1–67). The page numbers in parentheses in the text refer to this book.

4. Wrede's subsequent *Paulus* (1904; English translation, 1907) would call the apostle "the second founder of Christianity." Although many considerations have made this view of Paul untenable, it has been reasserted with ill-concealed animus by Hyam Maccoby, *The Myth-Maker: Paul and the Invention of Christianity* (San Francisco: Harper & Row, 1986). For a convenient summary and perceptive critique, see the review by J. Louis Martyn, in his collected essays *Theological Issues in the Letters of Paul* (Nashville: Abingdon Press, 1997), 70–75.

5. *Kyrios Christos* was first published in 1913; a revised edition, containing the author's rewritten first four chapters and incorporating his notes in the margins of his personal copy, was published in 1921. Not until 1970 was this important work available in English, when Abingdon Press published John Steely's translation of the fifth edition, for which Rudolf Bultmann provided an appreciative "Introductory Word." The page numbers in parentheses refer to this edition.

6. William Wrede's *The Messianic Secret* was published in 1901; not until seventy years later did an English translation appear, published by James Clarke in Cambridge and London in 1981.

7. Rudolf Bultmann's *History of the Synoptic Tradition* appeared in 1921. The English version, published in 1963 by Harper & Row and by Basil Blackwell Publisher in Oxford, translates the third edition of 1958 and includes Bultmann's notes that he had added to the second edition of 1931.

8. According to Bultmann, Mark combined the Hellenistic kerygma (like that in Paul, except for preexistence) with the Jesus traditions, but he was "not sufficiently master of his material to be able to venture on a systematic construction himself" (*History of the Synoptic Tradition,* 347, 350). This assessment of Mark's ability has been contested vigorously, especially by redaction critics.

9. The picture of early Christianity becomes even more complex when one adds the various opponents of Paul, the so-called Colossian heresy, those opposed by the Johannine epistles, and the various groups denounced in the Apocalypse.

10. See the broad-based study *The Christology of Jesus,* by Ben Witherington III (Minneapolis: Fortress Press, 1990). N. T. Wright prefers to speak of Jesus' "vocation," which he sees as symbolizing and enacting both Israel's vocation and God's coming. See N. T. Wright, *Jesus and the Victory of God* (Minneapolis: Fortress Press, 1996), esp. chap. 13.

11. Marinus de Jonge, *Christology in Context: The Earliest Christian Response to Jesus* (Philadelphia: Westminster Press, 1988), 26, 205.

12. I found the quip in Colin E. Gunton, *Yesterday and Today: A Study of Continuities in Christology* (London: Darton, Longman & Todd, 1983), 63.

13. For a fuller discussion of these observations, see my "Is the New Testament a Field of Study? Or, From Outler to Overbeck and Back," *Second Century* 1 (1981): 19–35.

14. For two attempts to grasp the character of Paul's thinking, see my "Paul and Apocalyptic Theology," *Interpretation* 38 (1984): 229–41, and "Paul as Thinker," *Interpretation* 47 (1993): 27–38.

15. For a more extended critique of the preoccupation with titles, see my "Toward the Renewal of New Testament Christology," *New Testament Studies* 32 (1986): 362–77; it is included in *From Jesus to John* (M. de Jonge Festschrift), ed. M. C. DeBoer (Sheffield: JSOT Press, 1993), 321–40.

16. My long-delayed book *Jesus in New Testament Christology* will apply this understanding to the Christologies of Matthew, Paul, Hebrews, and John.

CHRISTOLOGY
AND THE OLD TESTAMENT

Terence E. Fretheim

Without the Old Testament, there would be no adequate Christology. This claim may state the obvious, but it merits further exploration. The Old Testament has a contribution to make to Christology, not only through the New Testament's use of it but also through the way in which the church (led by the Spirit) reads the Old Testament anew in view of the total canonical witness to God. More continuity between Jesus and the God of the Old Testament is available than is commonly argued, and probably even more than the early Christians realized.[1]

In what follows, I make several introductory comments in relation to this claim and then suggest some ways in which the Old Testament understanding of God is crucial for proper Christological understanding.

SOME INTRODUCTORY ISSUES

1. The issue in my opening claim is not simply that the followers of Jesus sought to make sense of him by employing terms familiar from their scriptures. The basic issue at stake is not literary or historical. The early Christians make a theological claim on the basis of Old Testament texts: Jesus is the Christ whom God promised. Without the Old Testament and the presuppositions about God that it provides for that claim, Jesus is not the Christ. If the authority of that basis is diminished, as it often is by Christians, the claim that Jesus is the Christ is also diminished. The status given

to the Old Testament in the life of the church has significant implications for ongoing theological reflection regarding Jesus Christ.

2. Given the obvious incompleteness in our understanding of Jesus as the Christ, the Old Testament is indispensable for the *continuing* insight it gives regarding his identity. This means that it is insufficient to say Jesus is important for understanding the Old Testament; the interpretive traffic going the other way is even more fundamental. We continue to need the Old Testament in our ongoing efforts to understand Jesus more fully, both historically and theologically.

Just how to read the Old Testament so that it further elucidates the identity of Jesus is not altogether clear. Two factors stand in tension with each other: the particularity of the Old Testament in its pre-Christian time and place, and the experience of Christians who have for centuries heard the word of God addressed to them through these texts. The one reality that spans these times is God, the God of Israel and of Jesus Christ. In seeking to relate the two testaments, one is called to center one's interpretive strategies on the portrayal of that God.

Seeking out possible New Testament allusions to the kind of God of whom the Old Testament speaks (see below) will remain an important enterprise. But more is at stake. The explicitness of the New Testament references to these God themes may be minimal. Yet, as noted below, the reader still must ask about the effect these themes may have had more generally on the early Christian understanding of God (for example, claims about God in texts such as 2 Cor. 5:18–19 or Phil. 2:5–11). But even more, modern readers may discern significant connections between the testaments in this regard that early Christians may not have seen. The New Testament does not have the full and final interpretation of the significance of Jesus Christ (witness Chalcedon) or of the links between Jesus and the Old Testament. Postbiblical insights into the God of the Old Testament have the potential of enriching our christological reflections. In such cases, one might speak of the ongoing work of the Spirit, leading the church into all the truth (John 16).

3. The Old Testament has a status for the New Testament claims regarding the identity of Jesus that first-century Judaism does not. I discern some tendency in scholarship to collapse the Old Testament into first-century Judaism, as if to explicate the latter would accurately and adequately mirror Old Testament perspectives. For example, N. T. Wright, in a major recent work, undertakes a lengthy explication of "Israel's" worldview, beliefs, and hope in terms of what "first-century Jews actually believed."[2]

Aside from historical inaccuracies that this collapsing presents, its inadequacy is demonstrated in the fact that the New Testament authors almost always quote the Old Testament in support of their claims, not first-century Jewish sources that were available to them. It is not that early Christians were uninfluenced by contemporary theological and philosophical perspectives or disdained current exegetical methods. But apparently the experience of Jesus (including the tradition of Jesus' own use of scripture) propelled his followers into a new encounter with their scriptures in search for understandings that contemporary Judaism and its interpretation of those same texts was not believed able to provide. They read their scriptures with new eyes in view of their experience with Jesus and the faith in him that experience generated (see Luke 24). One might also speak of the gift of the Spirit (see John 16:12–15).[3] The effect of Jesus (and the Spirit) on the early Christians leads to a *rediscovery of the Old Testament itself* and to a "sea change" in seeing its interpretive possibilities. (A possible parallel to the depth of this change is the effect of the historical-critical method on modern biblical interpretation.) The early Christians encountered Old Testament and, more specifically, the God of the Old Testament in fresh ways. One effect of these new ways of seeing was that first-century thought may have colored their interpretation of the Old Testament to a lesser degree than might otherwise have been the case.

4. Such a perspective has implications for understanding the nature of early Christian claims regarding God. A common view is that the followers of Jesus engaged in what N. T. Wright calls "a radical redefinition" of their theological heritage.[4] Elsewhere, Wright speaks of a "radically revised Jewish picture of the one true God."[5] One reason for Wright's use of the word *radical* (in a context where he recognizes much continuity) seems to be apparent when he goes on to describe this Jewish God as the "transcendent God who is beyond space and time." But while this phrase may be an accurate portrayal of the God of first-century Judaism, it does not describe the God of the Old Testament. I hope to show that the God of the Old Testament has less "emptying" to do in the incarnation than does a God who is conceived in such "wholly other" terms. One may speak of an early Christian advancing (or filling out) of the Old Testament portrayal of God in speaking of the identity of Jesus, but more continuity is here than the language of radical redefinition or even revision seems able to acknowledge. In what follows, I use the language of *trajectory*.

To use the word *radical* is to stress distance and discontinuity. If one were working with perspectives in first-century Judaism, this theological distance might be claimed with some justification. (A question to be pursued would be how the understanding of God in first-century Judaism, under

under the impact of Hellenistic philosophy and historical experience, differed from that of the Old Testament.) But the issue of continuity/discontinuity with first-century Judaism should not be collapsed into the issue of continuity/discontinuity with the Old Testament. The religious and theological perspectives of first-century Judaism are an *interpretation* of the Old Testament (informed by other understandings). The question about Jesus' identity hinges most directly on differing interpretations of the *Old Testament*.

One could fall into the ditch on the other side of the road and simply flatten out the two testaments theologically or force christological readings of the Old Testament, claiming no newness or advance in theological perspective in view of the Christ event. The interpreter must live with the tensions entailed in staying between the two ditches. The theological tension between the testaments in view of the Christ event will never be overcome, but that tension in itself often generates a fuller understanding of God and God's ways in Jesus.

The early Christians, if asked about the kind of God in whom they believed, would have pointed to various Old Testament portrayals (see below).[6] In view of the fact that the God of the Old Testament is understood to be a certain kind of God, specific claims were made about Jesus' relationship to that God. Placing their experience of Jesus over the template provided by Old Testament understandings of God (and other matters), early Christians discerned a certain fit and the lights went on regarding Jesus' identity.

5. The Gospels have Jesus making some explicit claims about the place of the Old Testament in his self-understanding. Texts such as Luke 24:44–47 (compare 18:31–34; 24:26–27) are startling in this regard. "Then he opened their minds to understand the scriptures, and he said to them, 'Thus it is written, that the Messiah is to suffer and to rise from the dead on the third day, and that repentance and forgiveness of sins is to be proclaimed in his name to all nations, beginning from Jerusalem.'"

Jesus' followers, in turn, "argued . . . from the scriptures . . . and examined the scriptures every day to see whether these things were so" (Acts 17:2–3, 11; see 3:18–26). Paul testified that "Christ died for our sins [and was raised] in accordance with the scriptures" (1 Cor. 15:3–4). The reader can be forgiven for wishing that Luke and Paul had cited the specific texts to which they make reference. We would then not expend so much effort in seeking to determine which texts they had in mind and the approach they used in interpreting them.

In this search, textual blocks such as Isaiah 52 — 53 and various psalms have been brought into play, as well as numerous allusions and "echoes," which join the study of traditional texts, themes, and titles.[7] As important as this exercise has been and continues to be, more seems to be at stake than identifying and explicating specific passages. N. T. Wright's comment in this regard is helpful: "When Paul declared that 'the Messiah died for our sins according to the Scriptures' [1 Cor. 15:3] . . . he does not mean that he can find half a dozen 'proof-texts' from Scripture that he can cunningly twist into predictions of the crucifixion. He means that the entire scriptural story, the great drama of God's dealing with Israel, came together when" Jesus died.[8]

I follow Wright's lead in somewhat different terms: The "great drama" has to do with *two* stories that are woven into a single tapestry, namely, the story of Israel and the story of God.[9]

A fresh encounter with their scriptures in view of their experience with Jesus meant that the early Christians saw with new eyes not only the story of God's people (and their place within it) but also the story of God (and Jesus' place within both). As such, the Christ event is seen to be as much the climax of the story of God as it is the story of Israel. Jesus not only gathers up the people of God in his person and embodies this community. Jesus' story is not simply the story of *human* life and death. Jesus not only mediates the work of God on behalf of this people (as many Israelite "saviors" also did). Jesus is the climactic moment in *God's* own story. So, for example, the suffering of Jesus must be linked not only with the suffering of Israel but also with the suffering of God (see below; Mark 3:5; 14:33–34; compare Eph. 4:30). Or, the healing work of Jesus must be linked not only with the prophetic healers but also more directly with the healing work of God (see John 5:17).[10]

Hence, the interpreter who would understand Jesus through an appeal to the Old Testament must tend as much to God's story in the Old Testament as to Israel's story. God's story is more comprehensive, inclusive, and cosmic in scope than that of Israel. For starters, God's story has to do with the world, as does that of Jesus (witness Genesis 1; John 1; Colossians 1). (I wonder whether pursuing the idea of "story of God" has often not been possible because classical theism has for so long assumed that the word *story* does not really apply to God.)

The claims made regarding Jesus are fundamentally grounded in understandings of God and God's story from the Old Testament. For early Christians, the portrayal of God may have proved to be the sharpest point of continuity between their scriptures and their experience of Jesus. Old Testament God-talk provided a substratum of thought for ongoing reflection regarding God's act in Jesus, whether explicitly acknowledged or not. In other words, certain claims about God that permeate the Old Testament provided a theological matrix within which thinking about Jesus and his identity could develop.

If, for example, as Wright claims, everything Paul "said about Jesus was, for him, a way of talking about God," then it is important to ask *what kind of God* this is.[11] It is often said that the New Testament takes the God of the Old Testament for granted; but at least this key question remains: What kind of God is this God?

The following fundamental convictions about the God of the Old Testament, at the least, should be included in such a list. One may doubt that early christological formulations would, indeed could, have developed as they did without these theological convictions. I list these particular themes in view of my own experience of the witness of both testaments. A next step would be to gather still other New Testament texts in which there are quotations, allusions, or echoes regarding this kind of God.[12] But finally, the theological issue is not simply the use of the Old Testament by the New. The issue is a theological use of the Old Testament that is able to fill out our christological reflections even beyond that of the New Testament, though staying on the same trajectory.

JESUS' STORY AND GOD'S STORY

God in Relationship. First, the Old Testament witnesses to God as one who is *in relationship within the divine realm.* Israel's God is by nature a social being, functioning within a divine community (Gen. 1:26; Prov. 8:22–31; Jer. 23:18–23). These and other passages witness to the richness and complexity of the divine realm. God is not in heaven alone but is engaged in a relationship of mutuality within that realm and chooses to share the creative process, for example, with others. In other words, relationship is integral to the identity of God, independent of God's relationship to the world. A recognition of the sociality of God does not compromise the witness that God is one (Deut. 6:4). These Old Testament perspectives on the social nature of God provided understandings that laid the groundwork for later theological developments. Early Christian reflections about God that led to Trinitarian thought were not grounded only in New Testament claims about Jesus and the Spirit.

Second, this relational God freely enters *into relationships with that which has been created.* Biblical metaphors for God, with few if any exceptions, have relatedness at their very core (for example, king–subject, husband–wife, parent–child). Even nonpersonal metaphors are understood in relational terms (Deut. 32:18; Ps. 31:2–3). To characterize these metaphors generally: They are relational, usually personal rather than impersonal, ordinary rather than extraordinary, everyday rather than dramatic, earthly rather than "heavenly," and secular rather than religious. This type of language used for God ties God closely to the world and its everyday affairs. These kinds of images for God were believed to be most revealing of a God who had entered deeply into the life of the world and was present and active in the common life of individuals and communities.

This relatedness is also evident in the fact that God gives the divine name(s) to Israel, thereby identifying the divine Self as a distinctive member of the community of those who have names. Naming entails a certain kind of relationship. Giving the name opens up the possibility for a certain intimacy in relationship and admits a desire for hearing the voice of the other (see Isa. 65:1–2). A relationship without a name inevitably means some distance. Naming enables truer and deeper encounter and communication; it entails availability and accessibility. (In the Old Testament period, the divine name was pronounced.) But naming also entails risk, for it opens God up to an experience of the misuse of the name (see the commandment on the divine name).

The pervasive use of anthropomorphic/anthropopathic language is also important in this regard. God is one who thinks, wills, and feels. God has a mouth that speaks, eyes that see, and hands that create. This language stands together with the more concrete metaphors in saying something important about God—one who is living and dynamic, whose ways of relating to the world are best conveyed in the language of human personality and activity. It is ironic that Christians have at times had difficulty with this language, for in Jesus Christ, God has acted anthropomorphically in a most supreme way. (On God and human form, see below.)

The importance of such relational language is also evident in the prohibition of images. The concern of this prohibition is to protect God's relatedness. The idols "have mouths, but they do not speak; they have eyes, but they do not see; they have ears, but they do not hear, and there is no breath in their mouths" (Ps. 135:15–17). "They have hands, but do not feel; feet, but do not walk" (Ps. 115:5–7; cf. Jer. 10:4–5). The implication, of course, is that Israel's God is one who speaks and sees and hears and feels. With the idols there is no deed or word, no genuine presence. This understanding is continuous with that point where the Old Testament speaks of a legitimate concrete image, namely, the human being (Gen. 1:26). The human being, with all its capacities for relationships, is believed to be the only appropriate image of God in the life of the world. For the New Testament to use this language for Jesus (Col. 1:15) is testimony to him not only as the supreme exemplification of humanity but as one who reveals God most fully and decisively.

Israel's God is transcendent, but transcendent in relationship to the world, not in isolation from it. In the words of Abraham Heschel, "God remains transcendent in his immanence, and related in his transcendence."[13] God has taken the initiative and freely entered into relationships, both in creation and in covenant with Israel. But having done so, God—who is other than world—has decisively and irrevocably committed the divine Self to be in a certain kind of relationship. And so this God chooses to share power and responsibility with that which is other than God (Gen. 1:28), to exercise constraint and restraint in the exercise of power in the world (Gen. 8:21–22), and to honor promises made, even to the point of placing God's own life on the line (Gen. 15:7–21). The incarnation could be said to be on this relational trajectory, being the supreme exemplification of this kind of divine relatedness and its irrevocability.

This God of the Old Testament is not first and foremost the God of Israel but of the world. The opening chapters of Genesis make universal claims for this God. These chapters portray a God whose *universal* activity includes creating, grieving, judging, saving, electing, promising, blessing, covenant making, and lawgiving. God was in relationship to the world before there ever was an Israel, and so God's relationship with Israel must be understood as a subset within this more inclusive and comprehensive relationship. God's acting and speaking is especially focused in Israel, but this divine activity is a strategic, purposive move for the sake of the world (Gen. 12:3, "in you all the families [the families in Genesis 10] of the earth shall be blessed").[14]

The God Who Is Present. God's relationship with the world is comprehensive in scope. God is present and active in the *world*. God "fill[s] heaven and earth" (Jer. 23:24); indeed, the earth is "full of the steadfast love of the Lord" (Ps. 33:5; 36:5). God is a part of the map of reality and is relational, indeed lovingly relational, to all that is not God. Hence, God's presence is not static or passive but *an active presence in relationship,* profoundly grounded in and informed by steadfast love for the good of all.

Even more, the God of the Old Testament, in creating the world, enters into the space and time of this world and makes it God's own. For example, God builds God's own residence into the very structures of the created order (Ps. 104:1–3; compare Isa. 40:22; Amos 9:6), so that the heavens (or their semantic equivalent) become a shorthand way of referring to the abode of God *within* the world. God's movement from heaven to earth is a movement within the creation. God—who is other than world—works from within the world, and not on the world from without.

A comparable statement can be made with respect to time; God's relationship to the world is *from within* its structures of time. For example, the common language for divine planning and execution of plans (Jer. 29:11; 51:12) and being provoked to anger or slow to anger (Deut. 32:21; Ex. 34:6) assumes that temporal sequence is real for God. Timelessness is not descriptive of the God of the Old Testament; God's life is temporally ordered (at least since the creation). God has freely chosen to enter into the time of the world and truly get caught up in its flow. God is the eternal, uncreated member of this world community, but God too will cry out, "How long?" (Hos. 8:5).[15] To suggest that God first entered into time and history in the Christ event is to ignore this wide swath of Old Testament material. God's act in Jesus is an *intensification* of this already-existing trajectory of God's way of being present in and relating to the structures of the world.

Understanding divine presence in terms of varying degrees of intensification is already characteristic of Old Testament thought. In human life, differences in energy level, focus, direction, and attention, as well as the competing presence of others, determine our understanding of the intensity of the presence of someone. Regarding the divine presence, something comparable is at work; divine presence is not understood in a univocal way. For example, though Jonah flees "from the presence of the Lord" (1:3), he still professes belief in a Creator God (1:9). The departure of the tabernacling God from the temple (Ezek. 10:1–22; 11:22–25) does not mean that God is now absent (see 11:16). The psalmist prays to a God who has forsaken him but is believed to be present to hear (22:1). One might think of a continuum moving from general or creational presence to theophanic presence (see below), with accompanying and tabernacling presence being intermediate points. (Actual absence is not a divine possibility in the Old Testament.) God is believed to be continuously present, yet God will also be especially present at certain times; God is believed to be everywhere present, yet God will also be intensively present in certain places. The language of "glory," often used for an intensified divine presence, is used in connection with both theophanic and tabernacling texts (Ex. 24:15–17; 1 Kings 8:11; Ezek. 9:3).

Such texts show that the God of the Old Testament has taken a variety of steps at key times and places to be more intensively present in the life and structures of the world, and of Israel in particular. That this language is used to speak of Jesus Christ (John 1:14; 2 Cor. 4:4–6) catches him up in a trajectory of divine movement toward more intensified forms of presence in the life of the world.

God and Human Form. N. T. Wright states that the biblical God "became human without doing violence to his own inner essential nature."[16] He grounds this statement in an understanding of God as love, who by nature cannot "remain uninvolved, or detached, or impersonal." He also speaks of several Jewish "symbols" that spoke of their God coming to dwell in their midst (Wisdom; law; temple). But with respect to the human form, another Old Testament tradition is even more important, namely, the *theophany*. Throughout the Old Testament, God takes on human form and appears. God does not become human for the first time in Jesus.

Old Testament texts witness to various types of theophanies, but the most pertinent here are those where God appears in anonymous human form, as a "man" (*'ish*) or "angel/messenger" (*mal'ak;* see Gen. 16:7–13; 18:1–19:11; Judg. 6:11–24; 13:3–23). These divine appearances are brief, direct, and personal, usually to individuals. Moreover, they are usually not disruptive or extraordinary but occur within the framework of everyday life and experience. God appears, enfleshed in human form. In some theophanies (usually to the community), God appears enveloped in elements of fire, cloud/smoke, or light. These elements probably veil a human form; see the messenger "in" the flame of fire in Exodus 3:2 and the appearance of "the likeness as it were of a human form" with the fire round about in Ezekiel 1:26–28 (see also Ex. 24:9–11).[17]

In these theophanies, God appears in the life of the world in a way that is specific, articulate, and tangible; in this form, God speaks, listens, and even eats and touches. The assumption of human form is believed to be integral to the accomplishment of the divine purpose in each case. As such, the human form does not compromise divine transcendence. The finite is capable of the infinite. The empirical world can serve the task of "clothing" God. In these theophanies, God "wears" aspects of the creation in order to be as concretely and intensely present as possible. At the same time, the texts are devoid of speculation; the common partialness of reference (hand, foot, mouth, back) suggests a concern to convey a somewhat impressionistic picture.

In theophany, the personal and relational element is sharpened as the divine address to the whole person is made more apparent. There is greater intensity of presence, with greater potential effectiveness for the word spoken. Appearance makes a difference to words. A God who "appears," and appears in the flesh, says something more about God and the God–people relationship than does a God who only speaks. God's word is embodied; the speaking God is understood to share, if only for brief periods of time, the fleshly form of humankind. Hence, the human response can never be simply to believe or speak; it must also mean to re-embody the word in the world.

God's appearance in human form also reveals God's vulnerability. Appearance associated only with storm phenomena would suggest that God remained aloof, only to be feared, in total control of the situation. But for God to enter into the life of the world in human form makes for greater vulnerability; the human response can be derision (Gen. 18:12–13) or incredulity (Judg. 6:13–17). It is revealing of the ways of God more generally that in such key moments of revelation, God is enfleshed in bodies of weakness within the framework of everyday affairs, and not in overwhelming power. Even in those instances where the vestments of God's appearance are threaded with lineaments of power, they clothe a vulnerable form. (It might also be noted that theophanies witness to divine change, as do other themes, such as divine repentance. Depending on the topic, the Old Testament stakes claims for both divine immutability [better: constancy] and mutability.)[18]

Precritical interpretations of these texts often linked theophanies to the preexistent Logos or the second Person of the Trinity.[19] This is anachronistic language for the God of ancient Israel, of course, but it is significant that this linkage of theophany and Christology has a long tradition. I claim only that these theophanic texts may have provided a perspective on God within which incarnation could be naturally developed. The incarnation would not be a radical move for those steeped in Old Testament texts (see also on anthropomorphisms, above). To use an earlier formulation of mine, "there is no such thing for Israel as a nonincarnate God."[20] The Old Testament God is a God who is prone to incarnation, and once again, the interpreter can discern a divine trajectory of which *the* incarnation is climactic.

God, Prophet, and the Enfleshed Word. This understanding of God's appearing in human form is extended in the prophetic literature. From a canonical perspective, prophets appear at about the time that the messenger of God ceases to appear. Noteworthy are the significant continuities between them (human form; "man of God" and "messenger" identification; use of first-person singular and similar genres; membership in the divine council). Yet there are new developments (prophets have names and distinctive personalities; their ministries extend over time) so that they are called to function, in effect, as ongoing theophanies.

Thinking of the word of God as embodied in the prophet's person is particularly evident in Jeremiah and Ezekiel. In their call narratives, God does not speak what they are to say; the word of God is placed directly into their mouths (Jer. 1:9; 15:16; Ezek. 2:10–3:3). The prophet thus ingests the word of God, and "you are what you eat." Gerhard von Rad warns against taking these passages "in too spiritual a way. . . . The entry of the message into their physical life brought about an important change in the self-understanding of these later prophets. (We may ask whether the entry of the word into a prophet's bodily life is not meant to approximate what the writer of the Fourth Gospel says about the word becoming flesh.)" Samuel Terrien speaks of the prophet as a "living incarnator of divinity."[21] The prophets are understood to be vehicles of divine immanence; the word of God is enfleshed in their very selves. In some fundamental sense, the human figure *is* the word of God. The story of the prophet is a story of the word of God. The story of God gets caught up in the very life of the prophet.

The Old Testament does not finally come to the conclusion that God was incarnate in a human life in complete unbrokenness or in its entirety. Yet more decisive continuities between this material and the incarnation exist than has been commonly recognized. Those who had been steeped in the theophanic texts of the Old Testament would not have been surprised at incarnation.

God and Suffering. Messiah and suffering seem not to have been linked in pre-Christian literature; hence, the notion of a crucified Messiah is commonly thought to be a distinctively Christian formulation. At the same time, the Old Testament witness to a suffering God may not have been taken sufficiently into account in this discussion. God did not suffer for the first time in the Christ event; even more, God did not suffer for the sins of the world for the first time on the cross.

The New Testament witness to the finality and universality of Jesus' suffering and death is certainly an advance on Old Testament understandings. But it is an advance on an already-existing trajectory of reflection about a God who suffers. The Christ who suffers and dies on the cross for the sins of the many bears a strong "family resemblance" to the God revealed in the Old Testament, particularly in the Prophets. To see the face of God in a crucified man would not be a radical move for those steeped in Old Testament understandings of God. The *kind of God* whom the early Christians knew from their scriptures was a God who could know the experience of crucifixion.

The Old Testament witness to a suffering God is rich and pervasive.[22] This understanding of God is grounded in a God who has entered deeply into relationship with the world (see above), and with Israel in particular. In opening the divine Self up to the vulnerabilities of a close relationship, God experiences suffering because of what happens to that relationship. God suffers *because* the people have rejected God. In such cases, God speaks in traditional lament language (Isa. 1:2–3; Jer. 2:5, 29–31; 3:19–20; 8:4–7; 9:7–9); Jesus' words over Jerusalem stand in this divine lament tradition (Matt. 23:37). God suffers *with* those who are experiencing suffering (Ex. 3:7; Jer. 9:17–18; 31:20), to which the Emmanuel theme may be related.

Several texts witness to a divine suffering *for* (Isa. 42:14; 43:23–25; Hos. 11:7–9). Consider Isaiah 43:24–25: God here testifies to being "burdened" with the sins of the people (the verb is *'abad,* to which *'ebed,* "servant," is related). This divine carrying of the sins of the people issues immediately in the unilateral announcement of forgiveness "for my own sake" (43:25). To this text should be linked the "bearing sin" passages of Isaiah 53:4, 11–12 (compare 1 Peter 2:24). The servant of God thus assumes the role that God himself has just played. (See above on the relationship of God and prophet.)

Many of these divine suffering texts make clear that human sin is not without cost for God. For God to continue to bear the brunt of Israel's rejection rather than deal with it on strictly legal terms means continued life for the people. What does such suffering mean for God? In some sense, it means the expending of the divine life for the sake of the relationship with the people and their future life together. In the especially striking Isaiah 42:14 ("I will cry out like a woman in labor, I will gasp and pant"), God acts on behalf of a barren people, who are unable to bring their own future into being. God engages in such a giving of self that only one of the sharpest pains known can adequately portray what is involved for God in bringing to birth a new creation of Israel beyond exile. For this kind of God, the cross is no stranger.

NOTES

1. I am pleased to be a contributor to this book honoring Jack Dean Kingsbury. We started teaching together at Luther Seminary in 1968, and the helpful conversation begun there on the relationship between the testaments is here continued.

2. N. T. Wright, *The New Testament and the People of God* (Minneapolis: Fortress Press, 1992), 244. Another example of this tendency is the introductory New Testament section in *The New Interpreter's Bible,* vol. 8; it contains a "Jewish Context" chapter but none on the use of the Old Testament.

3. Several important works on the New Testament use of the Old Testament

have recently appeared; for example, Richard Hays, *Echoes of Scripture in the Letters of Paul* (New Haven, Conn.: Yale University Press, 1989); Robert Brawley, *Text to Text Pours Forth Speech: Voices of Scripture in Luke-Acts* (Bloomington: Indiana University Press, 1995).

4. N. T. Wright, *The Climax of the Covenant: Christ and the Law in Pauline Theology* (Minneapolis: Fortress Press, 1991), 115–16.

5. N. T. Wright, *What Saint Paul Really Said: Was Paul of Tarsus the Real Founder of Christianity?* (Grand Rapids: Wm. B. Eerdmans Publishing Co., 1997), 74.

6. For the importance of the issue of "the kind of God," see T. Fretheim, *The Suffering of God: An Old Testament Perspective* (Philadelphia: Fortress Press, 1984), 1. It is helpful to see that N. T. Wright uses this same language in *The Original Jesus: The Life and Vision of a Revolutionary* (Grand Rapids: Wm. B. Eerdmans Publishing Co., 1996), 79.

7. See, for example, Donald Juel, *Messianic Exegesis: Christological Interpretation of the Old Testament in Early Christianity* (Philadelphia: Fortress Press, 1988); Nils Dahl, *Jesus the Christ: The Historical Origins of Christological Doctrine*, ed. Donald Juel (Minneapolis: Fortress Press, 1991).

8. Wright, *What Saint Paul Really Said*, 48–49, 50–51.

9. The study of God in the New Testament has been neglected. See Nils Dahl, "The Neglected Factor in New Testament Theology," in *Jesus the Christ*, 153–63. This 1975 essay still pertains for the most part. The extended project of Wright is, in part, to "rectify" this situation (*New Testament and the People of God*, xiv). See also Brawley, *Text to Text*.

10. For a summary account of key New Testament texts regarding the relationship between Jesus and God, see Raymond E. Brown, *An Introduction to New Testament Christology* (New York: Paulist Press, 1994), 171–95.

11. Wright, *What Saint Paul Really Said*, 57.

12. Among the key texts that would have to be mined for such linkages are Luke 1—2; John; Acts 17; Romans 8—11; 1 Corinthians 1—2, 8—12, 15; 2 Corinthians 3—5; Galatians 4; Ephesians 1—4; Philippians 2; Colossians 1—2.

13. Abraham Heschel, *The Prophets* (New York: Harper & Row, 1962), 486.

14. For the importance of this theme in Luke-Acts, see Brawley, *Text to Text*.

15. For a discussion of the many texts that support this interpretation, see Fretheim, *Suffering of God*, 37–44.

16. Wright, *Original Jesus*, 82.

17. For a discussion of the pertinent texts, see Fretheim, *Suffering of God*, 79–106. A distinction is to be made between these theophanies where God is the bearer of a word and those of God as warrior in times of need, where no word is spoken and no form seen (Pss. 18; 29; 77; Habakkuk 3). On this, see J. Jeremias, "Theophany in the Old Testament," in the supplementary

volume to *Interpreter's Dictionary of the Bible* (*IDBSup*) (Nashville: Abingdon Press, 1976).

18. In the words of Walter Eichrodt, in the theophany "God's connection with the world is most clearly observed"; indeed, Israel's God is one who "can temporarily incarnate himself" (*Theology of the Old Testament,* vol. 2 [Philadelphia: Westminster Press, 1967], 15, 27). Some scholars downplay the form God assumes in the theophanies. For example, Walter Brueggemann ("Presence of God," *IDBSup*) states that there is "no interest in any form of appearance" (681). Brueggemann's lack of interest in this aspect of theophany is also evident in his *Theology of the Old Testament* (Minneapolis: Fortress Press, 1997), 567–77. Remarkably, he considers many theophanies to be "unmediated" (even in texts such as Gen. 18:1–2). Similarly, Samuel Terrien (*The Elusive Presence* [New York: Harper & Row, 1978]) devaluates references to the "seeing of the eye" in contrast to the "hearing of the ear" (112). Such is the impact of a narrowly conceived theology of the word of God.

In contrast, Edmund Jacob claims that "God always appears in human form," and that theophanies are "approaches to the biblical solution of the divine presence, that of God become man in Jesus Christ" (*Theology of the Old Testament* [New York: Harper & Row, 1958], 74). Gerhard von Rad (*Old Testament Theology,* vol. 1 [New York: Harper & Row, 1962]) speaks even more expansively; certain texts claim that, for Israel, "Yahweh has the form of man" (145; see also his "divine kenosis" reference on 367). That is, God does not simply *assume* the human form for the sake of appearance; there is, for Israel, an essential continuity between that form and the reality of God. Genesis 1:26 considers the human to be "theomorphic" rather than God being anthropomorphic (146). For further discussion of this issue, see Fretheim, *Suffering of God,* 102–5.

19. Eichrodt's arguments (*Theology of the Old Testament,* 28) in setting these Christian interpretations aside from Old Testament perspectives are largely beside the point. The point is not to "Christianize" the Old Testament but to consider the basic theological perspectives that informed Christian theological reflection.

20. Fretheim, *Suffering of God,* 106.

21. von Rad, *Old Testament Theology,* 2:91–92; Terrien, *Elusive Presence,* 241.

22. For detail, see Fretheim, *Suffering of God,* especially 107–48. The work of Abraham Heschel on the pathos of God in *The Prophets* is indispensable for this discussion.

THE SIGNIFICANCE OF NEW TESTAMENT CHRISTOLOGY FOR SYSTEMATIC THEOLOGY

Carl E. Braaten

THE CRISIS OF CHRISTOLOGY TODAY

Christology today suffers from the prevailing alienation between the disciplines of biblical exegesis and systematic theology. This situation constitutes a crisis with far-reaching consequences for theological education, the church's ministry, and the faith of ordinary Christians. This chapter aims to transcend the hiatus between exegesis and dogmatics with respect to the central concern of the New Testament—the identity and meaning of Jesus of Nazareth. Christology proper is what the church—the community of those who believe in Jesus as the Christ of God—thinks and says in response to the twofold question of who Jesus is and what he means for today.

The gaping rift between exegesis and dogmatics is the result of a complex development. Since the Enlightenment, biblical exegesis has taken pride in liberating itself from the church and its beliefs concerning Christ and instead has wedded itself to methods of historical criticism within the limits of a naturalistic and rationalistic worldview. Exegesis was controlled by the historical question "What really happened back there in New Testament times?" and it answered the question as if God had nothing to do with it. Dogmatics, for its part, became increasingly preoccupied with the apologetic question "Are the traditional teachings concerning Christ still believable and relevant in modern times?" To answer this question, theology often allied itself with some contemporary system of philosophy (for example, Hegel, Whitehead, Heidegger), using its categories and thought forms to reinterpret classical christological doctrines. While exegesis thereby tends to get bogged down in a myriad of historical trivia, systematic theology risks being imprisoned in the straitjacket of an alien system of thought.

Christologies oriented primarily to history center on the historical Jesus, inquiring not only into his time and place but into his life and teachings. Christologies oriented primarily to philosophy focus on the idea of Christ, exploring its symbolic meaning and function in Christianity and the religions. To explain just how the two poles—the Jesus pole and the Christ pole—belong inseparably united in Christian faith and doctrine is the perennial task of Christology. The crisis of Christology results from tearing apart what belong together. The most glaring current example is the approach of the notorious Jesus Seminar, led by Robert Funk and Dominic Crossan. Its emphasis on Jesus to the neglect of his divine identity repeats the ancient ebionitic heresy (a second-century Jewish Christian movement that proclaimed Jesus as Messiah because he fulfilled the law). Equally unsalutary is an emphasis on a Christ principle (for example, various shades of Hegelianism in D. F. Strauss and F. C. Baur, to some extent in Rudolf Bultmann and Paul Tillich, as well as the pluralistic theories of religion of John Hick, Knitter, and Raimundo Panikkar) not firmly rooted in the person of Jesus as a concrete figure of history—a repetition of the ancient docetic heresy. The christological confession is truly "the article by which the church stands or falls." The present-day crisis of Christology threatens to shatter the one foundation on which the faith of the Christian church rests.

To relate the two disciplines cited in the title of this chapter, I must say a few words of clarification about each of them. New Testament Christology has become a very slippery fish for systematic theology to lay hold of. While systematic theology possesses no independent resources to settle the many disputes in the field of New Testament Christology, it may engage in a critical assessment of the methods used and the findings achieved in New Testament studies. It must also reckon with the fact that there is no bare minimum of assured results on which systematic theology must conduct its reflections. The results are as multiplex as the methods. Grant Osborne writes, "Christological theory is in process of a paradigm shift in methodology."[1] And Carl Holladay concurs: "Recent study in New

Testament christology has become increasingly self-reflective about method. There is good reason to believe that until greater clarity is achieved in this regard, further progress in investigating many of the tangled questions of christology cannot be made."[2]

The situation is further complicated by the fact that leading scholars are not agreed on methods and results, nor even on the basic task of New Testament Christology. We may cite two examples from opposite ends of the ideological spectrum: the work of James D. G. Dunn and that of Robert Funk, the former a friend of Christian teaching about Christ, the latter an enemy. It is commonly agreed that modern biblical exegesis is bound to use the historical-critical method, understood in a broad generic sense; but this method does not exist as a neutral set of research procedures. A hermeneutical factor always comes into play, in either an open or a hidden way. A certain *Fragestellung* inevitably guides the research of any individual scholar. Robert Funk, the founder and leader of the Jesus Seminar, clearly has his own agenda, one that is hostile to Christian belief as the earliest apostles framed it in their preaching and doctrine. He writes in *Honest to Jesus:* "I do not want to be misled by what Jesus' followers did: instead of looking to see what he saw, his devoted disciples tended to stare at the pointing finger. Jesus himself should not be, must not be, the object of faith. That would be to repeat the idolatry of the first believers."[3]

In *Christology in the Making,* James D. G. Dunn professes quite the opposite intention, namely, to make sense of the earliest developments in Christology, even with a view to commending them for contemporary belief, ending with the high Christology of John's Gospel, which Dunn sees as the bridge to the classical orthodox Christology of the Creeds. Yet Dunn, too, is guided by his own theological agenda, which he forces on the text. He has in the back of his mind a desired outcome of his research—an understanding of the incarnation that does not overstep the limits of monotheism. Monotheism, not Trinitarianism, is Dunn's chief passion. Like so many of his dialogue partners in the myth-of-God-incarnate debate,[4] Dunn possesses a strong sense of the unity of God but a weak sense of God's triunity. He has shaped the New Testament evidence to mesh with his own theological sense of what is required for Christianity still to claim to be a monotheistic religion, along with Judaism and Islam. But why should a Christian scholar bend over backward to defend monotheism when it is precisely the doctrine of the Trinity that cries out for explication? The Christian doctrine of God does not favor a "radical monotheism" but an odd sort of monotheism that is radically tri-personal. The name of this God is Father, Son, and Holy Spirit. Regrettably, Dunn's book, for all its scholarly merits, does not succeed in identifying the root of the Christian doctrine of the Trinity in the incarnation. He is too busy trying to explain the incarnation within the framework of Jewish monotheism to acknowledge the extent to which it constitutes a radical departure, as Jewish rabbis saw very early on.

THE STARTING POINT OF CHRISTOLOGY

We have dealt with the crisis in Christology so far in terms of the methodological issues. When the church's interpretation of its own book is set aside as hermeneutically irrelevant, another set of presuppositions, a different religious agenda, is likely to fill the void. This is evident in the exegetical practice of both friends and foes of the Christian tradition, and it is a consequence of the long-standing divorce between exegesis and dogmatics.

Christology is a churchly discipline; it is the church's response to Jesus' question "Who do you say that I am?" It was Peter who first came back with the reply "You are the Christ." Peter's confession of Jesus as the Christ is the common ground of all communities that consider themselves Christian. They have built all their beliefs, rituals, and institutions on the foundation of his confession. All that is distinctive in Christian preaching and theology is centered in Jesus as the Christ. It is faith in Jesus as Christ that makes Christianity Christian. Jesus of Nazareth, as the Gospels portray him, is the starting point of Christology. However, the full confession of Christ continues to develop in the life and worship of the church through the centuries and continues to find expression in new language and symbols in the context of the apostolic mission to the nations.

When new Christology is written for the church in new situations, it will properly consist of three components: the Gospel narrative about Jesus of Nazareth, the New Testament kerygma, and the christological dogma of the church. Christology is thus like a three-legged stool; it cannot stand on only one or two legs. Since the rise of the historical-critical method of biblical interpretation, Christology took a turn to acknowledge the primacy and priority of the category of history. The modern search for the historical Jesus was inspired in part by the desire to reach behind the church's kerygma and dogma to locate in Jesus himself the beginning of subsequent christological developments. The church's preaching and mission and its conciliar dogmatic definitions cannot create Christology *de novo;* the subject matter of Christology must be Jesus himself, prior to what anyone later believed about him. It seemed important, for example, to discover whether

Jesus understood himself to be the Messiah, or whether he applied any of the other honorific christological titles to himself. In defending the messianic self-understanding of Jesus, one of my New Testament professors exclaimed, "If Jesus did not think of himself as the Messiah, why in the world should I?" Scholars who became skeptical of being able to discover any explicit Christology in the original Jesus still claimed, along with Rudolf Bultmann, to find an indirect Christology implied in his sayings or actions. Some material continuity between the Jesus of history and the Christ he was proclaimed to be by his earliest followers must exist. James D. G. Dunn is right on the mark when he writes, "For if we can uncover something at least of that self-understanding, and if it differs markedly from subsequent Christian doctrine of Christ, then we have discovered a serious self-contradiction at the heart of the Christian doctrine of incarnation itself."[5] It is not enough for Jesus to be *called* the Christ, functionally speaking; he must *be* the Christ in an ontological sense.

The history of dogma begins in the New Testament itself. Very early we encounter christological confessional formulas that say, "Jesus is Lord," "Jesus is the Christ," "Jesus is the Son of God." In the New Testament we have not only a Christology from below but also a Christology from above, which affirms what God has accomplished in history for our salvation. The road from New Testament Christology to the christological dogma of the ancient church represents an ongoing creative interpretation of the kerygma in new linguistic forms. The dogmatic statements that Jesus Christ is "consubstantial with the Father," at the Council of Nicaea (325 C.E.), and that he possesses "two natures in one person," at the Council of Chalcedon (451 C.E.), are examples of how metaphysical language can be appropriated to serve the gospel in a new cultural situation.

"Christology from below" takes its starting point in the Jesus of history, prior to later kerygmatic and dogmatic developments. This indicates that Christology, too, is not exempt from the pressure of the last two hundred years to understand things in terms of their historical beginnings and developments. However, starting Christology "from below" without reaching the heights of a "Christology from above" has often regrettably but needlessly resulted in a "low Christology," one that is incapable of bearing the weight of God's gift of salvation in Christ. I claim that both directions, from below and from above, are dialectically essential in a full Christology that does justice to its three blocks of material—history, kerygma, and dogma. As the proclamation of the kerygma was necessary to bring the story of Jesus to the nations, so the history of dogma was a hermeneutical necessity to translate the kerygma into the thought forms of Hellenistic culture.

Not merely as a concession to modernity but in terms of the internal logic of the matter, it is well to start with the historical method of interpretation, without, however, accommodating the anti-Christian and antitheological prejudices of a naturalistic or secular worldview. The historical point of departure honors the priority, authority, and normativity of the scriptural witness to Christ in relation to all later traditions of the church, including its most solemnly declared Trinitarian and christological dogmas and canonically established liturgical formulas.

The historical question "Who was Jesus of Nazareth?" has proved to be of broad popular interest even outside Christian circles. Jesus is a figure of world-historical significance, "the Man who belongs to the world."[6] The question of the identity and meaning of Jesus is the most useful place to begin interreligious dialogue with people of other faiths. For non-Christian people, Jesus holds more interest than do Christian dogmas about him. So the place to begin christological thinking today, for Christianity as a universal missionary faith, is exactly where it all began in the first place — with Jesus himself. This is what it means to start Christology from below.

Jesus of Nazareth existed as an eschatological prophet within the framework of Judaism and before the rise of Christianity. Prior to Jesus, there was no Christology. After Jesus' death, Christology is planted and grows in the hearts and minds of a handful of his friends and followers who experience his presence as the risen Lord. By the end of the New Testament period, a "high Christology" is in full swing.

How did it come about that this eschatological Jewish prophet who met his fate on the cross as a common criminal would soon after be confessed as King, Messiah, Lord, Savior, Son of God, and the very Word who was with God and who, indeed, was God? (John 1:1) Or to put the question the way Bultmann did: How did Jesus the preacher become the one who was preached about?

Very selectively, we can point briefly to three factors that help answer this question. The first is the event of Jesus' resurrection. Here is one key to all the titles of honor ascribed to the crucified Jesus, without which there would have been no good news of salvation to tell the nations. On account of his resurrection, Jesus was present in the power of the Spirit as the living Lord and the loving Savior. Starting from below with the lowly man Jesus, the conviction that God raised him from the dead eventually propelled the confession of Christ to the highest possible identification of Jesus as God.

Most contemporary New Testament scholars are of the opinion that Jesus did not explicitly claim christological titles for himself. Supposing that

these were confessions of the believing community after Easter, it would
be implausible to maintain that the earliest believers arbitrarily attributed
christological titles to Jesus without any motivating ground in his own public ministry. What did the first believers remember about Jesus that legiti-
mated their confession of him as the Christ? So the second factor lies in the
mystery of Jesus' most intimate personal relation to his Father, his Abba
experience. Jesus addressed God as "Abba," and the way in which he did
this was something new, in comparison with both the Old Testament and
the Judaism of his day. His relation to his Father implies his Sonship in an
exclusive sense. He is uniquely the one and only begotten Son of God, and
not merely one among the many children of the heavenly Father. Only in
and through Jesus do we gain access to God as our Father. This Father–Son
relationship is the foundation of the reconciliation of all people with God
and with one another. I share the view of many contemporary systematic
theologians who see the root of Christology in Jesus' Abba relationship.[7]

The third factor is Jesus' proclamation of the kingdom of God—the
nerve center of his message. Jesus announced the imminent approach of
God's kingdom; it is near at hand. Its advance signs are already visible in
his ministry. What is more, Jesus binds the coming of the kingdom to his
person. In a real sense, Jesus belongs to the gospel he preached. Origen
used the term *autobasileia* to express the idea that Jesus is himself the kingdom. He is in person the decisive event inaugurating the rule of God in
world history. The unconditional promise of eschatological salvation is expressed in Jesus' authority to forgive sins, to declare sinners acceptable in
God's eyes, to bless the poor and heal the sick. A prophet cries out, "Thus
saith the Lord!" But Jesus said, "Truly I say unto you!" A rabbi interprets
the scriptures, appealing to their authority. Jesus took authority unto himself and said, "You have heard it said of old, but I say unto you." He spoke
with immediate and direct authority, announcing the coming of God's
reign in and through his words and actions. The relation of Jesus to the
kingdom he preached is so close that his death on the cross was seen *ex
post facto* as his enthronement as King.

JESUS AND GOD

The Christian tradition has unanimously pointed to Jesus the Christ as the
answer to the question of where God has revealed himself in a definitive
way. Jesus of Nazareth is the person in whom the promises of the God of
Israel intersect with the human quest for meaning and fulfillment. There
are many "gods" in the pantheon of the world's religions. For Christians,

Jesus is the One who identifies the God of Israel as his Father. The identity of God is revealed in the history of Israel and in the person of Jesus. The question of who and what and where God is in the world is answered by his self-identification in Jesus Christ. The early Christian proclamation (kerygma) of the gospel concerning Jesus of Nazareth progressively yielded a new understanding of God. Philip said to Jesus, "Lord, show us the Father." And Jesus replied to Philip, "Whoever has seen me has seen the Father" (John 14: 8, 9). This means that knowing who Jesus is tells us who God is. God is the Father of Jesus, and Jesus is his Son. The identity of Jesus is key to the definition of God. Jesus the Christ is the sole medium through whom God reveals himself as the finally valid answer to the question of which God in a world of gods and idols we are to worship and trust regarding our human hope and destiny.

None of the contemporaries of Jesus directly called him God. The early church reached the confession of the Godhood of Jesus by way of a long development that reached its climax in the Nicene Creed, in the light of Easter, and in the context of worship. The resurrection of Jesus was an act by which God identified the divine Self as the One "who gives life to the dead and calls into existence the things that do not exist" (Rom. 4:17). At the same time, the resurrection was an act of God by which the mission of Jesus was vindicated and guaranteed a future in the life of the church and world history. The resurrection was thus the pivotal point by which God defined himself in the life of Jesus.

The classical Christian doctrine of the triune God was formulated in the closest possible connection with the centrality of Jesus Christ in the apostolic kerygma and early Christian worship. The Christocentric principle in faith, doctrine, and worship has come under vigorous attack by various schools of contemporary theology, especially process theology and the pluralistic theology of religion. They allege that the Christocentric character of the New Testament kerygma and ancient church dogma has rendered the doctrine of God too Semitic, historically limited, and anthropocentric. Their objection is that Christ becomes a "second God" alongside the one God behind the universe of faiths; the christological dogma turns a "mere man" into the object of faith and worship. Some of these theologians dub the Christ-centeredness of classical Christianity idolatry, Christodolatry, even Christofascism. Instead, they call for a "Copernican revolution" in which God would be put back into the center of the cosmos and the universe of religions, thus dislodging Christ from the central position he has held in the old Ptolemaic scheme of things. This would supposedly overcome the narrow parochialism of classical dogma that links the special self-revelation of God and the salvation of the world to the person and work of Jesus the Christ.

An old philosophical axiom asserts: The finite is not capable of the infinite (*finitum non capax infiniti*). It rules out beforehand the possibility of a real incarnation; it holds that the infinite God is metaphysically incapable of expressing himself in a finite human being. This axiom renders unintelligible the very concept of an incarnate being who is both fully divine and fully human. It breaks the ontological linkage between Jesus and God. Philosophy is permitted to play a trump card against the Gospel assertions that God became man, the Word became flesh, in Jesus of Nazareth. The central place of Christ in Christian worship is written off as pious fiction.

But what if the gospel is true? Then God is not a metaphysical prisoner of his own absoluteness. Then the infinite is capable of becoming finite, because that is exactly what happened in the incarnation. It is not metaphysical nonsense but evangelical truth that God reveals himself under contrary conditions, life through death, light through darkness, victory through defeat. The God of the gospel is capable of being open to the identity, attributes, and experiences of human life in a finite world.

If we take seriously the historicity of God's self-revelation in Jesus, we must abandon some ancient assumptions about God, stemming from Greek philosophy. In Greek metaphysics and Hellenistic religion, the eternal God had of necessity to be essentially immortal, impassible, and immutable. In other words, God could not die, God could not suffer, God could not change. But death, suffering, and change are the common lot of human experience. If we take our cues from the Gospel narrative, believing that Jesus is God in the flesh, we know as a matter of fact and faith that God did experience the reality of death, God did know what it means to suffer, and God did enter the changing conditions of historical existence. Dietrich Bonhoeffer put the matter so poignantly: "Only a suffering God can help." The idea of an absolutely immutable, immortal, and impassible God may fit the metaphysics of pagan antiquity and New Age mysticism, but it does not cohere with the picture of Jesus we have in the Gospels. If God did not really suffer and die in the person of Jesus of Nazareth, and if in Jesus' death only a good man died, then his suffering and death would be good for nothing. Jesus' death would be only his own tragic fate, and we might feel sorry for poor Jesus, but his suffering and death would be of no ultimate and lasting help to others in their suffering and dying.

Recent patristic studies have made clear that the prime motive in the development of christological doctrine was soteriological.[8] Athanasius was not interested in countering the Arian heresy with esoteric speculations about the nature of Deity. His concern was rather: If Jesus is not true God, then he cannot be our Redeemer. If Jesus were only a man, albeit a most perfect and holy man, or some kind of subdivine creature, he would not be able to deal with the problems of sin, guilt, and death. A Christology that settles for anything less than the true divinity of Jesus Christ, along with his full humanity, has ripped the heart out of the gospel. Since human beings are in no condition to save themselves, salvation must come as a gift from God. This is why Christology from above is needed to complement Christology from below. It is the answer to the most profound questions that arise out of the human experience of sin, death, and the devil.

Doing systematic theology within the horizon of the history of God's salvific acts has also led to a renewal of the doctrine of the Trinity. Nineteenth-century liberal Protestant theologians had no taste for the Trinity. Their low Christology had no need for such; for them, Jesus was nothing more than a man. Traditional Trinitarian language was seen as an arbitrary symbolic construct or the result of futile speculation. Albrecht Ritschl, Adolf von Harnack, and Wilhelm Herrmann argued that the Trinity was not essential to Luther's faith. It was only a piece of the eggshell that stuck to the theology of the Protestant Reformation from the old Catholic synthesis of biblical religion and Greek philosophy. Harnack depreciated the christological and Trinitarian dogmas of the ancient church as the "Hellenization of the gospel on Greek soil." Luther, he said, shattered the synthesis and rescued the kernel of the gospel from its philosophical shell, and so he became the founder of Protestantism.

Twentieth-century theology has witnessed a rebirth of Trinitarian theology. The new boost came from Karl Barth and Karl Rahner, one a Protestant, the other a Roman Catholic. They concurred that the Christian doctrine of God cannot be constructed on the foundations of natural theology or religious experience but must be rooted and grounded in the soil of the biblical history of revelation and salvation. This means that the three ways or modes in which God is self-revealed, as Father, Son, and Spirit, constitute the being of the One God. Threeness and oneness are inseparable. So the church has three articles of the Creed, each beginning with the confession of one Member of the triune God. At the base of ultimate reality is one God in three Persons; God's unity is a function of the mutual relations between the three Persons, revealing God as Love. Love is a transactional event occurring between two or more persons. Love requires otherness and difference in reality. There is no unitarian singleton at the top of the pyramid of all reality. The Trinity is the living God who, in his creative, redeeming, and sanctifying activity, is the mystery of the whole creation. Only the Trinity can make clear the identity and nature of the biblical God, the God of the gospel and of Christian faith.

I conclude with a word of contrast between "high" and "low" Christology. The doctrine of the Trinity presupposes the high Christology of Paul's letters and John's Gospel. The liberal modernist theologians and their present-day epigones who favor a low Christology usually appeal to the Synoptic Gospels or to some earlier stratum of primitive Christian tradition. Karl Barth eloquently spelled out the difference in contrasting the high Christology of the classical tradition with the low Christology of modern Protestantism: "Orthodox christology is a glacial torrent rushing straight down from a height of three thousand meters; it makes accomplishment possible. Herrmann's christology, as it stands, is the hopeless attempt to raise the stagnant pool to the same height by means of a hand pump; nothing can be accomplished with it."[9] A low Christology is based on belief that the tomb was sealed on Easter morning; a dead Jesus lay bound inside. Those who came to believe Jesus was alive were hallucinating or something like that. A high Christology is anchored in the Easter witness of the women and the disciples. Thomas, who had to be persuaded, blurted out: "My Lord and my God!" He acknowledged Jesus as more than a prophet. Nothing less than the divine name would do. From then on, God and Jesus were spoken of in the same breath. Mary's son was named Jesus, because he would save his people from their sins.

Finally, the decision for a low or high Christology does not only mark the dividing line between unitarianism and Trinitarianism but also determines the answer to the question of salvation. If there is no great need for salvation, a low Christology works quite well. Then we need Jesus only as some kind of role model. People can be counted on to save themselves, if they have good intentions and try hard enough. But if salvation is out of reach of human reason and strength, and humans are "dead in their trespasses and sins," help must come from beyond the human potential, from God's own coming into the depths of the human condition. Only a high Christology will bear the burden of the world's redemption and disclose the true identity of God as Father, Son, and Holy Spirit.

NOTES

1. Grant R. Osborne, "Christology and New Testament Hermeneutics: A Survey of the Discussion," in *Semeia 30: Christology and Exegesis: New Approaches,* ed. Robert Jewett (Decatur, Ga.: Scholars Press, 1985), 49–63.

2. Carl R. Holladay, "New Testament Christology: A Consideration of

Dunn's *Christology in the Making,"* in Jewett, ed., *Semeia 30: Christology and Exegesis,* 65–82.

3. Robert Funk, *Honest to Jesus* (San Francisco: HarperCollins, 1996), 305.

4. John Hick, ed., *The Myth of God Incarnate* (London: SCM Press, 1977).

5. James D. G. Dunn, *Christology in the Making: A New Testament Inquiry into the Origins of the Doctrine of the Incarnation* (London: SCM Press, 1980), xiii.

6. Jaroslav Pelikan, *Jesus through the Centuries* (New Haven, Conn.: Yale University Press, 1985), 220.

7. Among them are Karl Rahner, Hans Urs von Balthasar, and Wolfhart Pannenberg.

8. A. Grillmeier, *Christ in Christian Tradition* (Oxford: A. R. Mowbray & Co., 1975).

9. Karl Barth, "The Principles of Dogmatics according to Wilhelm Herrmann," in *Theology and Church,* trans. Louise Pettibone Smith (New York: Harper & Row, 1962), 265.

JESUS, CHRIST, AND ETHICS

Lisa Sowle Cahill

Perhaps the most significant development in Christian ethics in this century has been the shift from an ethic of personal virtue to an ethic of social change. As the social gospel movement of the late nineteenth and early twentieth century made clear, the Christian disciple must look toward more than personal faith and salvation expressed in a life of righteous works. He or she must, with the church, prophetically embody the kingdom of God in society. This means to live in transformative solidarity with those who suffer, even while awaiting the kingdom's decisive, future, and eschatological completion by God's act. "If love is the fundamental quality in God, it must be part of the constitution of humanity. . . . The atonement is the symbol and basis of a new social order."[1] This statement from Walter Rauschenbusch's classic work *A Theology for the Social Gospel* parallels the ethical hope of the modern Catholic social encyclical tradition that emerged,[2] as well as of the many subsequent theologies of liberation that have given Christian ethics a more global dimension and a voice "from below."

Both for the authors of the social gospel and for recent work in Christian social ethics, the teaching and example of Jesus, especially his preaching of the inclusive reign of God, have tended to figure more centrally than christological formulations, references to Jesus' supernatural origins, or promises of reward in an eternal life. What, then, is the relevance of New Testament Christology to ethics? What is added ethically when Jesus is understood as "Christ"? What difference does Christology make to a biblical view of moral discipleship?

The thesis of this chapter is that historical and social-scientific research on the life and death of Jesus is valuable in defining the distinctive orientation of Christian ethics, while to call Jesus "Christ" is to place his moral message against the horizon of a new reality that warrants and empowers the moral life. Although I make a distinction between the socially oriented "kingdom" ethic of the earthly Jesus and the Christian moral community's self-understanding as "body of Christ," I do not mean to separate the historical Jesus from the Christ of faith. Rather, the gradually developing proclamation of Jesus as the Christ—pluralistically expressed in the New Testament—is rooted in the experience and memory of Jesus during his lifetime. And, of course, Gospel depictions of the earthly Jesus are refracted through the experience of his resurrection and presence in Spirit. Nor do I intend to separate Jesus in any radical way from other prophetic ethical movements in first-century Palestine, especially in Judaism, or from other experiences of the Divine as mediated through earthly figures and communities.

THE HISTORICAL JESUS AND ETHICS

Recent research on the historical Jesus is important not only for what it reveals about the ethical, social, and political significance of Jesus and the early Christian movement in first-century context but for what it tells us about modern and "postmodern" opinions of Christology. To understand Jesus as Christ is to link Jesus to God as "God's anointed one" and to claim, at a minimum, that "God's saving and liberating power is manifest in Jesus."[3] "Christology" as a theological and hermeneutical category owes its existence to later conciliar and doctrinal formulations that move away from the symbolic and analogical language of biblical depictions, explaining Jesus' activity in terms of his being. These formulations use philosophical categories such as substance, nature, and person, and they claim explicitly that Jesus not only is a manifestation of God's power but is himself divine.[4]

One legacy of modern thought, with its privileging of empirical and scientific methods of investigation and construals of knowledge, is a deep skepticism, even among religious thinkers and theologians, about the credibility of belief in a transcendent or supernatural being or realm. Postmodern trends in Western culture and academia add to this skepticism a reluctance to make absolutist claims about the knowledge or superiority of any one social or cultural perspective, and so bring questions about the exclusivity and finality of the religious and moral significance of Jesus. On the positive side, authors reflecting these currents insist that the religious claims of Christianity, even those that biblical symbols warrant, must be subjected to some criteria of plausibility beyond the wishes, speculations, or possibly illusions of their adherents.[5] More problematically, they use models of knowledge, truth, and verification that are themselves culturally limited to undermine some of the most ancient symbols of Christian religious experience. This is particularly true of research on the historical Jesus.

It must also be recognized that these intellectual and cultural currents have affected even more traditional theologians, such as Karl Barth (neo-orthodoxy), Reinhold Niebuhr (Christian realism), and H. Richard Niebuhr (the cultural relativism of Christianity), who in turn have transmitted these currents in their work. Reconfiguring Christianity after the shock of the two world wars, these authors reaffirmed (in varying degrees) Christian symbols of transcendence. Nonetheless, they subjected sanguine, triumphalistic, and evolutionary views of Christian faith and ethics to stringent critique.

Biblical scholarship in support of the third quest for the historical Jesus reflects these critical trends. Its authors are, on the whole, remarkably uninterested in any attribution of divine identity to Jesus, in a supernatural source of salvation, or in otherworldly completion of historical events.[6] Instead, they center the meaning of Jesus *in* history, by referring back to the historical reality of Jesus. They stress not the transcendence but the *immanence* of God. Therefore, these scholars employ historical and social-scientific methods as appropriate to capture the reality and significance of Jesus. Jesus is compared to other historical figures and types by employing social history, social anthropology, and sociological analysis, as well as historical information about the ancient world and about biblical figures and events.[7]

For example, Jesus has been compared to a Mediterranean Jewish peasant (John Dominic Crossan),[8] a Hellenistic Cynic sage (Burton Mack),[9] a prophet of wisdom personified as Sophia (Elisabeth Schüssler Fiorenza),[10] a Jewish eschatological prophet whose expectations proved wrong (E. P. Sanders),[11] a charismatic but noneschatological Jewish healer and social reformer (Borg),[12] a Jewish miracle worker and eschatological prophet (John P. Meier).[13] There is variation among these authors in terms of both the strength and importance of Jesus' Jewish identity and his possible relation to a transcendent, divine power, but all share a commitment to use social-scientific methods to understand the impact of his life and message in his own historical context and to analogize (implicitly or explicitly) from that context to our own. Most important, especially for Christian ethics, is the shared conclusion that Jesus shattered the standard status markers of his world and overturned barriers to inclusion in a community characterized by forgiveness, compassion, and mutual service. The importance of this direction of thinking about the historical Jesus for Christian ethics can be illustrated with regard to two of the most influential researchers on the topic, John Dominic Crossan and Marcus Borg.

Crossan envisions Jesus as a Mediterranean Jewish peasant who preached that God's kingdom is present and open freely even to society's most despised and downtrodden. Jesus' iconoclastic practices of sharing the table with the sinner and the impure and healing without expectation of payment communicated his sense of the availability of God in experiences of compassion and solidarity. Moreover, Jesus' "ecstatic vision and social program sought to rebuild a society upward from its grass roots but on principles of religious and economic egalitarianism." It "was a challenge launched not just at Judaism's strictest purity regulations, or even at the Mediterranean's patriarchal combination of honor and shame, patronage and clientage, but at civilization's eternal inclination to draw lines, invoke boundaries, establish hierarchies, and maintain discriminations."[14] Crossan does not make much of Jesus' relation to a transcendent divine power, much less of the traditional Christian confession of Jesus as Christ.

Marcus Borg's picture is also highly social and political. He describes a "noneschatological" Jesus whose practices of table fellowship and healing communicated that the kingdom of God is actually present.[15] "In a world with sharp social boundaries, the inclusiveness of the Jesus movement was remarkable. As a boundary-shattering movement, it was a new social reality with an alternative vision of human life in community," a "community of compassion."[16] Borg agrees with Crossan that historical research helps keeps alive a "subversive memory" of Jesus that is essentially in accordance with the Gospels and available to all believers, scholars and nonscholars alike.[17]

Borg, like Crossan, rejects the traditional idea that Jesus expected God to fulfill the kingdom with an apocalyptic or eschatological act and so distances himself from supernatural overtones in linking transformed social relations with the arrival of a transcendent kingdom, eschaton, or eternal life. Yet Borg does strongly affirm that the inspiration of Jesus' activity is a personal experience of the Divine that cannot be captured in purely historical terms. Describing Jesus as a "spirit person," Borg names him as "one of those figures in human history who had vivid and frequent experiences of that reality which has variously been called 'the numinous,' 'the Holy,' 'the Sacred,' 'the Spirit,' or simply 'God.'" Borg circumvents the tradition and its christological doctrines in defining the presence of God to, in, and through Jesus but does see Jesus as communicating the possibility of "a relationship with the Spirit of God." "Without God at the center, the Christian life makes no important sense. If we are uncertain about the reality of God, we have no really important message."[18] Borg even describes "the post-Easter Jesus" as "the living Lord, the side of God turned toward us, the face of God, the Lord who is also the Spirit."[19]

Borg makes it especially clear that a dialectical relationship exists between our understanding of the historical Jesus and Christian discipleship now. Discipleship is profoundly ethical and political, since to believe in Jesus means to share in the relationship to God and to our fellow human beings to which he invites us. For instance, "if a Christian becomes persuaded that Jesus taught a subversive wisdom, it affects how that person sees the conventional wisdom of his or her own day; if a Christian becomes persuaded that Jesus countered the purity system of his day, it affects how she or he sees purity systems in our day; if a Christian becomes persuaded that Jesus indicted the ruling elites of his day, it affects how domination systems are seen in the present."[20]

The importance of this kind of research for Christian ethics should not be underestimated. Attentive readers or hearers of the double love commandment, the Sermon on the Mount, the parable of the Good Samaritan, and the parable of judgment in Matthew 25 have always realized that Jesus calls us to act compassionately toward neighbor, stranger, or enemy; to challenge social structures that define some as unworthy of our service; and to make a "preferential option for the poor." Even theologically traditional scholars writing about biblical ethics recognize much the same *content*.[21] But historical and sociological research fills out in vivid detail just what this call would have meant in the world of Jesus and his first followers. It serves as the latest in a line of necessary correctives to the perennial tendencies to domesticate the social radicality of Jesus' message, to focus Christian commitment on personal righteousness, and to delude ourselves that genuine faith need not have consequences for the redemption of the world and its oppressive institutions. In a postmodern atmosphere, the historical Jesus scholars aspire to protect the universal significance of Jesus, by means of the relevance and appeal of his ethical teaching. The transcendent dimension of social commitment is not necessarily eliminated (especially for Borg, Meier, and Schüssler Fiorenza), but what is most emphasized is the fulfillment of God's will through reformed historical communities of disciples who act transformatively in their social worlds. Believers today should have an effect on their communities and its structures that is *analogous* to the effect that Jesus produced in his historical setting, and that his first followers produced in theirs.[22]

THE CHRISTOLOGICAL MOVE

When Walter Rauschenbusch linked Jesus' preaching of the kingdom with the social gospel, categories such as "the Fall," "atonement," "grace," "salvation," "repentance," and "eschatology" were all still part of his working vocabulary.[23] Historical Jesus researchers today have evoked the admiration of some and the hostility of others precisely because they seem to convey their religious and ethical message quite effectively without these traditional touchstones of Christian faith. One hostile critic is Luke Timothy Johnson, for whom any admirable motive or valuable outcome in this research is quite overcome by its threat to "the image of Jesus held by traditional faith" and to "Christian faith" itself.[24] Johnson's basic and valid point is that the fullness of who Jesus is—"the real Jesus"—is not limited to what can be discovered by historical reconstruction. This is why it is important to understand Jesus through the lens of the Gospels, written after the resurrection experiences but based also in the memory of Jesus that extends back to his lifetime. That historical memory is connected with and reinterpreted in light of the experience of Jesus present in the community as Christ in the present. "Authentic Christian faith is a response to the living God, whom Christians declare is powerfully at work among them through the resurrected Jesus."[25]

A more developed treatment of essentially the same point has been made by Sandra Schneiders, who distinguishes the "actual Jesus" from the earthly Jesus (Jesus as he really was during his lifetime, a real person whom no literary text could ever fully recapture and who now no longer exists as such), the historical Jesus (a literary construct composed of selected elements of the Gospel writers' memory or knowledge of the earthly Jesus), the glorified Jesus (obviously not understood or communicated in his fullness), and the proclaimed Jesus (the variable, always incomplete, and often distorted image of Jesus presented to any specific audience).[26] The actual Jesus is the same person as the earthly Jesus of Nazareth but now resurrected and glorified. The actual Jesus is present to us "in the proclamation of the Word, in the celebration of the sacraments, in the unity of the Church, in our own living of his life through the gift of his Spirit."[27]

Schneiders rightly says that the actual or real Jesus is not a figure of the past whose life we attempt to recover using historical methods (however valid that enterprise is in itself) but rather Jesus in his present reality, which includes resurrection life and presence in Spirit. To what extent was the power of Jesus to mediate the saving and liberating power of God—the power that is named by calling Jesus "Christ"—already effective and visible during his lifetime? This issue bears on ethics insofar as it provides a transcendent and even eschatological dimension to the kingdom ethic of the earthly Jesus, that is, the ethic of inclusive community that the historical Jesus scholars identify as the primary significance of Jesus and his radical challenge to the sociopolitical order of his day and our own. If the naming of Jesus as Christ is a post-Easter development that in fact goes back to and is continuous with the way in which Jesus was perceived during his lifetime, then the kingdom ethic of Jesus is and always has been integrally related to an in-breaking experience of and trust in the Divine.

Any attempt to discern clearly what Jesus' own understanding of his mission was and what the responses of those who first interacted with him were to that mission is inevitably bedeviled by the fact that our primary access to the historical Jesus is through the Gospel accounts, and those accounts were written after the death of Jesus, when he was already being explicitly proclaimed as Christ. Although reasonable estimates of what Jesus said or did and how he was received can be inferred from large patterns of consistency among the Gospels, the estimates will always remain to some degree hypothetical. With this caveat, it may be said that a sizable consensus among many scholars is that an eschatological outlook characterized Jesus' teaching and deeds, and that this was well recognized by both his followers and his adversaries. A statement of Gerald O'Collins is representative:

> All three Synoptic Gospels recall not only that Jesus worked miracles but also that his miraculous deeds were powerful signs of the kingdom, inextricably bound up with his proclamation of the kingdom. His healings and exorcisms were compassionate salvific gestures, the first fruits of the presence of the kingdom which manifested the power of God's merciful rule already operative in and through his person. . . . As speaker of the parables, for example, he belonged to the kingdom and effected its powerful presence.[28]

Similarly, Rudolf Schnackenburg, after insisting that the Gospels "immediately draw all historical tradition into the faith-picture of Jesus Christ," still agrees that "the surest thing that can be established from the proclamation of the historical Jesus is his message of the coming and already in-breaking kingdom of God."[29] Or from Wolfgang Schrage: the "horizon of Jesus' ethics is realized eschatology in which the salvific kingdom of God is already at hand in Jesus."[30] Moreover, Jesus' experience of the kingdom has an indisputable "future-oriented viewpoint."[31] John Meier puts the point strongly: "It is clear that this future, transcendent salvation was an essential part of Jesus' proclamation of the kingdom. Any reconstruction of the historical Jesus that does not do full justice to this eschatological future must be dismissed as hopelessly inadequate."[32]

These same authors also concur that Jesus understands *himself,* in his healings and exorcisms, to be acting by the power of God (Luke 11:20/Matt. 12:28).[33] Jesus spoke in his own name to assert startling authority over the Sabbath, the temple, and the law.[34] John Carroll and Joel Green have recently argued that Jesus drew on themes and images in Jewish tradition to interpret his impending death in view of divine purposes, that is, to "forge a view of himself as the one through whose suffering Israel, and through Israel the nations, would experience divine redemption."[35] Although the Jesus of the Gospels is presented through the faith of the evangelists, O'Collins asserts that "it is quite implausible to think that Jesus was oblivious of performing a messianic mission. . . . Otherwise it is very difficult to account both for the charge against him of being a messianic pretender and for the ease with which his followers began calling him 'the Christ' immediately after his death and resurrection."[36]

Christology—theological interpretation of Jesus as the Christ—derives from the Christian community's attempts to understand the relation between Jesus of Nazareth, in whose activity God was already experienced as present, and Jesus now resurrected, exalted, and present in the life of the community. Christologies are notoriously and contentiously variable, both in the New Testament and in subsequent doctrinal history. I will simply focus on a few key aspects of New Testament Christology that have direct bearing on ethics. These include human sinfulness and salvation through Jesus' death; the resulting importance of the symbolism of the cross in defining the Christian life; and sanctification and eschatology, which I understand to be related.

"JESUS AS CHRIST" AND ETHICS

One thing Christology adds to ethics is a more profound view of sin and redemption than a study of the human situation as such can furnish, even if human relationships and social structures are subjected to as fundamental a critique as the historical Jesus scholars provide. An intransigent difficulty for social ethics is the ease and frequency with which human individuals and groups rationalize domination of others in the service of self-interest and cling tenaciously to power structures that support any privileges they may have already attained. It is for this very reason that Karl Marx, Reinhold Niebuhr, Michel Foucault, and liberation theologians all assert that more equitable balances of social power can be achieved only through the resistance of the oppressed themselves. Even on that basis, however, the past and present record of human history does not warrant much confidence that shifting power alliances within and among cultures are leading the human race toward a more peaceful, just, and cooperative future.

Sinfulness in human beings lies deeper than the provisional good intentions for moral and social reform that the prophetic ideal of a "preferential option for the poor" may evoke. Hence, a significant portion of christological symbolism concerns human sinfulness and the need for repentance, divine mercy and salvation. Jesus Christ's mediation of salvation is closely associated with his death, both in the New Testament and in theological tradition, and is frequently interpreted (especially under the influence of Anselm) as "atonement" or "satisfaction" for human sins.[37] While this kind of language reflects well the human experience of guilt and impotence, many have noted that it is problematic in suggesting that God exacts payment or propitiation in the form of an innocent death.

John Carroll and Joel Green caution against taking any one interpretation of the efficacy of Jesus' death in a literal or exclusive manner. Jesus himself and his first interpreters "searched the conceptual encyclopedias of their day" for a "range of metaphors" that could collaterally communicate that Jesus, in his death, represents not only sinful humanity but God.[38] The cross represents God's initiative and compassionate presence in human suffering and evil.

Jesus himself drew on images of Jewish tradition, such as the suffering of the prophets, the tradition of the suffering righteous, and the reconciliation of Israel to God through great suffering.[39] Using the Gospel of Mark, Adela Yarbro Collins shows that early followers "struggled to find meaning in the ignominious death of Jesus" and borrowed from many other rituals of sacrifice and substitution, both Greek and Hebrew, reinterpreted in light of Jewish scriptures and apocalyptic.[40] The salvific death of Jesus is represented in images drawn from public spheres of the first-century world in which he lived: the law court (justification), commercial dealings (redemption), personal relationships (reconciliation), worship (sacrifice), and war (triumph over evil).[41] The ensuing theology is an "interpretive quilt," whose "content remains amorphous" and suggestive.[42] Above all, the symbolism of atonement "repudiates ancient and modern attempts at segregating people away from the gracious invitation of God," which is for the whole world and not within the possession of any one individual or group.[43] Ultimately, as Jack Dean Kingsbury comments on Matthew, "the cross attests, not to the destruction of Jesus, but to the salvation that God henceforth proffers through Jesus to all humankind."[44] The theology of atonement and salvation is inseparably connected to ethics. "Believers—having been redeemed, reconciled, delivered, bought, justified, and so on—are now released and empowered to reflect in their lives the quality of life exemplified by their Savior."[45]

LOVE, CROSS, ETHICS

Many authors relate Jesus Christ to Christian ethics by placing the cross at the center of the moral life. Richard Hays is an influential example of those who propose that "Jesus' death on the cross is the paradigm for faithfulness to God in this world."[46] Hays does not use this image alone but combines it with "community" and "new creation." With these latter paradigms, Hays presents the church as a countercultural community of discipleship that embodies the power of the resurrection in "a not-yet-redeemed world."[47] But "the focal image of the cross" defines the content or substantive way of life of the kingdom of God in terms of Jesus' suffering and death.[48]

Certainly, the cross figures centrally in the Pauline proclamation of Jesus as Savior, and few would deny that this symbol communicates something intrinsic to Christian self-understanding. However, historical Jesus research helps raise the question of whether the cross is the center of Jesus' moral mission or of that of his disciples. Or is suffering the consequence of a life devoted to mercy, compassion, and the building of a community that represents the inclusive love and forgiveness of God? Indeed, when Hays takes up specific moral questions such as homosexuality, abortion, and ethnic conflict, his moral message seems to be not suffering as such but reconciling love.

Related to this question of moral content is that of the range of Jesus' vision and the effective extent of his salvific death. In what sense is the world really "not yet redeemed," and thus related to Christian ethics only in the mode of opposition? Somewhat in contrast to a position like that of Hays is that of Gerald O'Collins, who affirms that Jesus embodies a universal vision of God's pardon and salvation and calls all humanity to "a realistic love toward other human beings in need, a love which was willing to cross racial frontiers (Luke 10:25–37) and include everyone, even one's enemies (Matt. 5:43–48 and parallels). He called for a new brotherhood and sisterhood which denied any sacrosanct value to family or tribal bonds."[49] To interpret the kingdom as a universal vision of inclusive love is to encourage greater optimism about social change, as well as ecumenical cooperation in bringing change about.

But Hays asserts that "love is not a central thematic emphasis" in the

New Testament, and even that the foundational account of the early church (Acts) "neither commends love nor exhorts readers to experience or practice it." Instead, he reads the example of Jesus as "a rigorous, suffering obedience."[50] True, the symbolism of suffering is important in defining the Christian life. But the low occurrence of Greek equivalents for the English term *love* does not necessarily indicate that love is not the New Testament's central moral theme. One must look to the kind of behavior enjoined in the Sermon on the Mount, in Jesus' parables, and in Jesus' own fellowship with sinners and outcasts to see whether love or suffering is foundational in his vision of God's reign. Research on the probable impact of the historical Jesus' iconoclastic behavior and on the socially disruptive and reconstructive trajectory of early Christian communities allows us to see that suffering is the consequence or accompaniment of a certain kind of life oriented by responsibilities and purposes not subservient to the interests of society's powerful elites. The disciple risks suffering by active solidarity with the stranger, outcast, and enemy; but the heart of his or her life is participation in the merciful and forgiving compassion of God.

Seeking to understand the meaning of Jesus' death in relation to God's reconciling presence in history leads us properly and inevitably to consider Jesus' human death under the christological symbol of cross. But it is precisely *Jesus,* the historical person, that New Testament Christologies are reappropriating with the language of post-Easter faith. As Roger Haight notes, a "relatively adequate" Christology must explain how Jesus is "the bearer of salvation from God," but it must also be "faithful to the historical person of Jesus," and must do so in a way that empowers Christian discipleship.[51] Therefore the discovery of the cross cannot be allowed to obscure the shape of the new community that Jesus called into being. According to the Gospel accounts themselves, the cross is precisely the outcome of a life in which the power of the kingdom is already manifest in new relationships. Social-scientific explorations of early Christianity show that even Pauline cross theology can be understood against the backdrop of an "honor and shame" social system in which to seek prestige and respect is to align oneself with oppressive structures.[52] As the historical Jesus writers insist, this is not a situation limited to the first century.

A forceful example of the consequent nature of the cross in relation to love is Mary Solberg's *Compelling Knowledge: A Feminist Proposal for an Epistemology of the Cross*.[53] Solberg dedicates her work to "the poor of El Salvador" with whom she worked for several years. In dialogue with Martin Luther, Solberg develops a theology of the cross that unites knowledge of God and ethical struggle. An epistemology of the cross allows one to see, from within suffering, that God's purposes are not the purposes of the "systems and ideologies" that "thrive on racism, sexism, heterosexism, and gross maldistribution of economic resources and political power within nations and across international boundaries in all directions." God's purposes aim beyond suffering to liberation. The framework of the cross allows us to name, confront, and identify empathically with suffering. Then suffering can be countered "under conditions that protect, dignify, and empower."[54] Love defines the experience of compassionate solidarity out of which Solberg begins. Love defines her commitment to create conditions through which life-giving possibilities can be realized.

For the privileged, action to liberate from suffering requires love in the form of *metanoia,* acceptance of responsibility and a correction of course.[55] Knowledge of God through the cross makes us accountable to love insofar as it summons us to participate in "God's transformative solidarity" and to "affirm human dignity" through a committed and hopeful way of life.[56] Solberg's book illustrates that love of neighbor, cross, and social action should not be separated. But the key to Christian ethics is love. Frank Matera confirms that for both Jesus and Paul, "the moral life expresses itself in love for God, love for neighbor, and love for one's enemy."[57]

What difference for Christian ethics does it make to accent love rather than suffering as the touchstone of the moral life? I believe the centrality of love colors Christian ethics in three important ways. First, it conveys powerfully that the Christian life is a way of grace and joy. If discipleship is faith "truly active through love," then Christians do "works of the freest service, cheerfully and lovingly done," with "a joyful, willing, and free mind," rejoicing in the generosity of God.[58] Second, if the moral dimension of God's "reign" and of Christ's "body" is seen as active love of neighbor, that image encourages a confident and hopeful commitment to transform all relations and structures that oppress, hurt, and diminish others. Third, if the Christian life means accountability to social transformation, that self-understanding opens the door to positive, active, ecumenical cooperation with other persons and groups for the common good. Although the Christian message can be deeply countercultural, it can also—as a way of solidarity and service—radically engage all cultures with a summons to change.

A further important question for Christian ethics reflects a tension in the New Testament itself; in Christian theologies of sin, soteriology, sanctification, and ecclesiology; and between some major contemporary Christian approaches to social ethics. That question is whether moral and social change is a realistic expectation within human history. This question may be posed on two levels, that of the church and that of society. Does Christian faith transform believers, so that the moral behavior of the church and its members is truly and significantly different? If the church understands itself as a leaven for social change, can it really expect that its moral message will be accepted and effective in society in any significant or far-reaching way?

Christology is important in answering this question, but its answer remains contested and difficult to clarify, on both levels. A full discussion certainly exceeds the scope of this chapter, but I can here indicate some possible implications of Christology for Christian approaches to moral and social change. First, as Leander Keck noted in his presidential address to the Society of Biblical Literature, New Testament writers presuppose "the new reality created by the Christ-event" and assume that this reality has "an impact on the believer in the community that exists in Christ's name."[59] In the messianic ethics of Jesus, eschatology signifies not only that God's completion is to be awaited in hope but that even now the kingdom is becoming effective in the face of evil. Jesus mediates not only God's judgment on evil but the possibility of its conquest through the redemptive powers of the kingdom.[60]

To understand the life and death of Jesus in terms of his resurrection and sending of the Spirit is to coexist with others in a "story where death is not the ultimate answer to human life, irrespective of all appearances to the contrary."[61] It is to be able to see, believe, and act on the fact that "Jesus is the stronger one, stronger than any forces of evil, more powerful than any horrible problems that imprison and distress us." In Christ, "salvation means being delivered from death, absurdity, and hatred, and being redeemed for life, meaning, and love."[62]

As far as the content of Christian moral behavior is concerned, there are no radical departures from "the noblest social norms of the Jewish and Greco-Roman worlds."[63] But Christians are committed and empowered in a special way to include *all persons* within their sphere of moral concern, to overcome evil and death by living in radical solidarity with those whom they formerly despised or regarded as enemies. And this call to transformation is addressed to and realized by a whole community of disciples, not just by virtuous individuals.[64] The fact that the material content of the Christian moral life—the personal and social good realized by moral behavior—is substantially the same as that of other communities means that Christians and others can and should engage together in moral debate and action. The distinctive contribution of Christians is the "preferential option for the poor," rendered by the kingdom teaching of Jesus and empowered by the presence in Spirit of the resurrected Christ. This affects not so much the Christian understanding of good to be sought as it does persons to be served, securing good for others as well as for ourselves.

With what kind of confidence will Christians anticipate that the distinctive Christian commitment to resist the power structures of "the world" on behalf of the world's poor will evoke a corresponding *metanoia* from others? This question engages ethics with fundamental Christian theologies of sin and redemption. The absolutely gratuitous, and correspondingly *limited,* character of God's election in Christ has certainly been a strong theme in Christian tradition. Yet resources within Bible and tradition also affirm the *universal* character of the divine love, and thereby of the salvation mediated in Jesus' resurrection from the dead.[65] Premodern Christian authors, including Augustine, Thomas Aquinas, Luther, and Calvin, accepted the former position. Interest in universal salvation became greater after the Enlightenment, not only because of heightened value given to the individual and to the principle of equality but also because modern societies provide a context for theology and ethics that is self-consciously intercultural and pluralistic. As Christians engage discussion partners outside traditional Christianity about profound questions of human meaning and social relations, they also recognize more clearly the evils done in the name of Christianity itself. Christian triumphalism wanes, and a more inclusive vision of God's relation to humanity emerges. The pluralism of Christologies in the New Testament suggests variety and a certain open-endedness in models in order to understand transcendence, the Divine, salvation, the role of Jesus Christ as mediator, and the possibility of experiencing and being reconciled to God through other religious traditions.[66] To envision Christian discipleship as a cruciform conflict with a rejecting world is an effective strategy for reminding those who are participating members of privileged cultures that commitment to God requires a critical stance toward seductive cultural values. But further resources in the biblical literature need to be mined to respond to matters of local and global injustice for which Christians may be accountable. The urgent character of many ethical and social problems confronting humanity across the boundaries of cultures and religions—ethnic violence, economic globalization, and ecological damage, to name a few—seems increasingly to demand that Christians seek moral common ground with others and commit themselves with others to transformation as a real possibility.

NOTES

1. Walter Rauschenbusch, *A Theology for the Social Gospel* (Nashville: Abingdon Press, 1945), 273–74.

2. Leo XIII's *Rerum Novarum* (On the condition of labor) was published in 1891.

3. Marinus de Jonge, "Christ," in *The Anchor Bible Dictionary,* ed. David Noel Freedman (New York, London, and Toronto: Doubleday, 1992), 1:921.

4. See John P. Galvin, "Jesus Christ," in Francis Schüssler Fiorenza and John P. Galvin, eds., *Systematic Theology: Roman Catholic Perspectives* (Minneapolis: Fortress Press, 1991), 251–324; William P. Loewe, "Chalcedon, Council of," in Joseph A. Komonchak, Mary Collins, Dermot Lane, eds., *New Dictionary of Theology* (Wilmington, Del.: Michael Glazier, 1987), 177–78; and Elizabeth A. Johnson, *Consider Jesus: Waves of Renewal in Christology* (New York: Crossroad, 1990). Written by Catholics, these works are ecumenical in scope and tone.

5. See James M. Gustafson, *Ethics from a Theocentric Perspective,* vol. 1: *Theology and Ethics* (Chicago: University of Chicago Press, 1981).

6. In the words of Marcus Borg, "the image of the historical Jesus as a divine or semi-divine figure, who saw himself as the divine savior whose purpose was to die for the sins of the world, and whose message consisted in preaching that, is simply not historically true" (*Jesus, a New Vision: Spirit, Culture, and the Life of Discipleship* [San Francisco: Harper & Row, 1987], 7).

7. See *Interpretation* 50, 4 (1996), on the theme "The Historical Jesus."

8. John Dominic Crossan, *The Historical Jesus: The Life of a Mediterranean Jewish Peasant* (San Francisco: HarperCollins, 1991).

9. Burton L. Mack, *A Myth of Innocence: Mark and Christian Origins* (Philadelphia: Fortress Press, 1988).

10. Elisabeth Schüssler Fiorenza, *Jesus: Miriam's Child, Sophia's Prophet* (New York: Continuum, 1994).

11. E. P. Sanders, *Jesus and Judaism* (Philadelphia: Fortress Press, 1985).

12. Marcus J. Borg, *Meeting Jesus Again for the First Time: The Historical Jesus and the Heart of Contemporary Faith* (San Francisco: HarperCollins, 1994).

13. John P. Meier, *A Marginal Jew: Rethinking the Historical Jesus,* vol. 2: *Mentor, Message, and Miracles* (New York and London: Doubleday, 1994). Overviews of these and other authors are given in Marcus J. Borg, *Jesus in Contemporary Scholarship* (Valley Forge, Pa.: Trinity Press International, 1994); Michael E. O'Keeffe, "Searching for the Historical Jesus: Examining the Work of John Dominic Crossan and Marcus J. Borg," *Horizons* 24 (1997): 175–92; and Luke Timothy Johnson, *The Real Jesus: The Misguided Quest for the Historical Jesus and the Truth of the Traditional Gospels* (New York and San Francisco: HarperCollins, 1996).

14. Crossan, *Historical Jesus,* xii.

15. Borg, *Jesus in Contemporary Scholarship,* 166.

16. Ibid., 154.

17. Ibid., 196.

18. Ibid., 153.

19. Borg, *Meeting Jesus,* 137.

20. Borg, *Jesus in Contemporary Scholarship,* 194.

21. For instance, Wolfgang Schrage recognizes Jesus' "preferential option for the poor" and writes, "Jesus criticizes wealth radically, promises the kingdom of God to the marginal poor, and asserts their rights" (*The Ethics of the New Testament* [Philadelphia: Fortress Press, 1988], 100–101).

22. For discussion of this point in relation to Christian ethics, see William C. Spohn, "Jesus and Christian Ethics," *Theological Studies* 56 (1995): 92–107, especially 101–7; and Thomas L. Schubeck, S.J., "Ethics and Liberation Theology," *Theological Studies* 56 (1995): 107–22, especially 120–22. See also Pheme Perkins, "Jesus and Ethics," *Theology Today* 52 (1995): 49–65, especially 64–65.

23. All these and more can be found in the pages of Rauschenbusch's *Theology for the Social Gospel*—that much-maligned supposed harbinger of liberal Protestantism.

24. Johnson, *Real Jesus,* 40, 141.

25. Ibid., 143.

26. Sandra M. Schneiders, *The Revelatory Text: Interpreting the New Testament as Sacred Scripture* (New York and San Francisco: HarperCollins, 1991), 100–1.

27. Ibid., 101.

28. Gerald O'Collins, S.J., *Christology: A Biblical, Historical, and Systematic Study of Jesus* (New York: Oxford University Press, 1995), 55–56.

29. Rudolf Schnackenburg, *Jesus in the Gospels: A Biblical Christology* (Louisville, Ky.: Westminster John Knox Press, 1995), 318.

30. Schrage, *Ethics of the New Testament,* 37.

31. Schnackenburg, *Jesus,* 318.

32. Meier, *Marginal Jew,* 2:350.

33. Schnackenburg, *Jesus,* 318.

34. O'Collins, *Christology,* 59–60.

35. Joel B. Green, "The Death of Jesus and the Ways of God: Jesus and the Gospels on Messianic Status and Shameful Suffering," *Interpretation* 52 (1988): 34. This article recapitulates part of the argument of John T. Carroll and Joel B. Green, *The Death of Jesus in Early Christianity* (Peabody, Mass.: Hendrickson Publishers, 1995).

36. O'Collins, *Christology,* 57.

37. "Atonement and Scripture" is the theme of *Interpretation* 52, 1 (1998). For a theological history, see Francis Schüssler Fiorenza, "Redemption," in Komonchak et al., eds., *New Dictionary of Theology,* 836–51.

38. Carroll and Green, *Death of Jesus,* 278. See also, O'Collins, *Christology,* 67–81.

39. Green, "Death of Jesus," 34.

40. Adela Yarbro Collins, "Finding Meaning in the Death of Jesus," *Journal of Religion* 78 (1998): 196.

41. Carroll and Green, *Death of Jesus,* 265.

42. Green, "Death of Jesus," 35.

43. Carroll and Green, *Death of Jesus,* 278.

44. Jack Dean Kingsbury, "The Plot of Matthew's Story," *Interpretation* 46 (1992): 355. See also Jack Dean Kingsbury, *Matthew,* 2d ed. (Philadelphia: Fortress Press, 1986).

45. Carroll and Green, *Death of Jesus,* 277.

46. Richard B. Hays, *The Moral Vision of the New Testament: A Contemporary Introduction to New Testament Ethics* (New York and San Francisco: HarperCollins, 1996), 197.

47. Ibid., 196, 198.

48. Ibid., 197.

49. O'Collins, *Christology,* 77.

50. Hays, *Moral Vision,* 200–1.

51. Roger Haight, "On Pluralism in Christology," *Budhi* 1 (1997): 45.

52. See Wayne A. Meeks, *First Urban Christians* (New Haven, Conn.: Yale University Press, 1983), 180–83. Susan R. Garrett, "Paul's Thorn and Cultural Models of Affliction," in L. Michael White and O. Larry Yarbrough, eds., *The Social World of the First Christians: Essays in Honor of Wayne A. Meeks* (Minneapolis: Fortress Press, 1995), 82–99.

53. Mary Solberg, *Compelling Knowledge: A Feminist Proposal for an Epistemology of the Cross* (Albany: State University of New York Press, 1997).

54. Ibid., 164.

55. Ibid., 107.

56. Ibid., 125. Among others, several African American authors have also understood God's presence to suffering in Jesus as a call for social transformation through inclusive community. See, for example, Diana L. Hayes, *And Still We Rise: An Introduction to Black Liberation Theology* (Mahwah, N.J.: Paulist Press, 1996), especially chap. 7, "The Vision of Black Women: Womanist Theology."

57. Frank J. Matera, *New Testament Ethics: The Legacies of Jesus and Paul* (Louisville, Ky.: Westminster John Knox Press, 1996), 254.

58. Martin Luther, *Christian Liberty* (Philadelphia: Fortress Press, 1957), 28, 30.

59. Leander E. Keck, "Rethinking 'New Testament Ethics'," *Journal of Biblical Literature* 115 (1996): 11, 15.

60. Ben Wiebe, "Messianic Ethics: Response to the Kingdom of God," *Interpretation* 45 (1991): 29–42.

61. Sean Freyne, "The Quest for the Historical Jesus: Some Historical Reflections," *Concilium* 1997/1, Werner Jeanrond and Christoph

Theobald, eds., *Who Do You Say That I Am?* (Maryknoll, N.Y.: Orbis Books, 1997), 47.

62. Gerald O'Collins, "Jesus," *Church* 13 (1997): 9.

63. Daniel J. Harrington, "Biblical Studies and Moral Theology," *Church* 13 (1997): 17.

64. For instance, Wiebe, "Messianic Ethics," 31; Matera, *New Testament Ethics,* 250–52.

65. O'Collins, *Christology,* 299–303. Among other evidence that "Christ is redemptively present to all" (301), O'Collins cites the story of Cornelius in Acts 10 and passages from Galatians and Romans. Wiebe also sees Jesus' eschatological mission to restore Israel as "encompassing the nations" ("Messianic Ethics," 41).

66. Paul F. Knitter, *Jesus and the Other Names: Christian Mission and Global Responsibility* (Maryknoll, N.Y.: Orbis Books, 1996); S. Mark Heim, *Salvations: Truth and Difference in Religion* (Maryknoll, N.Y.: Orbis Books, 1997); and Haight, "On Pluralism in Christology."

THE SIGNIFICANCE OF NEW TESTAMENT CHRISTOLOGY FOR PASTORAL MINISTRY

David L. Bartlett

Writing about the Gospel of John and its "Christologies," Wayne Meeks has observed that a Christology is not a contraption that, once wound up, runs on its own. What we see happening in the fourth Gospel's controversies about Jesus' identity is not two Christologies struggling for dominance but an exegetical and interpretive process by which a new religious movement interpreted scripture, interpreted Jesus, interpreted its own history, and interpreted the world in one complex dialectic.[1]

In his exemplary study of Christology in the Gospel of Mark, Jack Dean Kingsbury uses two primary devices to help the reader understand how Markan Christology "works." First, he studies the Markan use of christological titles—Messiah, Son of God, Son of man. Second, he undertakes a literary-critical study asking how the narratives of the Gospel exemplify and shape its Christology.[2]

This twofold approach to the Christology of a New Testament writer not only is persuasive but provides guidelines for those of us who seek to understand pastoral theology in the light of the biblical paradigms, as we interpret scripture, interpret Jesus, and interpret our world, often especially our congregational world.

On the one hand, pastoral practice is a matter of appropriate theological and christological *understanding*. What can we say about this Jesus of Nazareth that is theologically appropriate and pastorally helpful? On the other hand, pastoral practice requires church persons to take part in an ongoing narrative, the story of God's dealing with humankind, and in particular God's dealing with the church. The enacted Christology of the New Testament points to contemporary possibilities of enactment, embodiment, in the practice of the churches.

In this chapter I study how titles and narratives work together to make christological claims in Mark's Gospel, in the Gospel of John, and in Paul's epistle to the Galatians. In each case I also suggest how the christological claims of these works might shape both pastoral understanding and pastoral practice.

Because this is an essay and not a book, I confine my study to the use of one title, "Son of God," in each of those writings and to one crucial narrative in each—Mark's passion narrative, John's twofold narrative about Christ as shepherd, and Paul's narrative of his own apostolic call in Galatians.

THE GOSPEL OF MARK

Kingsbury has reminded us that a right reading of Mark's Gospel depends on knowing whose point of view in the narrative is reliable.[3] Certainly we are invited to trust the narrator, who begins or titles his book: "The beginning of the good news of Jesus Christ, the Son of God."[4] Twice the voice of God affirms the validity of the title. In Mark 1:11 the heavenly voice speaks to Jesus directly (and probably exclusively): "You are my Son, the Beloved; with you I am well pleased." The first part of the acclamation echoes Psalm 2:7:

> I will tell of the decree of the LORD:
> He said to me: "You are my son; today I have begotten you."

The second part of the acclamation recalls Isaiah 42:1:

> Here is my servant; whom I uphold,
> my chosen, in whom my soul delights;
> I have put my spirit upon him.

It may be that Mark recalls and wants his readers to recall that the first reference is to the Davidic king and the second to the prophetic servant. Certainly, the reference to the gift of the Spirit in Isaiah ties directly to the descent of the Spirit at Mark's baptism. What this passage (like the use of the title "Son of God") does is raise in the mind of the reader the question of what it means to say that Jesus, who is Messiah (or Christ), is also Son of God.

God, that most reliable commentator, speaks again at the scene of the transfiguration in Mark 9:7. Now the voice speaks to Peter, James, and John and not to Jesus alone: "Then a cloud overshadowed them, and from the cloud there came a voice, 'This is my Son, the Beloved; listen to him!'" Here we have not only Old Testament echoes but also Old Testament figures. Moses and Elijah, representing the Law and the Prophets, treat Jesus as an equal—and then God treats him as more than their equal. While presumably the disciples need not stop listening to the Law and the Prophets, it is Jesus' voice especially that they are to hear.

In Mark's Gospel, to be Son of God is to be chosen, beloved, authoritative, Spirit-driven. To be Son of God is also to be demon-recognized. Perhaps strangely to our ears, not only God gets Jesus' title right but so do the demons. As is well known, it was a feature of the world behind Mark's Gospel that sensitive and sensible people saw the struggle between health and distress as a struggle between demonic and godly forces. In such a struggle, demonic and divine powers alike sought to gain control over the opponent by learning to name its name. And because demonic and divine powers alike knew the truth beneath the surface of things, they were apt to get the names right.

> They came to the other side of the sea, to the country of the Gerasenes. And when he had stepped out of the boat, immediately a man out of the tombs with an unclean spirit met him . . . and he shouted at the top of his voice, "What have you to do with me, Jesus, Son of the Most High God? I adjure you by God, do not torment me." . . . Then Jesus asked him, "What is your name?" He answered, "My name is Legion; for we are many." (Mark 5:1–9)

The strong exorcist wrests from the demons their name, Legion. But the wily demons have already recognized the secret name of the exorcist: "Son of the Most High God." What malignant Pharisees and befuddled disciples fail to get, Satan's minions recognize immediately. The one who torments them is Son of the Most High God. He is Son of the Most High God in part because he *does* torment them. Jesus is God's Son because he is God's adjutant in the struggle against destructive and demonic power.[5]

Important clues to the significance of "Son of God" emerge in the first nine chapters of Mark's Gospel. Jesus as Son of God is Messiah and more; kinglike and prophetlike as well, greater than Moses and Elijah, aligned with God against the forces of evil, Spirit-filled.

However, another motif has run through the first chapters of Mark's

Gospel. These chapters, set in Galilee, keep pointing toward Jerusalem. In Jerusalem, Jesus acts out the crucial narrative that helps us understand Mark's Christology.

Jesus himself (another reliable commentator) three times tells the disciples that what lies ahead for him is suffering and death (and resurrection too, of course).[6] Each time the term he uses for himself is neither Messiah nor Son of God but *Son of man*. Each time Jesus predicts his death, the disciples fail to understand or refuse to believe.

The narrative draws us to Jerusalem, where at last reliable testimony comes from a merely human voice, that of the centurion at the foot of the cross (15:39). Now even more clearly the christological title finds its function in a narrative setting.

The opponents ironically testify to truth they do not believe: "He saved others, he cannot save himself. Let the Messiah, the King of Israel, come down from the cross now, so that we may see and believe" (Mark 15:31–32). The reader begins to realize that only because he refuses to save himself can Jesus save others; and we are about to behold a witness who believes in Jesus precisely because he does *not* come down from the cross.

In scene after scene, the inner circle of Jesus' support disappears. In chapter 3, Jesus' family gives up on him; in the passion narrative, the disciples give up on him. At the end of chapter 15 it appears that God gives up on him: "My God, my God, why have you forsaken me?" Jesus cries (Mark 15:34). Even though Jesus is quoting Psalm 22, which ends with affirmation, it is striking which verse from that psalm he chooses to quote.

An outsider speaks the truth: "Truly this man was God's Son." Not only is Jesus Son of God because he is the chosen, king and more than king, greater than Moses and Elijah, Spirit-driven, exorcizing Son of God—now he is the abandoned Son of God, the suffering Son of God. What the inner circle never did get and the opponents mocked, this anonymous centurion sees and says: "Son of God." All the other titles are qualified by this stark fact, this suffering, this cross.

A note of universalism may also lie in the claim that Jesus is God's own Son. As Messiah, he might be God's gift to Israel alone; as Son, he represents and re-presents God to the larger world of Jews and Gentiles alike. It is a Gentile centurion who knows him for who he is; when he dies, the temple curtain that keeps God in the Holy of Holies is torn in two (as the heavens are torn in Mark 1:10 when the Spirit descends).

What implications for right pastoral theology and right pastoral practice are there in Mark's use of the title "Son of God" and in his telling of the crucifixion?

The title opens us to the richness of the gifts available in Jesus Christ. Right pastoral understanding acknowledges the authority that comes with Jesus' Sonship. His is the one voice we are to hear in the midst of all the competing voices (sometimes, as with Elijah and Moses, even when those voices are from the richest parts of our tradition). Right pastoral understanding knows that Jesus as Son of God represents and re-presents for faithful people the strong claim of God's victory over those demonic forces that drive us and can finally destroy us.

Yet the title and especially the narrative of the cross cut against all attempts at sentimentality and pastoral Pollyannas. The story enacts what faithful people and faithful pastors live out in our own lives. Sometimes the clearest sign of God is God's absence; the God-shaped void where assurance used to be. Pastoral theology acknowledges that—the cry "My God, why have you forsaken me?" and the astonishing reminder that the cry begins, "*My* God."

In Mark, Sonship finally requires suffering; and discipleship will require the same. Pastoral ministry becomes both the acknowledgment of the cost of discipleship and the willingness to acknowledge Christ's presence as Son in the midst of that suffering. Mark's Son of God always stands against our easy theologies of glory—marking fidelity by church growth, discipleship by press coverage, and loyalty to the gospel by the increase of the budget. Right theology is to acknowledge the suffering Son of God; right practice always knows that at any minute his followers may also be required to take up the cross.

THE GOSPEL OF JOHN

While the reliable narrator of Mark's Gospel begins by assuring readers that Jesus is God's Son, the reliable narrator of John's Gospel begins by assuring readers that Jesus is God's Word made flesh. That claim that Jesus is God's Word, glory dwelling among humankind, governs the christological claims and the narrative movement of John's Gospel.

Nonetheless, the affirmation that Jesus is Son of God also has its important role in the development of Johannine Christology and in fact becomes the claim toward which the gospel seeks to drive its readers: "But these [signs] are written so that you may come to believe that Jesus is the Messiah, the Son of God, and that through believing you may have life in his name" (John 20:31).

As early as John 1:14, the evangelist links the affirmation of the glorified Word made flesh to the affirmation that Jesus is God's only Son. (The NRSV reads the text as an unlikely analogy: The word made flesh is like *a* father's son who reveals the paternal glory—but what kind of sonship would that be? Surely, this is an affirmation about the proper relationship of *the* Son to *the* Father, not about the general relationship between fathers and sons.) To say that Jesus is Son of God in this Gospel, then, is to say that Jesus displays the attributes of God. John 1:18 says this even more explicitly: "No one has ever seen God. It is God the only Son, who is close to the Father's heart, who has made him known."

To say that Jesus is Son of God is also to say that Jesus is the one who was sent. He becomes God's representative for judgment and for mercy, standing in the Father's place at the crisis of the world (John 3:17). In chapter 5, the Gospel makes it even more clear that the Son who is sent comes into the world carrying the authority of the Father. Sonship consists in part in a kind of commission that enables the son to stand in the father's place.

> Jesus said to them, "Very truly, I tell you, the Son can do nothing on his own, but only what he sees the Father doing; for whatever the Father does, the Son does likewise. . . . The Father judges no one but has given all judgment to the Son, so that all may honor the Son just as they honor the Father. Anyone who does not honor the Son does not honor the Father who sent him" (John 5:19–23)

In the best known verse of this Gospel, John reminds us that the Sonship of Jesus also reflects the love of the father, and that the mark of the Father's love was the willingness to give the Son: "For God so loved the world that he gave his only Son, so that everyone who believes in him may not perish but may have eternal life" (John 3:16). The language recalls the story of Abraham and Isaac in Genesis 22, where Abraham finally is not required to give up his own son. Just as God provided a ram for Abraham, now, in Jesus, God gives up his Son for the sake of Abraham's children, his Son who is also the Lamb of God (see John 1:29). The Gospel reflects the connection between Sonship and sacrifice when John bears witness both that "here is the Lamb of God who takes away the sin of the world" and that "this is the Son of God" (John 1:29, 34). In the same passage, John's affirmations recall the affirmations of Mark's Gospel (Mark 1:8, 10). The Son is also the one on whom the Spirit rests (John 1:32–33).

Finally, the claim that Jesus is Son of God in the fourth Gospel is a claim about his unity with the Father, both in his ministry and from and for eternity. John 14:9–13 recalls familiar themes of Jesus being sent by the Father and authorized by the Father, the reflection of God's glory, but at the same time makes clear the familial unity that grounds the other aspects of Jesus' Sonship:

> Jesus said to him, "Have I been with you all this time, Philip, and you still do not know me? Whoever has seen me has seen the Father. How can you say, 'Show us the Father'? Do you not believe that I am in the Father and the Father is in me? The words that I say to you I do not speak on my own. . . . I will do whatever you ask in my name, so that the Father may be glorified in the Son."

That this unity is eternal is affirmed by Jesus' prayer in John 17: "Father, the hour has come; glorify your Son so that the Son may glorify you. . . . I glorified you on earth by finishing the work that you gave me to do. So now, Father, glorify me in your own presence with the glory that I had in your presence before the world existed" (John 17:1–5).

Indeed, *unity* may be too mild a term for the relationship of Son to Father in this story. As in Mark, Jesus' opponents often ironically infer truths, or half-truths that point to the fullness of truth. Here is what John writes at the end of a Sabbath controversy inspired by Jesus' willingness to heal the man at the pool of Bethzatha:

> Therefore the Jews started persecuting Jesus, because he was doing such things on the sabbath. But Jesus answered them, "My father is still working, and I also am working." For this reason the Jews were seeking all the more to kill him, because he was not only breaking the sabbath, but was also calling God his own Father, thereby making himself equal to God. (John 5:16–18)

The irony, of course, is that Jesus *is* equal to God in the Johannine scheme of things, but he does not *make himself* equal to God. By creating the world through him, by sending him as designated representative, by raising him up on the cross and from the tomb, it is God who makes Jesus God's equal. Yet the ironic thought of "the Jews" catches the depth of the claim in John's Gospel that Jesus is God's own Son. To be God's Son is to be God's equal: "We have seen his glory, the glory of the Father's only Son" (John 1:14, author's translation).

Sonship is therefore not a metaphor in John's Gospel but a description of the eternal relationship between Jesus and the One who sent him. They share in glory; they are one.

The term *Son of God* is not just a sort of pious formula for the fourth Gospel. The nuances of the title reflect the nuances of Johannine Christology. The Son is sent by the Father as his representative and speaks with his authority (as sons might be wont to do). The glory of the Son re-presents the glory of the Father (as we can often see fathers reflected in earthly sons). The Son is the unimaginable gift that the Father gives for the sake of the world—a sacrifice like that God demanded of Abraham but now completed by God. The gift is beyond measure because the Son whom the Father gives up lives in and with the Father from the beginning and to eternity.

Two narratives that echo each other help us further understand the Johannine Christology and see how it might shape Christian life and practice in our contemporary ministries. In each case, though Jesus is identified as God's Son, he is also identified as a shepherd. John 10:11–18 stakes out the fundamental claim in a parabolic narrative:

> I am the good shepherd. The good shepherd lays down his life for the sheep. The hired hand, who is not the shepherd and does not own the sheep, sees the wolf coming and runs away—and the wolf snatches them and scatters them. The hired hand runs away because a hired hand does not care for the sheep. I am the good shepherd. I know my own and my own know me, just as the Father knows me and I know the Father. And I lay down my life for the sheep. I have other sheep that do not belong to this fold. I must bring them also, and they will listen to my voice. So there will be one flock, one shepherd. For this reason the Father loves me, because I lay down my life in order to take it up again. No one takes it from me, but I lay it down of my own accord. I have power to lay it down, and I have power to take it up again. I have received this command from my Father.

Though this passage does not explicitly refer to Jesus as Son of God, the references to God as Jesus' Father carry the implication that the good shepherd is also the good Son (see John 10:17, 18). Furthermore, I read John 10:22–30 as an expansion on the relationship of shepherd to sheep. Then the dispute of 10:31–36 is a reaction to the parable's explication, and here the identification of Jesus as God's Son is explicit: "Can you say that the one whom the Father has sanctified and sent into the world is blaspheming because I said, 'I am God's Son'?" (John 10:36).[7]

What strikes us first about the narrative is that as a parable it stretches the limits of credulity. Does even the best shepherd really lay down his life for the sheep? The image has been stretched to make the christological point. Here is a good shepherd—and more!

The image of the shepherd sacrificed for the sake of the sheep expands on the image of the Son in John 3:16. There, recalling the story of Abraham and Isaac, we hear that God gives up the Son for the sake of the world. Here, the Son voluntarily chooses the sacrifice; it is his activity as much as it is the Father's.

Furthermore, the unity that we saw displayed between the Son and the

Father is now displayed between the shepherd and the sheep: "I know my own and my own know me, just as the Father knows me and I know the father" (John 10:14). The image of the Son as shepherd stresses the intimate relationship each believer has with him. The image of the community as flock makes the same point. The relationship of one sheep to another is not emphasized. Rather, what is emphasized is the communion that each sheep has with the shepherd. (As others have noticed, this works rather differently than the image of church as Christ's body, members dependent on one another as well as on their Lord. In the same way in the image of John 15:1–10, the branches belong to the vine; the image does not emphasize their relationship one to another.)

Indeed, it looks as though one problem with bad shepherds is that they get in the way of the right relationship between sheep and shepherd. They are interlopers who, by their cowardice, cooperate with the forces of evil; they do not really know the sheep, because the sheep do not really belong to them. Our impression is that there is no need for subsidiary shepherds; the flock relates to the one shepherd who is sent by the Father to care for them.

The narrative suggests something of the interplay between Christology and Christian community. Because believers and the Son are one (as the Son and the Father are one), the community relies directly on Christ and not on other figures who might serve as intermediary leaders. The relationship between believers and Christ is intimate, unmediated, strong. So strong is that relationship that finally the shepherd is willing to lay down his life for the sheep. If we think of the meaning of the narrative, not in Jesus' ministry but in the time of the Johannine church, we realize that it is because the shepherd has already laid down his life for his sheep that the sheep live in close communion with him.

Sometime after the first twenty chapters of John's Gospel were written, a member of the Johannine community added chapter 21. Raymond Brown suggests that this additional chapter represents a shift in the pastoral practice of the Johannine community, and perhaps a modest variation on its Christology as well.[8]

> When they had finished breakfast, Jesus said to Simon Peter, "Simon son of John, do you love me more than these?" He said to him, "Yes, Lord; you know that I love you." Jesus said to him, "Feed my lambs." (John 21:15)

It is perhaps indicative of the later origin of this chapter that while the identification of Jesus as shepherd remains (and shifts), Jesus is not here identified as Son of God but consistently as "Lord" — and God is not identified as "Father" but as "God." The diminution of the "familial" imagery corresponds to a shift in the vision of religious leadership—almost literally, "pastoral" leadership—in the emerging Johannine community.

Now the sheep are not fed exclusively, and perhaps not even directly, by the shepherd but by his intermediary, Peter. Love still orders church life, but a particular (apostolic) leader becomes mediator of that love. If, as some have suggested, Peter represents throughout this Gospel a kind of symbol for the leadership of churches that have been more directly and clearly ordered by apostolic leadership than John's own community, we may see here a shift in church order as John's community becomes at once more settled and more ecumenical.[9]

As Gail O'Day points out, the kind of leadership that Peter here embodies is congruent with the concerns and claims of the entire Gospel. No keys are given Peter, and no special authority; he is asked to embody the requirement made of every disciple, every believer, "I give you a new commandment, that you love one another. Just as I have loved you, you also should love one another. By this everyone will know that you are my disciples, if you have love for one another" (John 13:34–35).[10] Nonetheless, both the imagery and the import have shifted in chapter 21 from the earlier chapters. There, it is clear that there is one Shepherd; the love of disciples for one another imitates but does not re-present the love of the Shepherd for the sheep. Chapter 21 presents an intermediary, a subsidiary, a "vice-shepherd"; the sense of community has either developed or shifted.[11]

(Notice, too, that in the great feeding scene of chapter 6, Jesus feeds the "flock" directly. Unlike the story in the Synoptic Gospels, no disciples serve as intermediaries between Jesus' bounty and the hungry crowds.)[12]

Overall, the two narratives of the shepherd suggest two angles of vision on pastoral leadership, which may be complementary or may be in a kind of tension.

One vision of the church suggests that all Christians are directly related to the Son, as the Son is directly related to the Father. While all Christians love one another, the love of Christ for Christians is not mediated but direct—like that of the shepherd for the sheep, like the nourishment of the vine for the branches.

The other vision of the church (where the language of Sonship drops out) does not diminish the sovereignty of Jesus as Lord over the church but does suggest that as God has delegated to him particular responsibilities, so Christ delegates some of his loving oversight of the church to Peter—and perhaps through Peter to other church leaders as well.

Again, we can draw insights for pastoral theology both from the use of the title "Son of God" and from the two narratives that use, or avoid, that title.

"Son of God" in the fourth Gospel represents the strong sense of unity between Father and Son. It carries over into the strong sense of the unity of believers with the Son, and therefore with the Father as well. The identity of the community reflects the identity of Jesus and the God who sent him. The meaning of the life of each believer rests on his or her relationship to the Son, who is the way by which God leads believers to God; the truth about God, come in human form; and the embodiment of that life which God intends for all. That is, pastoral understanding based on John's Gospel is centered absolutely in the one Word through whom the world was created and to whom the world is being redeemed. Faithful pastoral teaching always points directly to him and invites others to believe in him. Faithful pastoral practice is always witness.

Contemporary enactments of pastoral leadership may represent something of that combination or of the tension we saw between the narrative in John 10 and that in John 21. How far do we understand believers as directly in contact with the Son, so that they are fed directly by him? How far do we raise up the image of church leaders as pastors, shepherds, those to whom the care and feeding of church members is entrusted? In this second image, it is fairly clear how important pastoral leadership must be; in the first image, believers seem directly to rely on the one Pastor and to rely on communal love for one another. The narrative of John 10 is the more radical—and probably the more difficult to embody. Hence the more structured vision of John 21 and of most church life today.[13]

GALATIANS

While Galatians 4:1–6 makes use of the christological title "Son of God" (and Galatians 1:12–16 employs the term in a narrative), it is also clear that the meaning of the term in Galatians 4 is determined in part by a kind of metaphorical or parabolic context.

J. Louis Martyn has helped us reconstruct the historical situation behind this epistle. Paul has founded the churches in the Gentile communities of Galatia. The gospel he preached there did not include any requirement that Gentile converts to Christianity take on the "burden" of following the stipulations of the Jewish law. Not long after Paul departed, other religious leaders arrived preaching a quite different interpretation of the good news: "They centered their message in the covenantal, Sinaitic law, identifying it as the venerable and permanent word of God, confirmed to eternity by God's Messiah/Christ. Telling the Galatians that, apart from this divinely ordained anchor, they were cast adrift on the stormy sea of life, the Teachers offered them a security that appeared to many an absolute Godsend."[14]

It is the issue of security that Galatians 4 addresses. Paul wants to assure the Galatian Christians that their relationship to God does not depend on observance of the Sinaitic law (especially as that relates to circumcision). He insists rather that the security of believers rests not on anything they do but on what God has done for them in Jesus.

In this passage, it is particularly important for Paul to affirm that Jesus is God's own Son, because as the Son, Jesus provides the means for others to enter God's family—through adoption:

> Now before faith came, we were imprisoned and guarded under the law until faith would be revealed. Therefore the law was our disciplinarian until Christ came, so that we might be justified by faith. But now that faith has come, we are no longer subject to a disciplinarian, for in Christ Jesus you are all children of God through faith. As many of you as were baptized into Christ have clothed yourselves with Christ. There is no longer Jew or Greek, there is no longer slave or free, there is no longer male and female; for all of you are one in Christ Jesus. And if you belong to Christ, then you are Abraham's offspring, heirs according to the promise.
>
> My point is this: heirs, as long as they are minors, are no better than slaves, though they are the owners of all the property; but they remain under guardians and trustees until the date set by the father. So with us; while we were minors, we were enslaved to the elemental spirits of the world. But when the fullness of time had come, God sent his Son, born of a woman, born under the law, in order to redeem those who were under the law, so that we might receive adoption as children. And because you are children, God has sent the Spirit of his Son into our hearts, crying, "Abba! Father!" So you are no longer a slave but a child, and if a child then also an heir, through God. (Gal. 3:15–4:7)

There is an implicit narrative here. In the time before Christ, Jews and Gentiles alike were under the guardianship of "elemental spirits," authoritative powers who were not to be confused with God. For Jews, those elemental spirits included the law; for Gentiles, the elemental spirits were honored by the keeping of certain feast days and celebrations. But law and celebration both belonged to the childhood of humankind. Children were not free; in some ways, they seemed no better than slaves.

But when the children reached maturity, they were eligible to be heirs of the goodness of their Father. Yet this inheritance would be possible only if they were ransomed or rescued from the elemental spirits, who should have no sway over the adult lives of these potential heirs.

For Paul, Jesus is the true Son of God who is "sent."[15] Because he is sent as God's Son, he carries all the authority of the Father who sends him—both as ambassador and as heir. Included in that authority is the authority to ransom, to rescue, believers. Included in that authority, precisely because he is Son, is the power to welcome, to "adopt" others into the family. Among those "others" are Gentile believers.

Their security does not depend on circumcision or keeping the law any more than it depends on the elemental spirits they worshiped in their own pagan infancy. Their security is based in their place as children and heirs of God's promises—as brothers and sisters of Christ, God's original Son.

This security is confirmed in two ways. It is confirmed by their baptism—which, unlike circumcision, does not make distinctions but recognizes the common humanity of all believers. Their security is also confirmed by the fact that in worship they call out the Aramaic word *Abba,* which means "Father." How could they cry, "Abba!" aloud if it were not true that God had adopted them as God's own children?

Liturgical practice therefore confirms the insights of the theological exposition. Baptism replaces circumcision—and unites what circumcision had cut asunder. The Fatherhood of God replaces the guardianship of the law (for Jews) and of ceremony (for Gentiles).

To designate Jesus as Son of God in this context is to recognize his authority and power, on the one hand, and to acknowledge that through him believers have access to the family of God, on the other.

An autobiographical narrative in Galatians further helps us understand the christological claim that Jesus is God's Son. Paul is recalling his own call to apostleship—and faith:

> You have heard, no doubt, of my earlier life in Judaism. I was violently persecuting the church of God and was trying to destroy it. I advanced in Judaism beyond many among my people of the same age, for I was far more zealous for the traditions of my ancestors. But when God, who had set me apart before I was born and called me through his grace, was pleased to reveal his Son in me,[16] so that I might proclaim him among the Gentiles, I did not confer with any human being, nor did I go up to Jerusalem to those who were already apostles before me, but I went away at once into Arabia, and afterwards I returned to Damascus. (Gal. 1:13–17)

Hans Dieter Betz, who has done the most thorough analysis of the structure of this epistle, reminds us that the narrative moves toward the argument. There is congruity between the life lived and the gospel declared. The congruity between Paul's call and his pastoral authority is not a matter of Donatism but of integrity.[17] In some ways the most astonishing reversal is that this persecutor of Christ should become apostle. So the apparently excluded are now adopted—become part of the family, too.

Looking back on this narrative in the light of the passage from Galatians 3 and 4, we can see why Paul stresses the role of Christ as "Son" in this story. As in that later passage, to say that Jesus is Son is to say that he has the authority given him by God to redeem all humankind. As Son of God he redeems Paul from the authority, tutelage, and perhaps even bondage of the law. So bound was Paul to that elemental spirit that he violently pursued Christians who seemed to deny it. Paul enters into his maturity as heir of God through the intervention of the Son (who is always fully Son and fully heir). Then the Son, as God's agent, sends Paul as *his* agent to redeem the Gentiles from the bondage to their elemental spirits.

The reminder that Paul did not confer with any human beings is not only a statement of his apostolic authority—it says what the passage in Galatians 3 and 4 also says—but also an affirmation that it is God and God alone who welcomes both Jews and Gentiles into God's family, redeeming them from that immature "slavery" in which they were bound to the elemental spirits of law and ceremony. This zealous Jew preaching the gospel to those Gentiles is himself a sign of the breadth and depth of the mystery of the family of God.

The use of the title "Son of God" and the story of Paul's call have at least two theological implications for pastoral teaching and practice. First is the reminder that the status of believers as children of God is always subsidiary and dependent on the prior status of Jesus Christ as God's own Son. Our status as children (for Paul) is not a given of creation but a gift of redemption. In pastoral practice this does not, I think, diminish the pastoral gift of asserting and affirming the worth of each person given to our care. It does remind us that this worth is given at a cost (as the love of any good parent for a child carries with it costs, sacrifices, loss—along with abundant joy).

Second, and in accordance with Paul's main theme, is the reminder of the radical inclusivity of the Christian claim. "Liberal" Christians in our time have rushed to "inclusivity" as the fundamental mark of God's intention for the world, while "conservative" Christians have bristled at what they see as a too-easy adoption of secular standards for openheartedness.

Liberals may forget that the inclusion of the gospel is an inclusion in Jesus Christ. He is the one in whom God has liberated Jews and welcomed

Gentiles. We are brothers and sisters, children of God, because he is God's own Son. The primary word of the gospel is that God has sent the Son. The derivative word of the gospel is that through the Son we are also adopted as sons and daughters.

Conservatives tend to forget that we really are—all of us—adopted as sons and daughters. The divisions we want to draw among ourselves are radically challenged and converted by Paul's gospel, which would not recognize even that ancient, biblical division between Gentile and Jew. More than that, Paul's strong insistence that Gentiles should not try to become Jewlike in their habits and practices challenges all Christians. Some of us are eager to welcome any-one into our communities of faith—just as long as those we invite become more like us. Others of us strive endlessly to imitate other Christians whose practice, theology, and lifestyle seem more acceptable than our own.

Paul insists that the community of faith is open to us by our adoption as sons and daughters through the one Son, Jesus Christ—and our pastoral practice needs to acknowledge and embody that claim. Whatever the litur-gical practice behind the Galatian church, we do well to remember that when they called, "Abba—Father," they did so bilingually. Monolingual churches miss the fullness of the gospel, and pastoral practice always opens us up to other languages, other voices.

Different (not, I think, conflicting) Christologies emerge from these apostolic writings. Christology shapes the lives of communities, and it emerges from those lives. Reading Mark, John, and Galatians, we get hints of different practices in early Christian communities and of the doctrines and narratives that informed those practices. None of us is bound simply to replicate our forebears in the faith; all of us will need to decide which christological claims and pastoral practices comfort us—but also which challenge, stretch, mature us.

The vocation of Christian ministry always requires a wrestling with these witnesses and with the tough and sometimes intransigent here and now. We can see how Paul, Mark, and John lived with tradition and with changing circumstance and wrestled out faith for their people—a light to their paths, and to ours as well.

NOTES

1. Wayne A. Meeks, "Equal to God," in Robert T. Fortna and Beverly R. Gaventa, eds., *The Conversation Continues: Studies in Paul and John in Honor of J. Louis Martyn* (Nashville: Abingdon Press, 1990), 311. The en-tire essay is found on 309–21.

2. See Jack Dean Kingsbury, *The Christology of Mark's Gospel* (Philadelphia: Fortress Press, 1989). For explicit attention to both elements of this program, see the preface to the second edition, ix–xi.

3. Kingsbury, *Christology of Mark's Gospel,* 47–50. See also Robert M. Fowler, *Loaves and Fishes,* Society of Biblical Literature Dissertation Series 54 (Chico, Calif.: Scholars Press, 1981), 156–70.

4. Textual evidence on "the Son of God" is divided, but with Kingsbury I think the manuscript evidence for its inclusion is convincing. See Kingsbury, *Christology of Mark's Gospel,* 14n. 53; see also Bruce M. Metzger, *A Textual Commentary on the Greek New Testament* (London and New York: United Bible Societies, 1971), 73.

5. James M. Robinson has helped us see the power struggle involved in Mark's Gospel and in his Christology, in *The Problem of History in Mark* (Philadelphia: Fortress Press, 1982); on demonic recognition of Jesus, see Susan R. Garrett, *The Temptations of Jesus in Mark's Gospel* (Grand Rapids: Wm. B. Eerdmans Publishing Co., 1998), 66.

6. Mark 8:31; 9:30–31; 10:32–34.

7. On the function of this passage in explicating the parable, see Raymond Brown, *The Gospel according to John (I–XII)*, Anchor Bible (Garden City, N.Y.: Doubleday & Co., 1966), 406.

8. Raymond Brown, *The Community of the Beloved Disciple* (New York: Paulist Press, 1979), 161–62.

9. But see Gail R. O'Day, "The Gospel of John," in *The New Interpreter's Bible,* vol. 9 (Nashville: Abingdon Press, 1995), 854–55.

10. Ibid., 861.

11. This does not decide whether chapter 21 is later redaction or a development by the evangelist within the Gospel itself, though I tend toward the former belief. In addition to reasons cited above, nothing in the "original" shape of chapters 1–20 leads me to think that the issue of the church's future should be related in particular to the role of Peter.

12. Compare John 6:11 with Mark 6:41, Matthew 14:18, and Luke 9:16.

13. For a fuller discussion of the Johannine options, see my *Ministry in the New Testament,* Overtures to Biblical Theology (Minneapolis: Fortress Press, 1993), 89–114.

14. J. Louis Martyn, *Galatians,* Anchor Bible (New York: Doubleday, 1997), 18.

15. The commentaries differ on whether this "sending" presupposes the Son's preexistence. Betz doubts it; Matera thinks it likely. The function of the Son in the passage does not depend on the answer to the question of preexistence. See Hans Dieter Betz, *Galatians,* Hermeneia (Philadelphia: Fortress Press, 1979), 206–7; Frank J. Matera, *Galatians,* Sacra Pagina (Collegeville, Minn.: Liturgical Press, 1992), 150.

16. I use the NRSV marginal translation.
17. Betz, *Galatians,* 61–62. "It cannot be accidental that, at the end of the *narratio* in Gal. 2:14 when Paul formulates the dilemma which Cephas is in, this dilemma is identical with the issue the Galatians themselves have to decide, 'why do you compel the Gentiles to judaize?'" (62).

THE SIGNIFICANCE OF NEW TESTAMENT CHRISTOLOGY FOR PREACHING

Elizabeth Achtemeier

It is a pleasure to contribute to the festschrift for Jack Dean Kingsbury, in honor of his sixty-fifth birthday.

In dealing with the topic that has been assigned to me, I must first say that we are speaking about the realm of faith—a fact not automatically taken for granted these days. The word *Christology* has as its root "Christ," *christos, masiah,* the anointed long-awaited Messiah of Israel, who is the object of Christian faith. In that faith we are joining in the biblical witness; for what else are the scriptures but a confession of faith? They are made up of the witness of thousands of persons who have preserved for us the record of what God has said and done in their lives. At the heart of that witness from both the Old and New Testaments is the proclamation that through the life, death, and resurrection of Jesus Christ, God has fulfilled his promises to God's covenant people Israel, redeemed humanity from its slavery to sin and death, and restored to all humankind the possibility of life and love eternally with God in the kingdom of heaven.

THE ROLE OF THE PREACHER

The Christian preacher, then, is one who believes the biblical witness. If the preacher does not believe that witness, he or she has nothing to preach. But the believing preacher becomes the proclaimer of that good news handed down to the church in the scriptures. The preacher joins the long line of biblical witnesses that runs through eighteen hundred years of Israel's history and two thousand years of the history of the Christian church.

In short, the preacher stands in a tradition. Like Paul, he or she declares what he or she has "also received" (1 Cor. 11:23; 15:3), and again like Paul, the preacher becomes the steward of that tradition, a steward of the mysteries of God (1 Cor. 4:1). In the role of a steward, the preacher preserves the tradition. Like a wine steward, she or he keeps the new wine of the gospel from becoming corrupt and spoiled. But also like a wine steward, the preacher "serves" the tradition; she or he proclaims it and passes it on. Through preaching and teaching, the preacher believes, the proclamation of the biblical tradition will bring its hearers also to join the long line of witnesses as believers in Jesus Christ. "Faith comes from what is heard, and what is heard comes through the word [by the preaching] of Christ" (Rom. 10:17).

In the proclamation of the gospel, the preacher is fulfilling the biblical prophetic function of releasing the active, effective Word of God to do its work among the gathered congregation. The Word of God does not just convey information or set forth new views, although it may do both. Rather, in the scriptures the Word of God works; it creates a new situation (Gen. 1:3; Isa. 55:10–11). As Paul writes, the word of the cross is the "power of God" (1 Cor. 1:18), working among his gathered people. The Word may convict of sin; it may call our lifestyle into question; it may comfort; it may forgive; it may confirm faith; it may create a new human being (2 Cor. 5:17). The Word of God *does* whatever God wills, and the Christian preacher, standing in the biblical tradition, is the mediator of that powerful and effective Word.

THE SUBJECT AT HAND

So in dealing with Christology and its relationship to preaching, we are dealing with faith's preaching of the good news of Jesus Christ. We are not treating the widespread practice of therapeutic preaching, in which the purpose of the sermon is just to make the congregation feel comfortable and reassured. We are not discussing the preaching of humanistic values or of exemplary ethical systems or of politically sagacious insights and moves.

We are not even dealing with the widespread practice of moralizing: A congregation that is enslaved to sin cannot "just get out there and do good." Above all, in discussing our topic, we are not dealing with the so-called third quest, with the critical hunt for the "real Jesus," to be discovered by historical, sociological, or psychological criticism.[1]

There is no doubt that several centuries of scholars' critical work with the scriptures have made vast contributions to our understanding and use of the Bible. Historical criticism has delivered us from the mental gymnastics required to reconcile the vast variety of witnesses in the Bible. Criticism has focused on the unique contribution of each of the biblical witnesses. And it has placed all the scriptures in their actual history, concerned with particular places, times, and persons, so that the Bible cannot be turned into a set of timeless principles or ethereal truths.

The witnesses to Jesus Christ, however, and therefore the subjects of New Testament Christology are indissolubly embedded in a narrative, and faith in Jesus Christ is dependent on that narrative. Even in affirming the Apostles' Creed, we cannot say, "I believe," unless we recount a portion of the narrative: " . . . born of the virgin Mary, suffered under Pontius Pilate, was crucified, dead and buried, on the third day he rose again from the dead, he ascended into heaven and sitteth on the right hand of God the Father . . . " If we begin to dismantle the narratives of the Bible, in all their continuity and diversity, then we have no firm foundation for faith. The Jesus who is separated from the biblical narratives' context ends up a totally unrecognizable figure, unknown to the church and indeed unknowable. He ends up as a Hellenistic Cynic sage or a Jewish Cynic peasant; as a subversive sage and social reformer who had visions and mystical experiences, as an egalitarian prophet of wisdom, or as an eschatological prophet of Jewish restoration. He even ends up in some critics' work as a metaphor or symbol or paradigm. But the Jesus who emerges from such criticism is largely the product of the critics' own inclinations and interpretations.

THE LOCUS OF INTERPRETATION

Jesus Christ comes to us, by the work of the Holy Spirit, through the Bible's narrative history and *through the biblical interpretation of that history*. In dealing with the scriptures, we cannot separate the biblical interpretation of the events recorded from the events themselves. The Bible sets forth a narrative for us — a narrative spanning some two thousand years — and at almost every point in that narrative, the Bible tells us what the narrative means. It gives its own interpretation of the history it tells, setting forth how God is related to the history and therefore what the meaning of the history is for our lives. And the preacher must not separate the events in the biblical history from the interpretation of those events in the Bible itself.

If preachers begin to tell the congregation "what really happened"; if they drag all their critical tools into the pulpit and, by them, try to get behind the biblical interpretation of some happening; if they replace the Bible's interpretation with their own modern interpretation on some biblical event, the Lord of the Bible disappears. For example, a preacher may attribute the plagues on Egypt in the book of Exodus to natural happenings, but the preacher thereby loses Exodus's witness to God's lordship over nature and history and other gods, and the point of the biblical story is lost. God uses a covenant people to tell his story, and we either accept or reject their witness. The events and words of the Bible together with the biblical interpretation given to both make up the content of the revelatory witness handed on to us, and it is that witness of which the preacher is a steward and to which she or he is required to be faithful (1 Cor. 4:2).

To be sure, there is great variety among the narratives that the biblical witnesses hand on to us. Some of those narratives contradict each other. We have two different views, in the Synoptics and in the fourth Gospel, of how often Jesus went to Jerusalem and of the relation of his death to Passover. We have two different views, in Acts and in Galatians, of Paul's relationship to the Jerusalem church and of the content and result of the Apostolic Council. We have differing views of how we are to behave toward ruling authorities, just as in the Old Testament we have differing interpretations of the wilderness period or of the kingship or of the covenant. But the faithful steward of the mysteries of God is the preacher who listens to all those interpretations, who lets the scripture interpret itself, and who then sets forth the Bible's interpretation of the event dealt with in the text for the morning. In assembling its canon, the church affirmed that it required all the biblical interpretations given to us to reveal the nature and purpose and activity of the God to whom they witness.

Ultimately, the whole witness of the canon becomes flesh in the Word incarnate Jesus Christ. He becomes the measure of all in Old Testament and New. For example, there are several different understandings in the Old Testament of the messiah. It is finally the Messiah incarnate who reveals who is the true One sent from God. Indeed, the New Testament serves as the final judge and reinterpreter of all that has preceded it in the Old Testament. Yet the Old Testament also interprets the New, and that brings us immediately to our subject of New Testament Christology.

WHO IS JESUS CHRIST?

In dealing with the New Testament's witness to Jesus Christ, the preacher must be aware of the fact that such witness is given largely in terms of the Old Testament.[2] Our Lord is not some mysterious figure suddenly dropped from the blue; nor was he understood in the first- to third-century Mediterranean world as just another mythical savior in a mystery religion or gnostic sect. No. The New Testament writers understand Jesus Christ as the completion and final reinterpretation of God's long, almost two-thousand-year history of working with Israel. He is inseparably connected with the concrete, specific history of his covenant people. If he is separated from that history, as he is in some solely theocentric theologies so fashionable today, he becomes simply an object of fanciful speculation. The New Testament churches understand Jesus Christ from the standpoint of their scriptures, namely, from the standpoint of the Old Testament.

Who is Jesus Christ in the New Testament? He is the long-expected Messiah, promised in 2 Samuel and the prophetic writings (Mark 8:29; Luke 2:26; John 1:41; 20:31; 1 John 5:1). Thus, many of the royal psalms of the Old Testament are used to describe his life. Psalm 2:7 is quoted at Jesus' baptism and at his transfiguration: "This is my Son, the Beloved." Psalm 110 is employed to describe Jesus' resurrection and exaltation to the right hand of God (Acts 2:32–35; 5:31; Rom. 8:34), where Christ reigns and puts all his enemies under his feet (1 Cor. 15:25; Eph. 1:22).

Kings were understood in the Old Testament as the shepherds of their people. Therefore, as the Davidic Messiah, Jesus is that good shepherd in John 10, who was promised in Ezekiel 34:23 and 37:34. By the time of Hebrews and 1 Peter, the reference to Jesus as the royal, Davidic shepherd has become one of the standard liturgical formulas used of Jesus in the church (Heb. 13:20; 1 Peter 2:25). Certainly, the fact that "shepherd" is a royal title should prevent the sentimentalizing of Jesus as the good shepherd.

THE NEW MOSES

Jesus is also the new Moses, according to Matthew, and the Moses of old forms the type or foreshadowing of our Lord. Just as Pharaoh of Egypt attempted to do away with all the Hebrew male infants, so Herod tries to do away with the infant Jesus by slaughtering all the male children under two years of age in the region of Bethlehem (Matt. 2:16–18). Just as Moses gave the covenant commandments to the old Israel on Mount Sinai, so Jesus as the mediator of the Word of God gives the new commandments to his disciples on the new mount (Matthew 5–7), and those are contrasted with the commandments in the law of Moses (Matt. 5:21, 27, 31, 33, 38). Just as Moses took Aaron, Nadab, and Abihu with him when he went up Mount Sinai to talk with God (Ex. 24:9), so Jesus takes Peter, James, and John with him up the mount of transfiguration (Matt. 17:1). But whereas Moses' face shone with reflected glory from talking with God in his glory on Sinai (Ex. 34:29)—an account to which Paul also refers (2 Cor. 3:13)— Jesus' face shines with his own glory (Matt. 17:2; compare 2 Cor. 4:6). And as the divine voice was heard at Sinai (Deut. 5:22–26), so it is heard once again on the mount of transfiguration (Matt. 17:5).

Such a use of Moses as the type of foreshadowing of Jesus can be further understood when we consider that Moses, in the book of Deuteronomy, is the bearer of the sins of his faithless people (Deut. 1:37; 4:21), dying outside the Promised Land so that Israel may enter into it.

Indeed, Jesus is understood in the New Testament as the fulfillment of the word of Moses in Deuteronomy 18:15, that God will raise up a prophet like him, whom the people are to heed. (For the latter phrase, see Mark 9:7.) Certainly, some of the classical prophets, and especially Jeremiah, understood themselves to be fulfilling this role of the Mosaic prophet. But in the post-exilic period, the promise takes on an eschatological dimension, and there arises the expectation of a special prophet like Moses. John 1:21, 25; 6:14; and 7:40 mirror that expectation, but in Acts 3:22–26; 7:37; and 7:52, Jesus is specifically identified with that eschatological Mosaic prophet.

THE PASSION

Paul states in 1 Corinthians 15:3 that Christ died for our sins "in accordance with the scriptures," and it is to the Old Testament that the authors of the New Testament turn to interpret Jesus' death on the cross. Very early Jesus is identified with the Suffering Servant of Isaiah 52:13–53:12 (Mark 10:45; Rom. 4:25; 5:18), and that identification is pervasive in the early and later portrayals of Jesus' passion. Jesus is the one who is silent before his oppressors (Mark 14:61), who is reckoned with the transgressors (Luke 22:37 and parallels; cf. Isa. 53:12), who is like a lamb led to the slaughter (Acts 8:32 = Isa. 53:7–8). He is the Lamb of God who takes away the sins of the world (John 1:29). His grave is made with a rich man in fulfillment of Isaiah 53:9 (Matt. 27:57–60), yet he has committed no sin and spoken no guile (1 Peter 2:22). Jesus is the one by whose stripes we were healed when we had gone astray like sheep (1 Peter 2:24–25). In short, Jesus is understood as the true Suffering Servant, foretold by Second Isaiah.

The New Testament also portrays Jesus' death in terms of the Old Testament exodus and covenant traditions, and this is especially true in the letters of Paul. In the Old Testament, Israel is redeemed, or bought back, out of slavery by the God who adopts Israel as his son (Ex. 4:22–23; Jer. 3:19; 31:20; Hos. 11:1). Paul picks up the figure and applies it to our redemption by the cross of Christ: "You were bought with a price"—that is, the death of Christ—therefore "do not become slaves of human masters" (1 Cor. 6:20; 7:23). As a result, through faith in Christ we, too, receive adoption as the sons and daughters of God, just as Israel received that adoption (Gal. 4:4–6). We are allowed to cry, "Abba! Father!" and we become heirs of all of God's promises to Israel (Gal. 3:29; 4:6).

In a different figure in the fourth Gospel, Jesus is slain as our paschal lamb (John 19:14, 31), recalling the Passover lamb of Exodus. Therefore, his legs are not broken on the cross, recalling Exodus 12:46; Numbers 9:12; and Psalm 34:20.

Jesus' words at the Last Supper, when he gives the new covenant (1 Cor. 11:25), hearken back to Jeremiah 31:31–34. Hebrews 9:15 and Revelation 1:5–6 and 5:9 connect this covenant tradition with the redemption of Israel from Egypt and her call, in Exodus 19:6, to be a kingdom of priests, so that the cross is connected with the whole of the exodus–Sinai act of God. Similarly, John 6 uses the tradition of the manna in the wilderness to speak of Jesus as the true bread of life.

To portray the details of Jesus' death, the Gospel writers turn to the individual laments of pious sufferers in the Psalms. Psalm 22 is employed to portray the cry from the cross (Mark 15:34), the division of Christ's garments and the casting of lots for them (Mark 15:24; John 19:24), the derision by passersby and the mockery of the chief priests and scribes (Mark 19:29, 31 and parallels), and Jesus' thirst (John 19:28). John also makes use of Zechariah 12:10 and Matthew uses Zechariah 11:12–13, while Luke 23:30 quotes Hosea. Indeed, Psalm 118:22 is used to interpret the entire Passion and resurrection (Acts 4:11; 1 Peter 2:7), while Paul interprets Jesus' death in terms of the stumbling stone of Isaiah 8:13–15 (Rom. 9:32–33).

Jesus in the Gospel according to John is the incarnation of the entire word of the Old Testament. As such he is the temple incarnate (John 2:19–21). First Peter 2:6 names our Lord as that cornerstone of faith (Isa. 28:16), who is the beginning of the new universal people of God. He is the incarnate Promised Land, the Old Testament's "place of rest," according to Hebrews 3 and 4. He is the incarnate covenant, replacing the bread and wine with his own person, in John 13; and as we have said, he is the incarnate Messiah, the holy Son of God.

THE TRUE ISRAEL

Jesus is someone else in the New Testament's portrayal of him: He is the true Israel. He is the son who is delivered out of Egypt (Matt. 2:15). He is the contrast to the first Israel in the wilderness who murmured and rebelled against the Lord, because Jesus in his temptations in the wilderness refuses to be a disobedient son. And the fourth Gospel emphasizes this replacement motif. There, Jesus is the only Son (John 1:14, 18), replacing the sonship of those unfaithful Jewish leaders who are children neither of Abraham (John 8:39–40) nor of God (John 8:42) because of their constant disbelief. In John 15:1, then, Jesus is the true vine, replacing the vine Israel that God planted (Ps. 80:8–11), but which yielded only rotten grapes (Isa. 5:1–7).

Jesus, the son of Abraham and the son of David (Matt. 1:1), fulfills God's promises to Abraham and to David, so that Paul can write, "In him every one of God's promises is a 'Yes'" (2 Cor. 1:20).

Thus, in many and various ways, using the narratives, the traditions, the metaphors, and the words of the Old Testament, the New Testament writers formulate their witness to the life, death, and resurrection of Jesus Christ, and through their witness, the one true God and his work are revealed to those who believe.

A RADICAL NEW ACTION

This is not to say that there is nothing new in the New Testament. The New Testament is not just an exegesis and extension of the Old. Rather, it testifies to an act of God that is radically new—the incarnation of his only begotten Son for the salvation of the world. Something greater than Solomon is here (Matt. 12:42 and parallels), something greater than Jonah (Luke 11:32), something greater than even Abraham (John 8:53–59) and Moses (Matt. 5:21–48; Mark 9:2–8; John 1:17). "Truly I tell you, many prophets and righteous people longed to see what you see, but did not see it, and to hear what you hear, but did not hear it" (Matt. 13:17). And so every believer in Jesus Christ who is least in the kingdom of heaven is greater than even John the Baptist (Matt. 11:11). But the new action of God in Jesus Christ, his radical in-breaking into human history, did not abrogate the past promises of God, just as Second Isaiah testified they would not (Isa. 40:8). Rather, God's work in his Son gathers up all the promises, all the words of the Old Testament, and brings them to their completion. The final meaning of the events of the Old Testament find their goal and their ultimate interpretation in the life, death, and resurrection of Jesus Christ. Yet it is precisely those words of the Old Testament that are used to tell who Jesus

Christ is. If the preacher wants to proclaim Jesus Christ in our day, then he or she is going to have to proclaim also the words and events of the Old Testament.

THE SIGNIFICANCE FOR PREACHING

It makes a great deal of difference in the proclamation of the good news of Jesus Christ as to whether or not the preacher sets the figure of our Lord in the context of the Old Testament and the canon as a whole. Let me illustrate.

Matthew 2:13–15. In Matthew 2:13–15, the Holy Family goes down into Egypt to escape the sword of Herod, and Matthew sees that as a fulfillment of God's word in Hosea 11:1 — a simple little example of how Matthew repeatedly understands Jesus to be fulfilling Old Testament prophecy. But unless the preacher knows the full setting of the Hosea passage, he or she cannot understand the deeper meaning of Matthew's testimony here.

In the book of Hosea, despite all God's sobbing love for his adulterous people who worship the baals, despite the fact that Israel is God's adopted son or his bride, Israel is unable to repent and return to the Lord. "Their deeds do not permit them to return to their God," proclaims the prophet, "for the spirit of whoredom is within them, and they do not know the Lord" (Hos. 5:4; compare 4:12).

God therefore promises through Hosea that he will begin his salvation history with Israel all over again. After his judgment on them, God will once again bring his people out of Egypt and woo them in the wilderness, speaking to their hearts, so that they answer him as in the exodus time. He will remove all baal worship from them and establish shalom in their community, giving them the bridal gifts of righteousness and justice, steadfast love and mercy, covenant faithfulness and knowledge of their God (Hos. 2:14–20). Thus will God reestablish his covenant with his people, despite their past sinfulness. That is the hope for the future that is held out to God's covenant people.

Despite that divine promise, the nation of Israel falls victim to the Assyrian Empire in 722–721 B.C.E., is deported to that foreign land, and finally disappears from history. Where, then, is the fulfillment of God's promise for the future, spoken through Hosea?

Matthew writes of the fulfillment in 2:15. Once again God calls his son out of Egypt, as he called Israel at the first; but this time the son is his begotten Son, Jesus Christ. In that calling, in Jesus' coming forth out of Egypt, God begins once again that saving history in the life of his people that he promised, through Hosea, he would bring to pass.

Matthew 1:23. Let us take another brief example, from Isaiah 7:1–4 and Matthew 1:23. The scene in Isaiah is the Syro-Ephraimitic war, when the two countries of Syria and Ephraim are attacking Judah in the effort to force King Ahaz to join in their alliance against the armies of Assyria. The prophet confronts Ahaz with the command from God to place his trust in the promise to David, in the belief that God will deliver the Davidic kingdom from its enemies if Ahaz will rely on the Lord. But, warns Isaiah, "if you do not stand firm in faith, you shall not stand at all" (7:9). Ahaz hypocritically replies that he "will not put the Lord to the test"—he has already summoned Assyria to his aid. The prophet therefore offers Ahaz a sign that God will protect his kingdom: "The young woman is with child and shall bear a son, and shall name him Immanuel" (v. 14). The reference is to an unknown woman of marriageable age, probably the wife of the prophet or of the king himself. But Ahaz does not need a baby; Ahaz needs an army. He will not trust, and Judah falls victim to the devastating armies from Mesopotamia in 733 B.C.E., becoming Assyria's vassal.

Once again Matthew picks up this promise from the Old Testament and applies it to Jesus Christ (Matt. 1:23). So what assurance is given the church over against all the worldly powers that threaten its life? As with Ahaz, it is given a baby, who is Emmanuel. And the words ring out from Isaiah, but we can put them in positive form: "If you do believe, surely you shall be established!"

John 12:32. Understanding Jesus Christ in the context of the Old Testament can lend enormous strength and depth to the preaching of the gospel. For example, in the fourth Gospel, Jesus tells his disciples, "I, when I am lifted up from the earth, will draw all people to myself." Obviously, Jesus is referring to being lifted up on the cross, which is understood in John as his exaltation over all (John 19). We also know that in John, Jesus is the temple incarnate, the one place and way to the worship of the Father (John 2:19–21; 4:21; 14:6). If the preacher puts that in the context of the Old Testament, then he or she can bring forth all sorts of passages.

First is the exuberant, royal Psalm 47, in which the emphasis is on God Most High, who ascends to his royal throne to be worshiped as the king over all the nations. "I, when I am lifted up from the earth, will draw all people to myself." That to which the psalm looks forward in the coming kingdom of God finds its amazing fulfillment in the dying figure of Christ on the cross, drawing all nations to worship him. Surely the celebration of that victory in the psalm becomes one of the proper expressions of the church on that day which is not Black Friday but Good Friday.

Another example is the use of Isaiah 2:2–4, in which Mount Zion is raised as the highest mountain and all nations flow to it to learn God's will and to walk in God's ways. God decides the disputes among them, and God's judgments are so right and just that the peoples beat their swords into plowshares and their spears into pruning hooks. Surely that is the universal peace of God and righteousness among all peoples that the church looks forward to when Christ draws all nations to himself and reigns over them. The use of the Old Testament helps fill out the meaning of John 12:32.

Illumining God's Purpose. In Genesis 12:3, God promises Abraham that through his descendants, God will bring blessing on all the families of the earth. Paul quotes that promise in Galatians 3:8, and it is by faith in Christ that such blessing is inherited. God's work in the world, promised centuries ago, is being fulfilled in the life of believers today.

In Philippians 2:9–11, Paul writes that God has exalted Jesus as Lord, "that at the name of Jesus every knee should bend . . . and every tongue should confess that Jesus Christ is Lord, to the glory of God the Father." But it was long before the time of Paul that God proclaimed that purpose through the words of Second Isaiah (Isa. 45:23). And it is in Jesus Christ that God is fulfilling that purpose, not only in Paul's time but also in the life of every congregation.

To preach Christ, which alone can draw a congregation to faith (Rom. 10:17) and hence to salvation (Acts 4:12), the preacher must bind himself or herself to the narrative and witness of the entire canon. Only through that narrative witness is Jesus Christ truly made known to us. But that narrative also includes the Old Testament preparation for Christ, and to be a faithful steward of all the mysteries of God, the preacher must proclaim the entire canonical story.

NOTES

1. See Luke Timothy Johnson, *The Real Jesus: The Misguided Quest for the Historical Jesus and the Truth of the Traditional Gospels* (San Francisco: HarperCollins, 1996); also the articles in *Interpretation* 50, 4 (October 1996), including M. Eugene Boring, "The Third Quest and the Apostolic Faith"; John P. Meier, "Dividing Lines in Jesus Research Today"; and John P. Galvin, "I Believe . . . in Jesus Christ, His Only Son, Our Lord: The Earthly Jesus and the Christ of Faith."
2. So, too, Brevard S. Childs, *Biblical Theology of the Old and New Testaments: Theological Reflection on the Christian Bible* (Minneapolis: Fortress Press, 1993).

INDEX OF SCRIPTURE PASSAGES

INDEX OF MODERN AUTHORS